Environmental Dilemmas

Toposophia

Sustainability, Dwelling, Design

Toposophia is a book series dedicated to the interdisciplinary and transdisciplinary study of place. Authors in the series attempt to engage a geographical turn in their research, emphasizing the spatial component, as well as the philosophical turn, raising questions both reflectively and critically.

Series Editors:
Robert Mugerauer, University of Washington
Gary Backhaus, Loyola College in Maryland

Editorial Board:
Edmunds Bunkse
Kim Dovey
Nader El-Bizri
Joseph Grange
Matti Itkonen
Eduardo Mendieta
John Murungi
John Pickles
Ingrid Leman Stefanovic

Books in the Series:

Mysticism and Architecture: Wittgenstein and the Meanings of the Palais Stonborough by Roger Paden
When France Was King of Cartography: The Patronage and Production of Maps in Early Modern France by Christine Marie Petto
Environmental Dilemmas: Ethical Decision Making
by Robert Mugerauer and Lynne Manzo

Environmental Dilemmas

Ethical Decision Making

ROBERT MUGERAUER AND LYNNE MANZO

LEXINGTON BOOKS

A division of
ROWMAN & LITTLEFIELD PUBLISHERS, INC.
Lanham • Boulder • New York • Toronto • Plymouth, UK

LEXINGTON BOOKS

A division of Rowman & Littlefield Publishers, Inc.
A wholly owned subsidiary of The Rowman & Littlefield Publishing Group, Inc.
4501 Forbes Boulevard, Suite 200
Lanham, MD 20706

Estover Road
Plymouth PL6 7PY
United Kingdom

British Library Cataloguing in Publication Information Available

Library of Congress Cataloging-in-Publication Data

Mugerauer, Robert.
  Environmental dilemmas : ethical decision making / Robert Mugerauer and Lynne
Manzo.
    p. cm. — (Toposophia : sustainability, dwelling, design)
  Includes bibliographical references and index.
  ISBN-13: 978-0-7391-2057-6 (cloth : alk. paper)
  ISBN-10: 0-7391-2057-3 (cloth : alk. paper)
  ISBN-13: 978-0-7391-2058-3 (pbk. : alk. paper)
  ISBN-10: 0-7391-2058-1 (pbk. : alk. paper)
  1. Environmental ethics. 2. Environmental responsibility. 3. Decision making—Moral
and ethical aspects. I. Manzo, Lynne. II. Title.
  GE42.M84 2008
  333.72—dc22   2007052120

Printed in the United States of America

♾™ The paper used in this publication meets the minimum requirements of American
National Standard for Information Sciences—Permanence of Paper for Printed Library
Materials, ANSI/NISO Z39.48–1992.

Dedication

To Jan and David McKinley,

who thought about environmental futures
before the rest of us

Contents

Foreword

This pioneering work by Bob Mugerauer and Lynne Manzo in the burgeoning field of what might be labeled, "Ethics of the Building Professions," promises to become "a classic." The value of this work lies in the fact that it will be quite accessible and useful to the highly trained professors/instructors in the building professions who may not have had extensive training in ethics, philosophy, or humanities, but are called upon to offer courses and seminars in ethics. Yet, in no way does this volume fall short of being informed of and firmly based in the methodologies of applied ethics and the long history of ethical theory. It will be thus amenable to both the building professional who in not the too distant future will regularly teach applied ethics courses and the ethicist/philosopher who more frequently may be called upon to tailor teaching acumen in ethics to the needs of the design and building professions. This book will also serve as an ethics guide for non-teaching practitioners who find themselves in a professional atmosphere that increasingly calls for a more developed code of ethics in the workplace and the ability to engage in ethical discourse. This volume has been written with a thorough understanding of the pragmatic need for professionals and professional school students to learn ethics while engaged-in-the-field, where it is necessary to learn "while on your feet." One of the book's strengths is that it can be implemented immediately and directly through its insightful strategy—hey, if you find yourself in this problematic circumstance, and it is likely that sometime in your professional career you will, you need to be apprised of these ethical parameters in order to deal with the situation effectively.

And while the professionals, teachers, and students are engaged with this volume as a kind of "hands-on/how-to manual," without the hassle of having to take time away from the commitment to the building professions, they will be learning about the nature of ethics, its application, and its theoretical orientations, without taking time away from the concerns of their fields. The rift between theory and practice is always operable and thus needs to be negotiated and addressed when devising curriculum. With every move toward theory, it seems that application suffers, and vice versa. Ideally from the point of view of an ethicist, a person acquires extensive training in the historical classics of ethical theory, in contemporary ethical issues, whereby ethical concepts and ethical reasoning can be engaged, and in areas of applied ethics germane to interests and profession. But, such an extensive training has not been implemented and may not be practical and perhaps not efficacious. Nevertheless, with the ideal in mind, authors of applied ethics can integrate these domains in a way that informs the text, and the training of professionals and future professionals through a single course in ethics can be made sufficient in a way that offers the best of possible worlds under the circumstances. They will be trained to engage in moral reasoning, to recognize theoretical positions/paradigms, and to deal with the ethical problems in their respective fields and as they arise in their own professional experience. This volume is sensitive to this ideal and I believe will be highly successful in its implementation.

Let me back up my endorsement with the following observations. I maintain that the proliferation of the discipline of ethics in the last forty or so years can be traced to the cultural revolution of the 1960s. Prior to those cultural changes hegemonic ethical controls were more firmly entrenched in the fabric of our institutions. Recall the formal and highly controlled character of college life prior to "the sixties." But no longer are paternalism, authoritarianism, and other behavioral coercions generally accepted by society, especially when those in power may be out of touch and/or corrupt. The environmental movement and the concern for consumer protection, for example Ralph Nader, emerged during the culture revolution's rejection of the top-down power structure, and were factors leading to the growth of applied ethics in environmental ethics, medical ethics, and in business ethics. No longer would the efficacy of the ethical dimension of life work in one direction, meted out by those in control directed toward those who do not have power. With empowerment and advocacy "the public" now became better equipped to participate in the tactic of ethical probing. Although it was no longer tolerated by society for ethics to be instituted in authoritarian ways, the need for standards of behavior and ethically responsible people and institutions obviously still then persists, and even more so, as the power to demand accountability became more democratized. The personal ethics learned in Sunday school has its own proper excellence, but a developed conscience is yet insufficient for meeting the complex circumstances of a highly diversified technical world.

Thus, the need for raising consciousness about ethics and for ethical training has become recognized by various professions. Formal ethical training has become a necessary requirement. More and more areas of college study have made courses in ethics a requirement for the major. Professions have taken greater steps in developing ethics committees and in requiring additional training in ethics. The fields of applied ethics have grown, not only with environmental ethics and business ethics, but also with bio-/medical/nursing ethics, and legal ethics. The applied ethics for the building professions has so far not enjoyed the progress of development as these other fields. But the time is more than ripe for its development and proliferation. This lacuna is a pressing matter given the severity of the problems that face the world today—architectural ter-rorism, the severity of environmental degradation, the disappearance of nature, and the loss of quality of life. This volume in ethics for the building professions functions as the vanguard and I believe as the exemplar for this exciting and pressingly needed field of study. It is now time to get started!

Gary Backhaus
January, 2008

Acknowledgments

The material in the chapters on principles and rules and major Ethical theories is the result of over thirty years of thinking about and teaching general and professional ethics, including medical, planning, architectural and environmental design ethics. As a result, the origin of what is said often has not always remained clear through dozens of sets of notes. I have made every effort to identify all the sources, but it may be that an occasional phrase has been used inadvertently without attribution. In such cases it is especially important to note that my thinking and writing have benefited especially from: Tom L. Beauchamp and James E. Childress' exemplary *Principles of Biomedical Ethics*, which I used in my medical ethics courses for years, and Michael D. Bayles and Kenneth Henley's *Right Conduct: Theories and Applications*, which was a regular support for my Contemporary Moral Problems courses taught to 250 students at a time. In addition, I have benefited from the many excellent specialized collections (cited in the text), such as Andrew Light and Jonathan M. Smith's *Space, Place, and Environmental Ethics* with its outstanding essays, as well as from the major primary sources.

We would like thank MacDuff Stewart and especially Patrick Dillon, editor, for support and guidance in publication.

Material in the Rincon Center example in Appendix III is used with permission of the University of California Press. The professional codes reproduced in Appendix II are used with permission of their professional organizations:

- The American Institute of Architects, *Code of Ethics and Professional Conduct*
- American Planning Association, *AICP Code of Ethics and Professional Conduct*
- American Society of Landscape Architects, *ASLA Code of Professional Ethics* and *ASLA Code of Environmental Ethics*
- Construction Management Association of America, *Code of Professional Ethics* for the Construction Manager
- National Society of Professional Engineers, Code of Ethics for Engineers

Introduction

The Dimensions of Decision Making

Ordinarily, we go about our activities in everyday life, making decisions and acting in a fairly smooth way. Even when we are faced with a problem or a disagreement with others, we operate with sets of beliefs and values that are ready to hand, so to speak; they are part of the largely unselfconscious way we exist in the world. In the ordinary course of doing things, we more or less consistently apply these beliefs and values, but do not pause to reflect on the fundamental assumptions and concepts on which our thoughts and actions are based, nor on all the implications of our operational "guidance system."

We know, of course, that we need to act responsibly, especially when what we do affects others. It is hoped that one acts responsibility not simply to avoid punishments, but rather because in personal growth one comes to respect others and because it is inherently worthwhile both for society and for ourselves that we act out of consideration for others' well-being as well as our own. But apart from such a mindful way of living (about which we will write more later) there are social modes of accountability. Whether it be informal explanations to clients, peers, or managers, or more formal responses within the court system, we are expected to be able to give an account of why we acted as we did, which amounts to being capable of justifying our actions. When the occasion arises where we find ourselves describing what we did and explaining our intentions, we enter a realm in which there is discussion about what criteria we used to guide our actions and whether we have properly applied these criteria.

In such a situation the very character of our beliefs and values may be called into question. An examination into the foundations of our actions would involve deliberation, through which the criteria for proper responsibility are discerned and articulated in a more explicit and rigorous manner than happens in our everyday practices. This combination of reflection and responsibility is what we mean by "ethics." Ethics is typically defined as a system of principles and rules that helps us determine which actions are right and which are wrong (Beauchamp and Childress, 1983)—but it is this process of reflection that is so critical for ethical decision making and that is integral to this book as we consider different environmental dilemmas and problems. Here, we are concerned with applied normative ethics rather than abstract theorizing, and consider the practical application of ethical principles in real-world situations and decision making.

The different modes of ethical decision making and consequential actions (including, as just mentioned, being able to give an account of our implicit or explicit criteria of what is right and wrong behavior) may be seen as forming four dimensions, all of which we will consider in this book and which readers can explore through its exercises. Whether one is acting responsibly may be seen to be a matter of:

1. *One's individual core values and touchstones* that are ready to hand and routinely put into practice in everyday life. These are both implicit and explicit.

2. *The commonly accepted norms of one's society*, either what is considered *right opinion* or *a consistent worldview* that has historically and culturally developed in one's own cultural context

Since these two dimensions are internalized and put directly into action in everyday life, they may indeed be adequate to define responsible ethical behavior, but deciding upon that would require the explicit reflection which usually—as is normal and not aberrant—does not take place.

In addition, since most societies have long traditions of examining the criteria for good and bad actions and pondering how right conduct can be taught and encouraged, much thought has been given to the foundations of ethics. Often these groundings have been formalized in rules and laws. In such cases, over the centuries and even millennia, behavior has been considered ethical when it is:

3. *Principled action*, that is, when what is done is grounded in socially debated and agreed-upon principles and rules.

Finally, there is considerable cross-cultural agreement that at the most profound level one acts ethically not by following a rational schema or set of rules, but by

4. *Mindfully and consistently living* in a caring, virtuous, or wise manner. [1]

Though this more profound pattern of living ethically shares with the first two dimensions the feature of being directly lived rather than formally judged against principles and rules in each case, it differs from them in that it goes beyond such formal systems—amounting to a deeper and more fully integrated way of living, of acting well. This fourth aspect—perhaps more a goal during one's life's course than an achievement at any given point—is what we call, in both ordinary and technical terms, wisdom, and certainly in the case of care involves reframing questions, assumptions, and what are considered relevant factors in ethical decision making. [2]

In this book we will consider all four dimensions of ethics—reflecting on environmental dilemmas that lead toward responsible action. The first two dimensions will be taken up in chapter 1, the third in chapter 3, the fourth in chapters 2 and 4. [3]

In this book we are particularly interested in the ethical problems and dilemmas that emerge in place-based professional practice—that is, within the fields of architecture, landscape architecture, planning, engineering and construction management. Thus we refer to environment and environmental in a broad sense, not just as nature or pristine ecosystems but as places involving an integration of both natural and constructed elements. In this sense we take an integrated approach to the environment and environmental problems, one that is interdisciplinary and seeks to understand the unique challenges that place-based problems and dilemmas pose.

The Social Character of Environmental Decisions

Environmental problems occur in specific places and involve multiple parties—and thus social relationships. Environmental issues, and the consequences of any actions related to the environment, unavoidably involve, at minimum, the many people who live there and the local ecosystem—all of whom and which need to be incorporated into legitimate decision making processes. Because many people and ecosystems share—or constitute—any given place, they all have a stake in the outcome of what any of us do. It is not surprising that issues are hotly contested given the many (frequently divergent) interests, needs, and preferences of many of a community's members, much less those of outside parties who play a part. (The latter include people "downstream" who are affected by the consequences of our actions, or even the animals, birds, fish, and other organisms—even whole ecosystems—that do not have a say though their well-being and even their lives may hang in the balance.)

After all, it only is when we have to act, or have to respond to proposed action in real situations in particular places that we are called upon to make responsible environmental decisions. But how we think of a given situation, what, if anything, we do about it, and whether and how we think about the implications will help determine what we think constitutes a responsible environmental decision. For example, imagine the following scenarios:

❑   I have a wonderful 100-year-old live oak tree in my yard that has its trunk and two-thirds of its crown on a steep ravine in my side yard (where its roots stabilize the soil therefore preventing erosion down to the neighbor below in the back). Should my side-neighbor be able to shave down the roots that have grown under the fence to his side, buckling the walkway to the side door and backyard, which, given his advancing age, is making it difficult for him to navigate the walkway? What happens if this then harms the root system or even kills the tree, quite possibly leading to a mud-slide that would damage our mutual neighbor farther down the hill?

❑   Should we agree to or oppose the development of the Lopez family's 40 acres (a combination of farmland and wetlands) that the heirs want to turn into a new urbanist subdivision, but that the conservation society says should become part of the adjacent wildlife preserve?

❑   A nearby city needs more electrical power. Should we dam the river, submerging some forest land and a small community, to generate what is needed, or contract for more coal to be strip-mined in Montana and shipped to us by railroad, or support the plan to build a nuclear plant, or increase the price charged to the community by 250 percent to reduce demand? What bearing do these choices have on global warming, and what will our actions do, not only to our region but to the entire planet?

Of course, over time, we may come to realize that the same sort of situations reoccur in other places; or we may need to consider whether we need new policies to adequately deal with new problems (climate change, for example), new technologies (such as mega-hydroelectric power systems), or new social realities (including population growth, globalization, and epidemics). But the starting point in a given problem and the practical outcome of any possible decision are normally a tangle of interconnected physical and social dimensions that occurs in particular places and times, with specific circumstances and details. But, even in a given concrete case, environmental changes typically involve diverse groups of people and the larger physical context, including the health of the ecosystems on which we all depend (often extending to a regional or even global scale). As we will see, these constitute a large part of the reason why there are environmental dilemmas. Consequently, in regard to the environment, not only must we make careful and better individual decisions, we need to improve the way we operate socially, especially given the many roles and responsibilities we have as environmental professionals, or as private-sector developers and public policy-makers and staff, or as engaged citizens.

The Book's Organization and Ways to Use It

This is a book about ethical decision making, which, as you will soon discover, is a multi-faceted and nuanced process. There are many factors and issues that swirl around the ethical choices we make. And just as there is no one objective "right" and "wrong" decision for every scenario, there is no one right way to delve into the discussion of ethical issues and dilemmas. Therefore, we have organized this book so that the reader can start anywhere, and then move to the material of most immediate interest. In a certain way, it is like a hypertext, where each chapter has links to all the others; one could start anywhere and then move to any other chapter, and the ideas would be coherent and make sense.

We've organized the book on the idea that we already start in the midst of many perplexing problems in the world, then can more or less inductively move through stages of ordinary individual and group ethical decisions, and then through more and more formalized formats (professional, logical principle, substantial theory), concluding with a concentrated set of cases in which the different procedures can be exercised. The reader can stop at any point or skip around, as is appropriate.

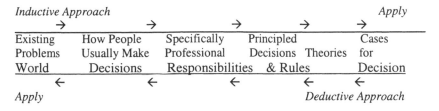

Inductive Approach				Apply
→	→	→	→	→
Existing	How People	Specifically	Principled	Cases
Problems	Usually Make	Professional	Decisions Theories	for
World	Decisions	Responsibilities	& Rules	Decision
←	←	←	←	←
Apply				Deductive Approach

The order of the chapters correlates with the viewpoint that an inductive procedure is the best empirical approach: we discover something in the world and try to understand it. When we encounter a question or a problem we think about it and try to address it while providing a responsible account of how we do so, at least to ourselves, if not to others. First we try to understand the situation with our own existing resources and viewpoints; then, organizational or institutional formulations of practices and norms become codified; such professional traditions could be more formally understood as the implementation of a coherent set of principles and rules; in turn, these principles and rules would come to be understood and finally legitimated insofar as they would generate general, coherent theories. Finally, the entire apparatus can be applied sensitively to new problems.

Or, considered from the other direction, working out matters more deductively, we can start with the theories that articulate the grounds that legitimize actions; these theories can be made more specific and applicable by elaborating the principles and rules that consistently follow from them. Decisions made in one's professional work can also be based on the codes of ethics of our individual professions. These codes, in turn, inform the social and individual viewpoints which we implicitly use on a day-to-day basis when we do not stop (nor usually need to) to deliberate on a course of action.

Because all the stages and formats of decision making are interconnected, it is perfectly fine to start with what is most interesting, most relevant, or strategically useful to you. Many people like to systematically move from general principles to more specific principles and rules, and then apply those to cases; others prefer to start where we usually operate every day and discuss cases, the deliberation of which enables us to move to the more formal principles or theories if further depth or substantiation of an argument is needed.

It should be noted that chapter 5 is especially important because it provides the occasion for the synthesis of environmental dilemmas and the many possible strategies for at least partial resolutions. Here, by focusing on sustainability as a complex, problematic realm, the book provides an extended example—and, more importantly, an opportunity—for you to practice integrating and applying all the elements involved in ethical decision making.

The Book's Goals

The book does not itself develop or advocate a position as most environmental ethics books do. That is, it does not develop the substantial content or arguments to try to establish what constitutes justice or allocation of resources for environment issues. Rather, the book focuses on the decision making process; and raises questions so that one can move to deeper reflection and to bases for responsible decision making. Our goal is to help readers be more aware of the worldviews, beliefs, and values that enter into the moral decisions they might make, and how these decisions might connect to larger ethical rules, principles, and theories.

To help readers think about their own positions and how they might approach certain ethical dilemmas, we employ a number of exercises and cases that each allow investigations into the choices and issues that different stakeholders might face. These cases allow investigation through different realms— there are those choices we make as individuals and those we make as members of particular groups either with shared worldviews or as belonging to the same professions. Then we can investigate those choices in terms of their broader and more formalized ethical principles and finally consider the theories that attempt to provide a comprehensive account of ethics.

Rather than select a large number of cases, we present several rather complex cases that bring up multiple issues as new layers of information and new facets of the scenario unfold. We present these cases in stages so that you may tackle them in increments through a series of exercises throughout the book. It will be helpful when doing the exercises to keep copies of your answers as we will return to many of these cases at different places in the book.

Skills: in reading through this book and working with the exercises you will learn about and practice (specifically) how to deal with environmental dilemmas and (generally) how to go about ethical decision making. By the time we have finished you will have:
- gained knowledge about the major ethical theories and principles[4]
- critically reflected on your own position (your values and worldview, including the assumptions and implications associated with them)
- understood and become able to engage with positions that differ from yours
- considered alternative approaches to resolving moral dilemmas, including identifying points of agreement/disagreement among alternative worldviews and stakeholder groups
- discerned differences are a matter of weight or interpretation given to a principle or value that parties may actually share, as compared to non-resolvable differences in assumptions or beliefs
- found a vocabulary and structure to discuss and work through differences
- exercised skills fundamental to moral reasoning and communication: specifically, you will have improved critical and active listening, read-

ing, thinking, writing, and will have increased your imaginative understanding of complex issues and problems.

Notes

1. There is some disagreement concerning the relation of care to virtue. The subtleties of care and virtue ethics will be treated in chapters 2 and 4.

2. That wisdom is the deepest realm from which one acts ethically is developed by traditional philosophers Aristotle and MacIntyre and recent care-ethicists, as well as by neuro-cognitive scientists Maturana and Varela, and, of course, Eastern traditions. See the end section of chapter 4, Theories, for more on this matter.

3. The relationships among these four dimensions of decision making: (1) our individual taken-for-granted bundles of values, beliefs, and attitudes; (2) socially shared world-views and norms about what is right; (3) formal sets of principles and (4) theories, including perhaps even glimmers of deeper wisdom—naturally vary dramatically among individuals, ranging from non-existent through fully coherent, as do the ways they are applied to actual problematic situations. One of the goals of this book is to provide the opportunity to work toward a more consistent integration of all these aspects and thus a more robust mode of decision making.

4. While the deeper analysis of subtle relationships among the major principles and theories is properly a matter of theoretical or meta-ethics, and thus not the focus of this book, the most important relationships and strategies for practical decision making certainly will be treated here—see especially chapters 3 and 4.

Chapter One

Reflection, Responsibility, and Decision Making

Ethics as Reflection and Responsibility

There are so many contested interpretations of ethics and morality that we do not believe it is useful to begin by arguing about *the* correct definitions. Instead, we propose to unfold the relevant distinctions and variations as we go—after all, one of the major tasks of any ethics is to come to an understanding of the complexities and subtleties of the subject matter, and this often happens incrementally. (As we proceed, it will become clearer why we have so many disagreements, and why those disagreements so often appear irresolvable. Such understanding also will provide several strategies for more successful decision making.) For all practical purposes it is sufficient to begin by thinking of ethics in terms of reflection and responsibility. As human beings, we are called upon to become conscious of who we are, of our relationships in the world, and to become responsible for our actions. The process of social deliberation about these matters is what we call ethics. While it is true that "every individual has a biography that consists in mature actualization of intelligent freedom and the manifestation of a unique personality," is also is the case that we belong within a social environment even before birth and during the course of our lives we can become fully human only within such communities (Ashley and O'Rourke 1982, 5).

"The intrinsic relation of persons to community implies that there is a *political* dimension to all human events. Therefore, ethics of the person-in-community must also be a *politics*," taking into account "the ways persons develop value systems socially—sometimes through debate and often through social conflict. . . . the problems of poverty, food, population, and pollution are central both to national and international political struggles" and, at the same time, are fundamental ethical issues (Ashley and O'Rourke 1982, 9).

Note that the personal and social process of making decisions and environmental choices does not end; rather, it goes on indefinitely, as long as a society remains functional. As the well-respected planner Peter Hall put it:

Decisions arise from a complex process of interactions among actors. All
these people think themselves rational, and are trying to behave rationally for
much of the time; but their conceptions of the rational differ. They have different goals, and different ways of achieving these goals. Some of them, particularly senior professionals and bureaucrats, have been trained according to
rational modes and will try particularly hard to apply these in decision making. Others, in particular politicians, will tend to follow more intuitive, adap-
tive, piecemeal methods. The most important definable groups are the community, or more particularly those members of the community who play an
active role in various formal and informal organizations that try to intervene
in the decision making process; the elected politicians, who must promise certain policies to the electorate in order to gain re-election and who will be subject while in office to pressures of events; and the professional and administrative bureaucracy which must administer policy but which invariably also
plays a large role in shaping it. Then each of these broad groups splits into
sub-groups. ... No outcome is ever decisive, since it can be reversed or can
wither away due to non-implementation. Thus the process of decision making
is not discrete, but is part of an ongoing complex of interrelated acts; and non-
decisions may be as important as decisions. (Hall 1981, 196–197)

Despite the fact that social decision processes continuously unfold (as Hall
just pointed out), ethical dilemmas are usually seen diachronically—as a snapshot of a moment in time suspended. Instead, dilemmas are perhaps best understood in a process-oriented way where questions, issues, and decisions are
continually interrogated, and actions are guided by reflexive practice. That is,
we start to identify and sort out the issues we see revolving around a dilemma.
We then begin identifying our values and concerns with each facet of the
situation, and consider a course of action by imagining possible outcomes and
implications. Then, based on what we might anticipate, we might go back and
re-think our strategies. Like the design process itself, the ethical decision making process can be an iterative one. Hence, a basic format for our exercises includes returning to the same complex problem or case several times with new
information, questions, or approaches; or some of them are presented incrementally, and we ask you to reflect and make decisions at a given point before
proceeding.

Dilemmas

We have chosen the title of this book carefully, stressing the decisions involved in attempting to deal with environmental dilemmas. What makes a
situation a dilemma? First, it is a concrete, real situation where a decision has
to be made. It is not simply a matter of discussing possible alternatives in an
abstract manner, debating the relative merits and demerits of various options
without having to actually choose a course of action. In such cases, the situation remains in the realm of the abstract, interminable argument. But in the

real world a decision has to be made; you have to resolve the dilemma to get on with your life (Harding 1985).

Second, and more importantly, a dilemma is essentially a no-win situation—or at least there is no win-win scenario. A dilemma is a dilemma precisely because each choice yields some negative consequences, so it is a matter of choosing between one set of sacrifices or drawbacks and another.

Third, and related to the second, dilemmas have a quality of contradiction to them. Different goals or courses of action are either in direct contradiction to one another or to some values we hold dear (Harding 1985). Thus, in a di-

---

A dilemma arises in a real, concrete situation where a difficult decision must be made—it is not merely an issue to be debated around a conference table—even though all the possible choices have some inescapable negative consequences and involve goals and values that contradict one another.

---

lemmatic situation, there is no getting around the fact that somewhere, somehow, something will be lost. Based on this we can also see how, in a true dilemma, there is no clear "right" answer that will present itself with adequate deliberation. In fact, a dilemma—even a moral one—is not a right-or-wrong situation at all. If a situation or decision were simply a matter of right and wrong, then there would be no dilemma to grapple with; instead it would be a matter of finding the right choice (Harding 1985). But this does not exist in a dilemma.

Fourth, all dilemmas have an element of weightiness to them. Making a decision in the context of a dilemma it is not like picking out a new suit. There are real consequences, and as we have established, when it comes to environmental or place-based dilemmas, these consequences, for better or worse, are shared across multiple stakeholders and communities.

How we understand a situation influences whether we perceive there to be a dilemma or not. Even if we conclude that we are facing a dilemma, how we frame that dilemma determines what questions we ask ourselves about the situation, how we understand what is at stake, and how we determine the right course of action. So different people facing the same situation may not all perceive it as a dilemma, and among those who do, subgroups may deliberate about it quite differently depending on what they think is really at issue in the situation. That is, we operate with many differing sets of premises.

Dilemmas—Good versus Good

"The essentially tragic fact," said the philosopher Hegel, "is not so much the war of good with evil as the war of good with good." In the engineered world this truth is brought home to us again and again. We try to do good and find that we are unwittingly damaging something we hold dear. Yet such dilemmas can evoke noble impulses and creative thought. It is often in challenge that we find the ultimate expression of our humanity.

(Florman 1996, 62)

Let us take the Heinz Dilemma for example, the classic dilemma raised in almost every Ethics 101 course.[1] In this scenario, a man called Heinz has a wife suffering from a grave illness. He cannot afford the medication that would make her well and without which she will die. The question posed is: should Heinz steal the medication to save the life of his wife? Depending on how one looks at this situation, it might not be considered much of a dilemma. Certainly the situation is weighty, and each option—to steal the medication or not—has negative consequences: possibly getting arrested, in which case Heinz will be of limited help to his wife, or allowing Heinz's wife to die. However, we might understand this dilemma differently if we change where we place our values. If we put human life above laws regulating the possession of goods or objects, even if they are controlled substances, then it might not be considered a dilemma and our choice is relatively easily made to steal the medication. This decision could be said to be a fairly logical one of prioritizing life over property, and it is that value that justifies its "rightness" (Harding 1985, Gilligan 1982). But this hypothetical dilemma could be significantly altered if the deliberator were to fill in some more details in the scenario, to consider further the nature of the social relationships involved, or the consequences of the various possible actions. Psychologist Carol Gilligan argues that if Heinz's decision to steal is considered not so much in terms of probable outcomes, but rather in terms of the specific consequences that stealing might have for a man whom we know already has limited means and power (since he could not afford the life-saving medication in the first place), then the dilemma itself changes:

> Considered in the light of its probable outcomes—his wife dead, or Heinz in jail, brutalized by the violence of that experience and his life compromised by a record of felony—the dilemma itself changes. Its resolution has less to do with the relative weights of life and property in an abstract moral conception than with the collision between two lives, formerly conjoined by now in op-

position, where the continuation of one life can occur only at the expense of the other. (Gilligan 1982, 101, as quoted in Harding 1985)

The nature of the social relationships involved in a dilemma and sense of responsibility and care we might have toward others is critical in the way we frame and deliberate on an ethical problem. As Gilligan points out, when we are dealing with real-life dilemmas, we typically know the people involved as well as something of their lives and their situations. And it is this social familiarity and embeddedness that makes a real difference in how we deliberate. For example, consider how your response to the Heinz dilemma might change if you were asked to steal the drug for him or if he were a stranger whom you read about in the morning paper.

Moreover, when we look at environmental dilemmas, there is an even greater level of social embeddedness. We know various stakeholders; they may be our friends, family, neighbors, our children's teachers, our religious leaders. We may like them or dislike them, agree with them or not, but either way we are in some mutual relation with them, and it is with all these fellow citizens that we must negotiate our own environmental decisions, either implicitly or explicitly.

Imagine the following scenario: You are a young engineer just out of school and you recently landed a great job with a reputable firm. You are put on a big exciting project, and although your particular tasks on the job are very modest, you are still pleased to be involved in the project. You are at the office late one night and you overhear your boss on the phone with the subcontractor. It seems they are discussing the supports for some of the beams in the new community center on the project you're working on. The subcontractor has suggested using different rods in their suspension for easier fabrication and to cut some costs. You know that such alterations mid-stream are not altogether unusual, and the changes are made. A week later, while you are on the construction site, one of the beams falls and nearly misses a worker. Being nearby, you help move the beam and notice that the problem seems to stem from the new rods used to support the beams. What do you do?

Now imagine that you tell your boss in the hopes that he might address the situation. He'll look into it, he says, and two weeks later, when you're on the site again, you notice the same rods and installation method were used. You talk to him again, hoping it was an oversight, and he explains that the senior engineers looked into it, there was an error with the installation of the one beam only, and there is no need to alter the overall fabrication of the holding rods. Now what do you do? And what would you do if three months later, when the center opens, a beam falls near some people during an after school arts program?

An unlikely fictional scenario, you might think. Well, this scenario is not much different than a real situation that occurred in 1981 when several walkways in the atrium of the Hyatt Regency in Kansas City, Missouri, collapsed leaving 114 people dead and 185 people injured. The problem was traced to the design of the walkways hung from rods connected to the atrium ceiling.

Upon the suggestions of the subcontractor, the changes were made. Then one night, when people were dancing on the walkways, the load became too much to bear and the connections that held up the walkways failed. The end result—apart from the loss of life—was that charges of negligence were filed against the engineering firm and both the architect and the firm lost their licenses (as summarized in Fleddermann 1999, 70).

To be sure, many environmental dilemmas that call for ethical decision making may not be life-or-death situations. Then again, it depends on what one considers legitimately a life-or-death situation and whose life is in question. Is it the lives of strangers many miles away, or the life of a loved one? Is it exclusively human life that is at stake? Is it a matter of survival or well-being? And is survival alone viable without any decent quality of life?

So then how do we, and should we, make choices about what to do? How do we, and should we, decide what is the "right" thing to do when faced with a difficult choice? We can begin to answer these questions by focusing on our everyday moral or ethical decision making, whether it concerns specifically environmental or other matters.

How We Make Decisions

Our Individual Bundles of Core Values: Pre-Reflective Yardsticks

As Harding (1985) points out, our acceptance of some set of premises over another is a function of the assumptions with which we live and where cultural differences (gender, age, race, ethnicity, religious inclinations, etc.) come into play. In other words, when making decisions, most of us do not start from scratch each time. Rather, we usually begin from a stable position, a more or less coherent and reliable view that has been absorbed from society and family that we then idiosyncratically modify through experience during our lifetime. This yardstick, as we shall call it, normally enables us both to make decisions that are in accordance with what others deem right, and to continue our communal way of life. Most of the time, we put our value system into practice in a quite consistent and sophisticated manner, which we are able to do because we have internalized it and it has become normalized to our social group (such normalizing is what constitutes the members of a society to be an "us," and enables at least the local world to appear intelligible and relatively coherent). Thus we operate pragmatically, without stopping to analyze or debate the principles or structures upon which our practices are based, and which in fact operate through, or are actualized by, those same practices—the way we live within the worldview we take for granted.

It would seem that all of us have our own ideas of what is right or wrong, even if we are not aware of this until a situation arises to elicit them or cause them to be examined. We can consider these values and principles our "ethical bundles." They are our own collection of values, beliefs, attitudes about what is right and what is wrong. Typically they operate on an implicit level, as we often do not interrogate or articulate our guiding motives or criteria until we find ourselves in an ethical dilemma or some moment of tension. In such exceptional instances, in order to move forward, to make a decision that we can feel good about, or at least accept, we can and do question our usual taken-for-granted world and interrogate our implicit values and beliefs, perhaps even going on to formulate these as general ideals or principles.

Identify Your Personal Ethical Yardstick

Try to identify some of the fundamental premises and values upon which you would operate when faced with a difficult decision:

❑ What do you depend on in your own conscience as your compass when you are trying to decide what to do?

❑ To live with yourself and do the right thing, what values and beliefs do you use as a yardstick to measure your choices?

❑ Are there any deal-breakers?—any basic rules of thumb that you would not bend (for example, Do not kill)? Jot down your basic rules. Now challenge yourself: Can you think of any circumstances where these rules actually could be questioned?

Such already internalized and accepted systems of interpretation, values, and practices normally allow us to make decisions without going back to square one because they select the relevant features to be considered (out of the mass of available information) and provide the measures by which we evaluate the possible outcomes. Because we begin with our core values and rules of thumb, we have a more or less reliable yardstick for decision making. As a result, unless the problem is exceptionally complicated or contested, deciding what to think or do can be a fairly short process. However, since the issues covered in this book are precisely such apparently unsolvable contested problems, we need to take a closer look at our implicit system of guideposts.

At the level of individual thinking and decision making, we need to situate ourselves. Where do our views come from? How much do we conform or rebel? How do we change? There are arguments that what we believe and take as our fundamental yardstick largely come from our family and society; but, certainly that is a complex matter that changes throughout different stages of our lives. Then, too, there are a variety of cognitive styles, and these have a bearing on why we see things as we do and on how we might improve the way we work with each other.

In analyzing the social source of our beliefs and attitudes about land use, Timothy Beatley contends:

> Particular values, land use values included, can be attributed to many sources, including parents and family, church, school, publications and the media, and political organizations. Research suggests, for instance, that parents influence to a considerable extent the political views and social outlooks of their off-spring. And, clearly, one's basic political and social views will, in turn, influence one's views about ethical land use.
>
> There is also considerable validity to the old saying that where you stand depends on where you sit. One's values and attitudes may be greatly shaped by the social and economic positions in society that one holds, and by one's source of employment. We can consider this in terms of land use once again: If one's livelihood depends on harvesting and milling old-growth timber, one is probably less likely to hold the view that such timberlands ought to be protected or set aside in perpetuity. If one is employed by the oil industry, one is less likely to support additional wilderness protection of those areas known to possess oil and natural gas reserves. Employment and economic and social position influence people's perceptions about what constitutes ethical land use (1994, 20).

But then what do we do with these differing perceptions and attitudes? How can we negotiate these differences? As Timothy Beatley points out, acknowledging the importance of different influences on the formation of values and attitudes does not automatically mean that land use ethics is simply the task of tallying up different values and normative positions and then organizing land use policy accordingly. Values and ethical positions about land use can change in response to both public dialogue and argument, and to private thought and reflection.

In regard to our individual decision making, it is important to understand our own mode of thinking and deciding. Many psychologists, sociologists, and educators have found that cognitive and learning styles are important factors in how we operate, and knowing more about them can facilitate success in decision making and satisfaction in our actions. Insofar as there is a correlation between cognitive style and career choice (a well-established phenomenon), there might be a correlation, however loosely, with the way different professionals—in their roles—go about deciding things. This might also explain some of the problems we sometimes have in understanding each other's different perspectives and values. Here we will note two different approaches to describing cognitive modes that bear on how individuals go about making decisions: a Jungian theory and the post-Kohlberg/pro-Gilligan recognition that moral reasoning involves a combination of cognition, feeling, and intuition—to be discussed in more detail at the end of this chapter. Of course, as with any psychological theory, different scholars take issue and provide important critiques of what is presented here; the point, however, is that these two theories show why not everyone thinks in the same manner and that adequate ethical decisions are not narrowly rationalistic.

First, the psychologist Carl Jung's work has identified four different cognitive styles, operative in two pairs: thinking (logical cognition) and feeling (subjective discernment and valuation, especially normalizing in relation to social groups and contexts); sensation (via physical senses) and intuition (of what is not explicit or even an aspect of the unconscious).

Thinking

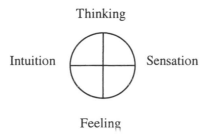

Intuition   Sensation

Feeling

We each have the capacity for all of these cognitive styles, but we often demonstrate strength and preferences toward some dimensions more than others. However, for Jung, ideally all four dimensions come into balance within each of us:

> For complete orientation all four functions should contribute equally: thinking should facilitate cognition and judgment, feeling should tell us how and to what extent a thing is important or unimportant for us, sensation should convey concrete reality to us through seeing, hearing, tasting, etc., and intuition should enable us to divine the hidden possibilities in the background, since these too belong to the complete picture of a given situation. (vol. 6, 1976, par. 900)

However, as Jung acknowledges, we typically operate with a combination of cognitive styles that involves one primary style and a secondary or auxiliary mode from the alternative pair. Given that the theory holds that within each pair one of the two is dominant and the other significantly subordinate, the corresponding two minor dimensions usually will be somewhat absent. For example, a person may be a thinking type (with little feeling) and an intuitive type (with little sensation). To be sure, there have been challenges to these various typologies, and questions as to how consistent one's way of thinking and acting really is across time and circumstances. Nonetheless, many such personality scales prevail and are applied in career counseling, among them the Myers-Briggs Type Indicator, the Gray-Wheelwright Jungian Type Survey, and the Singer-Loomis Inventory (Sharp 1987). These provide insights into modes of thinking and decision making; and, since we are cognizant of our individual approaches and worldviews, can facilitate our ethical decision making.

Shared Worldviews

While it may seem that everyone has a distinct personal set of values used in making decisions, there are patterns among us and commonalities across individuals about what we value and believe. This is evident when we consider our beliefs about which values take precedence over or outweigh others. At this level we are not denying the individuality of decision making, but pointing out that our individual positions can embody or constitute more general worldviews that normally are shared by many members of a culture (especially among those in the same given time and place). Thus, although there are a vast number of unique individual viewpoints, and while the decisions that individuals make will be unique, this does not mean we spiral into utter relativism. Because there are common threads across people's worldviews, there also are opportunities for collective action. For example, personal reflection and decision making, while being individual experiences, involve shared worldviews because they take place within the context of social networks and assumptions and because they involve our values, which, however, independent, nonetheless have been generated through interactions with others. At the least, then, we need to consider what common threads we may share in order to develop guidelines for ethical decision making (Ledwith 2005).

There are a host of ways that worldviews have been conceptualized and categorized over the years, and each leads us to different ideas about knowledge and action. These frameworks categorize and describe the coherent worldviews that appear in or through our actual routine practices, especially insofar as they provide the dispositions according to which we are likely to act in a given situation. Over the centuries, an array of different frameworks have developed, the most important of which we will highlight in this section. The following frameworks are examples only, and you will soon see that there is some overlap among them. There is little if any agreement about the precise descriptions of given positions, much less about the best classification system. Indeed, one of the authors has found that that in 30 books and 90 articles on the topic there is nothing close to agreement on common terms (Mugerauer and Murnane, 1992). What follows, then, are the major concurrent, alternative ways of trying to make sense of the different worldviews that scholars have identified over time.

Understanding various worldviews is crucial because they are the frameworks that define and delineate the relationship among the basic aspects of reality (the material world, humans, and the sacred, if there is such a thing), and thus includes an interpretation of nature and our relation to it. We first will discuss worldviews generally, then turn to particular views of nature. These are complemented by exercises at the end of the chapter.

There are different bases or fundamental premises for what we believe in that essentially have to do with what we see as the nature of reality. Fundamentally, three major or classic alternatives have been identified (with a significant subdivision within one of them), each of which specifies the characteristics of and relationships among human beings, the material universe, and the sacred.

❑ *Humanism,* in which human beings are understood to be either the most sophisticated organisms or unique (for example by possessing the capacity for reason and language) and thus as providing the measure of value and meaning in the world. What matters is what is generated by, or relevant to, human beings. This is an anthropocentric worldview. It does not necessarily hold that the natural world and nonhuman organisms are unimportant but that human life is central and takes precedence. It can be compatible with belief in some sacred beings, but only insofar as it sees humans as not subordinate or dependent upon them.

❑ *Naturalism,* in which reality is understood to consist of material and energy systems, whose physical-chemical laws and what evolutionarily follows from them are all that there is. Since what happens in the world is the product of these natural processes, human beings, too, are determined by them, and culture is understood as itself natural to organisms such as ourselves. Here humans are no more intrinsically important than nonhuman beings, and certainly not inherently more so than other organisms or ecological systems. Typically, naturalism holds that the idea of a sacred force or divinities is an illusion generated by psychological needs.

❑ *Theism,* in which a sacred force, a God or gods operate, especially as the creative source of the natural and human realms, which are thus dependent upon and subordinate to such divinity (and to which the natural and human world may tend or move back toward as a goal). Whether only originally or continuously actively involved in the world, the sacred would provide the ultimate measure of what is valuable and of how the material and human worlds are to be related, and thus of how we should act. Some theisms hold that there are beings other than humans and nature (for example, angels); some theisms hold that humans are created as superior to the natural world and to animals, others that humans do not hold a specially privileged position in the universe.

Note: here we use the term theism in the loose or general sense as just defined. We do not attempt to work out this worldview for all the differing and contested beliefs and definitions of God, deity and deities, and *the sacred.* To note the precise, technical definitions: atheism is the denial of the existence of a God or gods, polytheism is the belief that there are many gods; monotheism is the belief that there is only one God; deism is the belief in a God who set up the universe and subsequently left it alone; theism (a form of monotheism) is the belief in a personal God who created and sustains the world; and pantheism is the belief that God is identical with the natural world.

Within these basic views of how the universe is constituted, there are specific understandings of what nature is: in naturalism, it is the material realm of all that there is, a realm that includes but does not necessarily privilege human beings within the larger system or ecological network of beings; in humanism, nature is the physical basis or background to the subject that matters most— humans—and is to be used as we see fit; in theisms nature is the creation of sacred powers, to be understood in itself and in relation to humans according to the specifics of the divine directives. Congruently, we can see that in these various perspectives how we understand humans varies in the same way, with differing interpretations of our roles or places in the universe.

Alternative Characterizations of Major Worldviews

There is another way to characterize the major worldviews that explicitly describes their understanding of the natural environment and its relations to humans. This nomenclature may make clearer how the differing worldviews form alternative foundations for environmental decision making. The deep motives for environmental decisions lie in the meanings and values that are either derived from the natural, material world, from the human realm, or from the divine. Accordingly, the three classic worldviews often are described by alternative-complementary adjectives:

❑ *Anthropocentric* worldviews are the humanistic ones in which the greatest concern is for human needs. In different versions, what is considered to matter ranges from basic utilitarian needs to higher human cultural-spiritual developments (e.g. beauty-arts, play, justice, wisdom). A very important distinction that lies between individualistic and social anthropocentric positions (as we will shortly see).
❑ *Biocentric-ecocentric* worldviews are naturalisms, in which what matters ranges—widely—from the condition of matter and energy, to the basic needs of individual organisms or species, to the more complex needs of ecological-systems, or even to planetary life as a whole.
❑ *Theocentric* worldviews are the highly diverse theisms, in which, to note just a few versions, nature and the human are created or sustained within the divine (for traditional theisms), or where nature itself is considered to be the divine (pantheism), or where the generative forces of nature are the special province of feminine earth religions.

As you are now beginning to see, there is some overlap in these frameworks of worldviews. Moreover, not all frameworks comprise mutually exclusive worldviews. Many frameworks or specific positions within them cut across categories of worldviews. For example, those who hold that the world is a physical-mechanical, deterministic system, a version of naturalism, may also have either an inclination to anthropocentricism or biocentrism, depending on whether they hold to a social Darwinism that sees humans as the ultimate evolutionary achievement or to a less humanly centered materialism. Some forms of both naturalism and theism agree on the value of human life in a way that approximates a moderate humanism, though not for the same reasons. Your position in regard to these various worldviews will become clearer as we go through the cases and exercises in this chapter. Puzzling out how the various classification schemes overlap and relate to one another is an interesting challenge, and at the heart of intellectual history, but it is not our main task here. For now, we hope you think about where you might situate your worldview in relation to these frameworks to get you on your way to considering the multiple dimensions of ethical decision making.[2]

Hopefully, it is becoming clearer how the major worldviews involve assumptions and implications for environmental evaluations and decision making. For instance, some of the worldviews are frameworks built upon fundamental premises about the relationship of humans to other species, as well as to one another. An important dimension of this type of framework is about the distribution of resources. This revolves around whether we have a right to take what we want and need, and whether resources should be distributed equally across the population or according to some distributional logic, such as giving more for those who need more, or more for those who deserve more—however we might define need or deservedness

Social Darwinism—a naturalistic position with strong emphasis on, and lessons for, humans—holds that the world runs by way of competition and that only the fittest will survive. Within this framework, which applies not only to the animal kingdom but to humans, we can speak about the most ambitious and hard-working gaining the advantage and having—or deserving—what they accomplish. Included in this worldview are beliefs about the natural selection among ideas, economic systems, and so on, not just among people or animals. Here it is believed that the "best" ideas are most likely to catch hold and survive.

In contrast to social Darwinism we find the humanistic idea of fairness, or a belief that there must be some regulation of the distribution of goods, and the like. This worldview is based on the belief that we should follow a maxim such as: "From each according to ability," "To each according to her need," or "To each according to his contribution." You will notice that these are contending versions of one approach.

The Classifications We Will Use

Given the numerous possible alternatives and combinations of worldview frameworks that exist, we encourage you to be as precise as you can about your own position. For the sake of a clear and manageable format, we will develop the following categories in relation to the environment. These are the classifications of shared worldviews that we rely on in this text: anthropocentric (in which humans living in the natural environment—whether or not created by a divine source—provide the measure of meaning); eco- or biocentric (which takes the environment to be inherently valuable, containing humans as non-privileged); theocentric (in which the environment and human realms are grounded in and sustained by the divine).

Within the anthropocentric humanisms there are two important variations: individualism, or privatism, in which the natural environment is understood as a pure resource, controlled by and solely for the use of individuals. Here, value is placed on the idea of private individuals having rights and freedoms as individuals—primacy is given to that value. An obvious example of this is the idea of individual property rights—that individuals can do whatever they please with the property they own. In fact, the very idea of property ownership is a function of this worldview. The basic question is whether ethical behavior can be understood as the consistent pursuit of self-interest (within a minimal code of law and contract enforcement). In contrast, the idea of social well-being requires that humans need complex social networks to live and thrive (where the environment is taken to be the context for communal, cultural human development). This approach involves an appreciation that there are a large number of diverse communities, not only in historical relationships to specific ecological systems or regions, but often in tension or conflict with each other—such that social and environmental issues usually are inseparable.

Identify Your Personal Worldview

❑ How would you name your overall general worldview?

❑ Do any of the worldviews discussed here resonate in particular with you?

❑ How would you name your specifically environmental framework?

❑ Either use the categories in the box that follows or ones of your own choosing. Provide a working name for your view and list a few of the basic ideas identifying this position.

Information Box

Worldviews at a Glance

In this table we synthesize our categories of worldviews with others that have been identified in the literature by their most commonly used names.

This provides you with an easy worldview-at-a-glance so you may see how the various worldviews can be categorized and how they relate to one another.

Anthropocentric
A. Individualism – Privatism
❑   Free market
❑   Social Darwinism

B. Social Well-Being
❑   Technocracy
❑   Some Preservation-conservation-restoration
❑   Utilitarianism

Ecocentric – Biocentric
❑   Environmentalism
❑   Systems holism
❑   Animal rights
❑   Deep ecology
❑   Land ethic
❑   Eco-feminism
❑   Some preservation-conservation-restoration

Theocentric – Grounded in Sacred Powers
❑   Pantheism
❑   Earth religions
❑   Monotheisms including Christianity, Islam, Judaism
❑   Polytheism
❑   Hinduism
❑   Buddhism

In the information box we have synthesized the various worldviews that have been identified by scholars over the years, and in some cases millennia. As noted, there is nothing resembling agreement on common terms, categories, or definitions. But, it is an important start to know that such worldviews exist and to try to situate your own perspective among them.

Strategies for Decision making and Dealing with Dilemmas at the Personal Level

Core Values and Worldviews

We can progress in clarifying and understanding our own and others' personal core values and worldviews and in engaging strategies for environmental decision making by considering some of the major alternatives that need to be decided upon. We will explore the strategy of making decisions through honestly recognizing both differences and commonalities (by looking at the critical distinction between privatism and the other worldviews, by taking up anthropocentric and non-anthropocentric positions, and by making explicit the implications of the worldviews for the uses of the world. Then we will see how a focus on commonalities among worldviews may help dissolve dilemmas stemming from seeming differences among those worldviews. This also will provide a chance to unfold some of the more subtle characteristics of environmental decision making—often features that we need to accept rather than deny at perhaps our peril. It is important to note that while stressing commonalities is an important strategy, it only works if in the overall process there is honesty in acknowledging and dealing with genuine differences. (We will see this same tension between both necessities—differences that preclude false essentialism, and samenesses that genuinely do characterize some phenomena—when we deal with stereotypes, the historical features of different professional roles and attitudes, and also with the related varieties of aesthetics in chapters 5 and 6).

❑ *Step One: Privatism Versus Other Worldviews*
As Ashley and O'Rourke (1982, 14–15) point out, the most difficult position to bring to the table in discussion is the privatism that characterizes much of American thought and, with the spread of globalized capital and technology, more and more of the rest of the world. Privatism is the position that strongly emphasizes individual rights (over community responsibilities), to the extent that one holds that:

> I can do anything—anything is right—as long as it does not hurt someone else). This view derives from the tradition of individualism and contractualism developed by Hobbes and Locke [and Nozick, 1974] that holds: society exists only as a means to protect one individual from another, so as to leave each to pursue his or her private purposes. Moreover, any claim of one human being on another that is not contractual goes beyond the right to be let alone and is therefore unethical. Ethical behavior becomes the consistent pursuit of self-interest within a minimal code of law and contract enforcement. Proponents of this ethic argue (1) that in fact people really act this way and therefore other ethics are hypocritical, and (2) that this system of laissez faire actually produces more economic prosperity and human progress than do collectivist and altruistic ethics. In its more extreme though very common

> versions, the position embraces a social Darwinism that contends that even harming others is natural and acceptable, since life is a matter of the survival of the fittest. (Ashley and O'Rourke 1982, 14)

Obviously, such subordination of all values to that of the deciding (and contentious) individual makes discussion with others very difficult, to say the least. A further substantial difficulty lies in the contradiction inherent in the moderate version of privatism: since in fact no one's actions affect only the actor, harms and benefits to others are unavoidable—and thus communal impacts do need to be considered, even in individual decisions, if they are to be ethical. Privatism implicitly acknowledges the communal impacts in that it stresses the importance of family—one acts not just for oneself, in a grossly selfish manner, but for the sake of one's family or a specific set of one's loved ones since one has responsibility to provide for their needs. But, if we attend to the realities of how we consume goods and use the environment, it is easy to see that there is a spectrum of possible actions, ranging from providing reasonably for one's family without harming others to seeking to provide as much as to harm others.

The conflict with others would especially involve those in competition for the goods in question. It also would engage even those who, while not in direct competition, either produce or provide what is consumed from a marginalized position or who inhabit lifesystems that depend on such resources but find that their systems and ways of life become unsustainable (a point to which we will return in chapter 5). Whether privatism is grounded in religious, humanistic, or materialistic beliefs does not matter so much for our purposes as the fact that there is a wide gap to bridge between almost all other systems and the individual-centric approach. A non-conflictual relationship among these divergent pathways would only occur where the highly individualistic view takes more fully into account the fact that it actually has more connections to and implications for the communal good than often is the case. The key question is whether strong privatism stances can come to acknowledge and justify the harms or injustices that may follow from individual decisions.

Note, as Ashley and O'Rourke (1982, 13) argue, competition occurs when the resources in question are material, since "such goods can be shared among individuals only by dividing them up and giving to each a private share. What one gets, the other loses and vice versa." Obviously, this is not the case when the resources are cultural, spiritual or perhaps even ecological, since in these cases the values and goods are multiplied, not depleted, when shared or spread across many participants. "Thus the common good is not opposed to the personal good; rather it is the deepest heart of the personal good of each person" (Ashley and O'Rourke 1982, 14). We see this in the difference between distributing a truckload of timber and communally enjoying friendship, knowledge, or artistic beauty. Or, in the differences between subdividing a parcel of land and nurturing an ecological system where all the organisms and processes thrive together—a classic open network that can provide more and more goods as it moves toward greater complexity.

With the case of ecological systems, we see that even a purely natural or material worldview (that may be non- or anti-humanistic and non- or anti-religious) values participation in the network, since it makes little sense to focus on isolated individualized elements which in reality do not exist. Even competition for the same food or energy takes place within a system that itself needs to be sustained if any organism is to thrive. Indeed, it can well be argued that the self-fulfillment desired by extreme individualism "demands that people not isolate themselves in selfishness, but become open to community wherein lies this self-fulfillment" (Ashley and O'Rourke 1982, 15). Since "optimal functioning means not only an internal harmony and consistency of function within the organism, but also the capacity of the organism to maintain itself in its environment," in addition to our cultural spheres we need to open healthily to the natural environment (Ashley and O'Rourke 1982, 25).

One point of common ground (and a usefully shared ethical vocabulary) between privatism and most of the other worldviews can be found in the right to property—in a general sense, that which one has earned or that otherwise is legitimately one's own—and in the principle of non-maleficence. If non-maleficence is the principle that one ought not harm (or risk harming) another's "goods" including health, knowledge, freedom, reputation, happiness, and property [see non-maleficence in chapter three], then one clearly has the right to one's property and the rest of us have an obligation to respect that property. The ethical problem occurs when one person's right to good conflicts with the obligation to not harm another's goods. Thus we have developed the social justification to control another's property in the name of safety, health, and other aspects of public well-being. In cases where public well-being is seen to override the individual's property rights, it is generally agreed that the individual needs to be fairly compensated for what is lost—as in the case of land transferred under the assertion of eminent domain. (The term *eminent domain*, used especially in American property law and planning, refers to the government's power to take private property for public use—such as highway construction—without the owner's consent, but, in accord with the Fifth Amendment, with due process and fair compensation—defined as payment of the market value of the property.)

The issue of privatism marks a divergence of viewpoint and of operational criteria compared with the more social forms of humanism and with the other worldviews. For example, Ashley and O'Rourke argue that the values of "traditional Christian family life and a legitimate patriotism" should not be confused "with a privatism and nationalism indifferent or antagonistic to social justice" (1982, 15). Clearly, there is a parting of ways between individualism-privatism and other worldviews. Thus, in addition to being responsible for understanding the major points, in order to stay clear about how your view is related to others who agree or disagree, it is important to articulate your own position at this juncture where serious differences arise.

How Individualistic? A Fundamental Issue

The challenge of privatism is well worth group discussion.

Discuss how you would balance the private and public spheres. Tipping the balance one way or the other leads to very different outcomes when approaching environmental dilemmas.

- **Individualism-privatism versus**
- **Social well-being (a form of Anthropocentricism)**
- **Ecocentricism**
- **Theocentricism**

The basic question is whether ethical behavior can be understood as the consistent pursuit of self-interest within a minimal code of law and contract enforcement.

Strong individualistic views must also address how to deal with the wider impacts of individual actions. Is it credible to hold that one's environmental choices extend only to one's self? If not, how far does impact and sphere of responsibility extend: to one's family and immediate neighbors, one's close community, a larger regional-to-national realm, or globally in terms of resource depletion and extraction, pollution, acid rain, and climate change?

See exercise 1.1 at the end of this chapter for material on which to develop a discussion.

→ See the section on "Market Mechanism and Utilitarianism" in chapter 3 for more debates on the private-public realms.

Though our ethical principles and rules provide a framework within which decisions can be made given the concrete particulars of a situation, they are not at all a mechanical device simply to repeat generalized codifications in environmental decision making in the case of property rights. At least two things must be established from which we can proceed in most cases: it must be decided, 1) whether or not the right to a specific control of property is outweighed in a particular case by the obligation not to incur or to risk harming others; 2) whether or not compensation is due for the loss of property (or, perhaps of its potential value), and if so, how it is to be calculated. (As we will see shortly, though the legal and ethical spheres are closely connected in such issues, they are neither the same nor reducible to one another.)

❑ *Step Two: Anthropocentric vs. Non-Anthropocentric Worldviews*
If you have worked through reflection box 2, you should both better understand the implications that the alternative worldviews have for environmental decisions and be clearer about your own position. If you find yourself believing and acting upon a version of privatism, then you hold an anthropocentric position, as you also would if you subscribe to an emphasis on social well-being—in contrast with which the other positions have a good deal in common (though they have differences in regard to other matters).. As a next step, then, we need to continue to reflect on and sort out the distinctions and relationships among the versions of anthropomorphism from those of naturalism or theism, and especially to consider the differences among social anthropocentricism, ecocentricism, and theocentricism. When both steps are completed you will be able to more precisely proceed in regard to decision making.

As Timothy Beatley, an ethicist who writes about land use, explains,

> Another important dimension of ethics is the extent to which moral obligations are anthropocentric—that is, human or human-centered (sometimes also called homocentric). In the anthropocentric view, the costs and benefits associated with particular land use proposals are those that affect or accrue to human beings. In contrast, there has been considerable theorizing in recent years, particularly under the rubric of environmental ethics, that there are various non-anthropocentric moral obligations. The animal-rights movement in recent years epitomizes the non-anthropocentric view. Animals are owed obligations, not because they are necessarily the property of other humans, but because they have certain inherent rights.
> (Beatley 1994, 26–28; cf. Singer, Leopold)

In contrast, Samuel Florman, an engineer specializing in ethics, struggles with a non-anthropocentric perspective:

> From time to time, my engineer's zest for progress is tempered by profound concern for the natural environment. But, just as I'm about to give way to qualms and indecision, along comes some terrible natural disaster and my mood changes. Take, for example, the cyclone that attacked Bangladesh in 1991, killing 125,000 people and leaving some nine million homeless. That catastrophe aroused in me feelings of anger and betrayal as well as dismay. How can one cultivate a more compassionate attitude toward 'the environment', when confronted with such a violent reality?" (1996, 81)

→ See also the problem in the case of Hydro-Quebec, appendix III. This case also raises issues of how an anthropocentric or non-anthropocentric perspective can shift one's attitudes towards the dam.

❑ *Step Three: Worldviews, Interpretations, and Valuations*
The question of worldviews and the environment is not only a matter of the kind of value system or measure that we apply in making decisions—as if that were not enough. Even more deeply, beneath the way we see and understand nature, behind the way we operate in daily life, there are assumptions about

the natural world and the proper or desired relation it should have to the built environment we add upon and to it. Though for the most part we are oblivious to such fundamental orientations, to make responsible decisions we obviously need to reflect explicitly on the relation of the worldviews to what nature is. How does nature stand in relation to us—to our dreams, fears, needs, and obligations? Several major points need to be taken up here and then more material for discussion will be presented in the exercises at the end of the chapter.

Human Relationship to Nature

First, we must ask ourselves, what is nature?

❑   Raw material for human Use?
❑   The context of human life and culture?
❑   Energy & self-organization with emergent life?
❑   Divine creation?
❑   Something else?

Does nature have a right to well-being without having to be justified in terms of human use?

Your answer will depend, in large part, on how you view the human relationship to nature:

Are we dominant over nature, subservient to nature, or a part of nature? Are we superior or equal to other species?

As Anne Spirn asks in her book, *The Granite Garden*, if humans are equal to other species, then do we have any extra moral duty to care for nature? Do we have any special obligations to nature when we construct our built environments?

Different Worldviews Involve Differing Discernments of Space and Place.
    Many people feel that not all locations are the same. Consider where one was born or grew up (one's home town or region), or native country, or site of memorable life-changing events; often these are experienced as qualitatively different. There is an entire literature, in fact, that deals with place meaning, sense of place, place identity, and place attachment. As Yi Fu Tuan pointed out years ago, what begins as undifferentiated space evolves into place as we begin to know it better and endow it with meaning and value. Thus some locations might simply be demarked by coordinates in the spheres of science, technology, and commerce and be understood in terms of homogenous space, while those realms experienced as qualitatively distinctive and meaningful are called places. Architect Michael Brill used the wonderful term, "charged spaces, in order to refer to such places with a special spiritual or psychological power without identifying the charge as specifically religious, or even as ei-

ther positive or negative, for that matter. Such place experiences and meanings are not merely idiosyncratic, as is witnessed by groups' attachment to cities, regions, and even nations—to the point of fighting and dying over them.
Here, we see a strong connection between the physical space and one's identity, wherein one's customs and entire way of life have a coherent and distinctive spatial pattern that provide individual and social identity and meaning.

This is where ethics and decision making get tricky. When we so value
certain places that our identity and sense of self get intertwined with a place,
changes are easily perceived as threats to a place that can engender strong reactions and can create challenges in how to negotiate different meanings. This
not only happens on the individual level (individually held meanings and values), but also with shared place meanings as well. Even then there are challenges when various stakeholder groups have different attitudes and values
about a place.

Environmental decisions concerning contested uses of a place, then, often
involve at least implicit valuations of one way of life over another, and thus
contested anthropocentric or even theocentric worldviews. Given the importance of what hangs in the balance, it is necessary to make these different values and meanings explicit so they can be deliberated as part of ethical decision
making. Such differences in place, meaning and lifestyle are all too common,
as seen for example in what the Navajos say about cultural preservation of
their environment:

> Economic development is undermining Navajo culture by disturbing or de-
> stroying particular activities on the landscape through which people integrate
> the various places on their land base into the system of Navajo life and by se-
> ducing young people away from living in the Navajo way. . . . Preserving
> places important to Navajo people can help preserve Navajo culture, but to be
> most effective, preservation efforts must widen their focus from the specific
> places to the culturally significant landscape within which each place func-
> tions and from which it gets its power (significance) and to which it gives
> power. . .
>   Researchers [responsible for attempting to analyze the environment and
> recommend possible modes of development] reveal a sense of being caught
> between the go-ahead interests of developers that shape the realpolitik of
> "historic preservation" decision making and their professional responsibility
> to convey the concerns of the people they consulted. They compromised by
> focusing on places—not on whole landscapes, as the people want, but not on
> nothing either, as many developers wish. [But] the goal of the Navajo ap-
> proach is to keep entire, interacting cultural landscapes intact by keeping eco-
> nomic development from disrupting the full range of customary activities that
> keep these landscapes alive (Kelley and Francis 1994, 97–8, 101).

In the case of the Navajo, we see the proximity of spiritual concerns that
may be part of either certain forms of humanism or of theism. Just as there are
disputes among social groups concerning the use and meaning of places, so
too there are disputes about places that move beyond the sphere of anthropocentric concerns, and that are marked as sacred. Such places may be where a

god is said to have appeared, or where a special connection has been established between the sacred and profane worlds. In such cases, a mountain, cave, spring or well, or even an entire an landscape may be marked as sacred. Here special ceremonies would be performed and the site might be the goal of a pilgrimage. Williams and Stewart (1998) found this to be the case with the Devil's Tower in Wyoming. Considered sacred by local native tribes, it was also a considerable tourist attraction and destination for rock climbers. Clearly, for the believers, such places are charged with meaning, and a recreational use of the sites for activities like rock climbing are perceived as profane and disrespectful of the native culture and spiritual values. Conversely, hikers and climbers see the geologic formation as an opportunity to challenge their skills and quite possibly to connect with nature. Some climbers might even connect to Devil's Tower in a spiritual way, although usually the spiritual connection occurs on a more individual level and is not seen to be part of hikers' shared culture as it is for Native Americans. In such cases, we have a conflict between theocentric worldview and the others, a difference that extends beyond specific places to a consistent view of nature overall.

Arthur Versluis amplifies the difference between the dominant secular anthropocentric view and that of Native Americans or Australian aboriginals:

> Modern civilization is coming to recognize that it is destroying the natural world—but merely to see that this or that species is being obliterated is not enough. Nor is it even enough to observe rationally that we are destroying life in a given place, or on the whole earth. We have to look more deeply at why this destruction is taking place. From the perspective of the original peoples, we are destroying nature because we are blind to nature as theophany or divine revelation. Humanity has a spiritual relationship to the world, and our world destruction represents a spiritual blindness. (1992, 11)

Obviously, the positions of contemporary industrial and commercial society are well known and established in power. Precisely because of that, it is important to consider the ethical responsibilities that the differing groups have toward one another and to the natural and built environments.

→ For more on these topics, engage exercises 1.5, 1.6, and 1.7 at the end of this chapter; they focus on the contrast between secular (including mercantile) and spiritual views as well as on the difference between the legal and ethical decisions to be made in regard to lands that some consider sacred).

Dissolving Dichotomies, Accepting Uncertainty, Learning to Live with Wicked Problems

In making difficult environmental decisions, in addition to imaginatively thinking through and perhaps reframing differences and similarities, there are correlational strategies. Especially noteworthy among these are:
- ❑ attempting to dissolve dichotomies
- ❑ accepting uncertainty and controversy
- ❑ learning to live with wicked (unfolding) problems and the continuously unfolding character of social decision processes.

Why dissolve dilemmas? First, let us be clear about what a dichotomy is. Dichotomies are essentially pairs of opposites. They are distinctions that pose two individual elements or phenomena in binary, mutually exclusive, tension. One prominent dichotomy that is relevant here is the human-nature dichotomy that we have seen existing in many worldviews. Others include good-bad, reason-madness, reality-dream, and same-other. Many supposed dichotomies such as human-nature have been analyzed as false-dichotomies because they artificially distill a set of complex relationships into two broad and oppositional categories that are understood to be contradictory: they are posed such that one would have to accept or place an element in only one or the other. This can be disadvantageous when trying to appreciate the subtleties and complexities of certain situations. Thus one way to begin to solve dilemmas is to try to dissolve these dichotomies. The attempt helps even with those that cannot because: (1) they will be clearer or less complicated; and (2) will be closer to a solution to the actual problem about which decisions have to be made. In this section, we will identify and work through many of the relevant apparent dichotomies, discussing them in all dimensions of reflection and decision making.

Additionally, in making difficult decisions, we must accept the fact that while knowledge and understanding are essential, there is no way to know all the relevant facts; indeed, there is no such thing as "all the facts," since what is relevant unfolds as the situation unfolds, and the ways we think and interact with others can also change during the decision making process. Even if you were certain about the eventual outcome of a decision, it would still not solve the ethical difficulty because it would only enable you to see that outcome, and not whether and how that outcome was ethically legitimate.

Dissolve Dichotomies

A dichotomy is a division between two presumably distinct, mutually exclusive, even oppositional ideas. Dichotomies can be artificial and simplistic, making it more difficult to generate alternative approaches to a situation.

In order to get beyond dichotomies, you need imagination to generate alternatives.

You need knowledge and adequate concepts-theories to re-think definitions and categories, and to seek new classifications of elements that recognize and respond to differences but do not over-generalize or falsely essentialize members of a classification.

Think about multifaceted, flexible relationships.

Try to generate new complexes, new collaborations.

For example: The *nature*-versus-*culture* dichotomy does not stand up under close scrutiny: humans are part of the natural world; the natural world is inescapably shaped by what humans change and spare from change; culture is natural to humans, and so on.

Evolution and religion are not necessarily oppositional, as the work of Pierre Teilhard de Chardin shows—a French Jesuit paleontologist, he influentially argued (most famously in *The Phenomenon of Man*) that science and religion could converge in a great harmony.

Environmental protection and economic development are not exclusionary opposites.

Not all engineers are the same, nor are architects, developers, citizen or environmental advocates, and so on.

Uncertainty Is Unavoidable

There is a persistent misunderstanding that if we had all the facts, then we would know the answers—what to do and what is right in a given situation; but this is not true. More often, as a case unfolds, we can see of a complex web of possible harm and possible good also unfold, and thus the more difficult the issues and decisions become.

Of course, we need information to make decisions; but the information does not automatically lead to or suggest a decision. It merely forms part of the slippery terrain on which we are forced to operate.

The importance of imagination can not be overstressed, both to imagine the consequences of possible courses of action and to come up with new possible alternatives that might increase the positive aspects and reduce the negative.

In fact, Peter Hall (1981) identifies three types of uncertainty that have to be dealt with in environmental decision making:
❑ Uncertainty about the relevant environment (everything outside the immediate decision making system)
❑ Uncertainty about decisions in related decision areas (areas of discretion beyond the immediate problem and area of decision making)
❑ Uncertainty about value judgments (where final decisions depend not on information, but questions of value).

Another key to making difficult decisions is recognizing that ethical decision making unavoidably operates in the territory of what Horst Rittel calls Wicked Problems. Wicked problems are those difficult situations where decisions have to be made and in which there not only is no clear answer (i.e., a dilemma) but also, crucially, where the nature of the situation in all of its complexity unfolds only as we attempt to understand the situation and its many dimensions. As we come to understand some aspects of the situation, there is an unfolding of awareness of the potential choices and outcomes that may change with each step along the way. We could think of this as calling special attention to the changing, temporal aspects of the realities within which we live and of our own understanding and decision making processes.

Many of the environmental-social issues requiring decisions in which we have to choose between one set of goods-harms and different set of goods-harms only unfold their complexities as we engage them. It is only as we are underway, working toward a solution, making choices that usually preclude some possibilities as we actualize others, that the full nature of the problem emerges, along with its challenges and tangled consequences. Especially where the decision process involves collaboration among many diverse parties, those involved frequently work "simultaneously on understanding the problem and formulating a solution"—not *the* one and only correct or perfect solution, which does not exist (Conklin 2001, 4).

Wicked Problems are those in which:

- **A decision must be made**
- **There is not, nor will there be, an unproblematic solution**
- **Understanding the situation and problem can occur only in the actual process of trying to understand the situation and problem**

Here, linear problem-solving, proceeding from a clearly defined problem to a solution in a logical manner, is not possible. The requisite non-linear mode of decision making is virtually the same as what experts go through in the design process, with its iterations and dialogue among participants.

→ To practice dealing with a wicked problem that unfolds as you engage it, see the cases, Becoming a Planner, Rincon Center, and Hydro-Quebec in appendix III.

→ For a fuller analysis of wicked problems, so dubbed by Horst Rittel, see Conklin (1990 and 2001) and the CogNexus website www.cognexus.org.

Finally, the temporal character of natural and social conditions and relationships means that, even if well made, no environmental decision and subsequent practical action has narrow limits or a clear end point. There is no final situation. Correspondingly, the decision processes of specific individuals and groups never come to a final end: they always are both in the continuing processes of those individuals and groups and within the larger contexts of other social processes. (For more on the unavoidably unending character of decision making, see chapter 5.)

Toward Ethics Proper

Ethics, Religion, Law

Just as there are different worldviews, there are also multiple spheres of justification for decisions we make. There are valid modes of decision making outside of the realm of ethics and these include law and religion. Many decisions also concern realms of the aesthetic (beauty, form, etc.), politics (power, social relations), or epistemology (the nature of knowledge). Each of these is certainly complex, but especially in the sphere of the moral there is a good deal of complexity. In the first place, it is not easy to use the basic terms (morality, ethics, right, good, and so on) in a clear way given the tangled history of ideas and variety of cultural and technical uses. To remain grounded in common sense (rather than go astray into esoteric meta-theory), in this book we are concerned with decisions where right and wrong mean right and wrong in respect to what is morally acceptable, to what is good and bad or even evil in a given situation.

There are, in fact, a variety of ways that we might make decisions in regard to what is the good and not bad course of environmental action. For example, we may act according to individual conscience, to one's emotional response or intuition, to common sense or proper social custom (including legal systems), to secular or sacred authority, to divine directives, or to reason and rational-logical systems—which is what often traditionally has been meant by ethics in its precise historical sense, though that is contested (see the sections below on the role of emotions in the ethic of care)—or even to wisdom. The ethical would consist of critical reflection and robust discussion, integrating our cognitive and emotive dimensions, allowing us to be responsible in our actions because, as members of a social body to whom we are accountable, we not only are able to deliberate about possible courses of action, but are able to explain why we act as we do, and are thus able to sustain appropriate practices.

Given that people have made decisions on the basis of these various foundations for thousands of years, what is the reason to focus on ethics, that is, on reflection and justification of what are considered responsible actions (for example, through argumentation), implemented through the use of shared human capacities of experience and understanding? The basic answer lies in the pluralistic character of our world and the global impact of many environmental practices. For a group that shares a specific environment and a worldview, it may work well to make decisions on the basis of traditional authority or religious beliefs insofar as those are shared and consented to by all involved. However, there are few places in the world today where all those residing in an area with a given environmental problem actually agree on a specific religious perspective, or worldview for that matter. Nor are there many enclaves where a set of secular social customs is held by all—there is too much diversity and movement in our current world for that to be the case very often, particularly in advanced technological cultures. As a further complication, even for those few realms with a common set of customs or beliefs such as traditional villages or nomadic bands, voluntary communities, or professional groups under a common oath, the outcomes of environmental deeds and events impact others downstream who do not necessarily share the same views. Overall, the significant possible courses of action routinely are contested: social, ethnic, religious, and other differences would seem to be as much a source of conflict as of agreement. How then to find a way to deal with environmental dilemmas in a pluralistic world?

Ethics is distinct from religion, though often there is substantial connection between the two spheres. Clearly, some religious issues are not part of our society's moral-ethical realm, for example, whether or not angels exist, and what, if any, transactions they might expedite with the sacred. Further, even if one accepts moral truth on faith and assumes that one should act in accordance with God's commands or will, it is contended by many—though disputed by others—that beyond accepting proper authority we still need reason if we are to understand, interpret, and act upon religious directives. Already 2,300 years ago, the question was posed: "Is something good because the gods choose it, or do the gods choose something because it is good?" (Plato, *Euthyphro*). The debate about the relation of faith and reason continued throughout the history of Christianity, as can be seen in the differences between the Augustinian and Thomistic traditions (the former stresses the importance of faith and the relative inadequacy of human reason, whereas the latter emphasizes the complementary nature of faith and reason, since what would be true would be the same and accessible through multiple means, even if not with the same degree of certainty).

In addition, what is morally right or wrong could be connected with, but not reducible to, what is legal. That is because legal systems are the product of social or religious customs and thus subject to the same contentious problems just noted. The confusions between ethical and legal dimensions of environmentally related decisions are reflected in the shift in attitudes toward professional codes. At one time many professional codes were not really concerned with ethics in any deep way, but only with the ways in which professionals should conduct themselves in relation to each other (not competing by advertising, for example). When the courts ruled in the 1970s that many of the provisions of professional conduct in regard to other members of the professional community (such as protective limitations against advertising) were not legal, many concluded that what had been ethical problems no longer were problems because they had been settled. The complexity and subtlety of the categories seen by Florman, a sophisticated professional and ethical expert, promoted him to write:

> The morality we seek should be founded in the real world and be capable of practical application. It should be able to meet standards of both goodwill and good sense. To continue: I suggest that engineering ethics is not a set of guild rules. Once upon a time that is all engineering ethics was. The original codes

of ethics told engineers how they should deal with each other. Today society at large will not accept them as having anything to do with real ethics. [In addition, during the 1970s the Justice Department declared that many such restrictions violated antitrust laws governing unfair competition and thus] "radically changed the status of all professions—not only engineering. [As a result], the law has taken over many substantive areas [such as confidentiality] that used to be the province of professional ethics [controlled from within]. (1987, 86–87)

Though commendable in its appreciation of the importance of ethics, this reasoning concedes the conflation of the ethical and legal. But, since the issues that were legally settled and then set aside were not actually ethical problems in the first place, there was even more of an ethical vacuum in professional circles until the distinction between legal and ethical was clarified and developed over the last thirty years. Timothy Beatley puts the situation in perspective, arguing that the social practices of reductively categorizing problems as "only"-exclusively legal or economic or technocratic does not make it so:

Those involved in land use decision making must realize that ethical judgments are not optional. That is, the failure to view land use decisions as involving ethical choice is itself a de facto form of ethical judgment. Many land use decisions, perhaps most, are of the de facto sort, because they are defined in narrow technical, economic, or legal terms. . . .

Land use decisions affect the condition and quality of the natural and built environment, and the basic quality of people's lives. Land use decisions are thus not trivial, and should be the focus of careful thought on the part of those individuals and institutions responsible for making or influencing them. All decisions about the use of land, then, are inherently ethical judgments, inherently ethical choices. Land use decisions and policies raise questions of right and wrong, good and bad. (Our reordering for emphasis.) (Beatley 1994, 4)

→ For more on professional codes see chapter 2 and chapter 6, Professional Codes and Beyond.

More seriously, particular laws or orders from those granted power of authority can be socially destructive, immoral, or even evil. There have been numerous strategies to deal with the sometimes conflicting obligations to obey the law and yet not do evil: for example, the tradition of conscientious objection practiced by Henry David Thoreau and Mahatma Ghandi that holds that even a military person sworn to obey orders must not carry out a legal order that is immoral. This is exemplified in the deliberations in the Nuremburg trials of Nazi military leaders after World War II, when it was determined that it was immoral and criminal for soldiers to carry out orders dictating the mutilation and murder of Jewish prisoners.

In his examination of land use ethics, Beatley demonstrates that ethics and legality are distinct from each other in important ways. First, government controls and regulations are usually minimal and are often aimed at curtailing only the most blatant and repulsive land use practices: "While federal and state regulations substantially regulate development in sensitive wetlands, for instance, they clearly do not prevent development, and estimates are that we continue to lose some several hundred thousand acres of natural wetlands yearly, as a nation. To many, the destruction of natural wetlands is morally and ethically wrong, despite its being legally permissible. Thus, what is *ethical* land use may indeed conflict with what is *legal* land use." Additionally, what is required or mandated through laws or court interpretations is not necessarily ethical either. For example, while the U.S. Supreme Court may have established certain principles that apply to cases in which public regulation of land is so onerous that it requires just compensation, they do not determine or preclude examination of what constitutes an ethically just relationship between private property and public regulation. At the same time, Beatley maintains that "there is, in general, an a priori ethical obligation to respect and obey land use laws. Short of extraordinary circumstances, there is a moral duty to abide by existing collective rules" (Beatley 1992, 16).

In short, most decisions involve many people, given their legitimate roles as stakeholders, and because their lifeworlds will be affected by the decisions. Since in a diverse world there will be a plurality of often-competing worldviews and value systems, it is crucial to find ways to carry on open and reasonable deliberation within and among communities, which means that we need to become better at identifying commonalities and differences. As we began to see when considering the basic worldviews, reflection shows that, in fact, there is a not a chaos of disagreement across times, space, and cultures about the values that matter; the critical differences actually are systematic, and appear to be a matter of (a) the specific content-definitions of what those values entail in concrete terms and (b) the priorities among those values (Ashley and O'Rourke 1982, 2, 11). Using dialogue to locate commonalities of underlying value allegiances opens the way to imaginative strategies to satisfy multiple parties who may be disagreeing about specific details. Even identifying apparently irresoluble differences is useful because it makes explicit where the frictions lie, and enables attention to be effectively directed toward the points of contention instead of wasting time, energy, and what goodwill there may be in talking past each other or arguing without going anywhere.

Additionally, there is evidence that many of the world's major philosophical and theological systems have more in common than in disagreement. Thus, religious systems such as Judaism, Christianity, and Islam, as well as Eastern traditions such as Buddhism, while disagreeing on much (and often actually clashing in social practice), also hold very much the same set of deep values, though this may not be obvious without their being explicitly described in terms of rational categories and principles. Even non- or anti-religious systems such as secular humanism or Marxism agree that there is value in the material and cultural-social realms (while rejecting spiritual dimensions beyond the creative or productive human capacities). Thus people living within these frameworks can enter into responsible reflection—that is, ethically debate using the categories, principles, and responsive-caring strategies employed in this book. Now that we have gone through an overview of different worldviews and how they influence the way we understand ethical issues and value decisions, we can look at another set of plural perspectives that similarly influence how we approach ethical decision making.

Two Types of Moral Argumentation: Reasoning and Care

As we have noted, not all dilemmas are moral dilemmas. Moral dilemmas are a particular type that is unique in that it requires moral reasoning. Just as we will argue in the next chapter that no profession in itself is inherently ethical or unethical, we would also argue that events themselves, independent of context and motive, are neither moral nor immoral (Harding 1985).

In order to adequately address the process of ethical decision making, it is important to examine the nature and process of moral reasoning. Much of what is written about moral reasoning addresses the psychological dimensions, i.e., the cognitive processes behind logic, reasoning, and decision making. As we began to see in introducing cognitive and learning styles with Jungian theory, much of this is written from a developmental perspective that examines different stages of development of moral argumentation competencies, such as Kohlberg's now-classic theories on moral reasoning in boys. But this understanding has been expanded by theory and research outside of developmental psychology, which is why we return to it here. For example, Berkowitz organizes theory and research on moral argumentation into four general perspectives: the developmental—looking at the development of moral argumentation competencies; ethical—which looks at the ideal forms of moral argumentation; growth-facilitative—which looks at the functions of moral argumentation, especially its capacity to promote moral development; and finally the instrumental perspective, which looks at the practical functions of moral argumentation. The latter two focus on actual behavioral forms of moral argumentation; while the goal of instrumental argumentation is to change another's attitude or win an argument, the growth-facilitative goal is to grow to a more mature level of moral understanding. Berkowitz calls for an integrative approach to moral reasoning that incorporates all of these dimensions.

There are similarities and differences between moral reasoning and moral argumentation. Let's look at each separately. Moral reasoning is focused on how one understands a given circumstance; that is, how one thinks through a situation, as well as how one feels about that situation and what is at stake. Both thinking and feeling are part of moral reasoning—it is not only cognitive; it is also intuitive. It also includes thinking about the beliefs and values that we have and bring to bear in a situation where we need to make moral choices. Both thought and feeling processes are engaged to help us make sense of situations in which we may find ourselves. Moral argumentation is the explicit manifestation of moral reasoning. It emerges when we engage in discourse with one another and try to understand different viewpoints, confront and resolve differences in opinion and focus on different dimensions of a situation through verbal interaction. Moral argumentation requires us to be especially clear about our reasoning in order to maintain and substantiate our position to someone else. So in a certain sense moral argumentation is moral reasoning taken one step further outside the individual and into the discursive realm. Also, moral argumentation does not automatically mean that there must be opposition between two (or more) people—that there is an argument in the commonly understood sense of the word and that one must win it. However, moral argumentation does require explicating one's point of view and substantiating it in the face of alternative possibilities and viewpoints.

Reasoning, argumentation, and decision making all involve cognitive processes; reasoning is the mental, internal sorting through of information and choice, and argumentation is the external explication of that reasoning. And if circumstances require it, all of this would result in making an actual decision about what to do and how to do it. However, the fact of the matter is that reasoning as more strictly, traditionally defined (as logic) is not necessarily the way we deal with dilemmas. People are complex and life is messy. People are not always logical, we are emotional, we get inspired but we also get tired, cranky, and confused. We make decisions not only through logical calculations but also from our bundles of values, worldviews, and even more transient states of mind and the issues we might be grappling with at a given point in time. The following comment about design comes to mind: "Design for people as they are, not as you would have them be. Design for inefficient users. Design for creative, imaginative people who will do things with your design that you never have dreamed of, things both good and horrid. Design for people who are tired and stressed, cranky and irritable, sloppy and inattentive. In other words, design for real people" (Don Norman, product designer and educator).

Moral argumentation is a central component of human interaction. Berkowitz maintains that "even argumentation that is not explicitly focused on moral issues has a tacit moral component constituted by the fact that human beings have certain intrinsic rights and derivative duties. Hence one has certain ethical obligations when interacting with another person" (1985, 17). This has interesting parallels with the socially oriented ethic of care that focuses on a sense of morality inherently embedded in human relations. Berkowitz points out that moral argumentation is "doubly moral" in that there are constant, implicit moral obligations involved in human interchange.

Moral argumentation is not just a social skill for debating and discussing the dimensions of a situation, but a logical skill as well. Though it is unlikely that all moral disagreements might be logically resolvable given that we often disagree profoundly on the interpretations and meanings of the realities and terms involved, as well as about the assumptions and consequences involved, it is even further complicated in reality since people are not logical machines. To consider emotion and irrationality as obstacles that interfere with the logical resolution of moral arguments (Berkowitz 1985), is highly problematic. First, in such a view, emotions are seen as obstacles that impede successfully addressing moral problems, rather than as enhancing or bringing another dimension to moral reasoning and argumentation. Second, it implies that all moral disagreements are resolvable if only pesky emotions do not get in the way and that logic can automatically resolve any dilemma or debate. Since it is not possible to test whether moral dilemmas would be solvable if tackled only with logic, the point is moot in any case. Third, it ignores the power and value of the human emotional dimension for moral reasoning and argumentation. It portrays emotion in a limited and delimiting way, as an impediment, and not as a dimension of human existence that can support and enhance life, work, and the choices we make.

In fact, views such as Berkowitz's see emotion as negatively interfering with ethical decision making in contrast with the ethic of care. In this latter ethic, human emotion—and particularly a sense of care for other human beings, for maintaining relationships, for understanding things and events in relational ways, is critical to making careful and thoughtful choices about how we live and what is right and wrong. For example, in terms of moral reasoning, Marilyn Friedman (1985) notes the importance of care and context in all moral reasoning. She emphasizes the significance of contextual detail and argues that one's ability to engage in moral argumentation, and the manner in which one does so, is influenced by the level of detail provided in a hypothetical dilemma. That is, one's approach to a dilemma and the conclusions one draws in working through the situation can be different when a moral dilemma is specified in rich detail. This is what Gilligan called "contextual relativism," or sensitivity to the details of a situation.

The feminist (as noted, other-than-Heideggerian) ethic of care, was developed in response to developmental psychologist Lawrence Kohlberg's research on moral reasoning and development in children. Kohlberg believed his research demonstrated that boys have had a more highly developed moral sense than girls because of the way they negotiated among themselves while playing marbles. The boys were seen to have a better-developed moral sense because of their focus on principles of justice, whereas girls exhibited greater concern for not hurting others, and based their decisions more on this concern and on feelings of empathy and compassion. Gilligan challenged Kohlberg's framework and conclusions with her own research, arguing that there is a distinctive moral reasoning more commonly exhibited among females than males—that of an ethic of care. Gilligan maintained that instead of girls' reasoning ability being seen as more immature than boys', it was a different type of moral reasoning. She coined this a "morality of care" and notably, she also called it a "morality of responsibility." This became a significant but controversial alternative framework for understanding how people address moral dilemmas.

Gilligan's notion of contextual relativism and the ethic of care emerged from her research on gender and moral reasoning. Interestingly, she used the classic Heinz dilemma for her study that found women more often than men asked for greater detail about a situation before reaching a conclusion. Asking questions and requesting more detail about a situation had been interpreted as failure to fully comprehend a dilemma. But it emerged in Gilligan's work that women sought details about dilemmas to help them understand any suffering involved and engage feelings of compassion and caring. Therefore, Gilligan argued, these questions posed by female participants challenged the initial framing of the dilemma. Rather than the findings revealing shortcomings among the women respondents, they revealed shortcomings in the scenario for not allowing any real or meaningful choice (Friedman, 1985). From this research Gilligan (1982) famously developed her theory for an ethic of care. Additionally, from a substantially different direction in his later work, the philosopher Martin Heidegger contended that the notion of "care" names our primal relation to what is given to us, and thus simultaneously articulates both our fundamental obligation to the earth and the manner through which we might become authentically human—it is no accident that his emphasis on attunement and responsiveness to the relational dynamic that constitutes the world established him as one of the forebears of deep ecology (Heidegger, 1971a, 1971b).

Of course, this recognition of, and sensitivity toward, the situation in which ethical decisions are made has also been controversial. Skeptics have argued that if context were so important we could dangerously slide into utter relativism—we could get too situational and would have to start all over from scratch each time we encountered a moral decision. However, even if we agree that morality depends on the context, and that different approaches are best for different contexts, most would also agree that we need a general moral approach to indicate which types of contexts to handle in which ways, and to recommend how existing contexts ought to be transformed. This is where the ethic of care comes in.

The ethic of care is built on a recognition of the importance of human relationships where care for, and responsibility to, other persons is a more central concern than rights or rules, which is the traditionally understood foundation of morality according to many psychologists studying moral development. Indeed, Kohlberg acknowledges that Gilligan's work prompted him to take into account the importance of care and relationships to overall moral development, and to consider how these might augment his own emphasis on justice and rights. Later research continues to show that some people have a preference for what can be called "care reasoning" and others for "justice reasoning" (Friedman, 1985). These two different moral perspectives are now recognized by both Kohlberg and Gilligan. But a great deal of controversy remains about the relationship of care and justice and whether it is a false dichotomy (see the ethic-of-care section of chapter 4 on theory for more details).

Other research reinforces the importance and value of the emotional and relational dimension of moral reasoning and the interpretation of dilemmas. As Hinman (1985) points out, the emotions play a meaningful role in the interpretive process. He posits emotion as an integral part of our cognitive structure involved in ethical decision making, and that "emotions are a way of structuring and understanding our work, a way of making sense of it." He suggests an approach to educating the emotions, some of which, like compassion, he calls "illuminating" emotions that can be cultivated to promote not only moral reasoning but moral sensitivity. Additionally, for Hinman educating the emotions involves cultivating an entire worldview, not just single feeling in isolation, so loyalty is best cultivated in a context of compassion and sense of fairness, for example. In a different though related tradition of ethical analysis, the phenomenological sociologist Max Scheler also develops an emotive ethics, contending that our emotional experience of values has a unique cognitive structure and function—as a preference and evidence that directly intuits an order and ranking of types of values (Scheler, 1973; Deeken, 1974).

As we will see more fully in chapters 3 and 4, for deontologists, an absolute requirement is to respect people's autonomy and dignity as human beings. In contrast, the ethic of care posits that developing the capacity for affection and friendship (major elements of virtue) requires sensitivity to the needs of others and involves a whole pattern of emotional and psychological engagement (Cottingham 2000). If we want to achieve flourishing lives, we must cultivate our emotional sensibilities, and the cultivation of those sensibilities will not allow us to constrict our concern for some over others. Cottingham argues that moral commitment is seldom a matter of reasoning and argument alone, although other philosophers say that it does boil down to reasoning. Psychologists and philosophers aligning the self and morality with separation and autonomy (the ability to be self-governing) have associated care with self-sacrifice and feelings as an impediment. But care represents a fuller way of knowing, and a coherent moral perspective. Within a justice perspective, detachment is the hallmark of mature moral thinking; from a care perspective, detachment is the problem. The ethic of care, then, is sorely needed. Some have argued that an ethic that commands emotional as well as intellectual allegiance remains moral philosophy's greatest task (Cottingham 2000). In any case, there is ample room—and need—for both approaches. The objectivity and argumentation that traditional reasoning strives for, which can be accomplished by anyone who takes up the arguments and makes them her own, safeguards the possibility of universal rights and the processes of convincing one another, of coming into agreement, without violence. At the same time, an ethic of care provides an opening to each of us in our individuality (which universalizing formal logical reason and legal judgment, in principle, cannot), thus allowing a way to reflect responsibly on your and my irreducibly different situations and unique possibilities.

What Next?

Before moving to another chapter, it would be helpful for you to engage in the exercises and points of discussion here. Then, depending on your interests:

> Go on to chapter 2: Fundamentals and Frameworks
> (Dilemmas, Challenges in Environmental Professions; the Socially
> Responsive Self; Professional Codes of Ethics and Beyond)

Or go to chapter 3: Principles and Rules
(For direct application to cases, which can be followed by Theories)

Or go to chapter 4: Theories
(To review the major theories lying behind most individual and shared worldviews)

Or go to chapter 5: Reframing Sustainability
(Analysis of critical environmental issues facing us today)

Or go to chapter 6: Professional Codes and Beyond

Exercises: Discussion Points and Cases

In this section we present an array of cases and points for discussion. Reflecting the organization of this first chapter, these will help you articulate your own personal worldview and define the critical yardsticks that you might use for ethical decision making. In addition, the exercises will help you consider your stance on some of the shared worldviews we described earlier (anthropocentrism, biocentrism, etc.).

Exercise 1.1 Examining Privatism

When considering the relative merits and demerits of privatism as a worldview, it must be decided (1) whether or not the right to a specific control of property is outweighed in a particular case by the obligation not to incur or risk a harm to others; (2) whether or not compensation is due for the loss of the profit or other benefits from the property and, if so, how it is to be calculated. Again, we need to remind ourselves that though the legal and ethical spheres are closely connected in such issues, they are not the same nor reducible to one another. To consider the issue at a general level, particularly in terms of what is most just to all concerned, read the Case of "The State of Washington, Proposition 933" in appendix III and answer the questions there. In this case we see a dilemma, but different worldviews, regarding rights and property ownership, including questions of how to balance individual property rights and freedom with government restrictions to protect the public good. This is an increasingly pressing issue across the U.S today. Recently in Washington State this debate has played out via Initiative 933, which stipulates that the government must compensate private property owners for restricting development of their land (see case 5, appendix 3). Also, answer the following questions:

Liberalism versus Civic Tradition

In this exercise, ideally as a class discussion, we ask you to debate the following: Liberalism versus a civic tradition—which way is better?

John Short argues, "The problem with liberalism is a failure to assemble its rights-oriented individuals into a purposeful society. If people are all pursuing their own ends, how can they combine to reach agreement about wider social goals, such as the creation of more humane cities, let alone achieve them?"

1. First, consider the issue that Short raises here: Do you think that people can reach agreement about social goals and create humane cities if we all are emphasizing our right to freely pursue our own personal goals?

2. Next, let's add another layer. In contrast to liberalism, a civic tradition that runs from Aristotle to Hannah Arendt sees "people as essentially political beings whose individual capacities are fully realized only in the discussion and pursuit of collective goals. . . . From this perspective, classical liberalism [of John Locke, John Stuart Mill, and Adam Smith] is seen at best as an impoverished theory concerning private rights and not on the private-public set of rights and obligations and, at worst, as a justification for the continued inequalities of market society." (Short, 1989, 90).

Do you think this argument has any contemporary force in the face of the explosion of neo-liberal global-market policies? Is there still value in, or a desire for, a civic tradition? How might it be promoted through the forms of the built environment? (See Bess 1993).

Exercise 1.2 Challenges to Anthropocentrism

In addition to the Buddhist attitude of respect for all living beings, the views of many today challenge the limits of the "traditional anthropocentric set of moral conventions [that] privileges human preferences, interests, and needs over those of nonhumans" so that "when costs and benefits are assessed, anthropocentric practices weigh the harm to nonhumans or disruptions to ecosystems only insofar as these constitute a cost or benefit to human beings" (King 1997, 210). In contrast, supporters of a biocentric view affirm and defend the inherent value of other-than-human life, arguing that "humans are not the only ones who possess intrinsic value and deserve the respect of moral subjects" (King 1997, 211).

Which view do you agree with? Do you take an anthropocentric or biocentric view? Why? What are the implications and assumptions of this perspective? Are there any concerns common to anthropocentric and biocentric positions? Perhaps in enlightened self-interest we might see that a shift to a biocentric position is the best way to "protect even human needs and interests." (King 1997, 214). (For further reading—developing from King's excellent article and bibliography—see J. Baird Callicott (1989), Tom Regan (1981), Eric Katz (1992), Lauren Oechsli and Eric Katz (1993), Christopher Stone (1974), Bryan Norton (1987, 1995), Carolyn Merchant (1980), Paul Taylor (1986), Mary Midgley (1983), and opponents such as William Baxter, an anthropocentric theorist who rejects biocentricism and holds that the only relevant reason for preserving the environment is for "the benefit of man" (1974, 304–05; cf. King 1997, 213–14.)

Note, Karen Warren's "notion of a narrative relational ethic," in which "the locus of value is in the relationship rather than in the beings who stand in relation," directs attention to "the importance of first-person narrative as a vehicle for situating judgments of value as well as knowledge claims" (King 1997, 223, citing Warren's "The Power and the Promise of Ecological Feminism," (1990, especially pp. 191–193)). Here we find a connection to the feminist and contextualist approach discussed in our sections on an ethic of care. Again it is well worth following King's excellent bibliography, especially Basso (1987), Cheney (1995), Code (1995), King (1991a, 1991b), Ryden (1993), and Warren (1990).

Exercise 1.3 Place and Identity

Historic Preservation—Conflict and Respect for Others' Lifeworlds from an Anthropocentric Perspective

Environmental disputes may occur because there is a genuine dilemma and good-faith disagreements on all sides concerning what should be done. Being ethical, then, involves being sensitive to all those involved in decision making and action. But, more basically, we also (perhaps first) need to be careful to make sure that our differences do not arise out of an indifference to the interests and needs of others, a stubbornness concerning something we just do not want to do, even though there are good reasons why we should, or even a hostile, more-or-less overt aggression. Since bad faith can operate in subtle ways, and is not so easy to identify, especially in ourselves, the following dramatic (though unfortunately not so rare) cases may make the issues easier to see and think about. Wars have many causes and involve diverse motives, some directed toward values and lifeworlds that are more than merely pragmatic or utilitarian.

As an example, city planner Francis Violich has described how,

> In 1991 Dalmatia's revered symbols of human identity and love of place became targets as the walls of Dubrovnik itself—symbol of hard-earned freedom and self-sufficiency—were shelled. Zarar, Šibenik, Split, and dozens of villages suffered their share of medieval aggression carried out with twentieth-century military equipment.
>
> In times of peace these symbols of culture, history, religion, ethnicity, and tolerance represent an accumulated heritage that binds the generations to a place yet become taken for granted. But in times of war, especially when at-

tacks are sudden and unprovoked, these targeted monuments, which give form
and character to entire towns and villages, stand spotlighted by mind-piercing
experiences that are destructive to the community's collective consciousness.
Lasting wounds are created. Dark clouds of divisive aggression again settle
over the connectedness of people and place that Dalmatia has demonstrated
over the years. (Violich 1998, 293)

In fact, the hidden symbols, of local identity and sense of place were
known to all sides. Ironically the very designations, for instance as marked by
plaques, "signifying which buildings were to be exempted from war damage
according to the Hague Convention of 1954 . . . rather than safeguarding the
buildings, . . . highlighted them as priority targets for bombardment" (Violich,
302). In just one town, Zadar, air raids damaged 150 structures. In addition to
eight churches, twenty of the buildings with the greatest local importance
were targeted. Included were Sveti Šime Church (an especially valued instance of successful historical restoration), Sveta Stošija Cathedral (with its art
and windows from the twelfth and thirteenth centuries), and the Sveti Krševan
Church and its neighboring museum of archaeology (housing important collections of local history). In the density and siting of these buildings we see
the continuity of the urban fabric and sense of place, witnessed also in the
nearby scientific library and history archive building, the Gradska Straža
(guard house), and Gradska Loža (town loggia), shelled because they are important symbols of the city's heritage. Even the oldest thread of continuity—
the Roman pavement in the forum—sustained rocket destruction (Violich,
299–312).

Question: The scope of others' relevant lifeworlds clearly includes more than
individual monuments and buildings. To what extend does environmental responsibility extend to cultural, religious, and ethnic patterns of life? How
much territory and with what economic-political restraint would we be ethically bound to respect—and help preserve—a culture's place and identity?

Exercise 1.4 Are Some Places of a Different Kind?—a Theocentric Perspective

In *Sacred Earth: The Spiritual Landscape of Native America*, Arthur Versluis
claims:

Virgin nature reveals the timeless truth at the center of things, and her majesty
demonstrates to us how laughable are our theories and notions about her, our
absurd calculations. By *virgin nature* I do not necessarily mean nature wholly
free from human influences—for one could well argue that no such places
any longer exist on Earth. Rather, *virgin nature* refers to sacred wild places
that still maintain their numinosity, or spiritual power. . . . Increasingly rare,
virgin nature shows us an essential aspect of what it means to be human. (p.
11)

As examples of such specially charged places, to use Michael Brill's term, Versluis cites the Oneida Stone in New York State, ancient earthworks such as the Lyons Great Horned Serpent (160 feet long) on the Little Arkansas River, and the elevated rock outcroppings held sacred by the Yurok, Karok, and Tolowa peoples in Six Rivers National Forest in northwestern California known to climbers as Chimney Rock, Doctor Rock, and Peak 8. Would it be surprising that such places are not known to outsiders or, if they are, that they are called by other names? Williams and Stewart discuss Devil's Tower in Wyoming, which is experienced by some as charged and non-charged by others, or—and this is a critical question—perhaps charged differently (see *Step Three: Worldviews, Interpretations, and Valuations*, p. 20). If we do not even know the places of which the authors speak, how can we be competent to have a legitimate position on whether they have spiritual power or not? Or can we just dismiss such claims beforehand without any empirical basis in our own experience? Are there any examples of such powerful natural places that you have heard of and can introduce into the discussion? Have you yourself had especially charged experiences in nature?

Question: Do you think some places more worthy of protection than others? Why?
Based on what criteria?
What does protection mean?

Exercise 1.5 Secular Anthropocentrism and the Sacred

Arthur Versluis contrasts the dominant secular anthropocentric view with Native Americans' or Australian aboriginals' recognition of the sacred.[3] Does Versluis's position make any sense in today's world? Elaborate ways in which his distinction clarifies or confuses the opposing views about whether the environment is more than a raw material for human use. Is there any way for the two worldviews to find common ground? Versluis says:

> Humanity has a spiritual relationship to the world, and our world destruction represents a spiritual blindness.
> Nothing reveals this spiritual blindness more clearly than the attempted justification for the depredation of the last remaining wilderness areas on this earth. One finds corporation spokespeople arguing that we have an obligation to our economic system to go forth and extract 'natural resources' from wherever they remain. This kind of predatory language reveals a total incomprehension of the Earth's significance. The land is not merely a repository for 'natural resources'; it is a living manifestation of the Divine.
> Fundamentally, there are two kinds of people in question here. On the one hand is Promethean man, standing over a ruined land, filled with himself and his power over the earth. On the other hand is Reverential man, standing in humility and blessed with spiritual power. To Promethean man, the earth and sky and water are merely things to be used for his own aggrandizement; to

Reverential man, the earth and sky and water and all creatures bespeak their immortal spiritual Origin. This is why Reverential man bows down in reverence before all things; and this is why Promethean man, at heart, fears and consumes all things. (1992, p. 10)

Exercise 1.6—Ethics, Law, and Conflicting Worldviews

The Navajo nation's historic preservation department, created to help care for the cultural resources of the Navajo people—places and landscapes important to the Navajos and other American Indians," has explained that "American Indian concerns about preserving Indian cultures led Congress to enact a joint resolution, the American Indian Religious Freedom Act of 1978 (AIRFA), which affirms the inherent right of freedom to believe, express, and exercise the traditional religions of the American Indian, Eskimo, Aleut, and native Hawaiian, including but not limited to access to sites, use and possession of sacred objects, and freedom to worship through ceremonials and traditional rites. (U.S. Congress, 1978). But this law hasn't been effective or uniformly enforced. (Kelley and Francis 1994, 15–16; see also Deloria 1991, 1–6.) A case in point comes from northwest California:

> In 1988, the United States Supreme Court decided—in the case of Lyng v. Northwest Indian Cemetery Protective Association (1988) 485 US 439; 99L Ed 2d; 108 S Ct 1319—that despite the constitutional right to freedom of religious practice in the United States, and despite the absence of any compelling economic or social necessity, the United States Forest Service had the right to put a road through a Native American sacred place and could lumber forest land that had been sacred to tribal people for generations." (The dissenting opinions of Justice William Brennan, Thurgood Marshall, and Harry A. Blackmun are presented in the appendix to Arthur Versluis, *Sacred Earth: The Spiritual Landscape of Native America,* 139–44.)

Given that one has multiple obligations—to follow the laws of one's society, as well as to act ethically and to remain true to one's deep beliefs (in this case religious beliefs), a clearer understanding of these dimensions and their relationships is important even if it does not change our practical actions in a specific instance (though it might if one protested by means of civic disobedience). Either by general impression from the information in the paragraph above or by looking up the details of the Supreme Court decision, try to sort out the ways in which legal, religious, and ethical obligations are in complex conflict. Further, is there not an ethical obligation on the part of U.S. society to fulfill the promises of the American Indian Religious Freedom Act of 1978 (AIRFA), such that further consideration and action need to be undertaken?

Exercise 1.7. Christianity and Public Policy

Here are two statements from two of the many identifiable Christian positions about what an adequate environmental policy would have to include. In reading these through, try to determine to what extent other worldviews would be able to agree. What would be the reasons for agreement or disagreement?

A) To what extent can those of us without a religious view—that is, those of us who are humanists or theocentrists—agree with the conclusion of the following?

> At the beginning of a Christian natural ethics stands a firm commitment to nature's preservation. Since we did not make material creation, we do not have the right to destroy material creation. At best God has placed nature in our care, made nature subject to our responsible stewardship. When we escalate the chances for nuclear war, expose the seas to widespread oil spillage, or countenance the rapid development of wilderness areas and jungles, we fail a God-given trust. Nature does not exist simply for our good pleasure. The mystery of nature's being, . . , nature's intelligibility, the occurrence of nature in God, and nature's impersonal revelations of God all argue that nature has a right to be, a right to live, a right to flourish apart from its utilities to human beings. (Carmody 1983, 132–33)

We must ask ourselves: What does it mean to allow other beings a right to live and flourish? This may mean a paradigm shift in the way we understand the world or at least nature—but doesn't this have practical, behavioral implications as well? What does it imply that we have to do in our everyday practices? We can also consider these views in relation to public policy. How might public policy shift if we consider the rights of nonhumans to live and flourish?

James A. Nash (1991) argues that an ecologically sound and morally responsible public policy:

1. must continually resolve the economy-ecology dilemma. (p.197)
2. "will include public regulations that are sufficient to match social and ecological needs." (p. 203)
3. "will protect the interests of future generations." (p. 206)
4. "will provide protection for nonhuman species, ensuring the conditions necessary for their perpetuation and ongoing evolution." (p. 210)
5. "will promote international cooperation as an essential means to confront the global ecological crisis." (p. 215)
6 "will pursue ecological integrity in intimate alliance with the struggles for social peace and justice." (p. 217)

B) To what extent can those of us without a religious view—that is, those of us with an anthropocentric or biocentric view—agree with Nash's statements? What would be the reasons for agreement or disagreement? Could some versions of anthropocentric or naturalistic worldviews agree with Nash's criteria for what constitutes an ecologically sound and morally responsible public policy? Are there any other criteria you would add? To what degree is there overlap between these two characteristics of ecologically sound and morally responsible?

Exercise 1.8 Stewardship and Free Enterprise

Arguing on behalf of the tradition of stewardship, several authors grounded in biblical themes and Christian theology raise the following question: "Just how compatible or incompatible do you see stewardship with a free enterprise social system like ours in the United States?" (Jegan and Manno 1985, 162). How would you answer this question given your own set of beliefs and values? How would it be answered from several different Christian, Jewish, Muslim, Buddhist, or other perspectives (if members of the group at hand have enough knowledge or experience of various religions to discuss the issue fruitfully)? How might the question be answered from nonreligious approaches?

Exercise 1.9 Islamic Customs and the Urban Environment

Akel Kahera (1999) describes the way disputes over building and land use have been settled in the Islamic west. In cases involving public or private property, the Mālakī jurists of the Maghreb, or Islamic North Africa and Spain at the time of the Moors, "considered the public interest (*maslaha*)," which they found compatible with the "concept of causing harm or damage) (*darar*)," pp. 138–39, 162. Typically the issues involved the uses of streets and alleys, party walls and rooms, rooftops, or openings from or on to public and private spaces that became contested when people modified their buildings so as to change their relationships to neighbors. In addition to direct physical harm, there could be visual, auditory, and olfactory damage by creating a new window that invaded a neighbor's visual realm (especially critical given the culture's strong emphasis on privacy, especially that of women), or by creating a new workplace or toilet within the dwelling. "When called upon to give a legal opinion on infractions of space that culminated in *legal* harm, the muftī (appointed by the sultan, and thus with legitimately delegated authority) "invariably responds . . . with a fatwā" (legal opinion) that takes into account—is based upon—traditional religious teachings, law, the "rights of people, their customs and habits (*'urf*)," and his independent judgment (often consulting experts, who in the cases we are considering often were builders). Thus, Kahera concludes that "the environment contains important indigenous features reflecting the ethics of building, dwelling, and reasoning . . ." (1998, 133–35, 142, 161). That is, the built environment and the process of deciding on what was ethically acceptable reflects an entire, coherent worldview, in this case based on Islam.

To what extent might such an approach work in the U.S.? How similar is this to the process of local ward politics that has held sway in many of our cities?

To give an even deeper answer you may want to read works such as Kahera and Benmira (1998) and Kahera (1999), or by others. There are many current "international efforts to bridge, communicate, or otherwise understand the contributions of Muslim societies, places, and scholars" (Wescoat, 1997, 93). The highly diverse varieties of Islamic ethics followed by the more than one billion Muslims (about seventeen percent of the global population), including perhaps three to six million in the U.S., have many sources but are held together as Islamic traditions in that, "for practicing Muslims, the Qur'an and Sunnah (the life and sayings of the prophet Muhammad) constitute the primary sources of moral guidance and of shari'a (law). Theologians distill formal ethical principles from these sources for other theologians, religious leaders ('ulama), judges, and lawyers. The latter groups along with local preachers (e.g. mullahs) elaborate and enforce practical religious ethics for the community (ummah)." "Philosophical ethics intersect with religious ethics on matters of virtue and conduct (akhlaq). [The Arabs] build on Aristotelian and Platonic foundations and varying commitments to religious ethics . . ." [because they maintained a live tradition of scholarly interpretation of the original Greek manuscripts (that had been lost to the West and were passed only when the Muslims occupied Spain)] (Wescoat 1997, 98–99).

For the Muslim contribution to international environmental ethics and policy, a good start would include following the trail of references that Wescoat gives us in his fine essay: see especially Callicot and Ames (1994); International Union for the Conservation of Nature and Ethics Working Group (1994), Fakhry (1991), Hourani (1985), Hovannisian (1985), Nasr (1993), Afrasiabi (1995), Deen (1990)—an especially useful collection, with other important essays.

→ For more on Islamic ethics use of harms and benefits in regard to the built environment in comparison with Western theories, see the sections on beneficence and non-maleficence in chapter 3.

Exercise 1.10 Buddhist Ethics and Nature

It would appear especially hard to fully practice a Buddhist ethic in contemporary Western society. Even if most westerners would not hold such a view (because they are not spiritually inclined, because they think it impractical, because of their own theocentric position, or because of another reason), would what follows be a strong basis for an ecocentric way of life? On what grounds would it be legitimate to shift to deeply respecting life and accepting a more appropriately humble (less arrogant and destructive) view of ourselves than we generally display in western societies?

For the sake of this exercise, base your responses to the above questions on the following explication by Saddhatissa (1970) of what it would mean to attempt to practice the precepts of Buddhism (*Pañca Sīla*), among which one would affirm: "I undertake the precept to abstain from the taking of life" (*Pāṇātipātā veramaṇī sikkhāpadam samādiyāmi*) and "I undertake the precept not to take that which is not given" (*Adinnādānā veramaṇi sikkhāpadam samādiyāmi*) (p. 87). Following the first precept, the Buddhist would make the consistent effort to refrain not only from destroying any living being, but also from sanctioning such acts, since she "recognizes her relationship with all living beings [human or animal, regardless of size], a relationship which is so close that the harming of any living creature is inevitably the harming of herself" (p. 87). This would involve not eating meat, for example. Non-injury (*ahimsā*) has, as its positive counterpart, loving kindness (*mettā*) toward all beings, developed through meditation (pp. 89–90). Following the second precept, one would "'wait for the gift" (*dinnādayī*), abstaining, for example, from business transactions in which the other party is not fully aware of the value of what is being exchanged and thus is liable to being taken advantage of, as well as from more directly appropriating someone's property for one's own use (p. 100). This obviously is at the opposite end of the spectrum than the all too prevalent approach of *caveat emptor*—let the buyer beware.

Notes

1. The Heinz dilemma was created and first used in research by Lawrence Kohlberg in his studies of moral development. Later, Carol Gilligan re-examined this dilemma in light of her critique of Kohlberg's work. She and other scholars also introduced the Heidi dilemma, which is essentially the same scenario with the gender roles switched, to determine the degree to which gender identity might influence people's responses to the dilemma.

2. For further reading on worldview classification systems and how they relate to one another, see Mugerauer and Murnane, 1992; Drengson, 1999; Foreman, 1991; Kealey, 1990; Lester, 1989; Merchant, 1992; Milbrath, 1984; Miller, 1966; Naess, 1990; Oelschlaeger, 2002; Paehlke, 1989; Pepper, 1984; Petulla, 1980; Skolimowski, 1992; Swearingen, 1989; and Martin-Schramm and Stivers, 2003.

3. For an additional view of what Native Americans themselves say about environmental decision making, see Haudenosaunee [Six Nations Iroquois] Environmental Task Force, *Words That Come Before All Else: Environmental Philosophies of the Haudenosaunee*, 1995.

Chapter Two

The Environmental Professions, Reflection, and Responsibility

Reflection and the Socially Responsive Self

Having examined personal and shared worldviews as well as the nature of environmental dilemmas in the first chapter, we now turn our attention to what it means to be a socially responsive practitioner and then consider the most important features in relation to the particular fields of practice within the environmental professions.

Identify Your Role

How would you identify your professional role: landscape architect, urban planner, architect, civil engineer, construction manager, developer, public official (policy-maker or staff responsible for implementing policy), interested citizen, or?

What are, or will be, your special environmental concerns and responsibilities in that role?

What kinds of values and strategies might you advocate in that role?

What particular perspectives or values might the members of your particular profession share in common?

Values and Ideals behind Everyday Practice

To examine ethics in relation to professional practice in general, it is helpful to consider what motivates people to engage in the work that they do. One major driving force is people's fundamental values about what constitutes meaningful work, a sense of commitment to that work, and attitudes about how one maintains integrity. Personal commitments to ideals beyond rules or codes are often what guide our work and how we conduct ourselves and make work meaningful (Martin 2000). In this chapter, we explore some values that underlie professional practice in the environmental professions in order to establish a foundation for the development of one's personal set of ethics, which in turn provide guidance for principled action.

Personal commitments in professional life are often to ideals that are not mandated by rules or codes, but are based on our personal views of integrity and responsibility that go beyond duty. As we saw in chapter 1, these ideals influence our choices about what kind of work we take on and how we conduct ourselves in the development and implementation of this work (Martin 2000). The notion of professional ideals is a provocative one. Ideals most certainly go beyond rules that seek to limit behavior to maintain parameters of appropriate behavior in a given profession and beyond externally imposed regulations about what one ought to do. The ideal is what we strive for; it is what we personally perceive to be a standard of excellence. It is also an idea or a way of being that embodies that standard. When we think about ideals, we generally tend to think about the ultimate aim of an endeavor and achieving what is good and noble.

This last point is particularly relevant to professional ethics. We may strive for the ideal, but struggle in our efforts to attain it, and we certainly encounter situations where it is unattainable. Real, on-the-ground projects in which we engage in professional practice involve negotiating with others under circumstances that are not entirely in our control. This is particularly true when we work with multiple stakeholders and the general public. Moreover, none of us operate in a vacuum. As we have argued earlier, we are all socially situated, and because of this, negotiation is critical. We must negotiate not only with various stakeholders in our projects but within our own minds. We must decide what we are willing to do, what we are willing (if anything) to sacrifice and what we want to remain firm on. This can vary from project to project and within any given project over time. So again, ethical decision making is not static.

Holding our particular ideals and values is based, at least in part, on our conceptualization of our self in the world. Within a critical-theory perspective in particular, and the social-constructivist paradigm in general, the self is understood as socially constituted and, ideally, socially responsive. It is through an understanding of ourselves as socially constructed entities that we can perceive of our personal commitments and sense of integrity as going beyond the purview of the isolated individual conscience to being a shared enterprise based on a sense of social responsiveness and shared responsibility. Some have argued that social and moral responsibility is more a matter of responsiveness to others in need than a matter of following rules (May, 1996). In this sense, ethical practice is about what Habermas (1996) calls "the opening of communicative space." That is, ethical practice creates forums of communication wherein people (re)make the practices in which they interact and collectively develop new understandings of their worlds (Kemmis and McTaggart 2005). This line of argument has also been made by feminist scholars advocating for an ethic of care in conducting research, where ethical decision making is couched in terms of the situated self in relations with others (See chapter 5 for a fuller discussion).

Ethical dilemmas themselves are also situated. Not surprisingly, there is a tangled history of what situated means; the relation of concrete existential life to abstract, perhaps-universal principles, is further developed in chapter 5). In any case, while we are unique individuals with our own viewpoints and our own responsibilities on a project, we remain situated in a complex web of relationships and our sense of ethical responsibility hinges on or at least greatly affects those relationships. We do not make decisions about right action in a vacuum.

Professionalism and Excellence

Being a professional generally means having a set role involving specialized knowledge and training, autonomous decision making power and dedication to public service (Flores 1988). The latter two characteristics are particularly relevant for our discussion of ethics. Autonomous decision making power is perhaps the characteristic most obviously related to ethics, as the professional has the freedom or autonomy to make important decisions that will have a real impact on other people and the world around us. Apart from rules of conduct and codes of professional ethics that place parameters on what is acceptable and right, there is a good bit of latitude in what one can do in one's professional role. The other characteristic of professionalism, dedication to public service, suggests that the work of the professional is meant to be done to serve the public good. Thus, the decisions that one makes have a real impact on other people (and in the case of the environmental professions on the environment and other species as well), and those decisions must be made with those impacts in mind. As it relates to ethics, then, to be a professional means, in part, being committed to using one's expertise and skills in morally acceptable ways (Flores 1988). If this is the case, professionalism is a cluster of behaviors, attitudes, values and ideals that revolve around what is good and right in a given profession. It is about an idealized way of being and behaving. Given that, the notion of professionalism addresses the idea of goals and aspirations, beyond any formally prescribed codes of conduct. It is not that being moral means merely observing rules of conduct—otherwise professionalism is reduced to rule-governed behavior based on applying formal codes (Flores, 1988).

There are two approaches to professionalism, each with a different focus:

Professionalism as rule-governed behavior, morally achieved when rules are followed	Professionalism as virtue, morally goes beyond rules—may even mean breaking rules to adhere to a greater good

(Adapted from Flores 1988)

One way to consider the contrast between the two approaches to professionalism is to reconsider the Heinz Dilemma, in particular the role and responsibility of the pharmacist. On the one hand, the pharmacist can be said to be legally duty-bound not to take it upon himself to dispense drugs for free. On the other hand, the oath of his profession is based on doing good and not doing harm, which may lead us to think the pharmacist *should* give Heinz the drug to save a life. Should the pharmacist live up to his ideals or follow the rules? For a fuller discussion of the professional codes and their critiques, see chapter 6. What choice on the pharmacist's part would exhibit a higher level of professionalism?

Additionally, there also are two sets of issues related to the idea of professionalism: One concerns what kind of person one is or wants to be, and the other is related to how one should act. In other words, conformity to codes may only provide the appearance of ethicality but may be devoid of real substance (Flores 1988). Striving toward excellence in everyday practices is a major aspect of virtue—a critical issue on classical ethical theory of natural law (for example in Aristotle's ethical theory), that has stimulated new interest recently among theorists such as MacIntyre and Wasserman (for more on this topic, see chapter 4).

Gardner, Csikszentmihalyi, and Damon (2001) examine the idea of excellence and ethics in professional life in their book, *Good work: When Excellence and Ethics Meet*. Their notion of good work has to do with work of expert quality that benefits the broader society. It is not about money or fame or choosing the path of least resistance in cases of conflict. It is about being thoughtful about one's responsibilities and the implications of one's work (p. 3). The authors wisely point out that people can do their work expertly, but not necessarily responsibly. In stating this, they make an important distinction between expertise and ethical practice—that is, one can have all the specialized knowledge and technical skill there is to gain, but not necessarily employ them in socially responsible ways. We can also see how the authors equate ethical practice with socially responsible work. The challenge of doing good work defined thusly confronts every profession today.

> ## What does it mean to be a professional?
>
> Professional and Professionalism are common terms, readily used and understood, yet they warrant close examination, particularly when considering professional ethics. As with most familiar objects and concepts, we develop assumptions about them that remain implicit and go without questioning until something shakes up our professional life. In many cases, it's an ethical issue that arises in our work life. It is helpful to examine our beliefs about what it means to be a professional—to make the implicit explicit. What does professional really mean? What concepts and issues come to mind when you consider the term? How does this manifest itself in practice?

Within this framework of good work, Gardner et al. look at how professionals handle dilemmas—such as the HMO physician who wants to give each patient a proper evaluation and diagnosis but who must schedule at least six visits an hour or get penalized for not complying with requirements, or the high-school teacher whose approach to study is deep immersion into a limited number of topics but who instead has to structure her teaching to state-mandated exams that test recollection of discrete historical facts. Or the craftsman who believes in using only the finest materials while his contractor instructs him to use inferior materials to cut costs unlikely to be detected by a trusting purchaser (p. 9-10).

The Mirror Test

Part of the internal conversation people have about what they are willing and unwilling to do involves the mirror test, the name of which is said to have come from the story of a German ambassador who, when hosting a celebration for King Edward VII, was asked to provide prostitutes to guests. Unwilling to do so, he resigned his position. When asked about it he allegedly explained, "I refused to see a pimp in the mirror in the morning when I shave." (As retold in Gardner, Csikszentmihalyi, and Damon 2001, 11).

Whatever their chosen profession, at these moments of dilemma, thoughtful practitioners should consider three basic issues: (1) the mission or defining features of their profession; (2) standards or established best practices of their profession; and (3) one's identity, particularly one's personal integrity and values

(Gardner et al., p 11). Particularly interesting is how a person's background, traits, and values add up to her deeply felt convictions about who she is and what matters most to her as a professional, a citizen and a human being. They argue: "a central element of identity is moral—people must determine for themselves what lines they will not cross and why they will not cross them." (p. 11).

Dissolving Dilemmas

Dilemmas, as you now know, are by their nature very difficult situations that seem unsolvable. However, in some cases at least, shifting the way we understand the situation can help us see beyond the dilemma, in effect dissolving it. Now this is not to say that there is a way to review a situation so that the dilemma disappears, but rather that if we analyze the situation in light of worldviews and values we may be able to reconfigure the situation so that it is not utterly unsolvable. Gilligan's challenge of the Heinz dilemma and Kohlberg's theories of moral law are examples of how a paradigm shift refocuses our understanding of a situation to see new solutions and possibilities.

❑ Identify the frameworks involved in the way your question or problem is viewed. Continue reflecting on your and others' worldviews.

❑ Imaginatively attempt to reconfigure, redefining and recategorizing in order to undo dichotomies.

❑ A special perspective of environmental disciplines and professions: eliminating or reducing dilemmas by creatively eliminating what were thought to be inevitable harms. See chapter 5.

Dealing with Dilemmas that Stand

Naturally, not all attempts at dissolving dilemmas will succeed. When the dilemma remains, demanding a decision, some of the stakeholders will be called on to:

❑ Establish a hierarchy of values and sacrifice, compromise, or take different risks (see hierarchies or principles and rules in chapter 3).

❑ Act responsibly by maintaining and enhancing an ethic of care—or by parallel actions according to other forms of virtuous disposition or wisdom (see especially the ethic of care in chapters 3 and 4)

→ To think more about worldviews, you can return to the sections and exercises on worldviews in chapter 1.

→ To refine your sense of how to undo dichotomies, you can turn to the sections and exercises on the topic in Chapter One.

Gardner, Csikszentmihalyi, and Damon are all psychologists who draw on their training to develop an important perspective on ethics that incorporates issues of self-concept, identity, traits, and values as critical for ethical decision making. Damon is a developmental psychologist who has written definitive texts on moral development and, with Anne Colby, conducted pioneering studies of people who have led exemplary moral lives. Gardner is a cognitive psychologist who is known for his theory of multiple intelligences, which is notably quite popular in design education. Csikszentmihalyi is known for his work on flow experiences, which is relevant for ethics. Flow has to do with the circumstances in which we concentrate on a difficult task and use all our skills to get it done. These are gratifying experiences during which a person is totally immersed in the task at hand, fully committed and alive.

While flow experiences can happen in any aspect of life, Csikszentmihalyi found in his research that it happens often at work, when a job provides clear goals, immediate feedback, and a level of challenge that matches our skills: "When these conditions are present we have a chance to experience work as 'good'—that is, as something that allows the full expression of what is best in us." (p. 5). It is important to note, however, that flow experiences do not guarantee that someone is doing good work. As psychologists the authors view identity as that which is shaped by an amalgam of forces, including family history, religious and ideological beliefs, community membership, and idiosyncratic individual experiences. In the best of circumstances, these complement one another and add up to a coherent and positive whole. But this is an ideal, as we all suffer at some point from some fragmentation of identity, some diffusion and confusion. Thus, we must have continual internal conversations about who we are, what we want to achieve, where we are successful and where we fall short.

We all try to make sense of our experiences and understand what is happening around us (recall our contention at the beginning of chapter 1 that ethics is not merely a matter of armchair speculation, but instead involves decisions that are put into action and have serious consequences). We all also "have the capacity to frame experiences in certain ways—to construe them in a way that either motivates or paralyzes action," and we are all able to choose from a range of actions. Part of that ability to choose—and, we would argue, to perceive any particular range of actions—is related to one's personal capacities and resources. This is similar to Sandra Harding's arguments that whether we perceive a moral dilemma and how we make sense of that dilemma depends on how we frame the issues, which are at least partly based on our worldview. Similarly, Gardner, Csikszentmihalyi, and Damon use examples of how framing a dilemma depends in part on disciplinary perspective. So a historian might think about a situation in terms of trends in a field over time and how different periods emphasized different issues and in particular ways, while an economist might focus on market forces, contracts, bids, and the like. But there are other worldviews outside of disciplinary ones. So this is where frameworks for understanding nature might come in. If you have an anthropocentric view of nature, that will determine whether you even perceive a dilemma in a land-rights scenario, say, and, if you do, it will help determine how you would go about addressing the dilemma you perceive.

Complications of Practice in a Post-Modern World

We want to explicitly point out that recent social transformations in the way we think, in the global economy and telecommunication systems of today's world, and in our increasing awareness of the interconnectedness of ecological systems across the planet, all add layers of complication to ethical decision making and the environmental dilemmas we face. We need to consider how one can do good work (and be socially responsible). Today's professionals face particular challenges in carrying out their work since conditions change rapidly, market forces are so powerful, and our senses of time and space are being altered by technological innovations. Part of this condition is the "waning of an agreed-upon set of principles and of an ethical framework that has been designed to govern the decisions and behavior of all members of a profession" (Gardner, Csikszentmihalyi, and Damon 2001, xi).

As psychologists, Gardner et al. are "keenly aware of powerful economic, political, social and cultural forces and . . . realize that people often feel powerless to oppose them" but their main focus is properly on what is happening inside the heads of engaged professionals—how they make sense of their situations, and which plans and actions they ultimately pursue and why. They call out attention both to our personal values and to the relation of professional excellence to ethics. As to the first aspect, they contend that "all of us need to take stock of our own situations, weigh the various alternatives in light of our own values and goals, and make decisions that are both optimal under the circumstances and that we can live with in the long run. In the absence of this person-centered perspective, we are merely observers buffeted by the fates" (p. 13). But that leaves unaddressed the issue of the relationship between high-level performance and social responsibility—which is especially raised with their observation that experts primarily teach techniques to young professionals while ignoring the values that have sustained the quests of the greats. Clearly, professional life involves a social contract between the individual professional and the community since professionals agree to provide needed services and the community agrees to compensate them and recognize their right to perform those services.

How then would we know whether or not we are doing good work? In dealing with this question, Gardner, Csikszentmihalyi, and Damon, as well as Ledwith (to whom we will return shortly) (225), begin by elaborating the components of a professional realm, which would be comprised of individual practitioners, domains of knowledge, skills, practices, rules and values (thus domains have ethical dimensions). This realm includes institutions and other stakeholders both private and public, such as corporations and the citizenry. The researchers finally evaluate performance in terms of the realm's values compared to the practitioners' standards, with results describable in terms of degrees of alignment and misalignment.

Reflexive Practice

Clearly, moving to a deeper level in thinking about values, ideals, and one's views of professionalism and excellence requires reflexivity, as Schön has famously argued (1986). Reflexivity is the practice of incorporating reflection as an integral part of practice. It is a catalyst for collective change, a professional development strategy, a vehicle for designing in response to people's needs, and a way to facilitate partnerships. It is the inward-facing reflection that arises out of research and practice that attempt to respond to the social context and people's needs and values.

Schön advocates a new understanding and framework for professional practice that incorporates what he calls reflection-in-action. Interestingly, while Schön was writing about professional practice across many disciplines, discussing law, education, and counseling psychology in particular, he used the architectural design studio as the prototype for his model of reflective practice, as a way to understand competency and artistry in skilled practice. Effective practitioners, he argued, bring reflection-in-action to situations of uncertainty, uniqueness, and conflict. Designers model this well as they are regularly called to put things together in new and innovative ways, and to bring new things into being, yet there are many variables and constraints in the process of doing this. Some of the constraints are known at the outset of a project, others emerge during the process. Designers often start with messy situations that are uncertain, ill-defined, and complex, and they construct coherence as part of their design work, which Schön feels is particularly effective when it is done in a reflective way. This goes beyond professional practice as the application of privileged knowledge for instrumental problem-solving. It is a view of practice that is relational and emergent. We must understand ethical decision making in the same way.

Reflection can be an important catalyst for change since it often comes in response to dilemmas, problems, or even failures as "we have a natural tendency to want to troubleshoot; a desire to break down the ambiguity, resolve any paradox, achieve more certainty and agreement and move (back) into a comfort zone (Ghaye 2005, 177). Dewey (1933) argued that a function of reflection is: "to transform a situation in which there is experienced obscurity, doubt, conflict, disturbance of some sort, into a situation that is clear, coherent, settled, harmonious" (Dewey 1933, 100–101 as quoted in Ghaye 2005). Thus, Ghaye argues that reflection is an intentional pursuit and, like careful deliberation regarding an ethical dilemma, it is not a routine act: "Pervasive failure, avoidance norms, risk-aversion behaviors, self-protection, over- and under-responsibility, denial and defensiveness have to be confronted" (Ghaye, 178). These are key concerns that may influence ethical decision making on both the individual and collective (professional community, for example) level. Reflection can help us make decisions about what is the right course of action.

We need to critically examine our everyday practices, not to find fault, but to honestly evaluate what we do, so we can maintain high quality work and improve practice when need be. Naturally, what we usually do has significant limitations, many of which are beyond our control. As Ghaye acknowledges, "Often in our daily work 'being good enough' or 'doing the best we can in the circumstances' has to suffice. These expressions and many others like 'we did what we could' and 'this is all we could manage' occupy the ground between the extremes of 'success' and 'failure' and are all matters of judgment" (p. 179). In order to make such judgments, however, and in agreement with what we just considered with Gardner, Csikszentmihalyi, and Damon, and Ledwith, Ghaye suggests that "we need to ask ourselves three fundamental questions: (1) what are we trying to accomplish? (2) what practical action might we take that could lead to success? and (3) how will we know that something is a success?"

Here we find a shift, and a complex and interesting tension between two important views on reflective practice. Much of the focus on reflection and reflective practices during the1990s tended to emphasize three things—self-reflection, personal reflective writing, and critiques of that writing (Ghaye 2005, 181). More current thinking on reflective practices, however, focuses on a critique of the authority of reason, and emphasizes ends and values, rejects a technical-rationalist view of human worth, and enables us to exercise both autonomy and responsibility (Ghaye, 182).

More current thinking on reflective practices, however, focuses on the authority of reason, which favors a concern with ends and values, rejects a technical-rationalist view of human worth, and enables us to exercise both autonomy and responsibility (Ghaye, 182). Here we find a strong connection between dimensions of professional identity, responsibility, and reflection, and the more formal principles and rules to be considered in chapter 3.

We want to emphasize that reflective practice is necessary for ethical decision making. It is not just about reflection in some everyday sense of pondering this or that; rather, it is deliberate and systematic, significantly connected with moral decision making, and having significant pragmatic implications. Because the theoretical underpinning of the requisite robust reflection being considered here is critical theory, reflecting is not just thinking about the way we behave individually and our personal qualities, but it involves being critical and intentional, and taking history, power, and politics into consideration, since these also reflect how we think feel and act in particular circumstances (Ghaye 2005). As a mode of critical consciousness that enables us to see ourselves in new ways and begin to do things differently, reflection is also a creative process, as we have seen Schön argue (Johns and Freshwater 1998). This will turn out to be an important factor in learning to deal with ethical dilemmas.

Along these same lines, Monson (2005) calls for an inter-subjective and discursive professional ethics. He argues that studio education takes on a more egocentric view of design that inhibits this more ethical approach. Practical discourse could ground an ethical construction of practice, as more discursive processes are fundamental to environmental design in society. "The environmental design disciplines are especially bound to the social functions of 'practice', the positive action realized through cooperative activity that extends our conceptions of the world and human achievement within it." Similarly, Ledwith (2005) talks about the connections between personal narratives and the political dimensions of our lives. She addresses reflection in the context of community development practice, which she feels by nature is committed to a more just, equitable, and sustainable world. Personal experiences and choices have political consequences. So critical consciousness is needed for collective action for social change and social justice. She concentrates on the idea of personal narratives and the role of stories in the process of action for change.

As a profession, community development is central to countering what Peter Reason (2002) calls the "twin global crises of justice and sustainability" (p. 3). Transformative change starts in the deeply personal and reaches to the profoundly political, and this calls for "a critical praxis which Involves personal reflection on a continuum with collective action" (Ledwith 2005, 256). Ledwith goes on to argue that "it is essential that critical consciousness of everyday reality leads to a wider process of collective action for change on a local-global continuum" (p. 256).

Russell (2005), however, points out that there is more rhetoric than actual instruction on reflective practice. He argues that it is not enough just to advocate reflective process; there must be some indication of how it differs from an everyday sense of reflection. He believes that reflective practice is really a set of skills that can and should be taught. Drawing upon Schön's ideas of reflection-in-action, Russell emphasizes three elements that can provide practical guidance for reflective practice: (1) a puzzling or surprising event during teaching might stimulate new ways of perceiving or thinking about a situation or practice in general; (2) this new perspective might stimulate a novel course of action; and (3) actually carrying out the novel course of action might provide evidence for deciding if the new perspective and actions should be included in future practice (Russell 2005, 200). It is easy to see how these dimensions are also relevant for ethical decision making. An ethical dilemma or problem encountered in practice can certainly qualify for Schön's puzzling event that stimulates reframing the professional situation and perhaps even one's understanding of their professional practice as a whole. This new perspective can be gained from encountering dilemmas and navigating through them. Handling a dilemma often initiates new courses of action, which in turn can provide insights to transform one's practice—or even one's worldviews.

The Socially Responsive Self

So now we arrive at a set of pressing issues: What does it mean to be a socially responsive and responsible practitioner in today's society? Do we have an ethical obligation to be socially responsible? What is socially responsive/responsible design, planning, or engineering anyway and how is it achieved? In general, responsibility is defined as "a social force that binds you to your obligations and the courses of action demanded by that force" (WordNet® 3.0., from Dictionary.com website http://dictionary.reference.com/browse/responsibility, retrieved April 18 2007). As John D. Rockefeller Jr. noted: "Every right implies a responsibility; every opportunity, an obligation; every possession, a duty" (p. 13). These are provocative ideas—but if we look at definitions and dimensions of responsibility more closely we can begin to see how there are both similarities and distinctions between responsibilities and duties.

An Ethic of Responsibility Involves:

- a responsiveness to those who could help, especially those who are already in relationships with us or with whom we have taken on a particular role
- a sensitivity to the particular concrete circumstances and contexts
- a motivation to respond to others that grows out of the needs of other people
- a respect for the legitimacy of emotions as a source of moral knowledge, especially for guilt and remorse that are central to moral experiences
- a sense of responsibility tied more to who we are and what we can do than to what we have done. (May 1996, 88)

Larry May (1996), for example, examines the roots of the concept of responsibility and compares them with the notion of duty and obligation. May explores two possible roots of responsibility: first, the giving a response or being accountable to a person or group for what one has done; and second, being responsive for someone in need in a particular situation (p. 91). While the first root is more commensurate with the notion of ethics of duty and obligation, the second suggests that it goes beyond abstract rules impartially applied. He argues that "because of the discretionary aspect of responsibility, how people should be responsive for someone in need cannot be cast in terms of a simple abstract rule or formula" (p. 91). In particular, May considers the idea of social responsibility and argues that it is more than the opposite of self-interest; it is about a sense of responsiveness, the maintenance of relationships and caretaking among people.

It means being sensitive and responsive to those one may have harmed and those one may be able to help.

May examines these nuances of social responsibility and seeks to develop a more sophisticated conceptualization of responsibility that could be the foundation for a distinct ethic of responsibility. He traces the ethic of responsibility to Max Weber's 1946 essays, in which Weber calls for less attention to rule-oriented views of obligation and for more concern for how people and relationships are affected by one's behavior. Over time, however, responsibility has come to be understood as almost interchangeable with obligation and duty. May is calling for a return to this broader understanding that he then builds upon to develop an ethic of responsibility.

To be a socially responsive practitioner, then, is to be attentive and responsive to the social world within which one works. There is an awareness of the fact that people depend on us, that there are power differentials and also attendant vulnerabilities and dependencies that must be considered.

We have, to this point in this chapter, talked fairly broadly about professional practice. But this book is about ethical decision making in the environmental professions—that is, the suite of professional practice disciplines involved in the creation of space and place (architecture, landscape architecture, planning, urban design, construction management, and engineering). As such, we must consider the unique and important ways in which ethics and ethical decision making occurs in these particular professions.

Whistle-Blowing

Whistle-blowing refers to a situation wherein a person discovers that another individual or group has violated some code of ethics—often an established, formalized set of codes for a particular profession—and that person must decide whether or not to report the infraction. For example, you might discover some building-code violation in a construction project and you must decide whether or how to report it. Even a scenario that may seem like a simple choice at first glance can get enormously complicated depending on what code is violated, what is at stake (are lives or one's reputation at risk?), the implications of reporting the infraction, and so on.

We must constantly ask: How responsibly do we use our talents?

The Environmental Professions

Any book about ethics in the design and planning professions must explore the unique and fundamental ways that ethical issues arise in the everyday practice of these professions. As with most professional practice, there are a few, almost universal ethical scenarios like whistle-blowing, but ethics emerge most importantly in everyday decision making about the kinds of projects we undertake, and how we approach and navigate through them. Often these projects are substantial, lengthy endeavors involving multiple stakeholders with whom we must negotiate our relationships, responsibilities, and loyalties. Such projects cause us to think about, and continually reflect upon, the kind of practitioner we want to be. This is important for any critical practice, but in these place-based professions, and for policy makers addressing matters of place, public accountability and the nature of the impact of this work is what makes our obligations pressing, and we must constantly ask ourselves: How responsibly do we use our talents? What are our fundamental values and are we maintaining these values in our professional practice?

Emplaced Ethics

To understand the ethical issues arising from the practice and policies surrounding the design and planning professions, we must consider what distinguishes these professions from others. Most notably, they are all place-based. They are about creating and changing places, and because they directly influence the physical environment around us, they therefore influence the fabric and quality of our everyday lives. Across the built-environment professions there is a social responsibility that comes with directly influencing the creation and quality of the physical environment. Among the ethical considerations are concerns about physical safety and health—safe structures and sustainable environments—as well as important considerations for the well-being of people and other species. Damaged environments and poorly thought out design and construction diminish our experiences and potentials. In a certain regard, we can consider the ethical dimensions behind these professions to be about what Cameron (2003 2004) calls "place-responsiveness"—an approach of a society whose institutions and customs support a deep connection with land and place. This is a spatialized or emplaced ethics i.e. a realm or dimension of ethics that emerges particularly when addressing place, place-making, and the policies related to place. Such an emplaced ethics would require us to remain mindful of the complexities that unfold around place and address ethics in unique and context-sensitive ways.

For example, Stefanovic (2000) calls for a place-based ethics that "aims to guide us in our actions, not through the imposition of static principles and rules, but instead by teaching the meaning of attunement to a balanced fitting relation between human beings and their world" (as quoted in Cameron 2004, 117). Here, ethics is more about attunement than abstract principles. Similarly, Malpas

(2004) points out, "the articulation of place is also an articulation of ourselves—
it is thus that ethics enters centrally into the picture. But it is also an articulation
that cannot be undertaken in any general or abstract way. . . [It] is a matter of the
articulation of the particular pathways, activities, directions, and concrete relations in which we are already enmeshed" (p. 8).

Emplaced Ethics

**Emplaced ethics is the added dimension of ethics that
emerges when engaged in placemaking endeavors and policy
related to place. It is about attunement more than abstract
principles.**

Moreover, an emplaced ethics must address issues on both the local and
global levels. On the one hand, some explorations of the ethical dimensions that
emerge in relation to place focus on the unique value of the local. For example,
Cottingham (2000), following Levinas' now-classic ethics of the face, argues
that we have special concerns for those who are emotionally or geographically
close. When we are in face-to-face relations with people, we are brought to another, deeper level of responsibility in that other people and the impact of our
actions and decisions upon them may be more readily apparent and seem more
real. Similarly, we might feel more affinity with our local communities or feel
more strongly about projects that are happening in our own towns or neighborhoods because we see that they will have some immediate impact on our lives.

- How likely is it that we can turn to the values of
  an earlier era when human impacts on the land
  were more moderate?

- What are the trade-offs?

- What would we sacrifice?

- What would we gain?

- This calls into question the very notion of progress.

- What does it mean to advance society?

Numerous writers emphasize the importance of the local. Geographer Carl Sauer used the concept of *sequent occupance*, which looked at human impact on a particular geographical location through the lens of deep history. Sauer believed that human culture, in a continuum from the earliest reaches of prehistory to the present, has been actively changing the face of the earth. He called for "an ethic and aesthetic under which man [sic], practicing the qualities of prudence and moderation, may indeed pass on to posterity a good earth" (Sauer 1962, 557). "Bioregional philosophers from Dodge (1992) to Thayer (2003) add to Sauer's sequent occupance framework a prescriptive to not only live locally, but to reach back in time to an earlier era when the human imprint on the landscape was more moderate, and to emulate the values of those who were the bioregion's occupants at that time. In this way, present culture can learn to 'live-in-place in an area that has been disrupted and injured through past exploitation'" (Alexander 1990, 162, as quoted in Meredith 2005, 83).

However, Meredith critiques this micro-regional focus of the bioregionalists insofar as it limits our appreciation of the role and import of scales and localities: "The sense of regional identity spans several scales because our past narratives and present affiliations span several localities. Humans are not immersed in singular niches, nor is the bio-regionalist an existential, primordial localist, for his or her choice has been crafted" (Meredith 2005, 83).

Indeed, the reality is that we live in an increasingly globalized society where there are transnational flows of people, goods and capital. There is now a world culture as well as varied local cultures, and most people have allegiances to more than one culture, and are anchored in more than one territory (Lu 2000). More than ever, places are constructed through processes of interconnection and interdependence as well as through the process of creating meaning (Massey and Jess 2000). Similarly, Thomashow (1999) discusses cosmopolitan bioregionalism which integrates the local landscape with global systems and argues that the local landscape and the people who inhabit it "can no longer be understood without reference to the larger patterns of ecosystems, economies, and bureaucracies" (as summarized in Meredith 2005, 126). Such a view recognizes the complexity of scale and the need to bridge those scales, from the macro- to the micro-region. These overlapping webs of relation create a cosmopolitan community interwoven between global and local affiliations (Berman 2001). Thus, local issues are usually not exclusively local, and ethics must be conceived in terms of both local and global or far-reaching implications.

We must interrogate our practices in terms of ecological impacts. As Garrett Hardin points out, "There is no 'away' to throw to." (1993)

In addition to globalization, there is other evidence of the far-reaching impact of our locally based actions when we consider ecological impacts. Our actions in the temporal and geographic vicinity have more distant impacts—either because they are long-term and accrue over time or because they are less visible and impacts appear further away (in what happens downstream). In some way, all of our actions have reactions, many of which manifest themselves in the physical environment, some of which are more obvious than others. Obviously, lack of immediate or highly visible impact does not mean there are no real and serious ethical issues behind our actions. They may be more subtle and longer-term but we still make decisions that will benefit or harm others and therefore we must be thoughtful about the kinds of decisions we make (Markie 1994).

The value of understanding place and the impact of our place-related actions on both a local and global level is evident in the landscape ecology framework. Landscape ecology is an interdisciplinary approach to understanding the entire landscape that recognizes the importance of the larger context, patterns, and systems, and seeks to integrate nature and human settlement in a holistic approach. Interestingly, the term "landscape ecology" was coined by Carl Troll in 1939 in response to new technology—aerial photography (which, incidentally, also profoundly influenced the seminal landscape interpretations of J. B. Jackson). This enabled us to see landscape as an enormous puzzle and appreciate the interconnectedness of elements in the landscape. This more holistic approach opens itself up to an emplaced ethics wherein we can use culture to advance ecological health (Nassauer 1997). Here, culture comprises our collective choices and actions from what individual citizens do in their daily life (social practices) to the choices policy-makers and elected officials make and how resources are allocated (the political economy). All of these things affect ecological health. The challenge, according to Nassauer (1997), is that we may have difficulty achieving sufficient distance from our own cultural condition to see its consequences. Nonetheless, our individual and collective choices have significant ethical implications, and it is imperative that we interrogate these.

Design is essentially a normative activity in which designers present their vision of what the world should be. That's a lot of power. How can we use it responsibly?

Designers, planners, and other practitioners in the environmental professions have considerable and unique social responsibility. Thompson (2000) has argued that design is essentially a value-laden practice in which designers envision what the world could or should be like. This argument underscores the ethical dimension of the design and planning professions because what practitioners envision, once built or put in place, has a real impact on the quality of the lives of people who use the space—whether it be a particular structure, site, neighborhood, city, or region. While we all have social responsibilities as members of society, the level and magnitude of our professional responsibilities vary with our profession and our specific role. More accurately, with certain specialized roles come special responsibilities. Ethical decision making lies in how we interpret the responsibilities of our roles and what we do with them.

In contrast to Thompson's position, some posit that design (or at least architecture, as Wasserman et al. 2000 claim) is, by its very nature, ethical because it is directed to the well-being of humanity. However, we would argue that while the obligations and expectations for ethical behavior may be considerable in the design, planning, and construction professions, no profession is, in and of itself, either ethical or unethical. Rather, ethics emerge through our individual choices and actions as we live our lives and carry out our work. The important difference here is between intent and effect. While designers and planners may intend to work toward the betterment of the physical environment and the quality of our lives, there is no guarantee that this will be achieved. Whether one can say that they have improved the environment and the quality of our lives also depends on how betterment is defined and what courses of action we choose to achieve it. These can vary significantly, and herein lies the task of ethical decision making. For example, one designer's interpretation of the enhancement of well-being and the betterment of our world might be to make a creative statement with a unique, bold design that becomes the designer's signature, while another designer's notion of betterment is to develop green building strategies or small, infill development projects. Even if there were agreement on what well-being and betterment of our world mean and how these should be achieved, these alone would not be sufficient to make practice ethical. There are always opportunities to act in different ways, and, indeed, to not act at all. What matters ethically are the particulars of the choice of whether or how to act. Ethics emerge most sensitively and urgently in the context of needing to make difficult decisions—as occurs most obviously in dilemmic situations.

Ethical dilemmas often happen in the place-based professions because neither the boundaries of these fields nor those of the ecologically integral environments themselves are clear. It is not just a matter of where one's professional role leaves off and where another's begins, but that the parameters of each person's role in a given project might be fuzzy and that the co-determining dynamics of the natural and built environments are so complex that often we do not understand the consequences of intended actions. In the following sections, we will look at ethics in relation to the natural environment and then the built environment to get a perspective on the nature and scope of issues with which an emplaced ethics must grapple.

Emplaced Ethics and the Natural Environment

The ethical dimensions of our beliefs, attitudes, values, and treatments of the natural environment have been widely discussed and published for many decades, particularly since the environmental movement of the 1960s. Broadly speaking, the literature suggests there are three fundamental approaches to human-nature relationships: (1) people as separate and above nature, evidenced in language about "cracking the genetic code" and "harnessing" natural resources; (2) people as subservient to nature and subject to its whims and power, often evident in places and times of natural disasters—seen for example in the concept of Mother Nature and concerns about how to appease her; and (3) people in harmony with, or part of a larger continuum of, nature—an approach typified by the landscape ecology movement. The first (and some might argue the second) perspective constitute what are considered anthropocentric views of nature (the second and third are bio- or eco-centric). Within such frameworks, nature is "seen in terms such as: 'Wild' and 'uncivilized' [which] are often used as though they are synonymous and of lower rank than 'civilized' and 'cultured.' The wild part of nature can be seen as fearful and dangerous and needs to be tamed (Bunce 1994). This is evident through our way of controlling nature and cultivating the wilderness" (Hanssen 2000, 249).

As we began to see in chapter 1, each of these particular views of nature has ethical implications because the way we understand nature influences our actions in relation to it—everything from how we use the land and whether and how to harvest natural resources, to our everyday actions like recycling, and our choices of transportation and food consumption to name a few. In fact, one's view of nature would influence whether one considers there to be ethical dimensions to some of these choices at all, for example, whether we see it as our right, prerogative, or even our responsibility to harvest land and other resources, etc. What complicates things even further is that few people endorse one view of nature uniformly across all issues and situations. For example, one could have a deep respect for nature and spend a great deal of time in the backcountry enjoying the wilderness and perhaps even communing with it (suggesting a more biocentric view of nature), while being an avid mountain climber driving to and from wilderness areas in an SUV otherwise parked outside their single family suburban home with a lawn treated with pesticides (which might suggest a consumptive approach to nature). Then when a terrible storm downs trees that break through the roof of the same person's house, the climber might in that moment feel at the mercy of nature as an indifferent force (a human as subjugated by nature). As we began to see in chapter 1, people's attitudes and behavior toward nature can be sometimes contradictory and composed of different elements across conceptually distinct worldviews.

Much of the literature on environmental ethics written after the first wave of the modern ecology movement, Noel Castree (2003) argues, is written from the perspective of material essentialism, that is, from the viewpoint that entities in the world (lakes, trees, mountains, and so on) have properties that are autonomous from other entities—that is, they exist separately from people. So ultimately, debates about environmental ethics boil down into debates about ontology or the nature of being or existence. This has led to what Castree calls the "ethical invisibility" of nature which characterizes post-environmental thought. Because nature is not like people, the non-human has been absent from ethical consideration. Against this, some ethicists have searched for principles which assert that non-human entities have value independently of people. This is where arguments for the rights of animals and other species arise (the deep ecology movement); but as Castree notes, attempts to locate values in nature reinstate the distinction between human and non-human.

Material essentialism is the viewpoint that all entities in the world are autonomous—that is, they exist separately from people and have their own distinct, intrinsic value.

Instead, it is the connection rather than the distinction between human and nonhuman species that is more critical for ethical decision making in relation to place. As Stephen Jay Gould points out: "We can not win this battle to save species and the environment without forging an emotional bond between ourselves and nature—for we will not fight to save what we do not love" (cited by Orr 1994). This comment also illustrates how emotional connection and an ethic of care are so important for environmental ethics. But when considering nature, the notion of care gets complicated quickly. We must be clear about how we understand care and its implications for ethical action in relation to nature. Is care the same as stewardship? The questions in the discussion box that follows are critical for working out what an ethic of care means in relation to nature.

Nature in Relation to an Ethic of Care

- If humans are equal to other species, then do we have any extra moral duty to care for these other species?
- Should we learn to care for the earth, or should our goal be to enable it to have sufficient complexity to care for itself?
- In this context, what is care? Does it mean watching over the landscape? Intervening in change? Control?

—Adapted from Spirn's *The Granite Garden*

Within the specific fields of place-based professional practice there are distinct discourses that reflect particular values in relation to the natural environment. For example, Thompson (2000) examines the literature in landscape architecture in regard to environmental values and identifies three main areas of discourse: aesthetic, social and environmental. In each one of these discourses are implicit and explicit values that influence the kind of practice in which landscape architects engage. The aesthetic discourse includes a continuum of approaches from those which advocate for unspoiled nature, to approaches that sanction the manipulation of nature in the interest of utilitarian social needs or artistic expression. Embedded in this discourse are discussions of (1) conservation—natural landscapes are repositories of values to be protected; (2) accommodation—human elements are accommodated but usually to contain nature or to camouflage it; (3) improvement—the idea that nature can be improved, which is often couched in language of the picturesque and improving views; and (4) discussions of the tension of landscape architecture as a practical service-driven profession versus as an artistic pursuit. Along with these are social discourses about people's well-being, amenities, processes of consultation and participation, and the social change potential of the place-based professions.

Finally, the environmental discourse addresses concepts of harmonization, and considers the reconciliation of humans with nature as central to the health and integrity of all species. In his empirical research, Thompson found that practitioners, depending on their values, were more or less readily disposed to think about their professional practice (in this case landscape architecture) with most emphasis on either its aesthetic, social, or environmental dimension. This suggests values drive designers' choices about the kind of practice in which they engage. It could be argued that the choices of what we emphasize in practice have ethical dimensions as well; that is, we make decisions based on our perception of the right thing to do, of what we can and should do in good conscience in everyday practice.

All of these discourses and perspective can fuse however. For example, Anne Spirn, in *The Granite Garden*, describes a vision for how design and landscape ecology can be readily enmeshed. She argues that the natural environment has great potential for creating memorable urban forms and it remains an enduring framework in which we build and live. Thus, we need to understand the relationship between natural processes and human enterprise taken together. Solutions need not be comprehensive, but the understanding of the problem does. This is essential for ethical decision making where we need to look at dilemmic situations holistically and see the various stakeholders and issues at play as part of an integrated system.

When it comes to ethics in relation to the natural environment, landscape design, and ecology, the ethical principle of justice is quite prominent in the discourse (justice is fully addressed in chapter 4). For example Preston's (2004) work on environmental ethics builds upon Rawls' notions of justice and political liberalism to extrapolate ethical principles regarding nonhuman nature. In particular he examines Rawls' idea of reasonableness and a well-ordered society:

> [Rawls'] inability to provide a non-anthropocentric environmental ethic might threaten the stability of a 'well-ordered' society, and this possibility gestures to the potential 'problem' of pluralism in general . . . Environmentalists of a certain position might be deemed unreasonable in which case they are a threat to the well-orderedness of society. [However] if the group is 'reasonable', Rawls must hope that they will also agree with enough of the political conception of justice, and be swayed by appeals to reasonableness, that they will join in the overlapping consensus despite their environmental concerns. (Preston 2004, 73)

Let's break this down and examine what Preston is saying here. To begin, Preston considers Rawls' key question in *Political Liberalism*: "How it is possible for a just and stable society of free and equal citizens to exist and endure when its citizens 'remain profoundly divided by reasonable religious, philosophical, and moral doctrines?'" (quoted in Preston 2004, 73). This is where Rawls' notion of overlapping consensus comes in. Rawls' political conception of justice allows for the diversity that exists in a democratic society, and that could be accepted by many different and even competing moral doctrines so that some degree of overlap (agreement) can be achieved. But Preston argues that some doctrines, like those regarding environmental ethics, are so at odds with the principle of justice and a just society that this overlapping consensus is not achievable.

The well-ordered society is one where everyone accepts the same principles of justice, the institutions of society satisfy those principles, and the institutions are considered just.

Preston's argument seems to hinge on the idea of a well-ordered society, defined by Rawls as one "in which everyone accepts, and knows that everyone else accepts, the very same principles of justice" (Rawls 1996, 35). Two other conditions for a well-ordered society are that the main social and political institutions of society satisfy those principles and that these institutions are considered just. Initially, it might seem that pluralism would be a threat to the stability of such a society. As with almost any issue, there is a plurality of views about our environmental obligations. "Environmentalists might not want a de facto subordination of their values to background culture and this could present a stability problem since they might be disinclined to be part of the stable overlapping consensus of justice." Consider that Rawls did not extend the principle of justice to nonhuman animals, and that our views of our treatment of animals depend instead on our theory of natural order and our place in it. Less controversially, Brent Singer (1988, 207) very reasonably offers that such things as "regular access to potable water, shelter from freezing temperatures, uncontaminated food supplies, and safe air to breathe" be considered as primary goods . . . such things are needed for the exercise of the two moral powers and to further one's own conception of the good.... The same principles of justice that forbid disenfranchising one person for the social gain of another . . . would also forbid policies and practices that seriously contaminate the food, water, or air supply of one person for the social gain of another (Preston, 75).

If the environmental beliefs are not considered reasonable, then there is no consideration about overlapping consensus in the first place. In our non-Buddhist culture, the vegetarian who tries to convince others that meat is murder may not be considered reasonable. Michael Huemer (1996), using the example of a religious fundamentalist, argues that appeals to reasonableness will be effective only insofar as the dissident values reasonableness more than his or her "truth." If our vegetarian believes his or her doctrine to be true, what force does an appeal to reasonableness have on her or him? (Preston, 81). So Huemer argues that any countervailing value brought to bear on a comprehensive doctrine will be evaluated from the viewpoint of that doctrine. If, however, a citizen believes that a particular environmental policy or action should conform to the dictates of her doctrine regardless of what the majority of her fellow citizens reasonably believe—because the truth of her doctrine trumps the demand for reasonableness in political deliberation, this citizen is herself unreasonable.

If an environmentalist were to find him/herself in a society unjust with respect to environmental issues (for example, one in which citizens routinely and unjustly are being exposed to pollutants and in which this is known and permitted by the decision-makers of the society), justice might not only allow, but depend upon, that environmentalist doing more than simply attempting to persuade others, through the use of public reasons, to change the problematic policies. By definition, such a society is not a well-ordered society, and so our focus shifts from stability issues to the justice of civil disobedience: this is one scenario in which more aggressive measures might be appropriate. That our own society is not well-ordered raises some intriguing possibilities for moral argumentation around the issue (Preston, 82).

On Sustainability and Future Generations

In examining ethics in relation to landscape architecture, engineering, and landscape ecology, it is essential to consider the issues of sustainability and ethical implications of our actions for future generations. While chapter 5 and appendix IV are entirely devoted to sustainability issues, here we look broadly at the subject to begin identifying some of the ethical issues underpinning the discourse. First, since the literature on the subject matter has grown exponentially in recent decades, it is helpful to begin with a definition of sustainability.

Rooted in ecology, sustainability has been defined as "the nesting of human purposes with the larger patterns and flows of the natural world" (Orr 1994). It has also been defined more anthropocentrically as achieving a balance that allows economic well-being and social equity to be achieved across generations (Schaller 1978).

In looking across these and other definitions of sustainability, one can see several critical components emerge. First, sustainability is about the interrelationship of systems and the interconnectedness of all things. Second, there is a critical temporal component, about well-being over time. Third, there is the notion of balance and equity. One of the simpler definitions of sustainability is that it is ultimately about equity over time.

One of the most popular definitions of sustainability broadly states: "meeting the needs of the present without compromising the ability of future generations to meet their own needs" (Brundtland 1987)

In Preston's discussion of conservation, he examines the notion of justice between generations. He argues that people are often ignorant of the generation to which they belong—that is, they are blinded to the full impacts of their particular culture and cultural condition. In an effort to get past this, he calls for a notion of justice that goes between generations by appealing to the sentimental attachments of belonging to a family line: "Assuming a beloved line of descent for oneself, people could agree on some sort of ethic of conservation for the sake of those descendants. Brent Singer (1988, 209) points out that the problem with this approach is that it presupposes that having children is a part of every rational plan of life. Certainly many, if not most, people aspire to have children, but some people do not. Could this line of reasoning and appeal to family line still be effective if you do not have children of your own? It would seem that having children would be an aspect of one's conception of the good. Since participants are ignorant of their particular conceptions of the good [our blindness to our generation's cultural condition and its impact], they couldn't know that having children would be important to them in order to make justice-based provisions for descendants. Rawls might argue that children are included in the primary goods, but he doesn't make that argument and would probably be hard pressed to do so. Moreover, he needn't do so." (Preston, 76)

As an alternative, Singer (1988) suggests that it makes more sense in trying to determine what is just in one's environmental choices that we: "assume that the parties behind the veil of ignorance[2] [i.e. the parties affected by our actions] do not know to which generation [our emphasis] they belong in the stronger sense that they may turn out to belong to the current generation, or they may turn out to belong to any one of several future generations" (p. 209). How might that alter what we do in the here and now? Accordingly, people would not operate upon principles that would permit a current generation to consume all available air, land, and water, since participants might find themselves belonging to a future generation. This is consistent with the purpose of the veil of ignorance, namely, to ensure that principles are not chosen that favor the particular circumstances of any one person or group of persons (Preston, 76). Specifically, the veil of ignorance refers to a notion within Rawls' theory of justice, specifically a condition in which we are blinded to the specifics of who we are (rich or poor, bodily condition, ethnicity and gender) and of others who may be affected by our actions. We see this manifest in the expression blind justice.

The Veil of Ignorance

In theories of ethics and justice, particularly Rawles' theory, in an effort to be just we are encouraged to make decisions without knowing our specific identities or those of the others involved in order to minimize bias. Here the measure of justice would be that to which reasonable people would agree without knowing their own or anyone else's characteristics or situation in the world.

Within the larger sustainability discourse, the concept of social sustainability also has emerged. Socially sustainable programs have been defined as those programs and processes that promote social interaction, cultural enrichment, and respect for social diversity (Interface 2005). Thus, policies, institutions, and planning and social processes that can integrate diverse groups and cultural practices in a just and equitable fashion are thought to contribute to social sustainability (Polèse and Stren 2000). Concerns over social sustainability are also expressed to ensure that economic development does not deplete human and social capital.[1]

In these writings, social sustainability often is equated with social equality, but surely there are sustainable practices that do not guarantee social or economic equality for all members of society, for example, the use of recycled materials (sustainability as equality would make capitalism itself essentially unsustainable). Some critics have asked: Is social sustainability equivalent to social equality or is it more about the degree to which social (or any) practices enable a group to maintain itself and its way of life into the future, that is, to survive into the future? However, insofar as social sustainability is about addressing and trying to rectify social inequities, it can be argued that social polarization is inherently unstable and therefore unsustainable, or that while material wealth is unequal among members of society sustainability requires an equality of access and opportunity that is believed to be undermined by the spatial concentration of the poor.

→ For more on sustainability see chapter 5 and appendix IV.

Cultural Landscapes and Competing Landscape Values

Landscape values and our choices about what is valuable in the landscape are
also an important ethical issue in regard to the natural environment (Hanssen
2001). Tensions over cultural landscapes in particular raise interesting dilemmas
about land use—what should we preserve whose history and symbolism that relate to the desire and goal of taking care again of specific landscapes for current
and future generations. Hanssen talks about the value judgments in landscape
evaluations, pointing out that "selection criteria . . . are meant to be methodical
instruments for evaluating landscape in planning and administration, but the
formulations of such criteria also reflect basic ethical positions" which may or
may not be explicit (p. 249).

Hanssen further explains, drawing on the work of Skirbekk:

> We have obligations to take care of (preserve) landscape, related to the aesthetic
> experiences of humans and to protect landscapes with importance for social
> identity in a society. We are all parts of a society and a culture, and we also
> have an interest in their maintenance and survival. Converting such interests to
> duties requires us to 'filter' them [discursively], to be able to separate morally
> legitimate from morally illegitimate interests (Skirbekk 1994 as quoted in Hans-
> sen 2001, 250).

See the Cases on Landscape Identity and Conservation (Violich) at the
end of chapter 1 and the landscape ideas in chapter 5.

See the issues of Native American landscapes in chapter 1.

As Dolores Hayden (1997) points out in some of her writings on urban cultural landscapes, the significant question in considering preservation is whose
identity and history do we preserve and who gets to make this decision. How do
even the best intentioned among us begin to decide? According to Soper (1995),
when considering landscape ethics in regard to preservation and conservation,
we can consider three types of arguments: the aesthetic, the intrinsic worth of
the landscape or landscape elements, and utility, which stresses the importance
of landscape and landscape elements as necessities of human survival and flourishing (as summarized in Hanssen 2001). The first two arguments are used in
advocating for preservation, the third used more in arguments for conservation.
A discourse approach can also help us consider decisions regarding preservation
and conservation issues. Such an ethical approach would argue that irreversible
decisions about the landscape should not be taken, as they would be impossible
for future generations to correct. Further, discourse ethics suggests a particular
approach to landscapes that would

> reject analyses based exclusively on anthropocentric values, for instance from a
> utilitarian perspective. For example, economic analyses are exclusively based
> on a utilitarian perspective based on human preferences (transformed to market
> prices). In discourse ethics the utility perspective would not be regarded as a

more important criterion for decisions than other perspectives of the landscape. (Hanssen 2001, 251).

Clearly, an important challenge in cultural landscape preservation is in the development of criteria to evaluate various landscapes for consideration for preservation. Hanssen points out that when criteria in cultural landscape evaluations are formulated and used by experts, they are not part of any discourse or democratic dialogue where different types of interests have had the opportunity to participate in order to reach an agreement.

> The problem about using selection criteria to decide what are valuable landscapes for all of us is that just a few people define the rules to be followed and how to apply them . . . [but] neither economists nor ecologists alone possess the conceptual and evaluative tools to grasp adequately and to assess satisfactorily the urgent problems of how one should care for our common environment. Improved interdisciplinary collaboration and discussion is necessary.
>
> (Hanssen, 251)

Few would argue that cultural landscape preservation and conservation is unimportant—if hard-pressed to prove this, imagine what it would be like if any building or farmland could be destroyed, no matter how old or culturally significant, without any concern for its historic nature and cultural value. Suppose we knock down the Empire State Building or an old farmhouse, or we build a strip mall on a Native American burial ground. Many would be concerned by such activities. But beyond agreement that some things need to be preserved, the matter readily poses problems—where do we draw the line on what is preserved? For and by whom? Toward what end do we preserve a site? And how do we fairly develop the criteria for deciding? These are all legitimate ethical concerns worthy of careful debate.

Place, Meaning, Symbolism and Policy

When considering an emplaced ethics, another critical subject area that emerges in the environmental professions coalesces around place, meaning, symbolism, and policy beyond the previously discussed issues of preservation. This is something of considerable interest in landscape architecture, architecture, and urban design. Here, we explore these issues as they emerge in regard to the natural landscape. Some of the most intriguing writings on the matter emerge in discussions of the use of public lands and outdoor recreation. For example, some scholars writing on ecosystem management suggest bringing social concepts like sense of place into ecosystem models (see esp. Williams and Stewart 1998). One aspect of ecosystem management (and related public policy) is treating people as a rightful part of the ecosystem, but there is still a tendency to treat people as autonomous individual agents outside of the ecosystem. Williams and Stewart offer the sense of place as a concept to bridge the gap between the science of ecosystems and their management. They define sense of place as "a collection of meanings, beliefs, symbols, values and feelings that individuals or groups associate with a particular locality" (p. 19). By initiating a discussion of sense of place, they maintain, public-land managers can build relations with citizens that reflect the complex web of lifestyles, meanings, and social relations endemic to a place. This is an important alternative to the mechanistic view of nature that has dominated our technological society.

Sense of place is a useful concept for understanding the continually constructed, reconstructed, and contested meanings of public lands. Williams and Stewart offer two interesting cases of the debates surrounding the use and meanings of the Devil's Tower National Monument and Mount Rushmore (that enable us to further consider the related ideas introduced in chapter 1). The Devils' Tower National Monument is particularly popular with rock climbers, but this has been a source of contention as it historically has been a sacred place to local Native Americans. Clearly, these are two distinct approaches to this natural site. Similarly, Mount Rushmore is a contested public place, although not so much for use, but for its symbolic meaning. For some, it is a monument to American democracy, history, and manifest destiny and for others it is a symbol of the colonization and oppression of indigenous peoples. So a key question is: how do you negotiate different values, meanings, and beliefs? Williams and Stewart believe that a better management approach is to pay "careful, systematic attention" to the relationship between people and the land. They provide suggestions for particular strategies managers can employ:

1. know and use the variety of local place-names
2. communicate management plans in locally recognized, place-specific terms
3. understand the politics of place
4. pay close attention to places that have special but different meanings to different groups.

The urgency in managing special places is similar to the intensity of the debates to protect endangered species—both stem from a fear of irrevocable losses. The same issue is also evident in the preservation of built structures— particularly historic structures and neighborhoods. This is further explored in the section, "Diversity, Representation and Participation in the Urban Landscape" later in this chapter.

→ See the related material on sense of place and identity in regard to
   native peoples lands in chapters 1 and 5, and regarding
   the Canadian Hydro-Quebec Case in appendix III.

→ See the issues of the vernacular, environmental and social justice, and
   collaboration and compassion in decision making in chapter 2.

Emplaced Ethics and the Built Environment

An emplaced ethics would consider the ethical dimensions of place-based practice and policy in the constructed environment as well as the natural. One of the main challenges to exploring the ethical dimension of design in particular has to do with our general conceptualization of design. Architecture—and for that matter, landscape architecture and urban design—is often likened to an art because there are significant aesthetic concerns that are a part of these practices. To the extent that one views design as an aesthetic endeavor, the issue of ethics gets decidedly more complicated. For Markie (1994), a focus on aesthetics opens up a dangerous possibility that there are no important ethical issues in design, only matters of personal taste. This suggests that ethical issues are objective, and that once we talk about subjective assessments (of aesthetics, for example), it would preclude a discussion of ethics. But this view of ethics as objective contrasts with the post-modern, social-constructivist approach that recognizes the inter-subjectivity behind ethical principles—which is also commensurate with Aristotle's and contemporary theories of virtue ethics. The aesthetic dimension of design should not preclude appreciation of its ethical dimensions. Not only is there an ethical dimension to the aesthetic aspect of design, but there are ethical dimensions to all the other aspects of design. As we discussed earlier in the chapter, design in the built-environment professions is about place-making, and it comes with a significant social responsibility to create environments that support and enhance well-being of people, other species, and the planet as a whole. So we need to reconcile inter-subjectivity with ethical decision making.

In the next sections, we outline a few of the major issues in the built environment professions (and policy related to the environment) and explore their ethical dimensions.

→ See the related material on definitions and implications of various aesthetic positions and their relation to professional roles in chapter 6, the section Beyond the Codes

→ For more material on all these topics, see also chapter 5: Sustaining What? How do we Live?

Social versus Formalistic Design

There is a distinct difference between social design and more traditional formalistic design. Social design is an approach to architecture that is highly focused on users and designing for social causes. Here the mark of successful architecture is how it works for people and how sensitive it is to the larger socio-cultural context in which it is situated. For example, some of the work of landscape architect Walter Hood recognizes the value and humanity of homeless people and their rights to public space. In such approaches to design, meeting people's needs is a priority over making an artistic statement, although designers certainly still create innovative designs and address the aesthetic while at the same time considering social responsibilities of designers (for instance, Sam Mockbee's well-known work with his rural studio). In approaching architecture with this perspective, we can even consider buildings as citizens and evaluate them in terms of their contribution to society.

According to Robert Sommer, the goals of social design are: (1) to create settings that match the needs and activities of occupants—for example, habitability or goodness of fit; (2) to satisfy the users of a space—everyday environments are where we spend our lives; (3) to change behavior—as in the case of promoting socializing or enhancing sense of community; (4) to enhance occupants' personal control of the space to suit their needs—i.e. allowing for flexibility; and (5) to facilitate social support and encourage cooperation. In addition to the unique goals of social design, the design process itself is also different from that of traditional aesthetically-oriented design. It incorporates people, research, and feedback as essential elements, from the pre-design stage to post-construction. Even in the more traditional steps of the design process there is a distinct social orientation; for example, an essential part of programming is to learn about future occupants and community members if not by more formal research methods, then by informal conversations with people, observations, and simply spending time in the place.

→ For more material on this topic, see part 2 of chapter 6—Aesthetics and Roles and chapter 5

The steps of the social design process have been outlined as follows:
- *Needs Assessment*—Even before anything is designed, determine who will use the space. What are their greatest needs and concerns? Connect with various groups for multiple perspectives.
- *Design*—Actively seek input from community members through community-design workshops, focus groups and other participatory strategies. This requires reaching across disciplinary boundaries and developing skills to effectively explain design to laypeople.
- *Construction*—Discuss use of materials and construction processes with clients and users.
- *Use*—Once it is built, observe your design in action. This interaction of people with the physical space is a part of design itself. Do you observe any unintended uses? What might this mean?
- *Evaluation*—Based on observations of use, evaluate the design. Post-occupancy evaluations are critical to successful design and enable us to truly learn from precedents; they are an invaluable and essential part of the design process, not an add-on.

Social design suggests that there are ethical decisions designers must make about the kind of designer they are and want to be, the degree to which they consider social issues and other human dimensions, as well as whether and how to include users in the design process and whether and how to conduct research on uses after construction. Designers must ask: Am I trying to make a singular mark on a city skyline or create something in tune to the context? Are these two goals always in conflict? How does one express vision, and creativity through design? Can this be done while addressing social concerns at the same time?

How Much do Architects need Clients?

To emphasize the importance of people and the human experience of place, Robert Sommer argues that "without clients architects would become non-architects."

- Do you think that this is true?
- What is the primary goal/purpose of design?

Sommer also says that "the satisfaction of the occupants is critical for the moral justification" of the design professions.

- Is there a need for moral justification in the design professions today in regard to clients' or the public's needs?

Vernacular Architecture

Vernacular architecture is another useful area for exploring the ethical dimensions of architecture. Historically, vernacular architecture has looked at traditional ways of building with local materials. It is about material culture and how cultural identity is expressed in the landscape through objects, dwellings and settlements. This type of architecture is said to lie outside of canonical monumentality and instead highlight the cultural and contingent nature of all buildings and landscapes. In its narrowest definition, vernacular architecture is considered a method of construction that uses local resources to address local needs. It is a type of architecture indigenous to a specific time and place—not imported from elsewhere.

→ For more on this topic, see chapter 5

Whether or not to do vernacular architecture may also involve ethical choices. It may be that a project team member feels it is more ethical to use local materials. For example, Paul Oliver (1997), in the *Encyclopedia of Vernacular Architecture of the World,* has argued that, given the insights vernacular architecture provides into issue of environmental adaptation, such a way of designing and building will be necessary to "ensure sustainability in both cultural and economic terms beyond the short term."

Our Own Small Experience

Building, like poems and rituals, realize culture; . . . some
say they design and build as they do because it is the ancient way of their people and place. Others claim that
their practice correctly manifests the universally valid
laws of science. But all of them create out of their own
small experience.

- Henry Glassie

In a way, debates about ethical issues in the place-based professions in general are similar to debates about vernacular architecture. For some, vernacular
architecture means a fairly strict adherence to local resources and styles, but
others like Christopher Alexander have tried to identify adapted features of traditional architecture that could apply across cultures. Similarly in ethics, there
are concerns over the necessity to be sensitive to the unique challenges of each
particular situation, yet there are arguments on behalf of universal truths and
generalizable rules. The central problem is that in today's post-modern world
those of us educated and raised in the no-longer strongly regional world, or
building in a no-longer non-self-conscious indigenous manner, or trained as professionals in research-based, post-enlightenment colleges and universities, are
no longer vernacular people. Though we can learn from and utilize elements of
vernacular architecture and even ways of thinking, we ourselves can no longer
actually build in the vernacular mode.

→ For more on this topic, see the material on Hassan Fathy in chapter 5

According to an online encyclopedia, vernacular architecture is being used
as the inspiration to rebuild some communities after natural disasters. For example, Shelter Center, a non-profit organization in Britain, has explored the use of
vernacular architecture as part of a humanitarian response effort to provide transitional housing to communities that have lost their housing in disasters (Corsellis and Vitale 2005). Their strategy has been to use the vernacular so that familiar forms and materials might provide some reassurance and sense of continuity
to victims in this traumatic time (Corsellis and Vitale 2005). Here the use of
vernacular architecture goes beyond debates about aesthetics and local versus
universal qualities, and instead is part of an active strategy—and an ethical
choice—to maximize humanitarian responses by designers with this form of architecture.

Participation, Diversity, and Representation in the Urban Landscape

The potential political conflicts related to place values can be seen in communities that have been empowered or disempowered (often the same community experiences both simultaneously or in succession) in response to environmental problems (Edelstein 2003). In such cases, place attachments and meanings can be used to foster a partnership approach as different parties find common interest in their health and their neighborhood. When residents are able to take control of the situation themselves, and identify common interests and targets, they are more likely to be mobilized toward action and be empowered (Edelstein 2003; Rich et al., 1995).

The planning literature is a critical source for understanding neighborhood-based conflict because the planning process is rarely conducted without conflict (LeGates and Stout 1996). For example, in his effort to get racially integrated low-income housing built in white suburbs, Davidoff (1965) recognized decades ago the essential role that conflict plays in communities, arguing that "determinations of what serves the public interest in a society containing many diverse interest groups are almost always of a highly contentious nature" (p. 332). He argued that planners should act as advocates, so that the needs of underrepresented groups could be acknowledged and met. Equity planners today continue this tradition, as do those who employ participatory planning processes and advocate strategies for "planning for multiple publics" (Sandercock and Forsyth 1992, 45). Some planners even argue that conflict plays a necessary role in the planning and design of physical communities (Piven 1965). It is seen by some as a prerequisite for the existence and growth of public space, for example (Deutsche 1996).

Often we see conflicts in neighborhood planning processes and we can begin to understand these conflicts better by uncovering the fundamental values at issue in the different entrenched positions (Manzo and Perkins 2006). One typical example is the NIMBY (not in my backyard) response to what are often referred to as "locally unwanted land uses" or LULUs (Freudenburg and Pastor 1992). The NIMBY response is usually seen as organized community opposition to local environmental and/or social change—whether it is the development of a dumpsite, a wind-turbine farm, or a homeless shelter. Environmental psychologist Devine-Wright (2003) argues that policy makers and commentators who frame community responses in terms of a NIMBY reaction typically depict people as inflexible and irrationally opposed to change, while assuming self-interested and egoistic motives for behavior. In his research on one community's reaction to a wind farm, Devine-Wright (2003) notes that this pejorative label for resistance is "politically deployed to undermine the legitimacy of opponents' views by opposing symbolic/affective concerns with rational/instrumental ones" (p. 2). He argues that this has limited utility in accurately explaining the "important emotional and symbolic character" of community members' response to local environmental change (p.2). Perhaps most importantly, Devine-Wright (2003) points out that "NIMBYism fails to recognize that efforts to create better places to live are also likely to create the very social and psychological condi-

tions in which place change matters for people" (p. 2). We can see in these examples that how we frame a situation, and how we understand other players and
stakeholders within that situation, has a lot to do with how we would go about
resolving conflict.

Manzo and Perkins (2006) point out that a lot of conflict over land use issues and community development challenges comes from conflicts over place
meaning. Community development sociologists Flora and Flora (1996) maintain
that people within a community can disagree on the meanings and uses of places
and still respect one another if there is an "acceptance of controversy" (p. 221).
Once it is understood that meaning is not intrinsic to a place but is socially determined, then it becomes possible to accept diverse meanings as valid, air problems and discuss solutions. In their research, Flora and Flora (1996) examine the
creation of social capital in places where newcomers and old-timers clash in
their study of the in-migration of middle-class professionals from urban areas
into small towns. While longer-term residents look with favor on new retail facilities such as Wal-Mart for low-cost goods, newcomers interpret them as
threats to the picturesque nature of Main Street (Flora and Flora 1996). Here,
conflicts stem from focusing on *environmental* capital, and the importance of
social capital is ignored. Environmental capital, that is, the quantity and quality
of natural resources and the landscape, becomes the source of conflict, and neither side recognizes the value of the social capital they have together (i.e., each
group has skill sets, experiences and perspectives that can benefit the other
group). In this case, the newcomers had organizing skills and added new vitality
to the community; these could be seen as an important new resource to be integrated into the community (Flora and Flora 1996). Despite their different reactions to Wal-Mart, newcomers and old timers are still residents of the same town
and have its vitality and well-being at the center of their concern even if it manifests itself differently. This is their shared connection—the valuing of this community as a place to live. This can be the foundation of conflict resolution and
consensus building. Thus, when the focus is on social capital and the value of
fellow community members, conflicts can be effectively dismantled and the circumstances facing a community can be redefined in a more positive light.

Similar concerns also surround urban ethnic landscapes and their meaning,
construction and preservation. Long-standing, ethnically-diverse neighborhoods
are experiencing a new class of changes in their identity, meaning, and role in
the urban landscape, due to shifts in immigrant settlement patterns and the political economy in metropolitan areas (Abramson, Manzo and Hou 2006). Recent community-level planning and design studies have discovered diverse ethnic identities in places where they had been seemingly erased, denied, or hidden
(Dubrow 2002; Low, Taplin, Scheld, and Fisher 2002; Pader 2002). This work
has described how specific urban neighborhood spaces are used, altered and reproduced by different ethnic groups (Loukaitou-Sideris 2002). It further has
shown that in an increasingly diverse society, participatory processes, and multi-
culturalism in preservation and design are linked, and require new tools of engagement. This has significant ethical implications related to participatory de-

sign and planning. Here critical decisions must be made in at least two general areas: first, regarding what meanings, cultural identities, and histories get preserved and represented; second, who decides, that is, who participates in the design and decision making process, in what capacity, when and why. These areas are intimately linked because practitioners can employ a participatory process to ensure that important place meanings are understood and that community members' voices and histories are acknowledged and appropriately addressed. This is one of the particular strengths of genuine participation. The development of participatory practice "requires the articulation of what is implied when participants in a social setting decide to take the construction of their social reality into their own hands" via a participatory project (Kemmis and McTaggart 2000, 572). Such an approach necessarily involves the articulation of its ethical dimensions. But participation is rife with ethical dilemmas.

In order to examine ethical principles in relation to participation, and determine how they can be applied, we must first understand the unique characteristics of participation. While there are a great variety of interpretations about what constitutes participation and how it is best practiced, the full treatment of which goes beyond the scope of this particular chapter, there are a number of characteristics common to this kind of work that must be summarized here.[2] First, participatory practice by its nature is collaborative. It seeks to involve community members in the process and recognizes that each person or group involved brings something unique and valuable to the project. Such collaborations create a sense of shared ownership as well as a shared responsibility for the project and the relationships built through it. Second, in recognizing and interrogating design as a social practice, participation is a transparent process. In addition to collaboratively defining terms at the outset of the project, roles and responsibilities must be continually clarified and each individual must adhere to an agreed-upon standard of accountability. Third, participatory practice is an iterative process that is fluid and responsive to the social context, the changing needs of participants, and the consequences of previous actions in the research process. Fourth, participatory practice is also reflexive because successive efforts within and across projects respond to and build upon prior activities, methods, and findings. Fifth, participatory practice is critical. It is a deliberative process that interrogates social practices, including participation itself, in an effort to create positive change.

→ For more on collaboration see Part 2 of chapter 6.

While distinct, all these characteristics of participation are interrelated, particularly in their connection to underlying themes of transformation and democracy. For example, participatory practice, in being collaborative, transparent, critical, and iterative, transforms the way projects are carried out. It can also transform other social practices in which participants engage. Moreover, participation democratizes the process by shifting the locus of power not only among participants but also between the participation group and the larger social context in which it is situated. This in turn transforms both the participatory process itself and the lifeworlds of those involved. This occurs because participation involves what Habermas (1996) calls "the opening of communicative space." That is, participation creates forums of communication in which people (re)make the practices in which they interact and collectively develop new understandings of their worlds. (Kemmis and McTaggart 2005).

We could also argue that the decision whether to even employ a participatory approach is an ethical decision. Then there are myriad ethical decisions to be faced once we choose to do a participatory project. Importantly, the ethics that participation demands require a broader interpretation of the ethical standards and codes of a given profession than has been customary among the professionally oriented organizations which institutionalize them. It is no small problem that interpretations of ethical principles can differ considerably between the codes and participatory practitioners. For example, since participatory practitioners understand that their work is political, they recognize power in order to democratize the planning and design process. In contrast, professional-practice associations recognize power inequalities between professionals and the people whom they engage, but generally hold that it is not their task to transform that relationship.

Participation will not, in and of itself, make practice ethical. The approach can be deployed to support a project leader's agenda, or to further the interests of a particular group. Arnstein's (1969) "ladder of participation" warned us long ago that participation can range from manipulation to shared power, and it can easily languish in the realm of manipulation. The ethical challenge is that if one were to employ a participatory strategy, a way needs to be found to do so in a manner that does not set up unrealistic expectations of shared critical decision making that will only lead to frustration and disillusionment with the process if people's voices and concerns are not heard. Hearing people's ideas does not mean that all of them have to be incorporated wholesale into a project—certainly compromises and sacrifices are made in participatory projects. But it may be more unethical to invite participation and then ignore people's inputs than it would be to take a top-down approach in the first place and be clear that this is how the process will work.

→ Also see the critiques of the major theories at the end of chapter 4
→ For more on these topics see Part II of chapter 5: Sustaining What? How do we live?

Many real-world projects and even certain national policies and programs are good test cases for exploring the various ethical issues we have begun to raise thus far. Such projects involve practitioners from multiple environmental professions—architecture, landscape architecture, planning, urban design, construction management and engineering. One good example is the case of current public housing policy and the U.S. Department of Housing and Urban Developments' HOPE VI program. Designed to revitalize what the government considers *severely distressed* public housing, the HOPE VI program (Housing Opportunities for People Everywhere) has demolished public housing sites nation-wide and then rebuilt them as new, mixed income communities. For some, mixing incomes and deconcentrating poverty help avoid the stigma that usually enshrouds public and low-income housing. However, in this program tens of thousands of low-income families have had to relocate, and in many cases there has been a net loss of public-housing units. On the other hand, it has helped to revitalize truly troubled public housing and create a fresh start for communities. In regard to such a program there are ample ethical issues related to the environmental professions (both social and physical) as well as policies on housing and poverty. To learn more about the program and its ethical implications, or to consider your own ethical stance, turn to appendix III for a more detailed look at the HOPE VI case.

In this chapter, we identified some of the unique challenges that those in the placemaking professions face. Designers, planners, engineers, and construction managers not only face challenges in working with the physical environment and material world, but also must consider what it means to be socially responsive and responsible practitioners in today's world. In an age of globalization, constant flux and change, and increasing dynamism and diversity in our communities, we are called to practice Schön's reflection in action—to make decisions and get things done in a thoughtful and reflective manner that enables us—and our professions—to learn and grow, to become more effective and ethical.

Notes

1. Social capital, as defined in community psychology, refers to the extent and effectiveness of formal and informal social networks. Formal networks include participation in community organizations, and the links among those organizations, while informal networks usually refer to social relationships among individuals and mutual trust (Perkins, Hughey, and Speer 2002; Saegert and Winkel 1999).

2. These are adapted from Kemmis and McTaggart's key features of participatory action research (2005).

Chapter Three

Principles and Rules

Legitimacy: Proceeding by Principles and Rules

The use of principles and rules for ethical deliberation has the special advantage of assuring we fallible humans that our decision processes and outcomes are legitimate and thorough. Legitimacy is important because if an outcome is not considered legitimate by those it involves or affects it will not be implemented or it will be resisted, either in internal resentment or external social action. In an effort to move toward greater legitimacy and to help you with ethical decision making, this chapter outlines the major principles and rules that have been identified in ethical discourse over years. These principles and rules described in this chapter have been proven, across centuries, and even millennia, to include or take into account all of the many factors that constitute legitimacy—comprehension, trust, consent, knowledge-truthfulness—as detailed convincingly in Habermas' theory of communicative action (1979; cf. Forester 1982; Albrecht and Lim 1986).

As you will see in the next chapter on ethical theories, there are both significant differences and critical commonalities among them. While differences exist, the set of principles and rules presented in this chapter in fact represents an amazing core of agreement, historically arrived at through rigorous debate and testing in millions of people's lives. In other words, these principles and rules have been time-tested to be the most important by the cultures within which we live. Using these principles and rules for practical decision making does not guarantee that any particular decision is the best one possible; but one can rest assured of operating more responsibly and making valid decisions—as measured against the consensus of ethical heritage, even if there are many different ways in which the major ethical theories may elaborate the principles or their relation to each other, and given that there are other, non-western traditions as well.

As Beauchamp and Childress have demonstrated in their professional ethics pedagogy, utilizing the four fundamental principles of autonomy, beneficence, non-maleficence, and justice (and the attendant rules that go with each of these) is an effective way to discuss and decide upon sensitive, complex ethical issues in areas such as medicine. It makes good sense to proceed by following this approach, but of course adapting it to environmental disciplines, practices, and problems.

Principles:
- ❑ Autonomy
- ❑ Beneficence
- ❑ Non-maleficence
- ❑ Justice
- ❑ Care (as complementary to justice) and responsiveness

Rules:
- ❑ Informed consent
- ❑ Truthfulness
- ❑ Confidentiality
- ❑ Loyalty
- ❑ Conflict of interest

Though we cannot pursue the matter here, we wish to acknowledge the criticisms that could be made about our approach to ethics. A full investigation of all the ethical theories, their nuances, and how they relate to and are distinct from one another, is an important part of ethics. Indeed, adequate consideration of these theories is the proper business of general ethical scholarship. This is usually referred to as meta-ethics. However, in this book we are more concerned with what is called applied, normative ethics. Rather than remain in the realm of abstract theorizing, which is more the task of meta-ethics, we focus on the central issues related to ethical decision making in regard to environmental dilemmas. Of course, readers are encouraged to take up these larger topics on their own.

In utilizing principles and rules in ethical decision making there are three possible stances. First, there is relativism, a position contending that because there are divergent ideas and customs of different cultures throughout the world and history, not to mention the even more bewilderingly diverse opinions of billions of people, there is no possibility of any one objective truth or falsity in moral judgments or practices. Relativism, then, holds that what is considered right or wrong is simply what groups or individuals believe it to be—it varies and is relative to them. There also are more technical epistemological arguments involved in relativism—that is, arguments within formal theories of knowledge about why and how truth is relative. (Again, we recommend the reader to take up these critical questions with the aid of a teacher.)

The most common version of this position is cultural relativism, largely derived from anthropology, sociology, and more recently from cultural studies. Anthropology has long observed that what is considered right or wrong varies with different peoples, cultures, and times. From this it is concluded that what is right is what is right for them. That is, since society sets the norms, there can be no objective right or wrong—rather, it is a matter of prevalent belief. If this is so, then morality consists of descriptive statements only—for example, the cultural norm, "You can do whatever you want as long as it doesn't hurt someone else." What are considered moral beliefs of any society are by definition moral or right.

Relativism

Relativism holds that there is no one correct view of things—in regard to ethics, whatever is considered to be right or wrong is simply a function of the historical and cultural context within which the determination is made. Naturally, this will be highly variable across places and times.

In contrast to cultural relativism, individualistic or subjectivistic relativism holds the correlate: that what is good or right is whatever I decide. In ordinary terms, we would say that whatever a person decides is right is what is right for her or him. Here, morality is a matter of purely individual opinion, of personal preferences; moral statements are descriptions only (by definition, it would mean that no one could do anything wrong, (unless perhaps by total caprice and self-inconsistency). Of course, this is problematic insofar as ethics is a social phenomenon, or even necessity, and we need to have some sort of agreement in order to live together without being chaotically at odds with each other.

Absolutism

Absolutism holds that there is an objectively correct view—in regard to ethics that there is an actual right and wrong that is universal: it is always the same and applies in every place and time, transcending the differences in particular situations.

At the other extreme is absolutism, which holds that there is indeed a right and wrong that transcends the particulars of time and place, social and individual constitutions. This view is most commonly found in religions where it is held that the source of truth, of what is right or wrong, is the divinity that establishes the world and sets the paradigm for what should be done. A god or gods pass this understanding along to us through their manifestations in the world; their authority is continued by means of the specific religious tradition in question, for example, by religious leaders or institutions. There are non-religious versions of absolutism, based on the human ability to know reality in a finally objective and timeless manner, that is, in terms of ultimate truths that can be applied to varying situations in an appropriate manner through informed judgment. Such an approach can be found in (or is similar to) the objective universal truths sought in the physical sciences. An example might be the injunction: "Do not kill," which often is held as an absolute, though many cultures apply certain conditions or norms that modify it (such as "unless in self-defense").

From even these brief descriptions, it should be clear why we cannot cover these debates here. They can be considered what Alasdair MacIntyre (1981) calls "interminable arguments." They are interminable because, as they are presented from their respective starting-points:

> Every one of the arguments is logically valid or can be easily expanded so as to be made so; the conclusions do indeed follow from the premises. But the rival premises are such that we possess no rational way of weighing the claims of one as against the other. For each premise employs some quite different normative or evaluative concept from the others so that the claims made upon us are of quite different kinds. . ..From our rival conclusions we can argue back to our rival premises; but when we do arrive at our premises, argument ceases and the invocation of one premise against another becomes a matter of pure assertion and counter-assertion. (MacIntyre 1981, 8)

Interminable arguments are not only frustrating but leave us with no obvious pathway to a solution. However it is valuable to seek a middle ground between relativism and absolutism as a means to find a way to deliberate together and arrive at responsible decisions that can be implemented with a sense that they are arrived at legitimately. This is critical since genuine dilemmas involve choices in which all the alternatives involve complexes of goods and harms so that some harm is unavoidable when we finally act. However, because some of several different possible harms to different parties will occur in any dilemma, by definition, not just any decision will do.

The middle position between relativism and absolutism derives, in part, from the problems these other two extremes do not seem to be able to overcome. Relativism is not able to account for the conflicts concerning right and wrong except to say that such conflicts do occur and seem to correlate with social and individual differences. But this is precisely what is at stake in decision making concerning environmental dilemmas: many parties will neither concede that their position is merely subjective preference, nor that the right outcome is arbitrary or non-objective. Relativism, in other words, is of no help in settling moral, social, or legal disputes—nor is it helpful when people make decisions together as is necessary in environmental decision making. Since in relativism, what is considered right is what each party finds to be right according to their own criteria, the juxtaposition of different claims about what is right reduces immediately to a reassertion that each group has different criteria of truth and goodness. The result is a re-description of differences that merely returns to the obvious starting point—that the parties see the world differently and disagree.

To be ethical— appropriately reflective and responsible—we need to be able to give an account of our choices and actions that is satisfactory to others and that we are able to defend. We follow two congruent approaches in this book: (1) We proceed by way of the rationalist tradition in which principles, derived from or consistent with grounded theories, provide reasoned standards and processes. These provide guidelines for right conduct, by means of which we can understand and weigh the pros and cons of alternative possibilities, taking the context and empirical details into account in order to act consistently, but not mechanically; and, (2) we layer onto this tradition the natural law, which insists on the importance of taking more of human capacity into account than reason alone (especially since reason or cognition has come to be defined narrowly in the Western traditions, as in their strict scientific manifestations). Hence, emotion, intuition, and responsiveness to whole persons and contexts are especially important in this approach. (See chapter 4 for detailed treatment of this theory.)

Further, dilemmas exist within ourselves: even if we are individually the measure of what is true and right, we are not always of one mind. That is, we sometimes contradict ourselves or change our minds about issues over time. In addition, when we do not know what to decide in a given situation—we seek some basis on which to make a decision—even if that basis would be a personal principle, or set of principles so we could become clearer about which of our values (health, money, friends, respect, courage, truth) outweighed the others.

Thus, subjectivism leaves everything where it was to start with, with no practical suggestions for dealing with competing interests and values. But, because our views do have implications for others, and we do constrain and enjoin each other, we need to resolve and try to settle matters. We need social policies for environmental dilemmas, since without agreement on how to generally act when we do disagree, we find ourselves in a frustrating stalemate. For example, we wind up with such hardened NIMBYism (not in my back yard) that nothing gets done as differing factions refuse to cooperate.

Absolutism does not require as much comment. As we explained in chapter 1, we are considering processes of deliberation that are not based on religious authority—the main source of absolutisms. This is especially important because religious views are, in fact, part of the basis for social decision making for many people. Also, given the non-agreement in the world about religious authority, something other this is needed for an ethical approach. As to the philosophical or rationalist positions that are absolutist, it is notable that such absolutist positions have not served to move us past the dilemmas faced by our diverse and contentious society, nor have they been able to effectively address environmental problems. In terms of theories and methodologies of knowledge, the absolutist forms of post-positivist structuralism have attempted to consolidate a scientific approach in the social sciences, but have not led to further agreement on what is true—indeed, if anything, they have stimulated an emphasis on difference on the other side (even to the point where some of those arguing on behalf of relativisms wish aloud that there were some more universal position on human rights and environmental self-determination, for example, that would be creditable). Indeed, absolutist positions are often identified with political regimes that exert strong control over their populations and the environment, either resulting in paternalistically directed development of areas protected from popular access or use, as in Cuba, or in exploitation that displaces inhabitants, as in the cases of many of the rain forests of southeast Asia, (for discussion of these factors, see Mugerauer 1990).

At this point in the chapter we turn to the principles themselves and examine the fundamental premises behind each as well as the rules derived from them.

Autonomy

The Basic Concept

This fundamental principle posits that all people are self-determining; that is, they are able to choose their own life course and actions. It is not surprising that autonomy is a foundational principle for ethics since it is a necessary condition for decision making in the first place. Without autonomy, it would not be possible to decide what is wrong or right, nor would we be capable of being responsible for our actions. If what we did were strictly a matter of behavior stimulated by causes beyond our control, we would not be ethical agents at all, but merely part of a series of objects in a chain of cause-and-effect events.

Autonomy is not a regularly used word in English, since we tend to say "independence," or "free will," which connote the same concept. As synonymous with independence, autonomy is characteristic of the "self-aware, conscious, free, self-controlling subject or person" (Ashley and O'Rourke 1982, 39). Each individual person is understood to be able to make choices and plan what to do. We can think about or imagine what we might do in a given situation and decide to follow a choice accordingly (sometimes the phrase "free will" carries this connotation; as in "we will freely undertake this or that action").

Not everyone may be deemed autonomous; some humans are indeed dependent. An obvious case of this would be children, particularly those who are too young to understand certain situations adequately. In their case, some adult—typically a parent or guardian—is authorized by law and societal norms to make major decisions on behalf of the children. This is not just the case with children; even adults might not be considered autonomous if, for example, they have a significant mental illness. Such persons are considered not competent enough to decide matters for themselves, and guardians are appointed to make ethical and legal decisions on their behalf. Similarly, certain classes of those convicted of crimes and imprisoned have much of their autonomy withdrawn by the legal system and government: they are not able to exercise choice on matters that range from where they live to how they act, and they are not allowed to vote. Such cases give us an indication that there is a complex connection between rights and having the status of being independent—a point to which we will return.

Embedded in this principle of autonomy is the question of the very definition of a person. As we will see in chapter 4, ethical theories differ as to which features of a human being count and to what degree they count, as well as when autonomy begins and ends (i.e. where we cross the line between dependence and independence). Currently, for example, the question of whether a fetus is a person or not is the center of substantial social debate. In most rational ethical systems (that is, distinct from religious or legal systems) the concept person s not equal to being genetically a human being. In Kantian or deontological theory, the status of personhood is applied only to those human beings capable of competently making their own choices, while in natural law the status belongs to those human beings potentially capable of such competence, and not necessarily actually at a given moment (these theories are laid out in chapter 4). In any case, having the status of personhood carries with it different rights and responsibilities than does non-personhood.

The moral concept of autonomy is based on the idea of respect due to other persons. We need to respect their autonomy precisely because to be a person is synonymous with being autonomous: thus, to deny or ignore the latter is to refuse to acknowledge or accept someone as a person. Critical to this understanding is that persons and their choices are to be respected even when we believe that their criteria, mode of choosing, or judgments are mistaken. We are familiar with this belief from the many medical shows on television in which the medical team spends the first forty-five minutes trying to convince a patient to have a given procedure for his own good and he refuses for his own reasons. All along, the drama centers on the fact that it is his decision to make about his own treatment, even if it seems clear to the medical team, his family, or the audience that he is wrong and will suffer or even die if he does not do what the medical team prescribes. If the patient were a legal minor (a child), or deemed not mentally competent, then the family or a court-appointed guardian could make the decision on the patient's behalf and that patient would be subject to the treatment even if he physically resists—a major legal as well as ethical issue. Conveniently, in most of the television stories the patient decides to agree to the procedure in the last few minutes and all ends well. As we know, disputed issues in environmental decision making are perhaps even more complex given the large number of relevant persons involved and ultimately affected by the decision, and given that the dilemmas are seldom resolved in a way that satisfies all the parties.

In a more relevant example for ethical decision making regarding environmental issues, the principle of autonomy is also operative in debates about property rights (see also chapters 1 and 5 for a discussion of this issue). At least in the United States and many Western countries the idea of individual property rights that trump other rights or responsibilities is fundamentally based on the principle of autonomy.

The moral idea of respect for others is formulated in the major ethical theories as the more formal principle of autonomy. To preview what will be covered in detail in chapter 5, for Kant the general moral idea is that others never be treated as means, but only as ends inherently valuable in themselves. Consistent with this, in Kant's deontological theory the principle of autonomy appears in the obligation to respect the same right in others to make their judgments as we have in regard to our own. Mill, the major theorist behind utilitarianism is not as strong on this issue, although he certainly agrees with the principle of autonomy. He contends that persons should be free, for instance, when he emphasizes the right to be at liberty—by which is meant not being interfered with in our actions and lives. Natural law emphasizes the value of each individual human life. It specifically stresses how each of us is uniquely valuable, so that there is a fundamental incommensurability between any one person and another. (See chapter 5 on theories)

Finally, there is agreement across all major ethical theories that the category person cannot be understood as singular. To speak of a person is simply a way to begin to clarify the rights of and responsibilities toward persons. Despite the strong individualism in contemporary society, ethically the focus is on each of our responsibilities to others; that is, ethical issues are inseparable from community. The ethical principle of the autonomy of a person then neither implies nor justifies any self-centeredness or consideration of persons in atomized isolation (in contrast to the Social Darwinian worldview discussed earlier in chapter 1). Certainly our moral decisions and actions are taken in regard to others and the effect our actions may have on them. Ethical questions thus are questions of inter-personal rights, responsibilities, and obligations. In addition, persons have their autonomy within a community; that is, the community is the context necessary for autonomy to be generated and maintained. The key, then, to the possibility and continuation of autonomy is the free acceptance of the community in which one lives and the responsible carrying out of action within that community. In short, autonomy is a social and not an individual moral principle (Beauchamp and Childress 1983, pp. 60-61).

Autonomy

Autonomy is ultimately a social and not an individual moral principle. The focus is on how each of us is responsible to others. Ethical issues are inseparable from community.

Within the principle of autonomy, we also find the attendant issue of authority. If, in fact, there is a social dimension to this principle, as we established above, then we can say that beyond individual autonomy, in order for there to be not just me, but us, there must be some social acceptance of reasonable authority outside of our individual selves. The authority that we allow society over our individual selves may be delegated in the specialized complexity of social structures. For example, we often accept, at least initially, the authority of scientific experts or public health and engineering professionals, setting aside our potential individual insistence on making our own judgments in most cases.

An interesting issue for us to consider is how far this acceptance of authority extends to the environmental disciplines and professions as a whole. Obviously there are significant, unresolved problems in this area. Even if we all might be aiming at the same goal—for example, the well-being of those living in a given environment—there can be substantial conflicts between the autonomy of different parties on the one hand and the expert points of view on the other hand. It is important to note that there has been a shift lately in American society that places more emphasis on the rights of individuals to make their own decisions, compared to the former tendency to more passively accept and follow the directives of professionals. This shift has revolutionized the medical and health care professions, resulting in changes in education and practice. This can be seen for example, in the women's movement of the 1960s and 1970s, which affirmed the rights of women to make decisions concerning "our bodies, our selves," rather than obediently deferring to "father-doctor knows best."

Matters are not identical in environmental areas, but present their own complexities. 1 of the most dramatic examples is the pressing case of climate change, where the experts generally agree that this has become a significant environmental concern (although in the beginning there was less agreement among experts), but many social and political factions still vocally reject the dominant scientific position and advice. Central to dealing with these problems are decisions about what constitutes a reasonable individual choice and what its social limitations are, as well as decisions about more detailed matters, such as the conditions for and limits to consent and delegation of authority.

We can now begin to see how the principle of autonomy leads to a set of rules. These rules logically follow (are deducible) from and instantiate the general principles. Again, all the major theories agree that these rules are legitimate. They also enable us to act more readily, since they do not need to be reestablished in each and every case. However, there are more than enough complexities to interpreting and applying the rules in specific circumstances. Let us now turn attention to the rules that directly follow from the principle of autonomy. These include informed consent, veracity, confidentiality, and fidelity.

Informed Consent

Based on the principle of autonomy, the rule of informed consent says that it is the right of the autonomous person to not only be fully informed about a project or research in which she or he is participating but also to agree or consent to participate, knowing the implications. It is generally considered to be a right for autonomous persons, since one cannot be self-determining without being able to consent to a particular course of action, and one cannot make free, rational choices without being informed.

Moral justification to carry out construction or research would need to be based on the principle of autonomy because this principle "justifies allowing a person this option of accepting increased risk, and we therefore consider the protection of autonomy to be the primary function of informed consent regulations. There is a moral duty to seek valid consent because the consenting party is an autonomous person, with all the entitlements that status confers" (Beauchamp and Childress 1983, 68). There are particular challenges that arise regarding informed consent when it comes to non-autonomous persons such as those individuals we described above (e.g. children, those with severe mental illness, etc.). Most notably there are concerns about who is competent (here morally, not legally) and who is a non-competent person. What of nonpersons, such as animals (notably considered to be equivalent with human being in many indigenous traditions) that cannot speak for themselves—should they have designated guardians? What about nature itself? Should it too have a guardian? If so, who? When a person is deemed incapable because they are too young, in a coma, mentally deficient, or emotionally disturbed, a responsible second party makes the decisions. The parallel question of who decides for public lands and facilities often is vexed, especially when an action is politically contested. Here there are very difficult questions concerning the tangle of multiple clients and users—the person or institution that pays, the users, the impacted neighbors, people downwind, perhaps across the oceans. What are their rights? Who speaks for such clients? (Also see chapter 5, on stakeholders and roles.)

Autonomy is unquestionably applied to human individuals (e.g. autonomous persons), but what of non-persons that cannot speak for themselves—animals and all of nature?

There is a special connection of informed consent with the law since many suits assigning liability or seeking compensation for damages focus on failure of professionals to provide informed consent. Sorting out proper consent from nonconsensual action (usually performed upon a client's property or upon public lands or facilities) and from unauthorized actions (carrying out activities not allowed or authorized) are major legal issues. The legal dimensions, in fact, are much clearer than the related moral ones.

It is agreed that informed consent must be solicited whenever a process involves changes, or harms (or risk of harms) to property or environmental elements that are someone's, or when such actions have further consequences for others—increased risk of harm due to change in the amount and quality of water, heat, light, or wind for example. But sometimes it is difficult to know who will be affected by such environmental design decisions. In Los Angeles, the glare from Gehry's famous Disney Concert Hall was so strong on some of the surrounding buildings that the temperatures inside them rose to unacceptable levels, the remedy of which required scratching or rendering opaque the surfaces of the concert hall that caused the problem.

Who is the client?
To whom do we have our ethical obligations?

❑ Who owns what is built?
❑ The users?
❑ The public?

The general issue at play in these questions concerns the complex array of groups and stakeholders that will be impacted by our environmental decisions. The answer to the question: "Who is the client?" will not turn out to be simple. The difficulty is in finding ways to sort out the different rights and obligations of those involved and to find a way to legitimately balance them. Wasserman and colleagues sketch the issues at their widest: "Who ultimately do you design for: the contractual client, the project occupants, the public, the planet, the profession, or yourself? How does this affect the fundamental ideological, philosophical, and pragmatic premises of the design? Is there an ethical dimension to these questions?" (Wasserman, Sullivan, and Palermo 2000, 232.)

❑ What if there are multiple clients?
❑ What if all the groups above are the client? Could your responsibility to each require conflicting courses of action?

→ See the exercises in appendix III for further exploration of these problems.

On a wider, more diffuse scale, what does consent mean in regard to problems that do not appear in the dense urban and industrial areas that apparently are responsible for generating most of the greenhouse gases, but that appear in areas far distant and that impact residents not directly participating in consultative decision making? "The land areas north of the Artic Circle are frozen for most of the year. Subsurface soil that remains permanently frozen is referred to as permafrost. However, global warming has begun to thaw large areas of permafrost. Buildings are collapsing as the permafrost on which they are constructed gives way; the highways, and even pipelines, used for carrying oil out to markets are in increasing danger of collapsing or rupturing" (Gore 2006, 133–36). Examples of such widespread environmental impacts of global climate change complicate the rule of informed consent considerably. How would we properly obtain consent from all those impacted in cases such as these?

Elements of Informed Consent

There is some controversy and disagreement about what constitutes informed consent. Both terms need to be clarified: what it means to be informed, and what consent consists of and requires to be satisfied. Beauchamp and Childress propose that four elements constitute informed consent, each of which is a necessary condition for informed consent to be achieved. Two fall under the dimension of providing information; the other two concern issues of consent (p. 70):

A. Information
1.   Disclosure of information
2.   Comprehension of information
B. Consent
3.   Voluntary consent
4.   Competence to consent

As we suggested earlier, there remains the complex issue of who is authorized morally to make ethical decisions. First, let's look at these four elements of informed consent more closely, beginning with the last—no. 4, competence to consent, since this is most immediately linked to autonomy and because one's ability to consent is a key presupposition of informed consent directly and of ethical decision making in general.

4. Competence to Consent

Competence is the precondition for both understanding information and acting voluntarily upon it. According to Beauchamp and Childress (1983), there are three main standards for determining competence. Remember that these are moral and not legal standards of competence.

❑   the capacity to make a decision at all
❑   the capacity to reach a decision based on rational reasons
❑   the capacity to reach a reasonable result via decision making

As these three standards suggest, a critical issue in determining competence is one's ability to reason. There are many and varied definitions of what is reasonable, and these need to be discussed and agreed upon in any social setting.

On this issue, there is often agreement between ethics and the legal system, as with the reasonable person standard in law. Beauchamp and Childress combine the dimensions of what constitutes competence with the idea that "a person is competent if and only if that person can make decisions based on rational reasons" (1983, p. 72), a claim that parallels Habermas' conditions for acceptable communicative action.

The interpretation of competence here entails being able to:

❑ understand the situation or problem
❑ weigh the risks and benefits of different course of action
❑ decide what to do in light of such information.

Again, for those deemed incompetent, or those entrusted to public guardianship, there needs to be a second party who must act in the best interests of the primary party. Determination of competence is not merely an empirical question, but a value-laden judgment connected to larger belief systems (pp. 67–70). In property issues, often the second responsible party is whoever has power of attorney.

The Question of Competence and Public Lands

The question of the appropriateness and actual competence of those allocated decision making power is a major issue in regard to many public lands, as when there is debate over whether or not to drill for oil on the public lands of Alaska or to allow timber cutting or grazing on public lands.

We operate in the United States with the convention that the agency charged with responsibility, and thus able to commission and oversee projects, is the client. But, this is an uneasy situation, as we see in the frequent challenges by citizens who disagree with decisions by various branches of government. The issue is complicated by the very layering of government: citizens empower the government, by way of the legislative and executive branches, which regularly disagree and argue about the appointment of directors of administrative units. So, whether the client is an agency, such as the National Park Service, our elected representatives, or the citizens themselves, is a matter for debate in almost any case where there is significant disagreement.

After competence is established, we then must determine if consent is voluntary. Otherwise it is a matter of coercion, as was notoriously the case in the Nazi experiments conducted on Jewish prisoners in concentration camps in World War II. And lest we think of such atrocities as confined to that time and place, we can consider the Tuskegee syphilis study conducted in the U.S., where medical treatment was purposefully withheld from African-American men who had

the disease, and more recently the psychological research experiments on obedience, which were initiated, ironically, to understand the blind obedience to authority figures displayed by Nazi soldiers. What these latter examples raise is the
informational aspect of informed consent.

The Empty Lot Next Door

Suppose there is an empty lot next door to where you live—or
somewhere on your block for that matter. How might the rule of
informed consent apply to this situation? Wouldn't you and your
neighbors have a right to know what might be built there?
Would it matter if it were an apartment building—or a dump site
or waste-treatment plant? Does informed consent stop at merely
being informed, or do you want the right to have a say in what
happens? Who else should weigh in on this? In other words:
How far should informed consent extend?

Because voluntariness significantly depends on what information is disclosed and how, we now will look at the informational dimension of informed
consent.

1-A. Disclosure of Information

Disclosure of information is perhaps the most complex facet of the informational dimension of informed consent, especially in regard to whether there is
sufficient information to make a decision in a given situation. More specifically,
the critical questions concern whether there is adequate information regarding
processes, outcomes, risk-benefits, and opportunities for future questions or
withdrawal).[1] The degree to which one can be informed ranges across a spectrum: informed—partially informed—uninformed. In order to be more precise
and still allow a consistent application in varying contexts and circumstances,
the following standards have been formulated. The appropriate and ethically
obligatory stand is that the information disclosed in any situation must conform
to:

- ❑ The standards operative in the professional and disciplinary communities. The assertion that professional and research practices outweigh or
  take precedence over clients' rights normally is considered to allow too
  little autonomy.
- ❑ What a reasonable person would want to know. Although what is reasonable can vary from person to person, situation to situation, and culture to culture, here reasonable person generally refers to some idea of
  an average person or citizen with some degree of reason, as there needs
  to be some yardstick, some way to begin to arrive at an understanding
  of what is appropriate to expect of each other.
- ❑ What an individual client would want to know

Of these three standards of informed consent, the first position has tended to dominate; in the last thirty years or so there has been a shift to the second standard for two general reasons: because what is needed from clients (and for their own benefit) is not itself a professional-technical judgment, but a competent decision, and because there is perhaps unavoidably a vested interest in certain values and goals of the professions—a directionality or pre-judgment from which clients and their decisions need be independent.

Often, the first standard is considered too strong, since it amounts to requiring of laypeople the level of precision and detail of information expected in professional and research practices. But, this sets aside too much of the client's rights since most clients are not able to operate at this level of knowledge and interpretation; they have too little autonomy in decisions concerning their own affairs and possibilities. In the case of medicine, this resulted in the father-doctor knows best syndrome, which has since been socially rejected—in the same way expert paternalism has been resisted in the realm of environmental issues, which can be seen in challenges to accepting the Corps of Engineers as knowing best about flooding in the Gulf of Mexico and New Orleans, or urban planners and transportation engineers as knowing best about the means to the well-being of central cities as highways and urban renewal devastated stressed areas.

There is movement toward a rule with the second standard (the standard of the reasonable person) versus the third (what an individual client would want to know), which would appear to be too subjective or idiosyncratic. In this approach, the composite or ideal measure of what should be provided might especially involve both all necessary environmental and social impact information (as judged by a competent layperson, not by an environmental professional) and also the known risks (Beauchamp and Childress 1983, 72). Since the goal in informed consent is to provide those making decisions with what they need to know, no simple formula works. One must try not only to be flexible in different circumstances while still providing usable guidelines for action, but also to provide for an openness beyond the second standard of a general reasonable person—that is, to strive to meet the third standard: whatever else a particular individual would want to know. This would be done, for example, by providing opportunities for clients to ask whatever they wish and adjusting professional control, time, and patience to accommodate the new social expectation of environmental professionals. Obviously, this provision would be closer to a moral rather than a legal or business requirement.

1-B. Intentional Nondisclosure
The principle of informed consent raises the matter of intentional nondisclosure—that is, whether and when to intentionally withhold information from people in certain circumstances. Here, too, the matter has emerged more in regard to research. The distinct ethical issues in medical research revolve around the problems that arise when the researcher fails to obtain, or often even seek, client or subject approval. Though this can happen in regard to environmental phenomena, for instance when alternative pesticides or herbicides are used and results monitored, the obvious parallel with medicine is that the full conse-

quences and risks, or even full range of alternatives, are not revealed. Given the wide range of materials that can be selected in architecture and construction, for example, there is more than ample room to withhold information regarding performance, endurance, long-term costs, and so on. (See the case of Rincon Center in the appendix for several instances of material and financial nondisclosure.) Such withholding of information is a particularly difficult action to justify; clearly the responsible person cannot assume it is acceptable to do so; to the contrary—and especially given the related rule of truthfulness, it would be necessary to explicitly justify nondisclosure on the grounds that it prevents some other immanent harm (Beauchamp and Childress 1983, 81).

Arguments are somewhat routinely made that some nondisclosure or omission would be permissible if the intended outcome were benevolent. Physicians, lawyers, and environmental professionals, for instance, might make such arguments when they believe that knowing the whole truth would confuse the person making the decision, or that the person making the decision does not really want to know the whole truth for his own reasons, or that with only a partial understanding of the facts the person would very likely make the wrong decision compared to what the expert can clearly see is preferable. These arguments are all forms of what we popularly call paternalism in which we would do something not normally acceptable "for the person's own good"—which also means that we have made a judgment that we know what is good for that other person, perhaps better than they do and have chosen to act on that judgment with or without their consent. But, in light of what we have just considered, it is clear that such arguments would set aside autonomy and the related rights of competent persons. Even if one could accurately predict the outcomes of a well-intended action in the specific case and its overall direction within social relationships, it would be a deliberate violation of what we take very seriously as our right to self-determination. Note that at the opposite end of justifying paternalism, Mill argues for what he calls the harm principle: that preventing harm to others, not to oneself, is the only basis for interference with one's liberty (cited in Beauchamp and Childress 1983, 171).

On the subtle end of the spectrum, nondisclosure can mislead the parties making a choice when they depend on what they are told. While it is common, it seems, for humans to withhold information that may compromise a project in which they have become invested, such action is not warranted as ethical. Kim Dovey (1993) uses the memorable example of an architect providing what he calls a partial simulation of a building to a client, where the architect did not fully reveal to the client the intended color scheme of the building because the architect wanted to push the design as he imagined it—even though it was very likely that the client would have balked at large pink and green stripes across the building façade. Though "the architect's argument was that it was his practice to offer 'as little documentation as will be required,'" this was a public building and we can question, as Dovey does, whether the parties involved should be protected from architecture that is "markedly different from their expectations." Given the professional-client relationship and the obligations of the former to the latter, Dovey concludes that such nondisclosure would be unethical (1993, 32).

2. Comprehension of Information

Once information is presented to others or made public, there must be some effort made to ensure that this information is comprehensible to that audience in order to truly and properly obtain informed consent. Generally the core requirement is that the information be accessible in ordinary language. In addition to appropriate language, the manner in which the information is presented also must be comprehensible; for example, is there technology being used to present the information that is inaccessible to some—either literally or conceptually? Concern for the comprehension of information arises across the board in all professional relationships including the medical, legal, financial, and again most assuredly in the environmental professions.

Comprehension of Information and Participation: The Case of the Street Vacation

Informed consent is particularly an issue for planners and designers who engage communities in the planning and design process. Those who use participatory approaches are generally operating on a belief that participation is a critical form of informed consent and therefore is more ethical than other methods. But if the information provided to participants is not presented in a comprehensible manner, can it bring about truly informed consent? Not only might one need to consider the various languages spoken by communities, but also whether and how to translate more technical jargon. Would the average citizen understand the concept of "street vacation" as a planner or landscape architect would—or understand it at all? If we unthinkingly use such terms in community meetings, is that facilitating informed consent?

There is an array of challenges that comprehension of information raises including issues of education—yet at the same time avoiding undue influence—and remembering that adequately is not the same as totally in regard to what is informed and free or autonomous. Of course, there are problems of adequate translation of technical concepts and detailed scientific findings and with the method of presenting the information—both areas are liable to modulate the levels of fear of harm, acceptance of authority, or speed of the communicative interactions (p. 85). The regularly observed difficulty that most everyone has in reading building or site plans and blueprints indicates that what is correctly rendered and presented by professional standards is likely not to be comprehensible by laypeople. The environmental professions often compensate for this gap through alternate techniques such as perspective drawings, models, or computer-generated 3-D images that present things more the way they look. Yet, the danger of overly convincing graphics increases with digital visualization technology, where the virtual can be made to look any way that is desired and the client may be given a visual impression that is not so much a representation as a rhetorical stimulus—one that even substitutes for the core information needed.

3. *Voluntary Consent*

It is easy to see how concern for the comprehension of information leads to the requirement that the choice of action based upon this information proceed without undue influence, coercion, or threat. That is, once we comprehend the information provided, ideally it enables us to make a good decision or at least to act freely based on the information we have. The key ingredient here is the degree of voluntariness in consenting to or choosing a course of action. Again there is a continuum, in this case of voluntariness from broad latitude and freedom in decision making to excessive pressure or manipulation. Since normally there exist many pressures in decision making, few of which are hidden or even subtle, voluntariness is more than simply concern over influencing a person. The main concern is whether or not there is an unacceptable reward or punishment (or inference thereof) to induce a decision that people otherwise would not make. Manipulation can occur by means of the atmosphere created within which decisions are made (an intimidating location, controlled by someone other than the client), by the dress and manner of the professionals, by the way things are said or presented, and so on. The implied threat of hitherto unimagined disasters attending a wrong choice, or the insistence that the financial implications are more severe than they may, in fact, be compared to options of which the client is unaware, or even the way an eyebrow is raised in disbelief, or the voice that stresses that *"Well, its your decision. If you really insist* on taking *that* course, you certainly have the right to *take the risk* now that I have explained *the dangers involved"*—these all are forms of manipulation.

For more on informed consent (especially in wicked problems where the numbers of those who have a claim on participating in decision making change or only become disclosed in the course of events) see the
→ case on Rincon Center, appendix III
→ case on Hydro-Quebec, appendix III
→ Exercise 3.2 on Functionalism, at the end of this chapter.

Veracity—Truth Telling

In addition to providing comprehensible information in an accessible manner, another key ingredient for informed consent is that the information provided be actually true. In its simplest sense, the prima facie duty[2] variously named truthfulness, honesty, or veracity is fairly straightforward. The significant questions arise in regard to its relationship with other principles and rules, and the circumstances in which it might be overruled or modified. In other words, we begin assuming that the rule is to tell the truth; if there appears to be a compelling reason to consider not doing so, then an argument and justification would need to be made and evaluated.

Lack of truthfulness should not be construed in the narrowest way to mean only a direct falsification or deliberate lie. Rather, it can involve a range of actions from direct deception to failure to provide important information, that is deliberate withholding of information just discussed. The former would involve not only what we say, but what is written and reported (consider the popular book *How to Lie with Statistics*) and even maps.

Throwing Darts at Veracity.
A Challenge to Truth Telling

A notorious case emerged in Dallas, Texas, in the 1980s during the process of deciding whether the city should build DART (Dallas Area Rapid Transit). Some of the planners who advocated the approval of DART used deliberately misleading land use and ridership forecasts in an effort to persuade voters to approve the 100-mile rail transit system, then attempted to cover up more accurate alternative data, and finally continued to try to mislead voters by using out-of-date and incorrect material to generate even more inaccurate ridership and cost predictions. In addition to clear violations of the duty of veracity to the voters, DART's presentation of an extreme alternative as being moderate, through the elimination of the full range of options, obviously failed to allow informed consent since it exercised undue influence, if not coercion. (For good coverage of this case, see Kain 1990, pp. 184-196.)

Even with agreement on the properly broad definition of truthfulness, there is some disagreement among the major theories as to whether our duty to veracity is absolute and independent or not. For Kant and deontology (duty-based ethics) the answer is yes, our duty to veracity is absolute. For utilitarianism (or consequence-based ethics), the answer is not necessarily. There are three major sorts of reasons that come into play, as Beauchamp and Childress point out. First, it follows from the principles of autonomy and respect for persons that people have a right to be told the truth. For both deontology and natural law, if an autonomous person is to make good decisions they need to have knowledge; if they are to give informed consent, they have to be correctly informed. On both counts, ethical responsibility toward others depends on providing access to the truth. Secondly, for Kant, truthfulness is tied to the duty of fidelity. A necessary condition of keeping our promises is that we tell the truth about what we intend to do, and that in doing so we make an implicit or even explicit contract that needs to be true. (In this regard, philosopher Martin Heidegger notes the old sense of truth as "troth," which we hear in wedding or political vows wherein one says "I plight thee my troth." Here truth-telling and pledging one's fidelity are understood together.) Similarly, utilitarianism points out that social trust depends on being able to take people at their word, to be able to trust that what they tell us is true. Thus the social good and coherence that comes with confidence in each other critically depends on veracity.

Beauchamp and Childress, among others, argue that in today's ethical contexts veracity is a prima facie duty, that is, assumed to be right as we initially inquire into what should be done, but not absolute, in that it may reasonably be modified or overridden when in conflict with more powerful principles. As noted in the paragraph preceding, cases can be made that not telling the truth, or not fully telling it, would be justified in some circumstances. Whether we accept a set of particular arguments as convincing or compelling is, of course, the actual issue in ethical decision making. In the ordinary course of events, one tells a lie in order to deceive another, which is not acceptable practice. We would need to consider motives in order to try to legitimize such conduct, for example by contending that another's good depended on the truth not being told (that beneficence would outweigh veracity in a particular circumstance). Here there is significant agreement among ethicists, who largely maintain that we cannot withhold the truth or tell a falsehood to one who is entitled to the truth. That is, it is not the same to withhold truth, to be evasive, or to tell something false to an inquisitive party not directly entitled to know the truth as it is to do the same to someone having a right to the truth in question. Again, truth is connected here to fidelity: if in relation to an autonomous person for whose good we are obliged to work—say a client—we owe that person fidelity, and have the duty to tell them what they need to know in order to make a good decision, then they have the right to truth, and we the duty to provide it.

Competing Goods

Here in the exploration of principles and rules we see that dilemmas often involve competing goods, and we need to describe which principles outweigh the others in these circumstances. For example, when might beneficence outweigh veracity? It will partly depend on interpretation of who is entitled to what.

→ For some of the guidelines connected with attempts to justify
violation of truth-telling see the last section of this chapter
on weightings of principles and rules.

Confidentiality

Confidentiality, like truth-telling, is a prima facie duty. What is told to us in confidence or what we learn in the course of work belongs to those who relate to us and if they reasonably expect (much less explicitly affirm) that we keep the information private, then we are bound to do so. What belongs to persons, what is theirs privately, remains within their control, whether a matter of material property, intellectual property, or simply what they think and say. Clearly this is of major importance in the professional-client relationship, where the former acts as an agent for the latter and owes the duties of beneficence and non-maleficence.

That confidentiality is one of the most frequently, even casually, violated ethical rules is clearly not a justification to repeat or compound the improper conduct. Gossip conveying information learned in the course of working for a client is common, but unacceptable ethically. What is the client's is the client's, and the client alone has the right to decide who shall share material, including information.

Ethical dilemmas occur when there is conflict between confidentiality owed to one party and obligation owed to others. For instance, confidentiality owed to one party is not absolute; but neither is non-observance of confidentiality even when in the name of what one considers a better good. (Here, fidelity is involved, because if one does not share a client's values and goals, there naturally is greater likelihood of acting against the client's wishes.) In most serious cases involving conflicts with confidentiality we do not know with certainty about all the actions and consequences involved. For example, if we keep quiet about an intended development will an entire community be severely injured? If we take a shortcut in construction techniques or materials what is the likelihood that a user will be harmed? These are the issues of which cases are made.

→ See cases of Repaired Flaw and "Rincon Center," in appendix III

Beauchamp and Childress also note that while legal duties exist in regard to confidentiality (the obligation to release information if doing so might prevent serious harms to others), we need to remember that the legal is not the same as the moral (though perhaps it is not as dramatically demonstrated as by journalists spending time in prison for refusing to breach confidentiality by identifying their sources. As we saw in chapter 1, we clearly have an obligation to obey the law, while doing so may pose ethical dilemmas, rather than remove them. Beauchamp and Childress argue that the moral obligation to obey the law is not absolute, but prima facie 1983, pp. 213-14). Further, though there is no simple ethical transfer from one professional realm to another, it is worth noting what the American Psychiatric Association (APA) holds in regard to whether a client's confidentiality may be violated to prevent harm. The APA maintains that if there is substantial doubt about whether to break confidence, then the patient's right to confidentiality has priority (somewhat similar to the directions given to a jury whose members are instructed that to find the accused guilty, they must determine that the evidence is indicative "beyond a shadow of a doubt" Beauchamp and Childress 1983, 217). For environmental issues, we must also be concerned with balancing our social responsibilities and the degrees of uncertainly about what might happen based on what is told to us. Not only might harms not materialize, but harms can be created if one is an alarmist or generates undue worry.

→ For some of the guidelines connected with attempts to justify violation of confidentiality see the last section of this chapter on weightings of principles and rules.

Fidelity

With fidelity we again encounter the question of who is the client, particularly if there are multiple clients and there might be deemed primary and secondary clients. To whom do we owe fidelity? To whom truthfulness, confidentiality, respect of autonomy, the right of informed consent, beneficence, non-maleficence? From the professional point of view, the fundamental starting point is the special focus on and obligations to the primary client (usually the person or institution that hires, directs, and pays for the project and salaries. Then there are the connected and complicating issues of the users, especially if they are the general public who very often are not the owners or if they are, as in the case of environmental problems, they are the many unknown people living downstream (that is, those who will be directly affected by an environmental decision). For the most part, those beyond the sphere of the immediate client(s), especially in competitive economies and societies, enter into the ethical equation most seriously in terms of non-maleficence and justice.

The major issue of one's own values and conscience conflicting with an employer's or client's can seldom be avoided in the course of a professional career. This is certainly true in making complex environmental decisions. When we find ourselves on the opposite side of what a client wants, beyond the point of normal differences to the extent that the project, approach, or goals seem wrong, it clearly is time to question the propriety of remaining employed by that client, or working for that project.

→ see the case becoming a planner, appendix III
→ see the case of the Rincon Center in appendix III
→ see the cases concerning clients at the end of this chapter

Clearly, however, the major source of ethical earthquakes is the likelihood or actuality of harm to bystanders, that is, to the public. Often the public remains an abstract value concept; and general expression of concern for the public seems to be little more than a kind of reassuring hand-wave without much substance. Certainly understanding the full force of ethical dilemmas demands that we consider the other principles of beneficence, non-maleficence, and justice, which follow immediately below. (See Beauchamp and Childress' consistent emphasis on the importance of being sensitive to the public in terms of non-maleficence 1983.)

→ At this point in the reading, you may want to review the criticisms of the professional codes in regard to the public in chapter 6.

Beneficence

As with autonomy, the general principle of beneficence is an ancient one that has been absorbed into our popular consciousness. Its classic formulation is familiar to us in the form of the Hippocratic Oath, which in a contemporary translation states: "I will use treatment to help the sick according to my ability and judgment, but I will never use it to injure or wrong them." The first part of this oath speaks to beneficence: the idea of helping others. Beneficence is that which contributes to people's health and welfare, or provides overall benefits to others (the word comes from the Latin root bene which means good). The concept is basically positive, and thus naturally is paired with the complementary ideas of helping achieve or maintain a state of well-being by means of preventing or removing some negative element (non-maleficence). To assert beneficence as a principle is to claim that it is more than a matter of mere kindness and charity as is the connotation ordinary English usage.

Four Aspects of *Cost-Benefit* Analysis to be Considered.

1. the probability of the harms or benefits actually occurring
2. the potential severity of the harms and of the benefits
3. the nature of the harm (physical, material, psychological, social, or spiritual)
4. the nature of the benefit (physical, material, psychological, social, or spiritual)

There are two especially significant features to take into account in exploring beneficence: the provision of benefits and the balance between benefits and harms. First, the positive dimension of beneficence is relatively straightforward. For example, when the question arises about whose good should be satisfied or when there is a difference between the client and professional about what constitutes the value to be emphasized, since the professional has the primary obligations to the client, the client's good would have precedence (see also the sections in this chapter and exercises on who is the client). In the environmental and design realm beneficence can manifest itself in a number of ways related to how one sees professional responsibilities to clients. For example, in terms of a conflict between a client's social goals and an architect's aesthetic vision, Kim Dovey argues "in the end, the social values of the client must have priority over the private aesthetic of the architect" (1993, 30).

Challenges to beneficence start to occur when there is a conflict of rights and obligations among interested parties. Beauchamp and Childress, for example, argue that beneficence is a duty that we are obliged to carry out only if certain conditions hold:

1) if failing to provide the benefit results in serious risk to someone
2) if a person's action probably will prevent the harm from occurring
3) if the benefit to the person in need outweighs the risk to person undertaking the action to prevent the harm

(Beauchamp and Childress 1983, 153).

That is, the decision as to whether or not there is an obligation under the principle of beneficence involves evaluating the relation of benefits to harms.

We arrive, then, at the second important feature of beneficence: the balance of benefits and harms. There is another, broader balance to be considered regarding beneficence in addition to the question of actual harm (or risk of harm) versus benefit (or likelihood of benefit)—that is the overall balance of beneficence to non-maleficence—as is emphasized in the common approach of cost-benefit analysis, which seeks to calculate the final the balance between doing good or avoiding doing harm.

The Balance of Benefits and Harms

The measuring of benefit and harms is central to any major ethical theory—especially utilitarianism, which concerns itself with enabling the greatest good for the greatest number of people. We also see it in Aristotle's natural law theory with the injunction to nurture and not frustrate a person's potential. We also see the balance of goods and harms in deontology's perspective that the good of persons is paramount and that people are not a means to other ends but ends unto themselves. For more on this see chapter 4.

The obvious goal in ethical decision making is to consider possibilities that maximize benefits and minimize harms or the risk of harm, while also not violating other principles such as autonomy and justice. While there is no abstract formula to arrive at a proper measuring of the relationship between positive and negative impacts, utilitarianism offers a coherent procedure to follow.

Of course, the very concepts and empirical dimensions of costs and benefits are complex. In addition to the particular individuals and environmental elements involved in a specific case, there are large-scale economic and social approaches in which the macro-features of entire systems are factors. Those larger dimensions, including questions of economics and perceptions of quality of life, will be taken up in treating justice and public policy elsewhere in this book; here we consider the details of what is applicable in dealing with specific cases.

Integration of Multiple Facets

One of the major problems in considering and trying to balance harms and goods is that there is a great variety of goods (whose positive values we name with terms such as beauty, freedom, justice, truth, and so on). Further, for each good there is a great range of kinds. For example, there are different kinds of beauty, and thus also disagreements about what is good and what is neutral or harmful (formal beauty, functional beauty, symbolic beauty, and so on).

Thus, we can see how questions of what qualities of phenomena and experience to consider, and how to compare different qualities, are inseparable from worldviews, since the worldviews articulate how the various values are manifest concretely and further relate the values to one another in a consistent manner. Again we find that the material of chapter 1 (e.g. on worldviews, that of this chapter, and the theories of chapter 4 need to be integrated.

Obviously discussion and something approaching agreement regarding what is valued is important. This includes the social, philosophical understandings of a situation that usually are worked out among those involved. (See the issues of relational and absolute values and norms in the chapter 4 on theory). The major point made by utilitarianism is that we can work through and identify what matters in a given situation in some detail (Beauchamp and Childress 1983, 149) by evoking the principle(s) relevant to the decision and carrying out a standard analysis of probabilities in order to increase clarity in the judgment process. While uncertainly is not eliminated, this approach reduces the impact of purely intuitive responses or hunches, which are seldom transparent, consistent, or trustworthy, and thus not usually legitimate in rational decision making whose outcomes will be accepted over time. The drive in traditional ethics, then, is to formalize such analytic procedures, making them more systematic and less arbitrary without necessarily quantifying them (the ethic of care has its own procedures, distinct from the rationalistic model, but with its own precision nonetheless). Note, however, even if we make use of a formal analytic rationally, it is not clear that the net positive implications compared to the net negative ones necessarily justify accepting a particular procedure—that still requires discussion at the level of theory. Therefore, considering risks of harms in relation to the likelihood of benefits does not itself justify the approach: here it is only a decision-clarification tool that raises questions for moral decision making.

In Islamic tradition and law, the issue of weighing the costs and benefits of one's actions in terms of goods and harms is closely addressed. The Mālakī jurists of the Maghreb, or Islamic west, normally apply the principle of *hadīth*, "no harm shall be inflicted [on anyone] or reciprocated [against anyone]" ("*lā darar wa-lā dirār fī-l-Islām*") as well as "consideration of the public good (*maslaha*)" when called upon to give a legal opinion on infractions of space that culminated in 'legal harm'" (Kahera 1998, pp. 131, 138, 162). For example, in ruling on "a litigant's questions dealing with possible occurrence of collateral damage to adjacent property, [the mufti's] account concerns the principle of greater and lesser harm," specifically focusing on avoiding or minimizing *darar*—the "concept of causing harm or damage" (Kahera 1999, 139).

Regarding environmental and human well-being, the current concern with understanding buildings and environments not just in terms of up-front costs, but in terms of the long-term, is a big step forward. In part this helps overcome resistance to investing in higher quality environmental features by those concerned mainly with immediate profit—or at least by those who will be involved for a longer time—since over a thirty year period only one-half of a building's total cost is that of design and construction; the rest is allocated to energy use, maintenance, and related items. In the assessment or inventory of what matters in full life-cycle accountability, note how many factors are directly and obviously harms—harms that too often go unnoticed, much less checked.

Environmental Issues in Life-Cycle Assessment

❑   The exhaustion of scarce or finite resources
❑   The production of greenhouse gases
❑   The production of chlorofluorocarbons leading to ozone
     depletion
❑   The production of acid rain
❑   Habitat destruction and species extinction
❑   Materials or processes that harm plants, animals, and
     humans
❑   Air, soil, and water pollution
❑   Noise pollution with its deleterious effect on the human
     psyche
❑   Visual pollution
❑   To which we might add, light pollution at night

(Papanek 1995, 33).

→ For more on these issues, see chapter 5

Finding Common Ground

We are hopeful about the prospect that the ethical practitioner
can find common ground in regard to the criteria for decisions (such as harms and good) and for ways to dissolve
what may seem like non-compatible positions.

One way to do so is to find a procedure to actually agree on
priorities or hierarchies—a critical but daunting task.

In addition, we need to recognize the plurality of the ways
that values can be manifested historically by different
groups—particularly in multi-cultural societies where there
are multiple valid aesthetic, political, and epistemological
systems.

Principle of Non-Maleficence

The basic concept of non-maleficence, the complement to beneficence, appears along with the latter in the Hippocratic Oath we considered earlier, stated here again but now with a focus on non-maleficence: "I will use treatment to help the sick according to my ability and judgment, but *I will never use it to injure or wrong* them."

This term maleficence is another technical ethical term uncommon in English usage: we usually speak of harms or even evils. The Latin root is *male*, which means bad and also appears in terms like malicious and malfeasance, for example. Note, however, that the maleficence to which we are referring in the ethical principle of non-maleficence is not the same as malfeasance which indicates failure to act properly and incur legal liability or culpability. Maleficence more simply means harm. It is helpful to think of beneficence and non-maleficence together, in fact, as two ends of a spectrum; one is proscribed, the other prescribed:

Do not Injure ◄————————————————————► Do Good
(non-maleficence)   *(beneficence)*

There is wide agreement that we have a prima facie obligation of non-maleficence and that this principle covers a broad range of valued dimensions of our lives and the world. Specifically, the injunction of non-maleficence includes not harming or injuring reputation, property, liberty, physical and mental well-being, freedom of movement, and opportunity, just to begin a list. Nor should harm be taken narrowly. It includes not only actually inflicting or causing harm or injury, but intending or permitting even the risk of harm or injury. It is important to note that harm includes negligence. The failure to maintain facilities, for example, that leads to the leaking of toxins or the failure to carefully research and manufacture products that have unintended consequences (such as off-gassing), amounts to a failure to guard against risks to others. The importance of these issues has increased with the planetary spread of harms from emissions that have led to global warming. Our increased understanding of the complex relationships among ecosystems also makes us more sensitive to harms that occur originally as unintended consequences, but for which we are responsible once we know about them.

The general responsibility under the principle of non-maleficence is to remain careful and thoughtful. (This is somewhat similar to the principles belonging to the ethic of care addressed elsewhere in this book.) The standard in regard to this principle is that one comports oneself and conducts one's professional work with due care, which includes one's knowledge, skills, and diligence. (Due care is related to the concepts of the responsible person and the reflective practitioner who Schön describes in his work and we discussed in previous chapters). (Whether the standards to be met are more or less the same as the legal standards of the professions warrants serious discussion, as begun in chapter 3). Further, the question of an adequate standard would have to include deliberation as to whether the goals are weighty enough to justify the risks. Here there are also questions of magnitude and probability (see Beauchamp and Childress 1983, 112 for their list of ways to deal with or determine magnitude and probability in justifying risks).

Lack of Beneficence or Actual Maleficence?

"Consider a civil engineer I know who is remarkably adept at designing economical flat-plate concrete slabs for apartment houses. With careful study and hard work (always staying within safety features prescribed by code), he is able to de velop plans in which the reinforcing steel used is as little as four pounds per square foot. I also know an engineer who designed a comparable building that turned out to have seven pounds per square foot. It was a hurried, lazy, unimaginative piece of work, and when I pointed out to him how costly his design would be he merely shrugged. He could not be bothered to invest the additional effort in a more cost-effective design. The difference between the two designs represented 3 per cent of the total cost of the building, and since the projects I refer to involved housing for the indigent elderly, the harm done by the engineer . . . is too often overlooked." (Florman 1987, 105)

- In your opinion, was there actual harm perpetrated in this case?

- Would you say it was a failure to act beneficently?

- What is the ethical difference between failing to do good in one or another particular instance and always declining to do so?

The Principle of Double Effect
In the natural law tradition (see the next chapter for details), the principle of "double effect" has been developed to provide a further means of considering how we might deal with the fact that an act has both good and bad consequences. The principle of double effect posits that it would be ethically acceptable, in some cases, to allow an action that works on behalf of one party even though it would harm another. As startling as this might seem, it becomes more understandable when we look at the conditions under which this might be ac-

ceptable. The double-effect principle requires that four conditions be met in order to justify such action:

1. In regard to the act itself: the action leading to the result is itself morally good or neutral.
2. In regard to the agent: the agent or actor must not be motivated by a desire for the evil result itself, but sees the evil as to be avoided (that is, the person doing the action must intend only the good effect, and the evil effect is to be allowed only reluctantly).
3. In regard to the act: the good effect must not flow from the evil result. The evil is not the means to the good effect; rather both the good and bad effect follow together from the action.
4. In regard to the act: the act must involve a reasonable balance between the value that is preserved/gained and that which is lost/destroyed.
                                                            (Beauchamp and Childress 1983, pp. 113-115).

Justice

Issues of justice typically focus on what one needs, what one deserves, or what is fair when it comes to sharing benefits and harms. For instance, "to say that someone has a 'fundamental need' for or 'deserves' "something is to say that the person will be harmed or detrimentally affected in a fundamental way if that thing is not obtained" (Beauchamp and Childress, 1983, 174). Examples would include a non-toxic and safe environment, housing, nutrition, health care, and education. To successfully make environmental decisions we would require both adequate basic principles and a means for implementing them—but, for example, there appears to be disagreement on whether the Environmental Protection Agency (EPA), Federal Emergency Management Agency (FEMA), Occupational Safety and Health Administration (OSHA), or the U.S. health care and insurance systems are such instruments.

We do have a cultural stock of familiar characterizations or formulae to describe justice: an equal share to all, to each according to their need, to each according to their individual effort, to each according to their social contribution, to each according to individual merit, or the less-familiar, ancient idea that equals ought to be treated equally and unequals unequally. While the precision of these kinds of definition is vital to their truth or validity and force of application, they are highly abstract and general formulations that need to be filled in with substantive or material [sub-] principles that "specify the relevant respects in terms of which . . . ," that is, the characteristics or properties on the basis of which to decide what to do, how to distribute the benefits and burdens for instance (Beauchamp and Childress 1983, 187).

But, we have not resolved the conflicts among the possible interpretations of and practices regarding justice. As a society we do not agree about which definitions and modes of implementing justice to choose and why. Any resolution or further approximation to agreement regarding the specific relevant properties

Environmental Justice

Environmental justice emerged out of the environmental movement of the 1970s but only gained momentum in the '80s as it
became apparent that issues of race and poverty were intertwined with environmental problems and where harmful locations were concentrated.

Also known as environmental equity, environmental justice
deals with inequities associated with the burdens born by the
poor, racial minorities, women, or inhabitants of developing
countries. It seeks to redress unequal protection, decision making practices that systematically disadvantage groups or locate
undesirable or dangerous uses and facilities in proximity to their
communities (Roseland 1998, 154).

The environmental justice movement really began as many
smaller individual community-based efforts to mitigate environmental degradation in poor neighborhoods of color. It gained
fuller attention with the landmark book by Robert Bullard, one
of the leading figures in this field, *Dumping in Dixie: Race,
Class, and Environmental Quality* (1990).

In 1991, the First National People of Color Environmental
Summit convened and laid out specific principles of environmental justice. Notably, many of these principles build on the
traditional notions of justice in ethical theory, such as fair opportunity, but specify fairness in relation to environmental harms
and goods, e.g. the right to ethically balanced and responsible
uses of land and resources.

In 1992, the U.S. Office of Environmental Justice was created; in 1994, each federal agency was required to "make
achieving environmental justice part of its mission."

Critical resources on the subject include:
- Bullard's other important works (1993 2005 2007)
- *Environmental Justice Case Studies* (2000, onward), U.S.
  Department of Transportation, Federal Highway Admini-
  stration, Federal Transportation Administration, government
  document #0982-G-05 (on line)
- David Newton, *Environmental Justice: A Reference Hand-
  book* (1996)
- Julian Agyeman *Sustainable Communities and the Challenge
  of Environmental Justice* (2005)
- David Pellow and Robert Brulle, *Power, Justice, and the En-
  vironment* (2005)
- Eddie Girdner and Jack Smith, *Killing me Softly: Toxic
  Waste, Corporate Profit, and the Struggle for Environmental Justice* (2002)

and characteristics of justice would have to be grounded in supporting moral principles and thus the different ethical theories. Traditional theories may or may not provide adequate justification, which is one reason why new variations are developed, such as the renewed interest in virtue ethics, or why significantly new theories are generated, such as the ethic of care or the ethics of dependency and compassion.

Fair Opportunity and the Veil of Ignorance
Fair opportunity is another relevant aspect of justice, though there is disagreement about whether it is actually an independent principle. This concept covers aspects of persons that in fact often actually do serve as the basis for unequal distribution in societies even though, in terms of what is legitimate in principle, the differences in question should not be relevant. The reason they should not be acceptable as the basis for the distribution of goods is because they are differences over which one has no power and for which one has no responsibility. For example sex, I.Q., religion, or race are dimensions of who we are but are not properties one has, acquires, or overcomes (Beauchamp and Childress 1983, pp. 181, 184). If race or ethnicity is irrelevant in this principled sense, then it would not be proper to withhold the benefits of a safe environment from or impose excessive expose to toxins upon ethnic minorities. This corresponds to the commonsensical and technical definitions of justice as fairness.

John Rawls has famously proposed the "veil of ignorance" as the test of ethical fairness. He contends that if we start from a position of complete ignorance of who we might be, or when or where we are living, then what we would rationally agree to as fair or just would be conservative, in that we would not agree to substantial differences in allocation because of self interest. For example, given global demographics, it is likely that we would exist as a poor person of color in a difficult time and place, that we would not find it reasonable to privilege having a combination of a light skin color, being born into a prosperous family, and having the advantage of a good education. (Rawls 1981).

→ To engage issues of justice, see this chapter's exercises 3.6 and 3.7

Recurring Patterns of Conflict among Principles and Rules

There is a difference between the situation in which we act without much thought because that is the way things are done and the emergence of a tradition that results from careful deliberation using self-criticism to refine the appropriate criteria for decisions and proper actions. In the latter cases, patterns appear which can be utilized, at least as a starting point in reflection and debate. This would include the shared worldviews and even individuals' bundles of values and beliefs considered in chapter 1. The important distinction is between those patterns that are legitimized as deliberative and responsible and those that are not. As an immediate issue, we need to consider the recurring, unavoidable conflicts among principles and rules—these need to be reflected upon and argued out, lest we shirk our responsibility to be critically thoughtful.

However, since we do need to make decisions in the meantime, we can at least initially or temporarily rest on the current state of understanding while the larger discussion is underway. In fact, there is substantial agreement among ethicists on the basic relationships or weightings among the various principles and rules. Descriptively, this is to note the standard relationships that are taken to hold among principles and rules (you may have noticed, for example, that in addressing the ethical principles and rules throughout this chapter, we have also touched on some of the acceptable hierarchies among them). In judging that some principles and rules are stronger than others we logically are affirming that what is determined to be the weaker standard normally gives way and requires exceptional conditions to outweigh the stronger. Importantly, a given existential situation may indeed include such exceptional factors—which can and must be decided in each particular case. In addition, of course, the general weightings decided upon also need to be critically examined). To present these weightings, then, is not to posit a mechanical substitute for difficult deliberation.

Relative Weightings of Principles and Rules

Non-Maleficence > Autonomy > Beneficence

Overall, across ethical theories, it generally is agreed that non-maleficence outweighs autonomy, which in turn outweighs beneficence. However, this is only a rule of thumb and the details of each circumstance matter. Note that justice, our fourth principle, does not appear straightforwardly in this weighting scheme, though it usually is taken as the most important of all the principles. That is because justice would fall along the continuum in a place that corresponds to whichever of the other three dimensions is most primally evoked—that is, any given question of justice may be more fundamentally about preventing a harm (non-maleficence), affirming self-determination (autonomy), or bringing about a good (beneficence).

The importance of using principles and rules in dynamic tension for decision making partly lies in their relation to consequentialism (which, as will be seen in chapter 4, is significantly different for the various major ethical theories. However, it is neither obvious nor agreed upon that a good or bad result in itself provides a moral justification—whether it would do so needs to be decided in principle via a grounding theory and because the actual result of our decisions may be accidental, lucky, or a freak occurrence. The major issue in real decision making processes remains principled justification. Of course, in considering the details upon which the principles and rules will operate, it is necessary to do as much as possible to estimate the degree of probability of harm and the degree of severity as approximate knowledge bearing on the deliberation (as distinct from itself settling the matter). There also is the important process of exercising as much imagination as possible in seeking alternatives.

To become specific: in regard to the generally accepted weightings of principles and rules, the norm is that the obligations and effects under the principles of autonomy and non-maleficence outweigh those of beneficence. When the opposite is argued—that in a given situation the obligations and outcomes under the principle of beneficence outweigh those of autonomy and non-maleficence, we have the issue of paternalism, especially involving informed consent and sub-categories of truth-telling, confidentiality, and fidelity. Here the burden of persuasion falls on those who would make the case for setting aside the informed consent of those involved, which is possible, but not easy.

EXERCISES FOR CHAPTER THREE

Format for Applying Principles and Rules

Here, in outline form, is the basic format you can use in applying principles and rules to the details of a situation or dilemma to help you deliberate-several of which are provided in appendix III:

1. Whose interests are involved and what are they?
   Each of the significantly involved parties needs to be identi-fied as to how they would be affected under the most likely scenarios.
2. What values, principles, and rules are most relevant to the case?
   [These are explained in the remainder of this chapter.] At this point in the process, the task is to neutrally lay out all the principles and rules that apply from all parties' perspectives. Clarify which apply and how, given the details of the case. This needs to be done for each of the involved parties. Also try to identify at least the major points of tension or conflict that could arise.
   Then, given the alternatives,
3. What course of action do you recommend?
4. What are the major considerations in favor of your position?
   Make explicit the major reasons, arguments, empirical features and evidence (given the relevant principles and rules) that support your disposition.
5. What are the main considerations against your recommendation?
   How or why are they outweighed or overcome?

Exercise 3.1 Problems when designer and client differ

Papanek (1995) gives several instances of challenging ethical decisions he had to make in his career as an architect. In the story below, can you determine why he finds the client's proposal unethical? Try a group discussion to see if you can shed light on what he probably means. Then discuss: If you were the one in the situation, what would you have done? Why? Is this as easy as Papanek makes it sound, given that most of us need the jobs to make a living, support a family, pay down debt, and so on?

Values provide direction when decisions about alternative courses of action must be made. . . . To think dispassionately about what we design and why, as well as what the eventual consequences of our design intervention may be, is the basis of ethical thinking. It gets easier with practice.

When I first lived in Toronto in the 1950s, a client asked me to design a free-standing structure to house a florist's showroom. He said, "I know you have studied with Frank Lloyd Wright; well I want to have a showroom that looks as if Mr. Wright had designed it!" The last thing I wanted to do was a Wright pastiche, yet I felt that I could not turn down my first and only job offer. I have regretted my lapse of ethical judgment ever since, especially as it later turned out that there were several scores of my client's showrooms clear across Canada. This early, negative experience first turned my attention to the ethical dimensions in design.

Nearly everyone seems to feel that a designer, faced by a job that is ethically unsound or offensive, has only two choices: reluctant acceptance after much soul-searching, or outright dismissal. When discussing this in a seminar, my post-graduate students urge me to react differently. "Why," they ask, "don't you say, 'I feel that this commission is morally wrong, here let me explain why.'" It is a sad fact that I have never yet had a client willing to let me charge one hundred and fifty dollars an hour whilst I attacked his proposal and lectured him about pop-psychology, ethics, and personal value choices. Just unlucky, I guess. The fourth way of handling the situation is to tell him that I won't do the job (without going into details), then adding: "But George will be glad to do it, and is an extremely competent designer. Let me give you his address." This solves absolutely nothing. The job is still done (by someone else, it's true), your own office has lost income and helped the competition. (pp. 70-71)

Exercise 3.2 Issues within Professional Teams

Who has power in a professional team? What are the obligations within the new relationships between professionals and owners, especially in formats where the financial authority or engineers have final control or even daily oversight-management authority? What are the differences among the different modes of design, construction, delivery models—such as GMAC, design build, DBOM [design, build, operate, maintain, etc.]? (If you are not familiar with the major alternatives, do a bit of homework, or discuss the issues with construction, engineering, or management colleagues). Then, ideally with people from a variety of professions or disciplines, discuss:

> New Project requirements necessitate new architectural responses. Ethically, the architect must restructure several relationships that have been taken for granted for generations. For instance, who is the true client when the architect answers to the construction manager? How does the designer deal with design alterations by the construction manager, especially those that affect the public or occupant health, safety, and welfare? (Mitcham and Duval 2000, 39)

Exercise 3.3 Policy and Many Competing Clients. An Exercise for the Hydro-Quebec Case in appendix III

Hydro-Quebec

First read through the Hydro-Quebec case material in appendix III,

❑   Make a list of all the relevant parties (including distinctions among sub-groups, such as First Nations, et al.)

Then, for each of the groups:
❑   List the major principles and rules that apply or need to be invoked to reflect on the ethical responsibilities and rights of each group in this project.

❑   Make a matrix that allows you to display or align the agreements and disagreements among groups, and their basis in principles and rules.

❑   Analyze your matrix of principle and rules to figure out which principles and rules conflict or agree in the tangle of possibilities and required decisions.

❑   Make an argument for a solution, either on behalf of one of the groups or as a compromise for all.

❑   Consider the counter arguments. Perhaps classmates can take up the alternatives; if not, try to do it yourself.

❑   Consider whether you want to modify your position. When you are satisfied, defend why you hold that the one complex of principles and rules outweighs the other.

Exercise 3.4 Veracity: Debates Concerning Functionalism and Honesty of Materials

Debate for or against the following proposition:
"The design/form/appearance of an object/building/landscape should correspond to its use/function."

This proposition involves the following sorts of claims:
❑   Aesthetic values: an object, building, or landscape is more beautiful and better when its form does follow its function
❑   Truth values: for form and function not to correspond is in some way deceptive and false (bad)
❑   Social/moral values: for form and function to correspond is good for (promotes) a democratic way of life and society

Note, for a good discussion, a smaller focus needs to be made within the broad range of what we are talking about: machine mass-produced objects, handcrafted objects, large-scale/multi-party projects, and so on. Functionalism clearly is connected to the machine-produced, yet may not be identical with it, since not all machine-produced items exhibit a functionalist aesthetic. At the same time, some handcrafted goods fulfill the criteria or goal; but, not all do, nor perhaps need to. In the case of large projects such as building complexes or landscapes it is not always clear that there is either a discernable form or single function.

Counter-positions to the proposition stated above start from views and tactics such as:
❑   The functionalist view is merely one aesthetic preference among many
❑   Functionalism is inhumane or reductive
❑   Functionalism does not understand the nature of ornament
❑   The ideology of functionalists shows that they are wrong
❑   Functionalism is impractical in a capitalist world
❑   Functionalism is actually elitist and hostile to democracy

As you deliberate, explicitly address the following four dimensions of decision making:
1.   What position do you defend? Briefly state your view on the issue.
2.   What reasons, arguments, empirical features, evidence, principles, and rules support your conclusion? Have you also considered the basic assumptions and implications?
3.   What are the strongest reasons, arguments, principles, and rules against your conclusion?
4.   How do you overcome these counterpoints?

Exercise 3.5 A Classic Debate: Ethics and Honesty of Materials and Construction Techniques

There is a long tradition in architecture and engineering that it is dishonest to present materials that deceive us as to what they are or how they are used. (This view is an updated and more liberal position than that of theorists such as Schopenhauer and Ruskin in the nineteenth century who held that iron could not be used for true architecture because among its responsibilities architecture had to manifest the tension between (a) the human desire to use materials to resist nature and defy time, and (b) the inevitable force of time and gravity to bring the materials down—thus wood and stone were appropriate as natural materials, but iron was not.) The major argument of modernism is that architecture must be truthful in how it uses and shows materials and construction processes. For example, at the beginning of the twentieth century Loos insisted on the obligation for honesty and integrity of materials (reprinted 1982). According to this mode of thinking, a marble façade on a public building is acceptable because everyone can read the fact that the marble is decorative cladding, and does not mistakenly think that the entire building is constructed of blocks of marble; but, faux painting is unethical, as when columns are deceptively made to appear to be marble, which is a lie.[3] In another—regional—example of honesty in materials, Pacific Northwest Modernist architecture often uses wooden beams to span open spaces, deliberately leaving those beams exposed overhead (regularly treating the heating and air conditioning ductwork systems the same way).

Exercise 3.6 Design, Beauty, and the Spiritual

Some of our most difficult environmental decisions hinge on how we define things. Here is a question that picks up the controversy concerning the many definitions of beauty and design: What is your own position in regard to the viewpoint laid out below by Papanek? How essential or variable are the specific dimensions that he identifies to really deal with the issue?

> At first sight, there is no such thing as a piece of industrial design that is invested with spiritual values. There can be no transcendental refrigerator, no righteous chair, no moral tea kettle. We cannot find a spiritual advertisement, a soul-stirring logo or trademark. In the fields of fashion and textile design it is impossible to locate an immaculate cotton print or a saintly dress.
>
> The question of whether a design is spiritual or not seems easier to answer in relation to architecture. Architecture can—at times—touch the spiritual.
>
> Can the spiritual exist in design? The men and women working and studying in Germany in the 1920s at the Bauhaus (possibly the most influential school of design in history) would have answered affirmatively and without hesitation. Their conviction was: "If it functions well, it will be beautiful—and therefore have spiritual value."
>
> Looking at this proposition from the vantage point of the mid-1990s, things are less clear. . . [For all that can be appreciated in it], the Bauhaus style was

elitist and seen as alienating by many. To the statement, "If it functions well, it will be beautiful," we now add the questions: "If it functions well, doing what? It will be beautiful in what sense? Function and beauty in what context?" . . . [W]hat separates all industrial design from architecture: [t]hrough the manipulation and orchestration of interior spaces, it is possible to release transcendental feelings, hints of the sacred in people. This can't be done as directly in any tool, object or artifact. We may admire the pure lines of a birch-bark canoe, or a glider, but this aesthetic response—caused by simple elegance—may only infrequently release in us intimations of the sublime. (1995, 49–53)

Exercise 3.7 Justice as Fair Opportunity and Distributive Justice

The concept of justice as a matter of fair share—but not an unreasonable share—is integral to the principle of fair opportunity. For Kant, justice is not a matter of equal distribution of economic or other resources, but of whether there is a legitimate basis for unequal distribution. For example, everyone would have the right to a certain quality of education; if it costs more for some groups or in some circumstances (for example, because people live in thinly populated rural areas) then it is just to provide the greater amount where needed because the principle of fair opportunity requires that they receive it. It often is argued that the principle of fair opportunity may override effort or merit as a basis for different distributions. It is generally agreed that the principle of fair opportunity would revise the common practices of distributive justice, and that there are other better alternatives.

It is not settled whether the principle of fair opportunity is valid, or exactly what it would entail: How much to provide? In what circumstances?

It might seem at first glace that debates concerning property rights (for example, see the case of State of Washington, Proposition 933 in appendix III) fall within the category of fair opportunity because the argument is that one has a right to do what one wishes with one's own property, without interference, including profiting from one's property. But this is a misunderstanding based on the ordinary uses of English rather than the technical sense the terms have in ethics where fair opportunity refers to differences over which one has no power and for which one has no responsibility—again, things like race, ethnicity, or gender. Since property rights issues, which focus indeed are questions of justice, not only on issues of benefit and harm, but crucially on the question of who has a rightful stake—and thus a proper voice—in the action and outcome. There we can see how property rights are inseparably are bound up with questions of autonomy and informed consent, and of the balance of beneficence and nonmaleficence.

→ Now that you have covered the complex principles and rules of ethics, return to chapter 1 and reconsider the discussion points there concerning the two major varieties of anthropocentric world views: privatism and civic orientation. Also take another look at the box there on liberalism—do you still think about this as you did earlier? Why, or why not?

Exercise 3.8 Justice and the Indifference Map

As pointed out in the perceptive analysis of takings by Zev Trachtenberg, Brian Barry shows that "incommensurability of values does not lead necessarily to arbitrariness in decision making. . . . [Indeed], such trade-offs can fall into fairly consistent patterns" (1997, 83). As Trachtenberg explains, Barry "uses the economist's device of an 'indifference map' that consists of a set of curves that symbolize all the particular combinations of meanings (i.e. how much of each would be traded-off for how much of the others) that we would judge to be equally acceptable. . . . The indifference map thus expresses the range of distributions this society would consider just: given this pattern of meaning, these alternative combinations of criteria are equally acceptable" (pp. 83–84). As Barry explains, "Suppose that we imagine there to be only two very general principles which we may call 'equity' and 'efficiency'. Then for each person we can draw up a set of indifference curves showing along each line different combinations of the two between which one would be indifferent. . . . The problem of someone making an evaluation can thus be regarded as the problem of deciding what mixture of principles more or less implemented out of all the mixtures which are available would be, in his opinion, the best" (1990, pp.5-6).

Create an indifference map of your own for one of the environmental problems you find particularly intriguing or challenging. To do this, read the relevant sections of Barry's book *Political Argument: A Reissue with a New Introduction*, especially chapter 1: evaluation.

Exercise 3.9 Create Your Own Fiendish Cases

If Shiva was at the door, ready to destroy the world, and asked you where the most wonderful landscape was so that he could start by obliterating it, would you have to tell him the truth? Well, maybe that is not the most pressing question, but we all love to come up with devilish problems—as if reality did not present enough. So:

❑ Select a set of principles or rules that you want to set into tension in order to explore the issues concretely by use of case materials.

❑ Think about the most relevant features of the problem that would need to be involved. Imagine complications that make it very hard to decide what to do because all the choices have problems and damages associated with them, no matter what good they do—that is, try to create your own dilemma.

❑   Now, either with your imaginative powers, or by looking at news stories or other sources—or both, find a set of materials to put into case form. Most likely you will have to make a composite from several sources or select details from very complex material.

Notes

1. The term withdrawal highlights the research context in which the rule of informed consent developed, as suggested by our earlier references to the Nazi experiments on prisoners, the Tuskegee syphilis study, and Milgram's psychological experiments on obedience. In the research context, informed consent is required so that people know their risks, benefits, and rights as research participants, including the right to withdraw from a study at any time they choose. However, in the case of non-research situations, informed consent is still critical. We can readily see this in the case regarding locally unwanted land uses—or any land use issue for that matter. Residents have the right to know whether that empty lot is going to be developed into a multi-unit complex or a dump site or wastewater treatment plant, etc. and they have a right to a say in what happens to that property.

2. In ethics you will find much discussion of prima facie duties. This typically refers to those duties or responsibilities that could be considered obvious at first glance or readily agreed upon and therefore expected—for example veracity, gratitude, or fidelity. Ethicists from Aristotle onward have argued for the existence of such prima facie duties. As a more formal definition, Prima Facie (that is, at "first appearance" before investigation) connotes a binding principle in the modulated sense that it appears at first to be binding and remains as such unless a conflict with stronger duties leads to a judgment that it can be overridden.

3. We want to thank Justin Kliewer (2006), whose thesis is the source of these examples comparing Ruskin and Loos.

Chapter Four

Major Ethical Theories

Natural Law, Utilitarianism, Deontology, Ethic of Care

In this chapter, we turn our attention to the four major theories that have developed over time regarding ethics: natural law, utilitarianism, deontology and the ethic of care. Each of these represents a significant school of thought or conceptual framework about what is moral and what constitutes right action. The various ethical principles and rules of conduct that we have described elsewhere in the book are all in some way derived from at least one of these theories, although many of the principles and rules are based in more than one theory. These theories provide a helpful grounding for ethical decision making, providing conceptual structures and arguments that can help guide the choices we make. In looking over the fundamental premises, assumptions and concepts within each theory you can think about them in relation to your own worldviews as explored in chapter 1. You may find that some theories, or at least some arguments within the theories, are commensurate with your own approach. Thus, this chapter can help you connect your personal values and worldviews to a larger theoretic background. At the end of this chapter you will find a set of exercises that delve into different aspects of each theory more deeply and stimulate the reader to integrate these theories and take a stance on them. At a minimum, the awareness of the critiques poses for each major ethical theory in these exercises provide very helpful snapshots of the theories, their strengths and weaknesses.

Natural Law

Natural law[1] is a traditional approach to thinking about ethical issues and to deciding on practical ways of action. Begun by the ancient Greeks, like Homer and especially Aristotle (384–323 BCE), this theory was further developed by the

Roman Stoics, then adapted by medieval Christianity (Aquinas, 1224–1274). This approach to ethics continues today in several prominent traditions: as the fundamental viewpoint of major Christian religions (such as the Roman Catholic and Episcopalian Churches), in the recent virtue ethics identified with the work of Alisdair MacIntyre and the neo-Aristotelians (e.g., Martha Nussbaum).

Much of natural law has to do with the idea of human virtue. Popular culture and parlance might link the notion of virtues to religious views, but there are certainly treatments of virtue ethics that are separate from religious perspectives. So first let's look more closely at what is meant by virtue. While different theorists define virtue differently—for Homer, it is a quality that enables a person to discharge their social role; for Aristotle, it is a quality that enables a person to achieve the human *telos* (Greek for "end" or the ultimate goal of the good life)—the disposition or regular mindful habit. All these theorists define virtue as an acquired human quality, the exercise of which is a means to achieving the good for humanity as a whole. It is a dimension of our character that we can cultivate. MacIntyre (1981) describes the common thread across these various definitions thusly: "virtue is an acquired human quality the possession and exercise of which enables us to achieve those goods internal to practices and the lack of which prevents us from achieving any such good." (MacIntyre 1981, 178). In other words, we cultivate virtue to make good judgments and do the right thing at the right time in the right place. For Aristotle especially, the exercise of virtue is very situated and contextual; it is not a routine application of principles and rules. In addition to being context sensitive, the notion of virtue involves qualities that are for the benefit and well-being of society. It is a social phenomenon in which one seeks to cultivate these particular qualities of character for the good of society, not personal gain. While individuals may work toward personal excellence, an end goal unto itself, everyone exhibiting virtue will give rise to a "good" community.

Virtue and Practice
There are many different virtues identified by the theorists—courage, justice, truthfulness, agreeableness, faith, hope, love, humility, for example—and there is disagreement on what the most fundamental of the virtues are (faith, hope and love, for example, were added by Christian scholars like Aquinas) but most virtue ethicist, recognize that the virtues have to do with achieving excellence in practice. This is important for considering ethics in professional practice in the environmental professions. MacIntyre (1981) defines practice as "any coherent and complex form of socially established cooperative human activity through which goods internal to that form of activity are realized in the course of trying to achieve those standards of excellence . . . appropriate to, and partially definitive of, that form of activity" (p. 175). This is a lengthy and complex definition, but it has at its heart a desire for achieving a standard of excellence in one's endeavors.

In many ways, natural law begins in and is correlated with common sense—what we learn and share together as knowledge about the world in which we live. From this basis, we pass beyond common sense to deeper knowledge and ethical action by becoming more deliberate, rigorous, and consistent. But, even on the more scientific and philosophical levels, we are not estranged from common sense; rather, it is extended and elaborated to form part of our larger and continuing community heritage.

Virtue and the Slippery Slope

The common usage of the words virtue and virtuous in everyday language and for political purposes is very different from the way ethical theorists technically use the terms. It is important to keep this in mind when discussing virtue. The words often conjure up Images of the pious leader or saint who is or acts without fault. This is a slippery slope that may lead to judgments about superiority and about who is the better or more virtuous person. But such is not remotely what virtue is about—rather than calling us to be judgmental about others, virtue calls upon us to be good and do what we deem right and fair for the sake of others.

Natural law proceeds from the contention that the basis for ethical theory and action lies in the characteristics of the world, including the specific character of human life, a theory that seems commonsensical both as a logical idea and as something that we share together as a community living in the same world. A full ethics can unfold in the connection between the way things really are and what and how we know them to be theoretically and practically.[2] Another way to put this is to say that natural law theory posits that the world has three main features or assumptions, from which follow two major implications for ethics. Each of these is outlined below:

Assumptions about the World in Natural Law Theory

1) *The world is Inherently Intelligible.*
This affirms that we can understand things. For example, at the phenomenal level, science and the practical arts of farming and gardening can help us understand what corn, cabbage, and roses are. Science then gives us deeper and more systematic knowledge, especially of fundamental relationships, such as cause and effect.

2) *Things (Both Natural and Humanly-Made) Have Distinctive Natures.*
This premise asserts that things in the world each have their own essential and distinctive characteristics: planting a tomato seed will not result in a chicken growing, nor will an acorn become an elm or zucchini. This assumption lies at the basis of scientific taxonomies: we classify plants and animals, for instance, on the basis of shared and differentiated features. We see that among watery creatures a salmon and a seal are more alike in having a spine than they are like coral which does not, or that the seal needs to come up to breathe air whereas the salmon and coral do not. With these distinctions we already are on the way to zoology's classification systems of vertebrates and invertebrates. And because each thing is practically and theoretically related in specific ways to other things, we need to trace out the linkages among natural phenomena for proper understanding and successful practice. So too in natural law we understand that people have distinctive characteristics or natures.

3) *Life is Marked by Growth to Fulfill Potential.*
The essential characteristics of things actualize or unfold in the course of life—this is what we normally think of as development. Related to this is the fact that different dimensions of, and relationships among, things will differently come into play during the various stages of the growth during the life course of a plant, an animal, or a person. For example, once we learn that what we thought was an ugly duckling actually is an immature swan, it is not the case that the swimming creature actually changes its appearance. Rather, we are now more able to see it anew: to understand what it is right now, what it will become, and ways to nurture that development. Such knowledge obviously is crucial in environmental disciplines and practices. No planting-design project will be successful if we do not understand how far apart to plant seedlings with an eye toward how big the mature plant will be, how much sun or shade it will need, whether the plants around it will help or hinder its growth, and so.

What we learn is held and passed on by our traditions; but, a more systematic scientific elaboration is useful, even necessary, to maximize the positive relations among things that will enable each to maximally thrive in the ecological systems within which they belong. In short, these three assumptions about the world together lead us to understanding and acting on behalf of things. It is in this way that we are able to learn to do that which is most appropriate, most beneficial—what we normally would say is good for that thing or system of related things.

When we apply these three assumptions specifically to human beings, we find that humans have a distinctive set of characteristics or nature. While humans have many of the same sorts of biological features as other animals, we also have reason and self-determination, that is freedom to act and the ability to govern ourselves according to reason. In all these capacities—from learning to walk, talk and think and get others to respond helpfully, or to go along with our group or go a separate way—we find that we are social-political beings. Public life consists of education, work, and voting or holding political office, but in natural law theory, particularly for Aristotle, ethical-moral values and friend-ships that are now relegated to private life in our modern, individualistic world would also be part of the natural state of human beings as social-political.

In natural law, the idea is that people are essentially the same, human nature can be discerned by rational inquiry, and the characteristics of that human nature set parameters to what counts or is relevant to us. For example, the amount of mercury in the water we drink, a certain range of waves in the electromagnetic spectrum that we can perceive as visible light, and what our bosses think about our work all are relevant to what we do this week; the level of oxygen in the water matters to a salmon, but not to us since we neither need to nor are able to access it when swimming. Of course, what matters most for ethical decisions includes not only our physical features and needs to be healthy, but what is rele-vant to us in regard to private and public social life, learning to use language and to think, creative and imaginative activities, and so on.

Implications of these Assumptions

From the above three assumptions about the world that are made within the natural law framework, there follow two implications.

Our distinctive character indicates what we need for well being (what counts as human goods or values), and thus what are human rights and human obliga-tions.
Given that people, like all living organisms, dynamically grow and move toward their potential, we naturally have the capacity to make ethical decisions. But, given how complex and unpredictable life is, it is not easy to consider all the conditions that factor into a particular situation. Thus, in making a decision in any given situation we not only need to have a sound understanding of the case, we also need to be able make good pragmatic judgments—a capacity that Aris-totle called practical intelligence, as distinct from abstract scientific or philoso-phical knowing or more comprehensive wisdom. In the view of Aristotle, though we need legitimate knowledge of the way things are (in the rigorous sense of understanding the unvarying or universal laws of nature and mathe-matical-logical relationships), we also must be able to exercise judgment that remains bound up with the particularity of situations and differences that criti-cally matter.

Deciding on the proper ethical or political course of action in a particular cir-cumstance—how to put the multiple prescriptions into effect—is not a mechani-cal procedure; it requires subtle judgment or practical wisdom-intelligence.
There are no absolute grounds for deciding what is the right action, no fixed process for finding an answer. Rather, within the intricate web of actual circum-stances we are able to approximate the best answers and carry out the proper

actions when we have the disposition or regular habit (which is what Aristotle meant by virtue) as well as the supportive social context. Making and implementing ethical decisions depends on the capacity to judge and do the right thing at the right time in the right way. Such judgments require sophisticated understanding and substantial deliberation: judgment depends on knowing what is due and what is appropriate in each particular case, that is, a practical intelligence to discern and enact the right principles. (See Aristotle on prudence or practical wisdom (*phronēsis*) Book 2, v-xiii, MacIntyre (1981), chapter 12: "Aristotle's Account of the Virtues," and Nussbaum.)

Even Aristotle's famous dictum to follow the mean—the mid-course between extremes—is distinct from the mathematical sense of the term and much more a matter of experience and good judgment, as he makes clear:

> I call the mean in relation to the *thing* [anything that is mathematically divisible] whatever is equidistant from the extremes, which is one and the same for everybody; but I call mean in relation to *us* that which is neither excessive nor deficient, and this is not one and the same for all. For example, if ten is 'many' and two 'few' of some quantity, six is the mean if one takes it in relation to the thing, because it exceeds the one number and is exceeded by the other by the same amount; and this is the mean by arithmetical reckoning. But the mean in relation to *us* is not to be obtained in this way. Supposing that ten pounds of food is a large and two pounds a small allowance for an athlete, it does not follow that the trainer will prescribe six pounds; for even this is perhaps too much or too little for the person who is to receive it—too little for Milo [a famously strong wrestler from Southern Italy] but too much for one who is only beginning to train. Similarly in the case of running. In this way, then, every knowledgeable person avoids excess and deficiency, but looks for the mean and chooses it—not the mean of the thing, but the mean relative to us.
>
> (*Nicomachean Ethics*, Book 2 1106a20-b9)

Natural law holds that moral good and evil is a matter of promoting or frustrating the development of what we need to become fully persons, not only physically but in our social-political lives—a process that requires practical intelligence, that is, judgment based on experience.

Operationalizing the Dense Theory

Natural law posits that from the nature of individual and social human life a moral position follows that can be spelled out and operationalized in a relatively straightforward manner that is simultaneously rigorous and able to incorporate subtleties and differences within particular situations:

Given that human nature involves distinctive characteristics, we can describe our potential, our ideal possibilities. These are "goods."

If the human characteristic: *to be nurtured is*:	*The corresponding good*: *to be provided is*:
reason	knowledge
social life	love and friendship
biological health	proper diet and exercise

Elaborating the features that define human beings allows us to arrive at a non-arbitrary understanding of universal human goods: life itself, health, knowledge, freedom, dignity, love and friendship, property, reputation, happiness, and many others on which people have agreed for a long, long time. These goods are what we need to thrive as humans. From what is good for humans (what we need), our rights, obligations, and values follow. In turn, from these measures follow what we should *do*—prescriptive laws of conduct that all humans should follow. The application of the sequence of ideas to arrive at the conclusion, however, depends not only on scientific knowledge but also on practical judgment. In their simplest form, the basic elements and logic of practical reasoning that can help lead us to identifying the right action in a particular place and time are as follows. At base, however, it is extensive experiences with the subtleties and differences of things throughout their different states of development or modes of existing that need to be taken into consideration in determining what course of action to follow in a particular circumstance. Balancing conflicting needs among different parties affected by a possible course of action is commonly required, so that our practical judgments are political as well as ethical.

To take an example involving environmental decision making, Jim is a member of the city council, needing to decide how to vote next week on whether to support the regional transit plan that currently emphasizes a light-rail system with a new network of roadways. There have been two years of acrimonious debate, with parties making arguments on all sides, including the always interesting strange bedfellows whose usually divergent interests at least momentarily run parallel. There is a large and vocal "no more taxes" constituency that is opposed to mass transit on economic grounds, joined by various property-rights groups; at the same time, the overall region has a strong pro-environmental stance as part of its ethos, and thus supports mass transit in order to reduce energy consumption and pollution. The situation is complicated by the different points of view presented by special interest groups, advocates of all possible modes of transit, and dozens of expert analysts: the light-rail contingent and its consultants have one set of ideas and data; the bus advocates another; the bicycle and other-than-motorized groups their own social and environmental agendas. And, of course, there are the vendors, ranging from the asphalt and concrete lobbies wanting more roads to the German light-rail manufacturers and the high-tech companies touting computerized traffic control systems and remote-access to information about available parking spaces.

While he has studied the piles of reports and analyses, Jim also knows enough to be skeptical. It is not just that the different promoters have a vested interest in their preferred outcome—that is normal, it is just human nature to be biased in favor of self-interest or one's own value preferences. More than that though, from his time in office and from keeping up on similar projects around the country, Jim knows that the data presented, especially estimates of ridership and infrastructure costs—the financing analyses overall—are not at all trustworthy, principally because of unrealistic estimates up front about delays, design changes, materials costs, etc. And the environmental and social impact statements are controversial, no matter what they conclude. So, he knows that he does need to use such information, but finally will have to rely on his judgment, on his informed experience, especially because he wants his decision to balance a good choice among broad alternative visions that will impact the future of the region for decades with a practical focus on what will really work.

Old fashioned public-interest and common sense about costs are among his most important touchstones. Jim tries to explicitly keep track of the real goals he (and the citizens he represents) want to achieve: to reduce energy use, pollution, and frustration as people try to move around the area; to keep employment and the economy lively, which requires not only an efficient, cost-effective infrastructure but also a positive urban-regional image that attracts companies and talented people as residents. He knows from experience that getting stuck on a given technological solution—be it sexy and high-profile light rail or what seems obvious as "more of what works," with a deck added above the major highway lanes to double the capacity, coupled with a new system of suburb feeder roads—can make him lose track of the best way to get what is really needed, not just by the construction and particular user groups that will benefit from this or that outcome, but what will work best for the large number of taxpayers who will really bear the huge cost of the project.

Jim wants to explore whether the actual needs can be satisfied with another project, really another version of the projects already under consideration. The more he thinks about it, the more he is leaning toward advocating a big, dumb solution. A much larger network of smaller buses that would cover the city in a grid, allowing easy transfer without going downtown and no more than 10 minutes between buses, would go a long way to solving multiple problems at the same time. The solution is not sexy at all. But it uses the existing road system which is much, much cheaper than new roads or rail systems; a large part of the city bus system already runs on electric lines, limiting the vehicles' pollution, and the buses themselves (especially smaller ones) are not especially expensive. There is the usual reluctance to hire more transit employees—after all the U.S. is in an outsourcing, mood; but, opposite, there is a need for decent union jobs that really do some good locally. Not surprisingly, not even the bus advocates have proposed this approach, in part, it seems, because their consultants are promoting a combination of super-buses that would attract middle-class and suburban riders and a program of streamlined routes and fewer drivers to save costs.[3]

Key Elements of Natural Law

Natural law importantly is correlated with, and depends on, larger philosophical theories, especially traditional realist positions that distinguish between essential and accidental features of phenomena. Essential features of a person are those that define their character as human—classically that humans are rational animals (which includes sociability, friendship, and so on as Aristotle spells out in his Ethics and other works). In contrast, accidental features are those which vary from individual to individual, from society to society without making a difference in the fundamental characteristics that describe what a thing truly is. For example, if we hold that a person is a rational animal, then having a body and reasoning capacity are essential features, but whether one has red or black hair or is bald is only accidental and should not properly effect one's status, rights, and obligations as a human being (that what is proper in principle is frequently violated in human conduct indicates both that such actions indeed are unethical and provides a ground for appeal for justice, as happened regularly in the arguments for human rights).

A closely related distinction is between universal and conventional features. Some acts in society are done out of convention, or social habit and these are so ingrained or enculturated within us that we might begin thinking they are universal, but this is not necessarily so. For example, it is a convention that in some countries one drives on the right side of the road and in others on the left—what is proper is relative to the time and place. Such customs and associated obligations and liabilities (with possible sanctions or even punishments, like fines for driving on the wrong side of the road, for culpability in the case of an accident) are often woven deeply into the social fabric and can be taken for granted, even be assumed to be natural. There are various reasons why one should follow such customs—for social acceptance, to maintain order and safety, and so on. But, these relative and changeable conventions do not bind one everywhere and at all times: they are not universal. In contrast, we can say there is a universal obligation not to harm innocent people, which could also happen if one drove on the wrong side of the road. It is this deeper universal prescription that grounds the obligation to drive only on the side of the road that initially is arbitrarily and conventionally specified in a given place and time. Here we also can be sensitive to the fact that there are many cultural and historical variations to the way the essential features of humans are expressed and accommodated.

Of course, there is not full agreement on what essential features are—we have many areas of disagreement among people of good will and intention, and many dimensions of the world that we do not understand. The systematic theoretical and pragmatic discussion about essential features has been going on for 2500 years, which means that many issues have been resolved (a great strength of this ethical position); at the same time, lively debates continue and are vital to this ethical approach. It has been used as leverage against what successfully have been argued to be unjust or wrongful social systems. As the U.S. *Declaration of Independence* states: "All men [sic] are created equally and endowed with certain inalienable rights"—a universal natural law position—since all humans have the same essential nature. In this case, "men" would be interpreted by natural law theorists to mean human being, with the conclusion that women and people of all races and economic status should have the right to an education, to vote, and so on because their gender and race are only accidental and not essential human features. (This point is taken up in the Enlightenment as the ideas of universal human rights are being developed—though colonial projects clearly frustrate the ideal).

In fact, there currently is a resurgence of a variation on this view in postcolonial and human-rights arguments, especially in the move by figures who are politically leftist to a "new universalism" (Badiou 2003; Cheah 2006). Given the huge power and inertia of societies, with their many mechanisms of enforcing conformity and achieving continuity, it is not surprising, even if there is theoretical agreement on what is true, that implementing it by changing social norms and behavior is another matter. The processes of gaining more knowledge and using it in ethical decisions, and of reflecting on whether our categories and practices are consistent and adequate to what we know, are integral to natural law and a part of the environmental decision making we are considering in this book. For example, do we know how much of a given pollutant is substantially harmful and thus should not be allowed? Do we know how such pollution actually is spread so that we can specify who is responsible for stopping the practice and how they would do so? Would it make sense to say that just as persons have rights as persons, so also ecosystems or animals would also have rights?—remember that corporations are recognized to have rights and obligations and that Kant has a special or restricted definition of person as we shall see later in this chapter.

Despite theoretical and empirical differences of opinion on what constitutes an essential feature, there is agreement that if the essential features of a thing or a person are the same everywhere, at all times, then they can be considered universal. These essential, universal features are discernable—even if at a given point we do not fully know or agree on them since our knowledge necessarily is finite and incomplete at any specific time (this is part of what we mean when we say that knowledge is situated). Two important limitations are recognized and actively incorporated into the decision making processes of natural law, limitations that exist simply because that is the nature of our existence: there are limits to what we know and can know, and there are many unavoidable conflicts between incommensurables (choices and actions that have no common measure and are therefore incomparable or incompatible). One essential feature that is generally agreed upon by ethicists is that all persons have natural rights—the rights to develop their potential. This essential feature has a corollary—the universal obligation to behave in ways that nurture rather than frustrate these potentials. (For further reading, see "Descriptive and Prescriptive Laws," Bayles and Henley 1983)

Additionally, almost all cases that are ethically problematic involve situations in which some harms will unavoidably result, as we have discussed earlier in examining the nature of a dilemma. If it were not the case that some harm is unavoidable, the situation would very likely not be problematic in the first place, but only a matter of whether we would choose to act in one way or another.

Decisions become problematic in large part when and because some things are not clear or people disagree on a way to decide which harms to accept in the name of which goods.

- **Are the dangers to those cleaning up toxic waste sites, or living next to them, worth accepting in order to continue producing and using products that contain such toxins?**
- **Is the spatial, social, and economic organization of cities to be accomplished and maintained on the prospect of an increase in the dollar valuation of individual parcels of property?**
- **In such decisions which will simultaneously promote one value or potential while frustrating another?**

The difficulty of deciding what to do often is not only matter of deciding which values outweigh other values, but of encountering what lies behind that problem—that is, the types of value that are non-commensurate.

For example, there is no common denominator between the good of knowledge and that of health to which both could be reduced. Nor is there any commensurability between two human lives—there is no ethical reason why one person would have superior rights compared to another. (Incommensurability is also a point of contention within the theory of utilitarianism and will therefore be elaborated further in that section.)

Natural law's theory of the actual-potential nature of things, including humans with the capacity to reason and make informed, pragmatic judgments, not only provides an explanation of how we can discern the measure for ethical decisions but directly leads to the major principles presented in chapter 3. For example, the principles of benefiting others (beneficence) and not doing harm (non-maleficence) are alternative formulations of the obligation to nurture and not hinder, much less damage, the potential of our characteristic features. A parallel formulation to Aristotle's position is found in the ancient Hippocratic oath, in which a central passage stipulates (in a translation less modern than that which we used in chapter 3) that a physician must promise: "I will follow that system of regimen which, according to my ability and judgment, I consider for the benefit of my patients, and abstain from whatever is deleterious and mischievous." (Hippocrates [460–370 BCE], (1964, v).

Additionally, the principle of autonomy—independent self-determination of one's action and course of life—is in fact assumed in the possibility of making free ethical decisions in the first place. Finally, the principle of justice follows from the fact that human nature and rights are regarded as universal: in a society where inevitably there will be differences in wealth and prestige among citizens, each person's right would ordinarily be the same, modifiable only by one's historical, free decisions and actions. So, for example, if I acquire a fortune and decide to give it to charity rather than to my three already prosperous children, there is no injustice in their having less than they might have otherwise, even though several generations later this might be connected with a situation in which a great-grandchild is too poor to become well educated or eat well. (Aristotle's formal definition of justice specifies that "equals ought to be treated equally and unequals unequally." This obviously is an entirely abstract and general formulation of justice (a feature shared by the definitions of justice in utilitarianism and deontology) that needs to be interpreted in context, and requires thinking through changing cultural insights and blindnesses about human equality. For more discussion see chapter 2 on the principle of justice.) For discussion of the critiques of natural law's assumptions and approaches, see exercises 4.4 and 4.5 at the end of this chapter.

Utilitarianism

Utilitarianism is another major ethical theory and began as a movement in social reform by the social reformer and philosopher Jeremy Bentham (1748–1842). It was continued by the economist and philosopher James Mill, and substantially developed by his son, John Stuart Mill (1806–1873), who presented the classic formulation in his influential text *Utilitarianism* in 1861. This theory also is sometimes known as teleology from the Greek word *telos* meaning end or term of a goal-directed project.

This is often discussed in terms of means and ends—that our actions are means to certain outcomes or ends. The theory is often oversimplified and put in terms of the ends justifying the means, but, as we shall see, it is a bit more involved that that. The theory also bears certain features that reflect its birth in the modern era—the affirmation of reason and the rejection of political or religious authority as well as the idea that there are immutable truths. From the standpoint of utilitarianism, we can and must depend on reason and evidence to establish our ethical obligations.

Key Ideas

The grounding principle of utilitarianism is that of right conduct which is usually formulated thusly: "Conduct is right or wrong depending on whether it produces as much net utility as anything else that could be done" (Bayles and Henley 1983, 86). *"Net utility"* is the balance or sum of good (positive) and bad (negative) consequences. In common parlance it is often referred to as the greatest good. The definition of utility in general has caused much misunderstanding, especially in popularized reformulations of the basic ideas. Hence, it is important to use more precise wording to understand the basic view that an act's rightness or wrongness depends on whether it leads to what is useful, that is, to pleasure or happiness. In fact, Bentham's approach continues an older Roman tradition from Epicurus that holds that what is useful is that which provides the most pleasure and least pain.

Utilitarianism holds that moral good and evil is a matter of consequences. It is a form of consequentialism that posits that what is good and evil is determined by the outcomes of ordinary human intellect, sensations, and actions.

The creed that accepts "utility" or the "greatest happiness principle" as the foundation of morals holds that actions are right in proportion as they tend to promise happiness; wrong as they tend to produce the reverse of happiness. Thus, some scholars argue that the good consists of happiness or pleasure; but because this concept leads to oversimplification and considerable misunderstandings, sophisticated utilitarianism maintains that good or happiness amounts to the satisfaction of broader interests and/or intellectual and aesthetic preferences and social sympathy—much broader than physical satisfaction or pleasure only. Note, what is moral is defined and justified by non-moral values, or those values that are considered good in themselves, such as freedom or happiness. In other words, what is considered right conduct is based on what enables people to be free and fulfill potential. For example, even if professional environmental education is costly, involves academic disciplines and departments reorganizing what they do, requires long hours of study and internship, and results in a career with less pay than international finance, it would be useful-good for a person to be able to receive an engineering or design education that includes not only an understanding of materials, their energy implications, and the usual pragmatics of safety and endurance, but also of the pollution involved in their production, use, and disposal, and of the impact on community ways of life and the ecological environment.

As a consequence of the principle of right conduct, the conclusion concerning how we must act—our obligation—follows: "In all circumstances we ought to produce the greatest possible balance of value over disvalue for all persons affected (or the least possible balance disvalue if only adverse results can be brought about)" (Beauchamp and Childress, p. 20). If several alternatives have the same net utility, any one of them is permitted; if one alternative has the greatest net utility, it is obligatory and none other is permitted. A classic example of net utility is posed in the question of whether it is right to allow one person to die if that death means saving the lives of five other people. For strict utilitarians, the answer would be yes.

The above presents the basic theory of act utilitarianism, which is often modified by rule utilitarianism, which is intended to deal with the problem that we might accept immoral choices over common sense evaluations of an obviously wrong action in the name of a greater good. To keep with our example above, in applying the principle of right conduct to actual circumstances, it might appear that the greatest net utility involves breaking promises, telling lies, or even committing murder. As a preventative to this prospect, rule utilitarianism asserts that we must not compromise the rule of maximum utility just for the sake of individual or peculiar situations. In other words, we must keep utility consistent with common convention, that is, maintain general rules. Thus, it is held that "conformity of an act to a valuable rule makes the act right." Here a moral rule is interjected between the principle of utility and the individual action. In this framework, a professional code of ethics is a type of moral rule that is interjected between the principle of utility (greatest good) and what an individual practitioner might decide to do when working or a project with a client.

Where an act's rightness or wrongness depends on its consequences, we need to look for a first principle of moral conduct that would provide the standard of morality. We find this measure in the end result of human action, which itself is determined by utility. For example, happiness would be such an end result since it is taken to be inherently desirable or valuable for its own sake. In the course of time, our actions cause certain other circumstances to come about (ends), and the value of those results provides the measure of the propriety of those actions—which can either be evaluated after the fact or imaginatively when considering alternative possible courses of action. This can be diagramed in the following way:

The Act (the means or historical cause) → leads to the outcome or End
The Act is validated by ← the outcome or End

Further Clarification of Key Concepts and Objections
Utilitarianism has long insisted that the correct interpretation of its key concepts shows that common objections to them are misunderstandings of the theory. To the objection that the theory presents a degrading view in affirming that there is no higher end than mere pleasure, and displays only a low empirical description of what many people do, utilitarianism argues that, in fact, our human faculties are far greater than mere animal appetites, and that it is entirely proper to hold that the gratification of these complex and higher faculties is happiness (a position not unlike Aristotle's). This is evident in a utilitarian's choice of self-sacrifice for some perceived greater good. The theory does not intend to argue on behalf of some brutish pleasure, but for the pleasure of the intellect, of feel-

ings and imagination (for example, a well-performed symphony), or of moral sentiments such as charity or generosity. A purely physical contentment is not to be confused with what is intended here. People do act on behalf of higher modes of happiness and indeed can believe that it is better to have higher standards and be dissatisfied than to have low standards and be easily satisfied. As Mill puts it: "It is better to be a human being dissatisfied than a pig satisfied; better to be Socrates dissatisfied than a fool satisfied. And if the fool, or the pig, are of a different opinion, it is because they only know their own side of the question. The other party to the comparison knows both sides" (p. 10).

Further, the criteria for utility or positive value are not just a matter of what counts for the person acting; to the contrary, the theory stresses the social character of ethical issues and outcomes. Utilitarianism stresses the "greatest amount of happiness altogether," that is, that of the agent and others involved. The final goal of utilitarianism is only intelligible in terms of both good actions and the general cultivation of nobleness and character (as also with Aristotle):

> According to the greatest happiness principle, as above explained, the ultimate end, with reference to and for the sake of which all other things are desirable—whether we are considering our own good or that of other people—is an existence exempt as far as possible from pain, and as rich as possible in enjoyments, both in point of quantity and quality; the test of quality and the rule for measuring it against quantity being the preference felt by those who, in their opportunities of experience, to which must be added their habits of self-consciousness and self-observation, are best furnished with the means of comparison. This, being according to the utilitarian opinion the end of human action, is necessarily also the standard of morality, which may accordingly be defined "the rules and precepts for human conduct," by the observance of which an existence such as has been described might be, to the greatest extent possible, secured to all mankind; and not to them only, but, so far as the nature of things admits, to the whole sentient creation. (11–12)

To the further objection that happiness is not actually the goal of human life—and that utilitarianism thus is not a rational view because happiness is unattainable or not truly a higher value—Mill argues that pragmatically we do not seek some kind of rapture but, in a turbulent and difficult life, only some positive dimension, some reprieve. It is common sense that we try to have the best life we can. As to the objection that happiness would be a matter of intense excitement, such a view is based on selfishness, on finding more and more exotic experiences as we become jaded with the ordinary. In utilitarianism, this is to be set aside in favor of fellow feeling. Positively, utilitarianism holds that the evils of the world can be reduced by human care and effort, which can conquer many of the major sources of suffering. The emphasis is on the capacity of everyone to perceive and act on behalf of the greatest good. We often see that people do sacrifice their own happiness for the sake of the happiness of others. This would be the whole point of virtue: to gain what is good for others, to multiply human happiness.

As a correlate, decisions and actions need to be strictly impartial: disinterested and benevolent. Here we see the importance of social goods. Our ethical questions become "How do we put the interest of the individual and the whole into harmony (with ethical decisions, and finally with laws and social arrangements)?" "How can we learn to associate one's own happiness and conduct with universal happiness (a question of both education and social opinion and practice)?" In social good we find the relation of justice to utility. The tendency is to see justice as an absolute since it would appear a psychological and social fact that humans are disposed to think that our subjective feelings are a disclosure of some objective reality. But, if we inquire into the feelings that lead us to determine what is just or unjust, we can indeed see that justice is a kind of utility—that is, justice is a form of achieving the greatest good.

What would the feelings be like that would lead us to determine that something is either just or unjust? Can you give an example or describe some of them?

Empirical consideration, Mill contends, shows that we hold it unjust to deprive people of what belongs to them by legal right or moral right, in terms of what one deserves, or because it was promised, or because it is a matter of impartially determining what ought to count, or what is in the interest of equality. From these observations, we can induce the common linkage of law and morality, which we see in the connection of justice and law when we speak of "such laws as ought to exist" or think of moral obligations as more or less the same as legal obligations. Hence, we tend to consider right that which we think a person ought not to be punished for and wrong as that for which they should be punished. Here we see that morality is demarked from mere expediency. It would seem that the origins of such feelings lie in the impulse of self-defense and feelings of sympathy for others. These feelings become integrated into, and subordinated to, the fully social dimension of concern for the general good. Justice and rights, then, have to do with the general utility for the whole of society, for example, "When we call anything a person's right, we mean he has a valid claim on society to protect him in his possession of it, either by force of law or by that of education and opinion" (p. 52).

It is not surprising that different nations and peoples have different ideas of justice; but, within those differences about remuneration, taxation, or punishment, for example, one can distinguish underlying principles, such as whether the expectation and measure of what is just is equal effort or equal production. How then to decide among appeals to conflicting definitions of justice? Utilitarianism contends that practically it can settle "unresolvable conflict," as in cases where we are not deciding between good and bad, but between valid and irreducible obligations when the demands of the situation are incompatible. In these cases, Mill maintains that social utility alone can decide the course of action. However, this does not mean that justice is reducible to what is merely expedient, since it is "the most sacred and binding part of morality" and the route to peace. Following the maxim of treating all equally well (as deserved) will lead to the greatest happiness. The interests of all need to be considered, so that the social state might be a society among equals.

Though utilitarianism's application procedure is a calculus, it is not a simple calculus of looking at what directly would happen if we proceeded along a proposed course of action with predictable results. For example, it is not a matter of asking if it is right or wrong to build a dam across the river if it will produce so much electricity and profit at the cost of flooding so many acres and displacing such a number of farmers. Rather, the injunction to act so as to provide the greatest net utility requires that we act according to the best of all possibilities. That is, in deciding what we must do, we first must consider all alternatives. Though it is not always appreciated, utilitarianism requires that we be highly imaginative. We must imagine as many possible alternatives as we can, many of which will only emerge in the course of considering the most obvious ones and seeking to replace the dimensions that are most problematic (as one does in the process of combining features from multiple design alternatives or in reaching a negotiated agreement on the most acceptable course of action in the case of a dispute). See also wicked problems in chapter 1.

> *For each possible alternative in deciding on a course of right action within a utilitarian framework, we must:*
>
> 1. Sum up the positive consequences
> 2. Sum up the negative consequences
> 3. Subtract 2 from 1 to get the balance.

Generating a list of all possible alternatives raises the problem of aggregating the different possible consequences that we can conjure up when trying to make an ethical decision. We must have or find a common unit for different sorts of consequences—economic, political, psychological, health, aesthetic, and so on. (Note the contrast with natural law, which would contend that such values are incommensurable.) Mill argues that quantifying different dimensions into standard units can be done by experienced persons, that is, by experts. But would not each person need to do this for herself? Mill believes everyone can if they carefully follow social customs, which means that we do not start from scratch each time we have to make a decision. Rather, we can use what we have learned about and agreed upon though our common social experiences—which are held and implemented through laws and opinions—to come to a decision. In short, in addition to our fundamental principle of net utility we have as a set of secondary principles some general social practices (compare to Barry's indifference map as discussed at the end of chapter 4). This is the basis for distinguishing rule from act utilitarianism: while act utilitarianism involves measuring an individual act's rightness or wrongness by its consequences, rule utilitarianism is based on "consequences that generally, or as a rule, tend to flow from a certain kind of act (Punzo 1969, 87). As we have seen above, the point of the modification provided by rule utilitarianism is to ensure that individual decisions or acts do not fly in the face of social insights and beliefs. (In moving from consideration of an act in itself toward the consideration of the act as a general rule, utilitarianism comes closer to Kant and deontology.)

Apply Utilitarianism to the Interpretation of the Principles

We described above how utilitarianism addresses the principles of beneficence and autonomy. Now consider what you have learned about utilitarianism in light of the other principles and rules—informed consent, truthfulness, loyalty, confidentiality, and conflict of interest.

For example, how would utilitarianism approach truthfulness? How can we understand truthfulness in utilitarian terms? Try this for each principle and rule connecting each with the concept of net utility.

Because utilitarianism includes all the relevant outcomes, both positive and negative, in its calculations, it is argued by its advocates that this theory is especially useful in resolving conflicts among alternate claims and obligations, for example, in the case of resource allocations or in working out creative compromises among disagreeing parties.

Utilitarianism, as natural law and deontology, leads to the ethical principles considered in detail in chapter 3 (autonomy, beneficence, non-maleficence, and justice). For example, saying that good consequences must be chosen or followed over bad consequences, affirms the principles of beneficence and non-maleficence. In holding that human reason is perfectly well able to evaluate consequences and draw conclusions among alternatives, it is deeply affirms autonomy in its respect for persons. In contending that we are obliged, in our social context, to choose and act on behalf of the greatest possible balance of value over disvalue, utilitarianism asserts the importance of justice. (Without running through all the sub-dimensions and rules covered in chapter 3, the same can be shown for informed consent, truthfulness, confidentiality, loyalty, conflict of interest, and so on.) For discussion of the critiques of utilitarianism's core assumptions and approaches, see exercise 4.4 at the end of this chapter.

Deontological (and Contractarian)[5] Ethics

The basic ethical standpoint of deontology is that duty defines what is good. Since duty functions as the moral standard, the theory is called deontology, from the Greek word *deon*, which means that which is binding or a duty. Immanuel Kant (1720–1804) is the philosopher most prominently connected to deontology, which developed through his major works: *Foundations of the Metaphysics of Morals*, the *Critique of Practical Reason, Metaphysics of Morals, and Prolegomena to Any Future Metaphysics.* Later scholars also made significant contributions to the development of the theory, particularly W. D. Ross (1877–1971) with his works, *The Right and the Good* and *Ethic of Prima Facie Duties.* The leading contemporary work in this tradition is by John Rawls, especially his book *A Theory of Justice* (1971).

The major features of the theory are its goal for impartiality and reasoning, the recognition of the need to rise above self-interest, and clarity of motives when determining right and wrong, which derive from the major moral touchstones of deontology:

- It provides for universalization
- Duties follow from these universal principles (such as the principle of justice)
- People are seen as autonomously valuable, as ends in themselves, never as means only.

As do other modern philosophers, Kant emphasizes the role of universal human reason and—echoing the emphasis on science—seeks to articulate the universal laws of behavior. In arguing for practical reason he states: "the rationality of each person imposes on conduct, a requirement independent of our particular desires, passions, and feelings." A sharp critic of utilitarianism, Kant wants more austere reason to function as the ground of moral distinctions and decisions, with a sense of *duty* replacing the drive toward pleasure (remember that utilitarianism has counter-objections), arguing that a morally good will is neither augmented by utility nor diminished by uselessness. For example, in court we are obliged to testify truthfully, not on the basis of a desired outcome or in terms of likely personal loss or gain. To be morally honorable, Kant holds, we cannot look for the ulterior motive or end; rather, what is morally proper is done from a sense of duty.

Kant, as Aristotle and Mill, believes that his system corresponds to the common viewpoint. He argues that everyone has the experience of understanding that an act of kindness has moral worth, and though we properly feel satisfaction in performing such acts, we do not do so in order to obtain that feeling—such a motive would tarnish the purity of that act. As to the proper motive, Kant contends that it is the "fact that the character of moral duty is such that we are obliged to act morally, not for any extra-moral effect or consequence, but simply for morality's sake." (Punzo, 1969, 96).[6] The position wants to "give reason a primary role in moral life by taking the view that reason a priori provides the rules for moral behavior without any reference to possible objects of the sensuous indication" (Punzo 1969, 94). In short: an act is good precisely because it an act that it is my duty to perform.

For Kant, our moral obligations are what he calls *categorical imperatives*. An imperative is a maxim in the form of a statement or command. To say that a given action is required or categorical declares the "action to be *objectively necessary* in itself without any reference to any other end"—a clearly anti-teleological stance (Punzo 1969, 97). (Here we see a direct contrast with utilitarianism, which, as explained in the previous section, is teleological.) This does not imply that we have no freedom of choice, but that the grounds advanced to show that we must perform the action are rationally valid for all reasonable beings. In order to express the grounds for our obligation and simultaneously provide a way to test possible injunctions, Kant presented a formula to summarize the categorical character of our obligations:

> Act only according to the maxim by which you can at the same time will that it should become a universal law.
>
> (*Foundations of the Metaphysics of Morals*, 39)[7]

Since the formal statement is complex and difficult to understand, Kant provided four alternative versions and elaborations. Though we do not need to consider all the subtleties of these variations, we can note some basic differences in emphasis, such as his saying that "the categorical imperative states that we should make only those features decisive in our actions which we could at the same time make universal laws, that is, the factors governing all action."(Punzo 1969, 97). The value of the categorical imperative for Kant is that it presents an action as something binding because of the very character of the act itself. Such an action would not be conditional, as if it depended on achieving some other goal; rather, the unconditional character amounts to its being universal.

Deontology holds that moral good and evil is not a matter of consequences, but of the unconditional requirement that we do our duty. We are obligated to act in a way that would be universalizable—rationally valid for all humans.

We can rationally test possible statements to see if they can function as universal laws by examining their logical and practical consistency or contradiction. If we have the question as to whether we may lie, we can try out a statement, such as "One ought to always tell the truth," to see if we would reasonably agree on its validity as a universal law. Or we can try out a more extreme example to illustrate our point and ask, "Would breaking promises whenever convenient work to direct our moral and social practices in all circumstances?" Of course not. If we all broke promises whenever we wished, there would be no way to depend upon each other, accomplish much on a personal or public scale, or develop a society of trust in one another. The possible statement that it is acceptable to break promises when convenient fails as a maxim. What about the opposite: that we should keep our promises at all times? That would work as a maxim. Though it would sometimes be inconvenient or even problematic (if we were called on to testify about the wrongdoings of someone who threatens us), the overall system of human relationships and accomplishments would still work very well—perhaps, we would say, even depend on having the courage to do our duty. Thus, "Keep your promises" would be a categorical imperative.

Categorical Imperatives and Universal Laws

What are some universal laws that a deontologist might put forward? We already have identified several possible ones:

- One ought to always tell the truth.
- We should keep our promises.

What other maxims might you put forward?

Test them. Ask yourself tough questions to really determine whether you think they are truly universal—or do they have exceptions?

Or, to take another test issue, we can ask, "Is it right to tell a lie?" We can think this through as follows, starting with the extreme case: if everyone lied all the time—if it were a universal law that this is what everyone should do, everywhere and all the time—we would have chaos; such a practice could not possibly work. Thus "Everyone should lie all the time" is self-contradictory as a universal law and fails to pass the test. It is not allowed. (John Rawls, whose ideas are well worth exploring, further develops what we would need to pursue in regard to Kant's concept of justice, as treated above in chapter 3.) There are, then, for Kant and rule deontology, some absolute principles and rules.[8] In another formulation, Kant implies that we could think of the imperative as Positively, deontological approaches also successfully include the past accumulation and commitment of actions and obligations that still hold amongst us (another difference from utilitarianism). For a discussion of the critiques of deontology's concepts of universality and reason see exercise 4.7 at the end of this chapter.

Kant provides other formulations of deontology that stress the importance of persons as a measure. This has to do with whether we treat people as ends unto themselves or as means to some other end. For example, Kant says, "Act so that you treat humanity, whether in your own person or in that of another, always as an end and never as a means only" (FMM, 47). Here the categorical imperative focuses on humans as ends in themselves, and on society as a community of ends. The ethical realm and its universal laws, then, do not lead to some external goal. Instead, the end implied is inherent in the very character of humans as moral beings—persons have absolute and intrinsic worth. The unconditional character of moral obligations would require that rational beings have such status as ends in themselves, since unless something or one is of absolute worth there could be no absolute principle for reason and action (everything would be only conditional). But, for Kant, rational beings are just such unconditional ends.

Kant tells us: "Act so that you treat humanity, whether in your own person or in that of another, always as an end and never as a means only" (FMM, 47). Persons have absolute and intrinsic worth.

Given this very strong affirmation, to follow the consequences of his position, it is important to note that Kant has a particular and distinctive definition of a moral person. The question of who or what qualifies as a person is critical. For Kant it is not equivalent to being genetically a human being. Rather, it is a higher condition connected with having reason. Typical Kantian criteria for personhood include:
- reasoning: the developed capacity to solve problems
- self-consciousness
- self-motivated and self-monitored activity

You may notice that qualifications for personhood here are very different from the views of natural law, which are thought of in terms of the potential to actualize an essential nature, and not a certain already developed state of achievement, as deontologists do (though that would matter for the ability to make one's own decisions). Theory and empirical research investigating the stages of moral development have been elaborated by Carol Gilligan (who also has been involved in work related to the ethic of care as noted in chapter 1); others, such as Kohlberg, have worked to show that it is applicable cross-culturally, as would be required for the requisite Kantian universality.

Like natural law and utilitarianism, the deontological position also leads to a particular approach to the principles (autonomy, beneficence, non-maleficence, justice) and the rules (informed consent, truthfulness, confidentiality, loyalty, conflict of interest) that are articulated in chapter 3, though with some differences in definition and emphasis). For example, Kant develops an especially strong version of autonomy, since rational beings (and only rational beings) are precisely those who can propose ends to themselves, that is, serve as, provide, or be their own "ultimate limiting conditions" (FMM, 49). While other beings' goals are set by what they are (by their natures), as rational beings we can establish our own goals. In ordinary English, we would say "Humans do not exist for the sake of the goals that we set; goals exist for the sake of persons." We are not only subject to the moral law, we are its basis and its legislators. Note, the autonomous character of rational beings does not lead to their isolation from one another, but to community because we are autonomous precisely inso far as we are open to the inclusion of all other rational beings in community.

Beneficence and non-maleficence are stressed through the way Kant argues that the good—which we must do—is the same thing as our duty. When we act out of a sense of duty, we are acting for the good. Justice also is central since, as moral lawgivers, what rational beings legislate to themselves for their own ends needs to apply universally. What is just is precisely that which rational beings would decide upon and consent to as the basis for social governance of all actions without being based on moving toward to advantage or disadvantage of anyone within its universal sphere of application. A position congruent with the absolute and unconditional worth of all rational beings as ends in themselves (FMM, 49). (Again, this blindness to difference is consistently developed by Rawls as well.)

In a thoughtful, critical application of deontology to architecture, Kim Dovey applies Rawls' approach, "counter to both absolutist and utilitarian" positions, as a basis for establishing ethical criteria in practice. He finds that this approach is very compatible with the architectural profession's use of imagination, saying that Rawls' "'veil of ignorance' test should be easily incorporated into the practice of 'reflection-in-action' as one way of reframing problems. While this may or may not resolve the dilemmas, it offers the possibility of negotiating ethical positions in a manner that pays respect to the uniqueness of design problems and to the indeterminacies that both plague practice and keep it interesting" (1993, 27, 32–33).

Ethic of Care

The ethic of care has foundations in Sarah Ruddick's writings on the practice of mothering, *Maternal Thinking: Toward a Politics of Peace,* and particularly Carol Gilligan's work, *In a Different Voice,* on girls' moral development. Ruddick in particular argued that morality is gendered, and daily life is fragmented into a division of moral labor. The rationale for this is rooted in historic development related to family, state, and the economy, particularly divisions of labor in tasks of governing, regulating social order, and managing public institutions, that were men's domain historically. In contrast, the tasks of sustaining private personal relationships have been taken up by—or some might say imposed upon —women. The genders have been conceived in the first place in terms of special and distinctive moral projects. This has had the function of preparing us for our socially defined domains. Gilligan's moral theories stemmed from her concerns about gender inequity and the scientific tradition of the day: Piaget's studies of moral development were conducted with a sample of boys playing marbles. Piaget rationalized this gender-biased strategy by claiming that when they included girls in the study they "complicated interrogatory in relation to what we know about boys." Girls' different ways of negotiating simply were not seen as germane to the psychology of rules.

Similarly, Kohlberg's research on moral development also used an all-male sample, and he equated moral development with justice reasoning. In response feminist scholars argued that for women, morality is shaped more by caring relationships, whereas for men, morality is shaped more by compliance to rational rules regarding rights. There is competing evidence of the gender differences put forward by Gilligan. But as Marilyn Friedman (1985) points out, the "difference hypothesis" has significance for moral philosophy even if gender differences are debunked. The significance in this gender analysis is in revealing a lopsided preoccupation of moral theories with universal and impartial conceptions and the relative disregard for particular interpersonal relationships.

Thus what came to be known by some as a feminist ethics began with a critique of both gender difference and the nearly exclusive focus on justice, abstract rationality, rights and autonomy, which was said to be a masculine bias. As a result, feminists explored an alternative focus on care and a more relational ethic based upon it. However, as theory and research on the ethic of care has continued in the decades since its inception in the 1970s, it has articulated dimensions of ethics and moral reasoning that go beyond gender differences and are more fundamentally about articulating alternative approaches to moral reasoning that can be expressed by anyone.

The ethic of care posits that at the foundation of moral behavior is feeling and sentiment. This ethical principle is based in part on the idea that caring for people, being in tune to emotional needs, and taking a relational approach to decision making involves moral values. It sees people as interdependent and focuses on empathy and relationships. It posits that all human relationships can be characterized in terms of equality and attachment, and both inequality and detachment are grounds for moral concern. The ethic of care also offers important critiques of more traditional moral theories; it challenges the primacy of rationality, and the notion of the autonomous self. For further discussion and exercises exploring the critique of the autonomous self see exercise 4.2 at the end of this chapter. Whereas psychologists and philosophers aligning the self and morality with distance and autonomy have viewed feelings as an impediment, from a care perspective, feelings are a strength and detachment is the problem.

Since its inception in the 1970s the ethic of care has articulated dimensions of ethics that go beyond gender differences into a broader alternative and *relational* approach to morality.

Since its inception, numerous scholars have further outlined an ethic of care and have argued that it can and should be a distinct ethic (see especially Noddings, Gilligan, Baier). For example, Noddings points out that many women don't approach moral problems as problems of abstract principles and reasoning. Rather, they approach moral problems more through the concrete elements of situations and a regard for themselves as caring. Care locates morality primarily in the pre-conscious of the one-caring. Noddings argues that morality as an active virtue requires two feelings:

1. *natural caring*: An initial, enabling sentiment. We act on behalf of others because we want to. 1 way to understand this is to think of a mother's caring for her child—it is not considered ethical, but natural.

2. *a remembrance of caring and being cared for*: This is a matter of love and memory intertwined. Here we connect to a moment of "I must" in response to the plight of another. Even in cases where we feel conflicted ("I must—I don't want to") in response to another's plight, we can remember moments of caring and being cared for and we may reach toward this memory and let it guide our conduct.

If we talk about "I must," then we need to examine the notion of obligation. Sometimes when we automatically care, want equals ought; at other times, "I must do something" shifts to "something must be done." So when do we take this on as a personal responsibility? What creates this sense of "I ought," this sense of responsibility? For Kant, the ethical is what we do out of duty, not love. In contrast, an ethic of care strives to maintain a caring attitude, so ethics is dependent upon natural caring, not superior to it as Kant suggests.

Apart from attempting to address gender differences, the ethic of care is a philosophical attempt to see an alternative ethic because of the hitherto overwhelming dominance of justice and rights in ethical theory. It is a way to explore dimensions of moral reasoning and ethical decision making that are not adequately captured in terms of rights or justice. For example, Baier (1995) challenges the "assumed supremacy of justice" among the moral virtues, further identifying Alasdair MacIntyre and Alison Jagger as part of this counterculture. Of course, theorists focusing on justice do recognize that other things matter besides justice. For example, Rawls incorporated the value of freedom in his work so that the denial of basic freedoms is considered an injustice. Still, Baier points out, Rawls claims that justice is the first virtue (of social institutions), and more communitarian virtues and social ideals are simply justice.

Some scholars have questioned whether care and justice are really at odds, or whether we should be substituting an ethic of care for an ethic of justice, particularly because, in a gender-biased world, women need more justice than they have historically received. In this vein, writers urge caution about accepting the values of caring as an ethic. More recently, scholars are recognizing that care is not a substitute or alternative to justice, and that they can coincide and co-exist.

Key Questions to Consider about Justice and Care:

- Are they compatible or incompatible ways of interpreting the same moral situation?
- Are care and justice both indispensable for adequate moral understanding?
- Should care supplement justice? Or the other way around?
- Is one more fundamental?
- Do both apply to all domains equally?

Not all feminists share the view that there is something like a separate and different ethic of care, but many are convinced that there is—and that any adequate morality must include elements that have come to be considered ethic of care. Even Lawrence Kohlberg, whose psychological studies of moral development initiated Gilligan's counterpoint of the ethic of care, has come to agree that both care and justice are essential elements in ethical decision making.

Gilligan's work on moral development demonstrates two co-existing moral perspectives grounded in different dimensions of relationships: a justice perspective, and a care perspective. Shifts in focus either to care or to justice change the definition of what constitutes a moral problem: the moral injunction of justice is not to act unfairly, which contrasts with care's moral injunction not to turn away from someone in need. Thus, Gilligan's studies focus on relationships between moral judgment and action, and examine how people construct moral conflicts and choices. Friedman (1985), however, articulates some of the doubts and reservations of other feminists, using Gilligan's work as a springboard to extend her theories on whether and how notions of care and justice overlap. Friedman maintains that care and justice overlap more than Gilligan has realized. Morally adequate care involves consideration of justice, so the concerns are not necessarily distinct moral perspectives. Even so, there are other important differences in moral orientation—the nature of the relationship to other selves and the underlying form of moral commitment.

Unlike reversible figure-ground images, then, justice and care are not oppositional. Justice is not necessarily uncaring nor is caring necessarily unjust.

Justice and care are both organizing frameworks for moral decisions. The metaphors shift, though, when considering each principle individually. The viewpoint of justice focuses more on hierarchy and balance in human relations. The framework of care focuses more on networks and webs in human relationships. The moral dilemmas around abortion are often used as an example to highlight the differences in these two frameworks. Typically framed in terms of justice, the debate focuses on conflicts of rights of the fetus and the pregnant woman, seeking to determine whose claims take precedence. But framed as a problem of care, Gilligan argues the dilemma shifts. The connection between the fetus and mother becomes the focus, and the question becomes whether it is caring or careless, responsible or irresponsible to extend or end this connection. Within a justice perspective care becomes the mercy that tempers justice. (Note, there is no ready vocabulary in moral theory to describe care as a moral perspective in and of itself.)

Many among those who have explored the ethic of care juxtapose the cluster of principles of justice, rights, and obligations with a cluster of principles revolving around care, relatedness, and trust. Some have argued that justice should be assigned to the public sphere, and care to the private, but some feminists challenge that traditional public-private split, and maintain that a satisfactory morality should offer guidance for moral concerns in any context—public, private, or anything in between. Others have argued that justice sets the moral minimums under which we ought not fall as well as absolute constraints for our goals, whereas care deals with questions of the good life or human value over and above obligatory minimums of justice. There is a similar kind of argument regarding the professional codes of ethics that posits these codes as offering moral minimums, but that real challenges in ethical decision making happens on a higher level beyond the bottom line of what one absolutely ought not to do. This makes sense because traditional moral theorists usually see morality as composed of constraints that limit our pursuits. In contrast, few moral theorists stress good relationships.

It is important to note that many advocates of an ethic of care are not calling for a substitution for existing ethical theories necessarily, but an alternative prospective to one universal organizing framework. The ethic of care requires us to see morality not as reciprocal non-interference (typical of the justice perspective), but as positive, reciprocal attachment. Moreover, the critique embedded in an ethic of care posits that, when you consider power and power differences, the idea of non-interference becomes problematic. For the relatively powerless, non-interference could be neglectful and isolating (Held 1985). Further, trust and intimacy create special vulnerabilities to harm.

The issue of power is not a small one within the ethic of care. Another critique that its proponents make is that other ethical theories assume equal power or ignore imbalances of power negating rights of certain individuals altogether. Kantian morality is meant to regulate relationships primarily between equals—and those who have rights. Not everyone is seen as a right-holder, however. Rights have usually been for the privileged. For example, Kant saw women as incapable of legislation; they could not vote and were thought to need the guidance of more rational males (Baier 1985). The same could be said for people of other races and the rationalization for slavery.

Interestingly, even today, when following formalized ethical procedures and guidelines for research and practice concerning a relationship between unequals, there is usually some kind of promotion of the weaker so appearance of equality is achieved. For example, children are treated as adults-to-be, and the ill and dying are treated as continuing their earlier, more potent selves. This masks what our relationships are to those who are more or less equal. (This also is connected to professional ethics in that there is an imbalance of power based on expertise, which involves knowing ahead of time the possible implications of certain design choices.

Another main challenge posed by the ethic of care is to Rationalism and the idea that reason must control unruly passions. Interestingly, Kohlberg was heavily influenced by the dominant Kantian tradition and Gilligan's work critiques both Kolhberg directly and the tradition as a whole. The rationalism of Rawls' contract theory is also deemed problematic in this critique. For example, Rawls posits that each of us has our own rational life plan, which may or may not include other people. For Rawls, individuals are also assumed to be concerned for the advancement of their own interests and care about the interests of others exists only insofar as it helps their interests. And, in matters of ethical decision making, Rawls requires that all parties be mutually disinterested in order to blind us to biases and enable justice to prevail. In contrast, Gilligan speaks of a satisfactory life as providing progress of affiliative relationships and argues that contracts and rationalism are less useful when we consider close relationships. For example, once we begin to consider notions of parental responsibility then the idea of contract seems to be an inadequate paradigm.

Noddings (1995) argues that different ethical systems are not equivalent simply because they include rules concerning the same issues or categories. We have already seen this in comparing the other major ethical theories described earlier in this chapter. Noddings considers the debates over whether an objective morality (that is, a set of universal categories and rules based on common human needs and characteristics) is possible. While she agrees that morality is somehow rooted in common needs, feelings and cognitions, she maintains that this commonality does not mean an objective morality is possible. It may be that a subjective caring—a longing for goodness—provides whatever universality and stability there is to what it means to be moral. And while she argues that there is a form of caring that is natural and accessible to all, Noddings is not trying to develop a set of universalizable moral judgments.

It would seem preferable to place an ethical ideal above principle as a guide to moral action because principles are meant to be universalizable. As Nietzsche points out, this generalizability depends on some notion of sameness. So to accept the principles we have to establish that human predicaments exhibit sufficient sameness. We can't do this without abstracting out larger issues and principles from concrete situations. In doing this we lose the very qualities that give rise to the moral question in the first place. So where does this leave us? Well, Noddings does say that we can still receive guidance from attempts to discover principles. She mentions the doctrine of prima facie duty developed in deontology but says that this does not give any real guidance for moral conduct in concrete situations. It just guides us in abstract moral thinking. But we don't have to be cast into relativism either, because there is still an ethical ideal that is universal: maintenance of the caring relation.

An ethic of caring implies a limit on our obligation—we cannot care (or care deeply) for everyone equally. At the same time, we cannot refuse obligation in human affairs by merely refusing to enter or acknowledge a relationship. Since, by virtue of our mutual humanity, we are unavoidably and perpetually in potential relations (Noddings 1995). So, instead, we limit our obligations by examining the possibility of completion. What governs our obligation? Noddings argues that there are two criteria: (1) the existence of, and potential for, present relations; and (2) and the dynamic potential for growth in relations. Traditionally the study of ethics has not been relational, and this has had disastrous results. The encounter induces obligation. Importantly, the ethic of caring is not like universal love; it is contextual, specific, and related to particular others. It is situational. For example, Noddings and others who advocate for the ethic of care make an important distinction when addressing the initial findings of how men and women respond to the Heinz Dilemma. They maintain that, while we may legally punish one who has stolen, we may not pass moral judgment on that individual until we know why that person stole.

When the ethical theorist asks, "Why should I behave thusly?" the question is aimed more at justification than motivation, and at a logic that resides outside of the person. In this case, you are looking for reasons you can find through logical demonstration. For further discussion of the critique of the rational actor model, see part 2 of exercise 4.2 at the end of this chapter. The contention is that abstract arguments about relativism versus absolutism are irrelevant to moral conduct. They are of considerable intellectual interest, but they are distractions if the primary interest is ethical conduct. Noddings finds the search for justification especially problematic, considering that justification requires us to concentrate on moral judgments and statements. So we are led to explore the language and reasoning used to discuss moral conduct, leading us away from concrete events. Paradoxically, in looking for justifications, we are usually led far beyond what we feel and intuitively judge to be right, whereas we are not justified—we are obligated—to do what is required to maintain and enhance caring.

Toward Practical Wisdom

If we consider, as we do in this book, there to be different levels of ethical reflection and responsibility that become increasingly more self-aware and critical, then beginning with (1) individual values and (2) the social consensus or world views about what is right, we then come to (3) principles and (4) theories. From all of these emerges yet another domain, long recognized around the world as a deep basis for conduct, and which goes by multiple names: care, compassion, and virtue in a deep sense, something Aristotle called practical wisdom.[9]

In addition to the classic western tradition of wisdom and practical action as developed in the Aristotelian tradition, recent enactivist and autopoietic theories developed respectively by biologist Francisco Varela and neuroscientist Humberto Maturana contend that beyond applying a rationalist matrix of principles and rules, finally ethical behavior is motivated by wisdom. In this way, both scholars' views of ethical cognition and action are parallel to the Eastern traditions of Taoism, Confucianism, and Buddhism. In developing a way for current neuroscience to account for how only humans are "capable of commenting on their activities, or asking themselves critically whether they are acting in the right and proper manner," Maturana opposed the idea that objective knowledge can be obtained by increasing scientific distance. Just the opposite: he stresses the value of the lessening of distance "when we are completely immersed in our activities and situations . . . [in order that] an action may be described as responsible or irresponsible" (Maturana and Poerksen 2004, 35 and 77).

Maturana clarifies this by noting: "To act responsibly, then, means to care for someone else and, at the same time, to reflect on the consequences of what one is doing in relation to the circumstances in which one does what one is doing" (2004, 78). This particular argument is fairly commensurate with the ethic of care theories described above. Maturana also uses the term "mindfulness" to characterize "ethical behavior, which includes the responsible reflection of the consequences of actions . . . on another human being."

In order to make clear the connection with Eastern traditions, Maturana's colleague Varela develops what he terms an enactivist ethical position in the congruent [Asian] terms of "our ability to attend" (*ssu*)—which also needs to be understood in tandem with Eastern views (Varela 1999). Varela's theories of cognition describe the unfolding of our ethical capacity, which needs to be understood in relation to our development as virtuous persons, as understood by the traditions of Taoism, Confucianism, and Buddhism (Varela, 26, 65; this position is much more fully developed in Varela, Thompson, and Rosch, *The Embodied Mind,* Cambridge, MA: MIT Press 1999). In contrast to the dominant western metaphysical positions (or the Eastern tradition of Mohism) in which ethical reasoning consists of choosing among alternative courses of action by applying rules and principles to judge possibilities, Varela argues that we learn in the course of practice. That is, he contends that knowing is effective action in novel situations. This view of cognition being a matter of what we enact in the course of living in the world parallels Buddhism's teachings about learning how to actualize compassion, or Confucian views about learning to actualize virtue (Varela, 72). Specifically, Varela contends that Meng-tzu (Mencius), an early Confucian (the fourth century BCE), is correct in holding that "people actualize virtue when they learn to extend knowledge and feelings from situations in which a particular action is considered correct to analogous situations in which the correct action is unclear" (Varela, 27).

An enactivist ethics sees cognition as a matter of effective practices learned and carried out in the course of living in the world. Since we are immersed in our activities and relationships, we need to develop the intelligent awareness and dispositions that enable us to act in an adequately reflective and responsible manner in novel situations.

This position raises two fundamental questions. First, how do we first arrive at a definition and adequate understanding of what correct means? This is an issue that also emerges as we navigate within our four levels of ethics, cycling back and forth between concrete experience and theorizing. Secondly, how is such extrapolation of knowledge and feelings from situation to situation possible? According to Varela, it depends on the fact that we are capable of using intelligent awareness. That is, adequate reflection and analysis that ultimately arise through the practice of mindfulness or awareness (*samatha vispasnya*) (Varela 1992, 66).

"For Mencius only truly virtuous people attend to their nature sufficiently well to understand an event in terms of their experience and thus ensure that the appropriate extension follows easily . . . Only people who act from dispositions they have at the very moment of action as a result of a long process of cultivation merit the name of truly virtuous. Such a person can be said to have 'acted through benevolence and rightness'" (Varela 1992, 29–30). Clearly, as mindful, fully internalized, practice that arises out of virtue, authentic care, or wisdom is not at all a matter of mere habit, understood as routinized, unthought activity. Quite the opposite: "Thus truly ethical behavior does not arise from mere habit or from obedience to patterns or rules. Truly expert people act from extended inclinations, not from precepts, and thus transcend the limitations inherent in a repertoire of purely habitual responses" (Varela, 1992, 30–31).

Locating ethical reflection and responsibility in the sphere of practice, virtue, and wisdom, as Maturana and Varela do, is not only in agreement with several Eastern traditions, but is also much the same as what Aristotle did.[10] Indeed, for Aristotle, ethics is finally a matter of enduring but subtle practical understanding and disposition, as already seen in the fact that the proper title of the work we now know as [*Nichomachean*] *Ethics* actually (in the words Aristotle himself used, *ta ēthika*) translates to *matters to do with character* (Barnes 1976, 27). Especially the famous Book 6 of *Ethics* develops the terms *phronēsis* and *sophia* to explicate the unique blend of knowledge and action that characterize ethics and to distinguish this sphere from the other three modes of thought that aim at truth: from *epistēmē* (scientific knowledge that seeks the demonstrable and universal), *technē* (artistic or practical skill), and *nous* (intuition of first principles) (Book 6, iii, iv, vi).

For our purposes, *phronēsis*—prudence, practical wisdom, or proven practical common sense—is the key ethical term, complexly related to *sophia*—wisdom in the most finished form, wisdom without qualification—and virtue (Book six, v, vii, xii). Aristotle argues that though there is, in fact, a principle that regulates conduct, this principle is not abstract or scientific in the proper sense, but a matter of practical intellect, which combined with character (a particular moral state), generates appropriate choices and, in turn, actions (Book 6, i–ii, 1139a16-b2). Aristotle explains that "It is thought to be the mark of a prudent person to be able to deliberate rightly about what is good and advantageous . . . [or] conducive to the good life generally" (Book 6, v); practical wisdom is itself a virtue, and not merely a rational state, and as constantly exercised is an integral part of one's character (Book 6, v). The correct deliberation also is resourceful.

It is important to notice that, for Aristotle, "*phronēsis* is not concerned with universals only; it must also take cognizance of particulars, because it is concerned with conduct, and conduct has its sphere in particular circumstances. That is why some people who do not possess (theoretical) knowledge are more effective in action (especially if they are experienced) than others who do not possess it" (Book 6, vii). Similarly, the young "are not thought to develop prudence" because "prudence involves knowledge of particular facts, which become known from experience, and a young person is not experienced, because experience takes some time to acquire" (Book 6, viii). Here we find that what Aristotle himself originally says coincides with Maturana's emphasis on doing and Varela's focus on enaction, as well as with Eastern traditions of practice. In addition, in contrast to the more general character of scientific knowledge, ethical deliberation and action are considered to be contextual, as Maturana and Varela also argue in their neurologically based ethics: "Ordinary life is necessarily one of situated agents, continually coming up with what to do, faced with ongoing parallel activities in their various perceptual-motor systems. This continual redefinition of what to do is not at all like a plan selected from a repertoire of potential alternatives; it is enormously dependent on contingency and improvisation, and is infinitely more flexible than any plan can be. A situated cognitive entity has—by definition—a perspective" (Varela, 55).[11]

Practical Wisdom and the Environment

It may be good to conclude our consideration of theory with what might be considered words of wisdom in regard to the environmental dilemmas we face. At the least, environmental dilemmas call on us to reflect and respond deeply and carefully, which is always the next step in responsible, ethical decision making.

The Dalai Lama counsels us:

Today's challenges are so great—and the dangers of the misuse of technology so global, entailing a potential catastrophe for all humankind—that I feel we need a moral compass we can use collectively without getting bogged down in doctrinal differences. One key factor that we need is a holistic and integrated outlook at the level of human society that recognizes the fundamentally interconnected nature of all living beings and their environment. Such a moral compass must entail preserving our human sensitivity and will depend on us constantly bearing in mind our fundamental human values. We must be willing to be revolted when science—or for that matter any human activity—crosses the line of human decency, and we must fight to retain the sensitivity that is otherwise so easily eroded.

How can we find this moral compass? We must begin by putting faith in the basic goodness of human nature, and we need to anchor this faith in some fundamental and universal ethical principles. These include a recognition of the preciousness of life, an understanding of the need for balance in nature and the employment of this need as a gauge for the direction of our thought and action, and—above all—the need to ensure that we hold compassion as the key motivation for all our endeavors and that it is combined with a clear awareness of the wider perspective, including long-term consequences. Many will agree with me that these ethical values transcend the dichotomy of religious believers and non-believers, and are crucial for the welfare of all humankind. Because of the profoundly interconnected reality of today's world, we need to relate to the challenges we face as a single human family rather than as members of specific nationalities, ethnicities, or religions. In other words, a necessary principle is a spirit of oneness of the entire human species. Some might object that this is unrealistic. But what other option do we have?

I firmly believe it is possible. The fact that, despite our living for more than a half century in the nuclear age, we have not yet annihilated ourselves is what gives me great hope. It is no mere coincidence that, if we reflect deeply, we find these ethical principles at the heart of all major spiritual traditions . . . We must all keep in mind the primary goal of the well-being of humanity as a whole and the planet we inhabit. (2005, 187–201)

Exercises, Problems, and Challenges to the Theories.
Issues for Analysis and Discussion

Exercise 4.1 Connecting Worldviews and Theories.

In this exercise we would like you to consider the connections between the worldviews outlined in chapter 1 and the theories just outlined in chapter 4. In trying to sort out the implicit or even hidden bases for oppositions and environmental disagreements, Timothy Beatley contends that, "Disagreements over land use policy have often been the result of clashes between teleological (utilitarian or Aristotelian) and deontological views, although the holders of these positions would not likely describe them in these terms" (1994, 24). He then goes on to align the following concerns and approaches with utilitarian and deontological (duty-based) ethical theories.

Utilitarian:
1. anthropocentric:
   - cost/benefit analysis
   - market failure
   - contingent valuation
2. expanded-anthropocentric:
   - expanded utilitarianism (perhaps recognizing the importance of nature for maximum general social good)

Deontological:
1. anthropocentric:
   - culpability and prevention of harms
   - land use rights
   - distributive ethics, social justice
   - duties to future generations
   - duties to larger geographic publics
   - duties to keep promises
2. non-anthropocentric:
   - duties to animals and sentient life
   - duties to protect species and biodiversity
   - holistic, organic views
   - biocentrism
   - deep ecology
   - Christian stewardship
   - traditional Amerindian views
                              (Beatley 1994, 25)

Consider the following questions:
1. Given what was said about the anthropocentric and non-anthropocentric world views in chapter 1 and the theories presented in chapter 5, how accurate is Beatley's descriptive taxonomy?

2. His description portrays deontology as complexly, but very positively, oriented to environmental decision making. Do you think that is correct? Why or why not?

3. In developing his own position, Beatley explicitly argues that "many of the ethical theories and principles described in later chapters [of his book] are deontological in nature" as a counteraction to "land use policy [that] has historically been inappropriately driven by a relatively narrow utilitarian/market failure theory of what is morally correct." Do you agree that such a counter-move is a good strategy against a market-based viewpoint? Why—what arguments support or refute his evaluation?

Exercises 4.2 and 4.3 Moral Challenges in a Post-Modern World: Two Traditional Ideas Contested

Globalization has brought to the fore the complexities of multiple, contested identities, place meanings, and senses of place. This is part of the post-modern condition that requires us to cope with an increasingly complex worked filled with ambiguity and multiple role demands, temporal and spatial discontinuity, and a fragmented lifestyle. This is what Kenneth Gergen (1991) calls the saturated self. In today's world, flux and change is standard—transnational flows of people and capital influence even the mundane aspects of our everyday lives.

Post-modern society causes us to question some heretofore accepted premises related to ethics: (1) the notion of the autonomous self—a time-honored conceptualization; and (2) that humans are uniquely rational and that this rationality enables us to engage in ethical decision making. Let's look at each of these in turn.

Exercise 4.2 Critique of the Autonomous-Self Model

Some contemporary theorists argue that instead of thinking about moral judgment from the perspective of the autonomous self, it would be more fruitful to talk about if from the framework of the socially responsive self posited by May (1996) and outlined in chapter 2. This is very useful for understanding ethical decision making today, particularly within the challenging arena of the environmental professions. For example, Kuentzel (2000) draws on Anthony Giddens' (1991) existential (sociological) theory and David Harvey's (1999) post-modern theory to argue that individual action and social structure are mutually constitutive of one another. In particular, Kuentzel focuses on Giddens' notion of the "project of the self," which is to maintain the narrative of our self-understanding in moments of ambiguity and anxiety, and to anchor our sense of self across different situations and over time:

According to both Giddens and Keuntzel, in everyday interaction people re-flexively monitor their conduct and the conduct of others. This is what Giddens calls discursive or practical consciousness. It is not so much that these theories explicitly deny the autonomy of the self, it is a more inclusive re-thinking of the self in a relational manner. This theory is important for ethics because it recog-nizes the socially constructed nature not only of the self but of the situations in which we find ourselves. Moreover, it addresses dilemmas in its discussion of moments of ambiguity and anxiety, suggesting that the decisions we make and the action we take are at least partly based on a desire or need to maintain a con-sistent self-concept.

One could argue that holding our particular ideals and values is based on our conceptualization of our self in the world. But as critical theory and social constructivist paradigms posit, the self must be understood as socially consti-tuted, and ideally, socially responsive. It is through an understanding of our-selves as socially constructed entities that we can perceive personal commit-ments and integrity as going beyond the purview of the isolated individual conscience to being a shared enterprise (May 1996). This line of argument has also been made by feminist scholars advocating for an ethic of care in conduct-ing research, where ethical decision making is couched in a sense of the situated self in relations with others. The ethic of care is predicated on the notion that we are, by virtue of our mutual humanity, perpetually in relation with one another (Noddings 1995).

Other scholars, such as Lopes de Souza (2000), also extend the parameters of autonomy to include the concept of collective autonomy and consider auton-omy overall in a more politico-philosophical way:

> The idea of autonomy embraces two interrelated senses: *collective* autonomy, or *the conscious and explicitly free self-rule of a particular society,* as based on politico-institutional guarantees as well as the effective material possibility (in-cluding access to reliable information) of equal chances of participation in rele-vant decision making processes; and *individual* autonomy, that is *the capacity of particular individuals to make choices in freedom* (which depends both on strictly individual and psychological circumstances and on political and mate-rial factors. (2000, 188)

Lopes de Souza adopts Doyal and Gough's (1994) conceptualization of per-sonal autonomy as something that depends on: "first, the 'degree of understand-ing that an individual has about himself [*sic*], about his culture and about the expectations which are addressed to him as a member of his society'; secondly, 'his psychological capacity to formulate options for himself'; and thirdly, the 'objective opportunities for action on this basis' (Doyal and Gough 1994, 90; as quoted in Lopes de Souza 2000). This conceptualization of autonomy is at the basis of much ethical theory, as we have seen. At the same time, however, Lopes de Souza points out that in a strict sense individual autonomy is not entirely achievable in a society where people have different levels of access to resources and power. This is where the notion of a collective autonomy comes in:

The vital issue is whether a particular society is more or less heteronomous or autonomous (collective autonomy), because strong individual autonomy in a proper sense will be a fiction—at least, as far as the majority of the population is concerned—in the framework of a society which is characterized by structural asymmetry in the distribution of power and by inequality regarding opportunities. (Lopes de Souza 2000, 189)

This collective autonomy, then, forms the basis for empowerment and social change that can be initiated by average citizens in response to inequities:

There is no reason to assume that professional politicians and "experts" necessarily know what is good for individuals and groups better than the individuals and groups themselves. What is at stake here is not technical competence, but freedom: who decides about the *ends*? Can "experts" and so-called "representatives" legitimately define the needs of ordinary men and women in the place of the citizens themselves? (p. 190)

Where does this leave us regarding ethical decision making in professional practice? How do you respond to Lopes de Sousa's arguments? To what extent does autonomy—the traditional cornerstone of ethical theory, especially in the modern era with Mill and Kant—remain a valid foundation for ethics? To help you answer this, review the sections on the socially responsive self in chapter 2 and on autonomy in chapters 3 and 4.

Exercise 4.3 Critique of the Rational-Actor Model

As we have seen in the section on the ethic of care, there is also a burgeoning critique of the rational-actor model within ethical theory. But the critique comes from post-modern theory as well as feminist theory. For example, Giddens (1991) critiques instrumentalist theories that rely on assumptions about people as goal-directed rational actors calling this "the imperialism of individual experience." (This also bears on the principle of autonomy. Part of this critique is a disagreement about a functionalist approach to self identity that tends to see thoughts and actions as logical and goal-directed.

In the section on ethic of care, we described how Rawls argues that all of us have our own rational life plan, which may or may not include other people. Do you agree with this?

Rawls also asserts that each individual is concerned for the advancement of his own interests and cares about the interests of others only insofar as it helps his own interests. What do you think of this argument? On what basis might you say this is true or false?

Some environmental ethicists, especially those concerned with the notion of rights of other species, challenge the rational model in that they would acknowledge rights of other species that are not typically considered rational beings. It is not just that we are uniquely rational but, as Rawls argues, that good ethical decision making hinges on rationality foremost. Kuentzel and others question the idea of whether all action or all people are always goal directed. What is your position on this issue?

Exercise 4.4 Critique of 2 Utilitarian Assumptions and Approaches

Do you agree that the following are fatal flaws in utilitarian theory?

1. Critique: given the actual incompatibility of the most important values, utilitarianism's assumption—indeed requirement—that it is possible to aggregate and compute something, such as a greatest good, is simply impossible. It is neither possible nor desirable to try to reduce or translate heterogeneous values to a common measure (such as money).

How would it be possible to find a proper, common metric for incommensurables (health, freedom, and wealth; or among different persons)? In the case of environmental issues, wouldn't utilitarianism, at the least, need to go to full-cost accounting?

2. Critique: utilitarianism is not a complete ethical theory because it provides no basis for making ethical, rather than sociological, decisions. Rather than clarifying and grounding what should be the case as a moral goal, utilitarianism does no more than summarize the given status quo, describing what a given society in fact values. Is this not sociology, rather than ethic? Isn't it too relativistic to provide an adequate ethics in the age of globalization?

Could utilitarianism avoid merely describing and then replicating the status quo and relativism? (Also see the material on act- and rule-utilitarianism in this chapter.)

Exercise 4.5 Critiques of Natural Law

As the oldest of the major theories, natural law has drawn a substantial number of criticisms, many of which have led to the formation of the alternative positions we have considered in this book. Chief among concerns today is the way natural law depends on the conceptual ideas and empirical content of what is termed essential. Post-structuralist opponents have been especially vocal in arguing that what often are claimed to be essential groups or features in fact are arbitrary social constructions and not anything resembling timeless natural kinds. Feminists have contended that natural law's emphasis on the "rights of man" has been too literally taken in societies of the last several thousand years insofar as patriarchal structures have excluded women from full human status and rights. These two critiques both argue that conceptual mistakes have led to serious misunderstandings and injustices for those who are different, but whose differences are excluded from homogenizing universal categories and the corresponding general deployments of cultural power.

On the other hand, defenders of natural law contend that they can fully agree that social-historical limitations mean that the best available classification at any given time may be wrong, or improperly inclusive or exclusive. But they contend that the tradition of continuing to think and debate about such categorizations is, in fact, one of the major foundations upon which moral rights historically have been accorded to a widened population—that is, that from the limited (and thus mistaken) early Greek belief that such rights accrued only to free, male citizens of a polis, the same sort of epistemological and ethical arguments, especially through the Enlightenment, established that women, Africans, Native Americans, and other indigenous and colonialized peoples could not rationally be excluded from universal ethical rights.

What is your view about whether it makes sense to speak of the essence of human persons? What about wolves, or forests? How does such talk seem harmful or helpful to ethical decision making?

Is natural law challenged or obliged to find ways to incorporate theoretically and practical-empirically established differentiations into its theory? Can you identify a contentious point or possible shortcoming posed by critics and see whether natural law has or could respond adequately.

Exercise 4.6 Questioning Deontology's and Natural Law's Definitions of Person

As noted earlier in this chapter, an obvious, fundamental question in ethics is: "Who qualifies as a person?" For Kant, it is not all human beings genetically defined, but a matter of who has reason, which according to Kantian criteria, means who has reasoning as the *developed* capacity to solve problems, who is self-conscious, who is self-motivated and self-monitoring. Natural law differs in that it focuses on potential rather than actualized capacity. As a result, though internally consistent, both theories are critiqued: deontology because it may exclude humans who are young or not developed to the degree the theory would specify, and natural law because it includes as persons those in the earliest phases of life (the controversy of whether the fetus is a person with rights, of course, focuses on just this determination).

What is your view? Who counts as a person, with ethical rights?

Exercise 4.7 Critique of Deontology's Concepts of Universality and Reason

At the heart of deontology is the possible universalization of what might serve as a moral law—the critical, determining factor of whether something is an ethical obligation.

Can we think in universal terms in today's post-modern era in which we affirm and even emphasize multicultural differences? Wouldn't deontology need to develop a more culturally inclusive and respectful idea of legitimation, autonomy, and reasonable person in light of cultural diversity?

In addition, it has been charged that deontology, partially because of its operation within the historical-cultural context of Western scientific modernity, uses an overly-narrow definition of reason. The problem is that with a reductive view of reasoning, important modes of understanding and facets of decision making are excluded; significant features of human life (such as emotions, empathy, etc.) are omitted from ethical consideration, both on the part of those making the decisions and in regard to those who will impacted by the decisions.

Wouldn't deontology have to be modified in light of more fully humanistic and recent broadened understandings of cognitive processes? What changes would you make to this theory?

Exercise 4.8 Critiques of the Ethic of Care

This chapter raises issues about whether care is distinct from or complementary to justice. What is your position on this important issue?

The ethic of care, like all other theories, has to account for its epistemological assumptions and their implications; so it also faces special challenges. In comparison with the other three theories that are more within the mainstream of western thought's claims to a foundational rationality, the ethic of care's idea of knowledge as situated unquestionably involves "the abandonment of the ideals of certainty and of the permanence of knowledge" (Zammito 2004, 219). The concern is not only epistemological, but ethical and political, since the worry is whether the ethic of care would too subjective to provide an environmental ethics adequate to the age of globalism, especially where it seems necessary to argue for universal rights for colonized peoples and environments and not depend on the good will of the caring few (which is partly why post-Enlightenment thought sounds so legalistic). Thus, both the harsh critics of the post-modern concept of situated knowledge and many post-positivists sympathetic to it recognize the importance of dealing with the charge that the ethic of care inevitably leads to a substantial epistemic relativism. (Among the critics is Noretta Koertge, who contends that the idea of situated knowledge repudiates a universal and rational framework and thus is finally dangerous to democracy (1996a 1996b); among the supporters of an ethic of care is Helen Longino, who argues that the contingency of knowledge is not to be feared since, as the actual condition of human inquiry, it is unavoidable (about which positivistic views are in denial) and indeed is mitigated by the members' normative agreements that actually constitute the scientific thoughts and values and, we would add, ethical community (1990). Either by reflecting on your own or by considering some of the relevant literature (Koertge 1996a 1996b; Longino 1990), try to address the question: "Can (or how does) the ethic of care provide more than a subjective emotional impression or vague 'holistic' response to how we might act?"

Exercise 4.9 The Role of the Emotions in Making Rational Choices.

What perspective would you be willing to defend concerning the proper role of emotional factors in decision making? Articulate a position that deals with the following two sorts of questions:
1. Whether emotions should be included or excluded from legitimate decision making:
    - Should emotional factors be set aside in order to make sound and unprejudiced ethical judgments?
    - Should emotional factors be included, but limited to providing a check to determine if we are satisfied that a decision is within the bounds of what we can accept?
    - Should emotional factors be seen as opening us to ethical issues in the first place and as a crucial component of what we actually do when we make ethical decisions?
2. Are emotions similar enough across time periods and cultures that your position can be taken as generally creditable or applicable?

Before finalizing what you want to say, consider the following provocative view of Martha Nussbaum, a classicist and legal scholar, who contends that we can be sensitive to cultural and situational contexts, holistically include emotional factors in our practical understanding and decision making, and still arrive at a common view across cultures (thus avoiding both unsupportable universalism and overly-limiting relativism).

One of today's major ethicists, Nussbaum makes the subtle—but important—point that we should distinguish a neo-Aristotelian position from that of Natural Law. Specifically, she devotes considerable effort to elucidate Aristotle's concept of *phronēsis* in contemporary terms in order to try to provide a bridge between the classical tradition and the emerging ethic of care, especially in her insightful essay, "The Discernment of Perception: An Aristotelian Conception of Public and Private Rationality" (1990). In that essay, she explains how Aristotle himself agrees with advocates of an ethic of care that the Western tradition emphasizing rationalization (when defined as certain knowledge of universals) is an exaggeration that distorts practical life. In large part, he argues, such an understanding depends upon an overly narrow conception of knowledge, ignoring the legitimacy and importance of practical knowing or *phronēsis*.

From among Aristotle's arguments, Nussbaum calls our attention to two theoretical and pragmatic reasons why we need to remain sensitive to the role of emotion in decision making. First, strictly scientific knowledge is not appropriate for real ethical and political decisions: "Aristotle tells us that practical mat-

ters are in their very nature indeterminate or indefinable—not just so far insuffi-
ciently defined. The universal account fails because no universal can adequately
capture this matter" (Nussbaum 1990, 70). Further, "to argue that emotion and
imagination are essential components of practical knowing and judging is to
suggest very strongly that good judgment will at least in part be a matter of focusing on the concrete and even the particular, which will be seen as incommen-
surate with other things" (Nussbaum 1990, 83). It would follow that insofar as
emotion and imagination "are indeed closely linked with our ability to grasp
particulars in all of their richness and concreteness, then perception will disregard them at its peril" (Nussbaum 1990, 77). Second, in our practical social
lives, usually we initially see what is the case and what is needed by way of experience and feeling, rather than by pure intellect. As Nussbaum puts it, "We
might say that a person of practical insight will cultivate emotional openness and
responsiveness in approaching a new situation. Frequently it will be her pas-
sional response, rather than detached thinking, that will guide her to the appropriate recognitions" (1990, 79).

In fact, then, there is a strong tradition within Western ethics which opens
common ground to contemporary neo-Aristotelians and some feminists (and
others) who advocate an ethic of care. These object to the idea that emotions
and imagination cloud rational choice. Further, they not only argue that these
faculties neither distort our judgment nor are self-serving—on the contrary, they
are essential both for us to be sensitive to what is valuable in a given case and to
be able to comprehend the particulars of the matter. That is, emotion and imagination are critical to exercising good judgment.

Having considered Nussbaum's arguments, what are your final answers to
the questions posed at the beginning?

Notes

1. The like-sounding idea of natural rights, comes from the heritage of modern
thinkers in the seventeenth century, such as John Locke, who broke with traditional
natural law's contention that humans are social by nature, insisting instead that individual liberty is what is natural and primary. Natural rights theory (from Benjamin
Franklin to Robert Nozick) actually is part of deontological theory, considered later in
this chapter. Nozick's *Anarchy, State, and Utopia* (1974) is important to those advocating that property rights are a matter of the free choice of the title-holder, to be un-
encumbered by limitations of distributive justice.

2. The technical, philosophical studies of reality and of knowledge, respectively,
are called metaphysics and epistemology.

3. This example is drawn from a combination of Seattle's recent transit initiatives,
Bent Flyvbjerg's *Megaprojects and Risk* (2003), and the thoughtful and practical dissertation research of Ralf Brand (2003). Flyvbjerg explicitly works out the contemporary application of Aristotle for planning theory, research, and practice in his *Making
Social Science Matter* (2001).

4. All quotations from Mill are from *Utilitarianism*, originally 1861 (New York:
Hackett 1979), throughout cited by page number only.

5. There are many substantial reasons to consider contractarianism as deeply connected with Kant's theory and deontology. For example, John Rawles' theory of justice (though it also draws on Locke and Rousseau) develops closely from Kant's ideas of persons as ends in themselves and the fifth formulation of his categorical imperative: "Every rational being must act as if he, by his maxims, were at all times a legislative member in the universal realm of ends." The same connection is found with theories of individual rights, such as Robert Nozick.

6. One of the best, concise explications of Kant's dense theory is Punzo, 1969.

7. Abbreviated as FMM in all following citations.

8. As in utilitarianism, a distinction can be made within deontology between act deontology and rule deontology, though the former has not been successfully defended because it inevitably loops back around to affirm a rule, and thus makes sense only as a problematic version of rule deontology. Proponents of the former consider rules as something inducted from particular cases that can function more like rules of thumb that can help guide what one can or should do (Beauchamp and Childress, 36; cf. Frankena (1973).

9. Though we can not take it up here, Heidegger's vision of care as central to authentic human existence emerged in his first major works in the 1920s and was refined in his later work (1971a 1971b). As noted in chapter 1, his ideas of care and mortals as the shepherds of what is given by the heavens and earth has had a profound influence on deep ecology.

10. As Heidegger has definitively shown, Aristotle's originary insights are not at all the same as those that have come down to us in the 2500-year-old tradition of Aristotelianism, especially as translated through Latin and then the representational concepts of modern European languages and metaphysical systems. (Nor are they the same as what has developed as natural law.) Heidegger himself developed his own ideas about the importance of the decisive moment in life-defining, ethical-political decision making and action, from Aristotle's concepts of *kairos*.

11. Hence, it is ironic that among the strongest critics of Aristotle we find those who themselves begin by insisting on the contextual or situated character of knowledge and ethical decisions. Clearly it should be those at the other end of the spectrum—who argue that knowing needs to be atemporal and aspatial (universal and transcendental) in order to count as any kind of genuine knowledge—who should object to Aristotle's distinction between science proper and ethical prudence.

Chapter Five

Reframing Sustainability: Toward Environmental and Social Responsibility

The Mode of Analysis

In this book we have considered several methods and strategies to help make better ethical decisions concerning environmental problems and dilemmas. One's usual starting point of a personal position or a shared worldview always can be improved if more fully reflected upon and enacted as responsibly as possible. Beyond that, we can strive to move to a deeper and more explicit mode of deliberation by considering how we might live as reflective and socially responsible selves, by seriously practicing professional excellence, by systematically engaging the powerful grounding theories, and the principles and rules that consistently develop from them, or by attempting to enact an ethic of care. In addition, any of these modes of decision making benefit from proven approaches to undo dilemmas (especially false or unnecessary ones), and even dissolve these dilemmas by reframing issues. We can do this by carefully (re)defining key terms, recognizing differences, not over-generalizing, conceptually recategorizing and including multi-faceted relationships, changing historically constituted differentiations, and creatively changing the material conditions and consequences of action with new technologies. Where dilemmas cannot be resolved, decisions may be clearer when we systematically apply principles and rules, and particularly their initial hierarchies of rights and duties, to the complexities of involved parties and details of issues.

Applying these strategies, however, is neither simple nor mechanical; it requires understanding the relevant dimensions, assumptions, and implications of different approaches and strategies, gaining knowledge about the empirical realities of the case, and exercising good judgment (as Aristotle's *phronesis*, practical-contextual judgment), empathy, and imagination. Some of these capacities come from experience and development of character; others, such as the understanding just mentioned, are difficult because they require sustained reflection, for which we seldom have either time or the opportunity to focally question and discuss the subject. Hopefully, this book provides one such site. That is why, in addition to the ideas the text presents for consideration, there are opportunities for further practice and to tie the practices back into the concepts.

Since both the general theoretical bases and particular strategies are very complex and often difficult to understand, we would like to apply the full repertoire of theories, principles, rules, and so on to a complex of problems and do a test case to explore how we might deal with environmental problems and dilemmas. This chapter, then, is an advanced laboratory to try out ethical decision making, both by what we say and by what we show in the way we approach the problems. While we do present positive ideas and tactics, we do *not* claim that these are *the* only ways to approach the topics; rather, the intent is to give an example of an attempt to deal with problems in order to stimulate debate about this and other processes. In addition, by focusing on sustainability as an example of a complex, problematic realm of decision making, we do not imply that all environmental problems reduce to this, but only that the nested problems are central and well worth being used as a prototype for further exploration.

This procedure also will enable us to return to our starting point, to what has been said about the many specific facets of decision making and dilemmas such as those in chapter 2, including the reflexive and socially responsible self; professionals and excellence; identities, roles, and codes of environmental professions; emplaced ethics for natural and built environments; sustainability and the future; cultural landscapes and competing landscape values; place meaning, symbolism, and policy; social versus formalistic design; vernacular architecture; diversity and participation; and the principles, theories, worldviews, and personal touchstones with which we began. Since we are whole persons, changes that occur in one dimension ripple through all of what we think and do. This chapter will enable readers to re-gather themselves, hopefully now with a more robust, complete, and consistent capacity for ethical decision making.

Following are two lists. The first is an overview of the array of reframing approaches and strategies that we will continue to use in this chapter, though these are not listed or used in any particular order. This list is more of a reminder of what we can do when faced with an ethical decision or dilemma. The second, however, has items listed in the order of a logical relationship that we will follow—that is, it is an outline of the way the questioning will unfold. The outline provides a roadmap to show how and where we will go (and to enable the readers to proceed directly to any portion that is especially interesting or important if they wish). Because the outline makes explicit the sequence of phenomena to be considered in this chapter, which also is a way of systematically thinking through some of the linkages among the facets of the overall problems (such as climate change and pollution) and possible responses, this main sections of the chapter's text are marked correspondingly.

Reframing Approaches and Strategies:
- Consider definitions
- See how problems are posed
- See need for better distinctions
- Undo dichotomies
- Recognize differences
- Recategorize
- Open new perceptions
- Create new empirical conditions
- Simplify issues
- Redistribute factors as shared
- Identify core conflicts
- Find we may be able to live with some problems
- Make trade-offs
- Share burdens
- Take different risks
- Compromise
- Make a sacrifice
- Reconsider personal guidelines
- Reconsider conflicting worldviews
- Imaginative variation

Outline of Subject Matter and Unfolding of Reflection:
A) Sustainability as an example of complex decision making
  1. Many definitions of sustainability
  2. Problems of climate change and pollution
  3. Sustaining what?—how we live, energy, waste
B) Built environments
  4. Cities
  5. Suburbs
  6. Rural areas
C) Some of the major elements
  7. Infrastructure: cars & highways
  8. Buildings and housing
  9. Poverty and the disadvantaged
D) Positive alternatives
  10. Positive positions and contributions toward sustainability
  11. Lessons of the vernacular
  12. New forms and materials
  13. A new environmental professionalism and aesthetics
  14. Environmental and social justice
  15. Who decides?—toward collaboration, compassion, and care

Sustainability as an Example of a Complex Sphere of Decision making

1. Many Definitions of Sustainability

As already considered in the section On Sustainability and Future Generations in chapter 2, sustainability has been defined as "the nesting of human purposes with the larger patterns and flows of the natural world" (Orr 1994), and more anthropocentrically as achieving a balance that allows economic well-being and social equity to be achieved across generations (Schaller 1978), and as "meeting the needs of the present without compromising the ability of future generations to meet their own needs" (Brundtland 1987). There are many variations to naming a sustainable approach: sustainability, green, ecological holism, high-performance, and others. Additionally, we do not always agree on what these terms mean and people continue to use different definitions of sustainability; our concepts of sustainability are also not as clear as they might be.

A first strategy, then, is to strive for a clear, adequate definition. Though the Brundtland definition has served surprisingly well as a point of commonality, given the wide variety of positions, it is not likely that we can find one definition to which all parties can agree and that would include all the factors that prove to be relevant to the phenomena. Thus, we need to (a) work toward the best definition of which we are capable and (b) develop a complex enough definition (or definitions) that will enable enough agreement to move fruitfully forward.

What Does Sustainability Mean?

These questions are related to the exercises at the end of the chapter, but in order to be an active reader and participate in thinking through the critical issues, don't wait until you get to those exercises to reflect on the problems. Please begin now.

What does sustainability mean?—the answer is multi-faceted:
- Can you find patterns in the proposed definitions, perhaps related to the world views we considered in chapter 1?
- How shall we frame the problem? As a matter of saving energy, with a technological, behavioral answer? As the result of human action at the scale of the worldviews that lie behind our actions—if so, what strategies might change those views and the actions of many people?
- What are the distinctive responsibilities of the different professions regarding sustainability? What are the shared or common ones? What part of these are the responsibility of each and every one of us as moral beings?

As we work to clarify our individual and shared definitions of sustainability, we can make some progress by attending to the functional dimensions that need to be included. This would help us arrive at an identification of what we can point to as a common ground when we use the term sustainability. The *Gaia Atlas* is helpful in providing a starting point at least. It says, "In an urban context sustainability means a wide range of things," such as:

- Resource budgeting
- Energy conservation and efficiency
- Renewable energy technology
- Long-lasting built structures
- Proximity between home and work
- Efficient public transport systems
- Waste reduction and recycling
- Organic waste composting
- A circular metabolism
- Supply of staple foods from local sources"

(*Gaia Atlas* 1992, 72 and 179)

These aspects of sustainability are closely related to the economic dimension, but there are other facets of sustainability that can be included and their roles clarified. We must remember that sustainability is a broader way of life that goes beyond how we construct buildings. For example, any discussion of sustainability on the larger scale must also include consideration of the health and well-being of ecosystems as a whole (i.e., other species along with humans), so even within the urban realm there must be some recognition and allowance for urban habitats, how to create, enable and protect habitat corridors and engage in ecological restoration and remediation efforts as part of a vision of sustainability. Even in terms of built structures, we could also benefit from clearer definitions of green building: There are persuasive arguments that such definitions need to include both the technological and social dimensions:

> Beyond an apparent consensus of concern for the environment, it is often less clear what factors might define or constitute a green building. You only have to look through the numerous books on green or sustainable architecture and the myriad of building reviews in architectural periodicals and journals to identify a bewildering array of contrasting types or styles of green building, each emphasizing different aspects of the sustainability agenda . . . Clearly, if we are to progress towards a more sustainable built environment, policy-makers, researchers and designers have to begin to make sense of the conceptual challenges raised by an apparent variety of pathways towards sustainable design.
>
> (Guy and Moore 2005, 16)

At the same time, however, a variety of approaches yields a rich array of options so that green buildings don't all have to have the same aesthetic or emphasize the seam strategies.

Moore and Guy additionally argue that it is a mistake to follow "the popular view of sustainable architecture [that] renders it roughly synonymous with energy efficiency" and that would reduce the issues facing us to "radically simplified checklists that itemize 'best practices' or concrete things-to-do." They do hold that it indeed is important to learn from and share experiences, which is why they cite such sources as Edwards and Hyett who argue that a "large part of designing sustainability has to do with energy conservation," while also recognizing that it is also about "creating spaces that are healthy, economically viable and sensitive to local needs" (2001, 97). The problem with this view, however, is in its limitations: it also is necessary to assess "the wider social and political issues" that underlie our environmental views and actions, that is, that enable us to "understand how [these views and actions] are created, legitimated, and contested (Hannigan 1995, 3)" cited in Guy and Moore, who emphasize that we must critically analyze our fundamental values and "the process of environmental knowledge making" (2005, 4–7).

To begin, the U.S. Green Building Council, a national coalition of building industry leaders developed the Leadership in Energy and Environmental Design (LEED) Green Building Rating System™ to offer a national benchmark for the design, construction and operation of green buildings. LEED promotes a whole-building approach to sustainability by recognizing performance in five key areas of human and environmental health: sustainable site development, water savings, energy efficiency, materials selection, and indoor environmental quality (http://www.usgbc.org/DisplayPage.aspx?CategoryID=19). The LEED rating system is for both new construction and for the management of existing buildings. LEED certification provides independent, third-party verification that a building meets national standards for sustainable design. There are different levels of certification that a building may be granted, from silver to gold to platinum. Embedded in such a categorization system is a view that there are different levels of sustainability, or at least that different building construction and management strategies can achieve different degrees of sustainability. While not a flawless system—some have even argued that it does not go far enough or that the criteria are problematic—it is an important first step in developing some consistent, credible standard for sustainable design. Debates continue about what are the best criteria for sustainability and how much they should focus on economic solutions. But at least we are engaging in these debates that are ultimately and arguably about human accountability. (For information on LEED certification, see the U.S. Green Building Council website: www.usgbc.org).

In addition, at the time of writing, a joint initiative that looks at the sustainability of sites and landscapes has just produced the first report on practice guidelines and metrics for landscape sustainability. Launched by a interdisciplinary partnership among the American Society of Landscape Architects (ASLA), the U.S. Botanic Garden, and the Lady Bird Johnson Wildflower Center this initiative seeks to bolster LEED certification by looking at hydrology, soils, vegetation, and materials for a site www.sustainablesites.org.[1] Another goal for the Sustainable Sites Initiative is to create standards and guidelines sensitive to the unique needs of bioregions; while LEED standards are national (i.e., applied uniformly across the country), looking at site-sustainability requires standards that would respond to regional needs.

How Serious are Environmental Problems? How Serious are Our Responses?
Do Environmental Problems Exist on the Global Scale?[2]
On the largest scale, we find that the many decisions and actions of billions of individuals, especially as shaped and implemented by corporations and governments, are drastically impacting the planetary ecosystem. Not everyone agrees that these changes are primarily due to human actions, so there remain important debates to be carried out; but there is increasing agreement that we are responsible enough that we need to begin corrective action. In what follows, the authors take the position that the problems are major and do need a response; for readers who differ in viewpoint, this is the place to engage with each other.

How do we Address Environmental Problems?

In considering environmental issues and dilemmas, there are several fundamental questions we can ask ourselves:

- How should we continue when we do not even agree that there is a problem for which we are responsible?

- What do you suggest as a means to move to the next level of dealing with global environmental problems when there is no consensus that there is a problem that we need to deal with? For example, as of early 2007 the Bush administration's official position is that even if there is a problem with global warming we should not take significant action to change because it might negatively harm the economy in ways we cannot predict. Beyond the environmentalists who take precisely the opposite view, the recent reports out of Great Britain and United States argue that, in addition to environmental concerns in themselves, economic damage already is underway because of climate change and will substantially increase unless we act.

- What is your position on whether we have a global problem? How do you recommend that the two sides find a way to move forward together, at least to deal with the most threatening dangers?

→ See appendix I for websites on global climate issues.

2. Problems of Global Climate Change and Pollution

The phenomenon of global climate change is so important that it would be negligent and irresponsible to leave it unmentioned in a book on ethics and the environment. At the same time, not only does a proper treatment of this issue go beyond the scope of this book, there are also experts whose knowledge on the subject matter far outweighs our own. We therefore mention the issue here to identify some basic background about the debate and mark the issue as requiring the most serious environmental decisions and action.

Internationally, there have been debates about whether global climate change is indeed happening, and if so how, why and what to do about it. Not only is the scientific community debating the extent, causes, and potential solutions, governments around the world have taken different official positions on the causes and best solutions. The most significant international treaty, known as the Kyoto Protocol, sought to mitigate global climate change and assigned mandatory emission limitations for the reduction of greenhouse gas emissions to the signatory nations. Opened for signature in 1997, it entered into force in February 2005. Countries that not only sign but ratify this protocol commit to reduce their emissions of carbon dioxide and five other greenhouse gases, or engage in emissions trading if they maintain or increase emissions of these gases. The United State is among the signatories of the Kyoto Protocol. At the time the protocol was put into effect, the United States was the largest single emitter of carbon dioxide from the burning of fossil fuels – the prime cause of global climate change (United States Country Analysis Brief. United States Energy Information Administration 2005 www.eia.doe.gov/emeu/cabs/usa/full.html). While the U.S. has signed the protocol, the government has yet to ratify it, which means that the country is not officially bound to comply with the restrictions and policies it entails. There are numerous and complicated reasons why this is so, ranging from earlier conflicting research data (although now there is much more widespread agreement within the scientific community about the human causes of global climate change) to concerns for not having binding targets and timetables, as well as concern over exemptions of developing countries.

Apart from official national positions on the Kyoto Protocol, there are several important local initiatives taking place around the U.S. For example, as of March 11 2007, 418 cities in 50 states, representing more than 60 million Americans support Kyoto after Seattle Mayor Greg Nickels started a nationwide effort to get cities to agree to the protocol.

Global Climate Change and Flooding
Science has shown us that global climate change has real effects, as documented in Al Gore's book, *An Inconvenient Truth*: "We are raising the planet's average temperature and creating the dangerous changes we see around us" because of excessive greenhouse gases, "which allow light from the sun to come into the atmosphere, but trap a portion of the outward-bound infrared radiation and warm up the air . . . CO_2 usually gets top billing in this because it accounts for 80 per-

cent of total greenhouse gas emissions. When we burn fossil fuels (oil, natural gas, and coal) in our homes, cars, factories, and power plants, or when we cut or burn down forests, or when we produce cement, we release CO_2 into the atmosphere (2006, p. 28).

> We are dumping so much carbon dioxide into the Earth's environment that we have literally changed the relationship between the Earth and the Sun. So much of that CO_2 is being absorbed into the oceans that if we continue at the current rate we will increase the saturation of calcium carbonate to levels that will prevent formation of corals and intervene with the making of shells by any sea creature. (Gore 2006, 10)

With global warming, the earth's polar ice caps are melting at an increasingly alarming rate (especially in Greenland and Antarctica), which also means that the level of the oceans is rising. As that happens, since a larger percentage of the world's population lives on coastlines or on large rivers, there will be significant displacement. "In 1995, 2.2 billion people lived within 100 km of a coastline, nearly 39 percent of the world's populations" (Roaf, Crichton, and Nicol 2005, 190). In addition to the obvious problems of relocating millions of refugees and creating urban environments for them, there will be increased conflict over where the refugees can go and very likely wars over territorial and resource control (Roaf, Crichton, and Nicol 2005, pp. 207–216).

"Many residents of low-lying Pacific island nations [such as Tuvalu] have already had to evacuate their homes because of rising seas" and even London is threatened, since "the Thames River, which flows through London, is a tidal river. In recent decades, higher sea levels began to cause more damage during storm surges." While the Dutch have begun to reconsider their strategies of using dikes to control the seas and have seriously improved the floating house that can rise with higher water levels to mitigate the damage, in many places lack of resources and technology will require abandoning many developed areas. (Roaf, Crichton, and Nicol 2005, 186–209). It is not an exaggeration to say that the major flooding along the heavily populated coasts of the world is very, very likely to lead to wars as large numbers of people are forced to move and neighbors are not able or willing to accommodate them (Mugerauer 2005).

At the same time, even well-intended scientists and professionals disagree on the immediacy and scope of the danger. A case in point is Samuel Florman, who holds that:

> A generation ago, Rachel Carson, in *Silent Spring*, used the distress of birds to alert the public to the dangers of chemical pesticides. Her warning had its good effect . . . The present crisis, however, is more widespread and can't be traced to a single cause. The main problem seems to be "development"—development in North America where many species nest and breed, in South America where may species spend the North American winter, and on the flyways between the two . . . [But], it is a fact—less known than I think it ought to be—that human development has serendipitously helped many species of birds to thrive and in-

crease in number . . . When timberland is partly cleared, the "edge" that is created, with plants in various stages of growth, provides habitat for our most
cherished songbirds. There are, according to Roger Tory Peterson, renowned
dean of birding, perhaps a billion or two more songbirds in America today than
there were before the arrival of the Pilgrims ("Long After Columbus"). [We
learn from] the birds that nature is resilient, but only up to a point. We also
learn that our forebears treated the environment more sensitively than we might
have thought, that we have reason to be thankful to them, and that we had better go and do likewise. (1987, 43 and 45)

Our Response—How Much Responsibility?
No matter what your own position on the overall issue of the degree of danger
from global climate change and the extent of our responsibility for environmental problems overall, there is much evidence that our responses—
individually, professionally, socially, politically—are not always as thoughtful
as they should be. We mainly have in mind the indifference and even delibera-
tively harmful actions that characterize some of what humans do. In addition,
part of our environmental dilemma is that some actions clearly are called for, but
we do not agree on which actions or by whom. In contrast to the position advocated above by Samuel Florman, Victor Papanek, a designer and educator,
makes a rather different but equally strong argument: "The agenda . . . can be
put simply. It is vital that we all—professionals and end-users—recognize our
ecological responsibilities. Our survival depends on an urgent attention to environmental issues, but even now there still seems to be a lack of motivation, a pa-
ralysis of will, to make the necessary radical changes" (Papanek 1995, 9).

This is where the distinction, well established in fields like environmental
psychology, between environmental concern and pro-environmental behavior
comes in. Many people articulate environmental concerns, but this does not necessarily mean that we all act on those concerns. In other words, environmental
attitudes and concern do not always translate into action. Nonetheless understanding environmental attitudes is an important start for living in more sustainable ways. There are three main areas where understanding attitudes is helpful:
first, they are useful for policy-makers, environmental managers, officials and
program coordinators to inform them of the level of support they might receive
for a particular program or for the environment in general. Second, they can help
in setting environmental goals (60 percent of newspaper to be recycled in two
years) and third, they can indicate with some accuracy what people are doing in
regard to the environment and what they at least intend to do (Gifford 2002, 57).

Environmental attitudes are made up of cognitions (thoughts and knowledge), and emotional responses/feelings about the environment and one's behavioral intentions. The challenge is that, while people can be concerned about the
environment, there are a number of reasons why that might not translate into action or why the concern won't necessarily alter behavior. To begin, we like convenience, and when the negative impacts of doing things that are convenient for
us (driving to work or the store instead of taking the bus) are not readily apparent, or are literally invisible—at least for the time being—then we may be less

likely to alter our behavior: our choice to throw out a plastic water bottle in the park garbage can rather than take it to a recycling bin may seem small and innocuous in itself. Moreover, our appreciation of the impacts of our actions can be difficult to wrap our minds around, especially when more obvious and visible impacts are not anticipated for three more generations. Further still, in our everyday lives we may have more personally pressing concerns over jobs, health, safety and well-being that might take precedent over longer-term concerns for the natural environment. It has been argued for example, that if one is struggling to pay the rent and keep a roof over one's head, one may be less concerned about global climate change. That said, however, the argument within the environmental justice movement is an important one to remember here: while these other basic needs may require attention, this does not diminish our desire, right, or concern for equal access to such things as clean air and water. So concern for meeting one need does not preclude the concern or ability to care about other issues.

Are we committed to dealing with emerging environmental dilemmas?

People's attitudes toward the improving environmental conditions often are disconnected from their actual behavior. That is, while many people express concern about the environment, they do not always act on those concerns.

Why do you think that is?

What can be done about thus?

Don't we, individually, finally have to question our own actions or inaction?

"We must examine what each of us can contribute from our own specific role in society. We must ask the question: What can I do as a professor, construction worker, taxi-driver, school-teacher, prostitute, lawyer, pianist, housewife, student, manager, politician or farmer? What is the impact of *my* work on the environment? There is an ecological and environmental dimension to all human activities." (Papanek 1995, 17)

The treatment of environmental concern just summarized operates largely on the individual level. However, there are group-level concerns as well, and for our purposes in this book it is helpful to look at professional practice groups. One complication in regard to the environmental professions is that it often is unclear whether pro-environmental statements, missions and goals are made because it is good business or what indicates deep personal or disciplinary commitment to the environment itself. There certainly is growing social pressure to think green. "Within contemporary architectural discourse and practice there seems to exist a wide consensus on the urgent need to promote environmental innovation in building design . . . Deyan Sudjic has gone so far as to suggest that, as a result, 'for any architect not to profess passionate commitment to green buildings is professional suicide'" (Guy and Moore 2005, 16). To what extent does the character of the conviction matter ethically?

Discuss: How Deeply Green?

To what extent will the environmental profession genuinely embrace ethical environmental decisions?

or

Do many just shift with public opinion and economic pressures—acting green only when and because it is expedient or necessary?

How can we tell the difference—and does it matter?

---

3. Sustaining What? How We Live, Energy, Waste

We have begun to address environmental problems by implementing some of the strategies we have developed in this book (and that we re-listed at the beginning of this chapter). Specifically, we have started by identifying and considering alternative definitions of sustainability, by seeing how these definitions lead to asking different questions, and to seeing the problems, like climate change or professional responsibility, differently.

We need to continue examining how environmental problems are posed. For example, some have argued that sustainable development actually is an oxymoron, that we cannot talk about or achieve sustainability and still operate within a growth paradigm. Regardless of where you stand on that or any other attendant issue on sustainability, one thing is clear: We need to work toward greater clarity in defining and articulating the nature of sustainability, its components and implications. That is the next step, and it will help us to undo at least part of the problem—of creating false dichotomies or binaries—such as economic development versus environmental protection—on which the seemingly impossible choices are based. It is essential here that we recognize differences—make more subtle distinctions to eliminate over-simplifications, over-generalizations—and appropriately insert new complexities and collaborations.

Five Arguments Concerning Sustainability

1. Most of the various definitions and discourse on sustainability avoid the key question: "Sustaining what?"

2. There is good evidence that all we mean by sustainability is continuing our current ways of life indefinitely, without distress. But the way we now live is demonstrably unsustainable.

3. We implicitly answer what sustainability is when we ask either-or questions (based on dichotomies) such as "Should we preserve the spotted owl or support the logging industry?" because decisions about ecological action and sustainability are actually choices between differing—and likely competing—worldviews, all of which involve some version of the inseparable dimensions of economic-physical development and environmental integrity.

4. Distributive justice is a major challenge in ecological decision making. In dealing with the results of economic development and interchanges with the environment, there is an enormously uneven distribution of goods and harms, with very few receiving a disproportionate amount of the former and a very large number bearing most of the latter.

5. In today's post-modern world, it can be argued that the only motive for ethical behavior is likely compassion-care.

Mugerauer 1996, "Theories of Sustainability: Environmental Ethics, Mixed-Communities, and Compassion" in appendix IV.

→ Also see Engel and Engel (1990)

Sustaining the Unsustainable? How Do We Live?
If we consider sustainability broadly, we make little progress, a point already clear just by considering the extent to which definitions of green buildings amount to questions of energy use or of issues of human practices and cultural-political value systems.

One way to gain greater clarity on what to sustain and how to do it is to begin to explore the major types of human settlement and some of their defining characteristics. The descriptions that follow mostly have to do with cities in the United States because that is the primary site of the authors' and many readers' lives. Obviously, other parts of the world also need to be explored in more detail—precisely what we each need to do in our own decision making process.

For example, according to the *New Atlas of Planet Management* (2005), in the U.S. alone, if every fifth consumer purchased one of the most energy-efficient refrigerators available, the electric savings would eliminate the need for four large coal-fired power plants.

4. Cities

It is appropriate to begin a consideration of how we live not only by looking at today's cities but also by projecting into the future, which surely will be explosively urban: "A great migration is under way. Some 20 million people move to cities every year, a human transmigration unprecedented in history. By the year 2000, almost 50% of the world's population was urbanized, compared with 14% in 1900. By 2030 60% will be urbanized. Until the Industrial Revolution, only 1 in 5 people lived in a settlement with more than 10,000 inhabitants. Today, we talk about 'mega-cities'—urban conglomerates of 5 million or more. In 1950 there were 9 such mega-cities; by 1980 the number had risen to 26, of which 19 exceeded 7 million. By 2015 there likely will by 39 mega-cities worldwide. By that time Tokyo will reach 36 million people." (Myers and Kent 2005, 226.)

No matter what the problems of life in cities, they continue to draw large numbers of people who perceive that they harbor more opportunities for a chance at a better life. With the continuing increase in population, the environmental impact of urban phenomena, already problematic, will become an even more critical issue. What are the most relevant dimensions of cities about which decisions are needed? What are the major environmental issues?

What makes a good city a healthy city? What are the elements? How would they appear in the lifeworlds of all the organisms that compose the living environment and would they be experienced by us? (cf. *The Gaia Atlas* 1992, 104). The *Gaia Atlas* examines what they call the metabolism of the city, and identifies several critical dimensions that are part of this metabolic system: the processes of energy and materials (energy, food, water, air, and waste) in and out that keep the city and its residents alive.

Urban well-being would include such well-functioning
and integrated dimensions as:

- Energy provision
- Waste management
- Economic resources and viability
- Food supply and urban agriculture
- Water resources
- Healthy air quality
- Appropriate density
- Public transportation
- Communication infrastructure
- Affordable housing
- Supportive work places
- Open and green spaces
- Social justice

→ For further consideration of each of these factors, see
Myers and Kent, *The New Atlas of Planet Management
(2005); Myers, Gaia: An Atlas of Planet Management
(1992);* Giradet *The Gaia Atlas* (1992); Roseland, *Toward
Sustainable Communities (1998)* and *Eco-City: Healthy
Communities, Healthy Plane (1997).*

Chief among the most important urban factors, of course, is energy: "Modern cities are products of cheap energy . . . In recent years energy consumption
has gone up faster and faster: commercial energy use in U.S. cities went up by
an average of .56 percent per year between 1960 and 1980, closely following
rates of economic growth . . . Cities are also responsible for a colossal wastage
of energy. Electricity is supplied from power stations that can be less than 30%
efficient; over 70% of their fuel energy is wasted in the generation and transmission of electricity" (*Gaia Atlas* 1992, 106). Waste comes in many forms. For the
U.S. alone, appliances left in stand-by mode (computers, TVs, microwaves, etc.)
cost consumers more than $4 billion a year. Worldwide, other energy is wasted.
For example, only 40 percent of the energy released from burning fossil fuels
produces a useful service; the rest is lost as waste heat (Myers and Kent 2005,
141–143). Here we see that the point of the two classic tactics—conservation
and innovative technology—is to lessen the difficulty of the problems. At least
we can begin to see that there is very little sense in asking the either-or: Should
we reduce use or find new energy sources? As stated earlier, if we shift away
from such dichotomous questions we can more sensibly ask how we can do both
more effectively and we can ask deeper questions about why we consume the
way we do, what prevents us from changing, and so on.

Given the processes and materials that we have chosen to use over the last century and a half, and our recent historical patterns of consumption (which certainly were not those of frontier society nor of the Great Depression), there naturally are specific kinds of by-products and waste, which increase with the size and prosperity of the population. On the other hand, the very industrial processes that produced huge quantities of goods and the vast modern cities in the nineteenth century also generate enormous pollution. Now globalized, "One-fifth of humankind, over one billion people, live in places, particularly mega-cities, where the air is not fit to breathe. Atmospheric pollution in cities comes from a number of sources: . . . factories, refineries, power stations, airplanes, cars [and is] a new cause for respiratory diseases and conditions such as asthma" (*Gaia Atlas* 1992, 108). In São Paulo, Brazil, 90% of the smog stems from motor vehicle emissions. In Bangkok, where cars spend an average of 44 days each year stuck in traffic, one million respiratory infections are linked to air pollution. (As we can begin to see, further discernments are necessary. Not only are different nations, regions, and cities variable in the amount of pollution suffered, but within given cities there are disparities, with places of neglect and environmental degradation.

Further, just as the environmental problems caused by factories were bad enough to motivate well-intended industrialists to create company towns in healthier rural environments, today pollution continues to be problematic in established areas, and is newly troubling in hitherto rural areas as they become industrialized. This is dramatically evident in countries outside of the U.S. with little or no restrictions or governmental controls on air pollution. Consider the case of China:

"The plumes of smoke over Chinese cities are so dense that sometimes the cities are not visible on satellite photographs: the people call the smog the 'yellow dragon'. China burns 900 million tons of coal every year, about 80 percent of its total energy consumption. The price of coal is very low, so there is no incentive to burn it efficiently. Since the coal has a very high sulfur content of some five per cent, urban air pollution in China is highly acidic." (Gaia Atlas 1992, 108). As is well known, and as discussed at the beginning of this chapter, one of the consequences of our energy use and other productive activities is that we generate enough atmospheric pollution to increase global warming.

Given that these are the conditions we have created for ourselves and other species, we are faced with enormous ethical questions on both an individual and societal level. And in between there are decisions we can make that contribute to the ethical practice of the environmental professions to which we belong. For architects, landscape architects, planners, urban designers, construction managers and engineers, a critical decision making point comes already when they decide what kinds of projects they undertake. Then, in working on each project, there are key decisions about materials and strategies—will you use recycled materials and other green strategies? Will you use permeable materials in your pathways? Use native species in your planting plan? Will you build new neighborhoods in the foothills on the edge of town or work on infill development and neighborhood revitalization projects within the city? In each way, then, every project we work on, and each choice that we make within it, contributes to the larger whole of how we live our lives and the well-being of our cities.

One of the most troubling phenomena is that the decisions we make to deal with environmental problems often further contribute to or complicate the matter, exacerbating the situation for all of us. For example, slowing or stopping the trend in increased temperatures cannot be done by continuing the practices of consumptive North American culture and technology—which, of course, is spreading across the world, with especially problematic impacts in climatic zones that already are hot and humid. We are not going to make much progress in examining either the problem of climate change or the responsibility we bear through our practices and the range of options we normally consider without focusing on our assumptions and patterns of energy use—which again are very different for the facets of North American culture most aggravating the problem.

What Role Can Engineers, Landscape Architects, Architects, Planners, and Urban Designers Play?

What can these particular professions contribute to environmental problem-solving?

To what degree do such practitioners have an ethical obligation to mitigate environmental problems?

Can we make successful changes incrementally or do we need revolutionary, sweeping changes? How feasible are the latter?

Do your agree or disagree with the following?:

> Rather than tinkering with small incremental improvements in the efficiency of air conditioning systems, we need a step change to new paradigms for cooling buildings. Just as with the cars, we need super-low-consumption, dual fuel, eco-buildings that are naturally ventilated in spring, winter, and autumn, and in summer are run on solar air-conditioning when the sun is out topped up by small amounts of grid electricity when it is not. This is the way forward.
>   (Roaf, Crichton, and Nicol 2005, 233)

→ For more on the roles of engineers, environmental designers, and construction professionals see Roaf, Crichton, and Nicol (2005), including the sections on vernacular and new materials.

Increased temperatures lead many in prosperous countries like the United States and parts of Asia to deal with the problem by increasing the use of air conditioning—which increases the amount of greenhouse gas emissions, further warming the atmosphere, exacerbating a vicious negative cycle. "Buildings consume over 50% of all energy generated around the world and produce over half of all climate change emissions globally. In the United States alone air conditioning uses around 30-40% of all building-related energy, so say a fifth, or 20%, of all energy in the United States is used for air conditioning. The United States uses around 25% of all the world energy: that means that potentially around 5% of all greenhouse gases in the world come from US air conditioning alone" (Roaf, Crichton, and Nicol 2005, 223–24; cf. pp. 217–39).

The City: Great or Awful?

The City—great or awful? and the city versus the suburbs are two dichotomies that have dominated discourse in urban studies, planning, geography, and sociology. Research in this area falls into different camps. Certainly there are merits and demerits to urban, suburban and rural life alike, and cities have their share of greatness and awfulness as well. But still dichotomous questions persist. In a 2002 *Seattle Times* article, journalist William Deitrich, argued that people's options are basically either to stew in traffic or live in a box. Presumably, the suburbanites who must commute to the city for work will stew in traffic but live in something larger than a box, and the urbanites who opt to live in the city and presumably live nearer to their workplace than their suburban counterparts will be stuck living in small quarters. While many would agree that such a dichotomy is simplistic and misleading, it would seem that overall we are not fully aware of different options in between. What is your opinion of this argument? Do you see any other alternatives for where you live?

---

5. Suburbs

Suburban Sprawl

If the tensions between the city and suburbs are not new, neither is the over-simplified dichotomy embedded in the attitude that we should prohibit further suburban growth because it destroys the environment. In fact, wherever we develop large amounts of land for habitation—especially in the mode in which we recently do live, a critical point to which we need to return—we destroy the environment that was there. But, despite attempts at global population control (with some successes) there are more and more people who need a place to live. Moreover, despite attempts to discipline ourselves not to settle in especially delicate or critical environments, such as the fragile-soiled hill country above the aquifers of central Texas or the foothills of the Wasatch Front by Salt Lake City, Utah, people of means continue to prefer such places and use their resources to occupy them because they are considered desirable and beautiful. (Think, for example, of how the real-estate industry markets such places—"commanding views!"—they are called "manors" and "estates" and often are named after the very eco-system or habitat they destroy, such as "Fox Hills" or "Big Oak Creek"). How then can we move beyond a not-very-helpful dualism and not blanket-vilify the suburbs or those who live in them, or blindly defend them either?

There is no shortage of public discussion about the continued development of suburbs as a social and environmental problem, especially in the United States, England, and Australia, and increasingly in other parts of the world. Critics have long charged that the suburbs undermine social cohesion and promote isolation of individuals and social-racial exclusion, that the sprawl of continual suburban development is irrecoverably consuming natural landscapes and farmland at an alarming and environmentally harmful rate. At the same time, the suburb is a form much-loved by many, and a successful social-economic form of development. Since one of this book's central guidelines is that better environmental decisions would result if we could remove false or misleading dichotomies, we need to be especially careful not to over-generalize or essentialize. Although we might still speak of *the* suburbs, in fact, there is no one kind of suburb.

This is not to deny that there are particular problems connected with suburbs, but confusing the different sorts of places, and the way people live there and use them, will only muddle our understanding of the already complex relationships that suburbs have with neighboring cities (and each other). That makes it that much more difficult to make decisions that best fit the exact local situation at hand as well as the embracing global context. Recent research has helped us to discern the many operative distinctions that we need to take into account when making decisions, especially if we are to avoid facile generalizations and stereotypes. Distinct from the most familiar type of suburb, those built during the post-war boom of the 1950s, there now are a variety of recent new forms and of revived older ones, with various mixtures of the residential and business-commercial dimensions. As one recent study argues,

> The confusion, if not chaos, of contemporary suburban reality fits uneasily with the idealized image of suburbia as a never-never land of stable middle- and upper-class white families living with their young children in ranch-style homes surrounded by wide yards of green. Today suburbs are this and much more. They also contain the elderly, single parents, blacks, Hispanics, high-rise buildings, most of the nation's household and personal trade, the bulk of the nation's manufacturing plants, and a growing share of the nation's offices. In the years

since the 1960s, suburbia has become remarkably diverse, both in terms of residents and the variety of land uses. (Palen 1995, 3)

Palen demonstrates the utility of the more complex typologies of suburban
areas that convey a sense of the true diversity of such settlements, citing Michael
Weiss' 12-item classification of ethnographic areas and their associated characteristics:
1. Blue-Blood Estates – The wealthiest neighborhoods, largely suburban houses
2. Furs and Station Wagons – Newer-money metropolitan bedroom suburbs
3. Pools and Patios – Older upper-middle-class suburban communities
4. Gray Power – Upper-middle-class retirement suburbs
5. New Beginnings – Outer-city or suburban areas of single complexes, garden
   apartments, and well-kept bungalows (single or childless)
6. Two More Rungs – Comfortable multiethnic suburbs
7. Blue-Chip Blues – More affluent blue-collar suburbs
8. Young Suburbia – Outlying child-rearing suburbs
9. Young Homesteaders – Exurban boomtown of younger mid-scale families
10. Levittown, U.S.A. – Aging postwar working-class tract suburbs
11. Rank and File – Older blue-collar industrial suburbs
12. Norma Rae-Ville – Older industrial suburbs and mill towns, primarily in the
    south.
    Drawn from: Palen 1995, 112–113; also see the larger source work, Weiss 1988.

6. Rural Areas: for example, the Arid American West

Beyond the suburbs, rural regions are home to a smaller and smaller percentage
of the residents in the United States. This dwindling landscape reflects a long-
term effect of the political economy that has made family agriculture difficult to
sustain economically. If we reflect momentarily on the decisions that have
shaped settlement patterns in the U.S., along with our collective cultural identity, there is little doubt that environmentally unsound decisions were also a part
of this process and continue to operate today. This is manifest in the unsustainable places and ways of life to which many are attached and which form part of
our national consciousness (e.g. many living in neighborhoods that are zoned for
single-use residential with minimal requirements surrounding each single-family
house. This has created the very home places that suburban dwellers have grown
to love and desire). It is also manifest in the ideologies that underlie our culture
(such as the wild west and the "family farm") and in turn have influenced many
of our land use decisions. Think also of the example provided in chapter 2 of
manifest destiny discussed in the Stewart and Williams' article on people's perceptions of Mount Rushmore as a symbol of manifest destiny—European settlers destiny, right and moral duty to expand across the continent. In addition,
we pointed out in chapters 1 and 2, our ideologies have led many of us to frame
issues in a way that dichotomizes multi-dimensional issues —such as whether to

use the national parks to the degree that doing so yields considerable environmental damage, or to leave them alone and risk losing connection with nature—when in fact the reality of this and most phenomena lies somewhere in between.

We are not trying to tackle the entire complex of environmental-social-economic issues in its entirely, but simply identifying this area as part of what needs to be reflected upon when thinking about sustainability and ethical decision making. In questioning the choices that led to the development of rural regions and the challenges such development can place on delicate eco-systems, we can consider the case of the substantial development that has occurred in the arid region of the Southwest in the past 100 years, particularly the fastest growing metro-areas of Phoenix and Las Vegas. According to the U.S. Census Bureau, the population of Arizona grew by about 423 people per day during the five-year period between July 2000 and July 2005. That is a net figure that also takes into account how many people left Arizona or died during that time. Most of this growth occurred in Phoenix.

Explosive Desert Development

Urban development seems to fly in the face of any reasonable idea of sustainable environmental or landscape use. Yet it seems unlikely that explosive new desert development will cease, since one of the areas of the U.S. where urban development is most visible is in the sunbelt and desert regions. For example, cities like Phoenix and Las Vegas have grown exponentially in the last five years.

To what degree do you think this urbanization is environmentally destructive? If it is destructive, is it socially improper or unethical? If harmful or unethical, is there any way to mitigate, if not dramatically change, these settlement patterns?

After you formulate your initial answers and discuss the matter, keep a record of what you said; then we can return to the issue after we consider ways in which the lessons of the vernacular and new technologies and designs can contribute to positive solutions, unknotting at least part of what is now typically posed as either-or alternatives.

The two largest and fastest growing cities in the U.S. are Phoenix (2005 population: 1,461,575) and Tucson (2005 population: 515,526), known as Arizona's Sun Corridor. Researchers and community leaders alike believe that these two cities will merge into one megalopolis in as little as a decade, engulfing several small towns along the way (Reagor 2006). While the downtowns of the two major cities are separated by 120 miles, the existing suburbs reach much farther along Interstate 10. Moreover, planned developments for both cities— one stretching sixty miles south of metropolitan Phoenix, the other heading forty miles north of Tucson—will leave only a twenty-mile gap between the two cities in the next handful of years (Regor 2006). No one likes to think that the desert is disappearing or being compromised, but the sheer growth in population, accompanied by expectations in achieving and maintaining a certain lifestyle is driving a demand for housing that is spreading farther and farther out into the desert.

In terms of sustainability (water and energy use, and so on) these desert cities are not naturally able to sustain current populations and land uses, much less those of the projected future. As one group of biology students from Earlham College noted in their report, "The Ecological Impacts of Human Development in the Southwestern United States":

> In the last two centuries, humans have found more and more efficient ways of making the desert livable for an increasing number of people. Technological advances, in the form of enormous dams, miles of water canals, and millions of air-conditioning units, have resulted in the desert becoming an extremely comfortable environment for cities, as well as for agriculture and grazing industries. However, these advances have had negative effects on the desert ecosystem. Increased grazing have degraded riparian zones and altered the desert plant community and agriculture and irrigation has altered streams, rivers, and canyons. Exotic and sometimes invasive species have been introduced that can quickly colonize and dominate the landscape. Increased visitors to parks and natural areas have affected the biotic soil crusts of even the most preserved areas. Finally, the growth of cities and ensuing suburban sprawl is replacing the once-desert landscape with extensive pavement, grassed lawns, homes and picket fences. (Cox, Kauffman, Hart, Lund, and Wagner, www.earlham.edu/~biol/desert/impacts.htm, accessed April 20, 2007)

There are two especially pressing problem areas here: first, the seemingly unsustainable patterns of urbanization; second, the competing uses contributing variously to environmental degradation/conservation and the question of how better protection might be accomplished by the public and/or private sectors.

Of course, in these cases of rapid urban development, the environmental issues are not in the least merely factual matters; rather, they are tangled with deeply held and contested individual core values and group worldviews, some of which operate at a full-blown mythical level, as we can see with the cases of Progress and manifest destiny.

7. Infrastructure: Cars and Highways

We can gain a better understanding of the problematic aspects of different settlement patterns, and the way their commonalities knit together into a larger set of environmental problems, if we continue to unfold the important physical and social features that make them what they are. Within each of the three main landscapes—cities, suburbs, rural areas—we have made decisions about settlement patterns, which include the physical and social relationships among residences, work places, recreational areas, and so on. In each case we have continually affirmed the importance of freedom enacted as mobility, and an especially individualized form of movement at that (minimally constrained by time schedules or spatial separation).

The forms of long-distance mass transportation have shifted from train or bus systems to automobile and airplane. Local travel, as we all know, has largely abandoned pedestrian modes (people once commonly walked miles to work within towns), and buses (to which, earlier, once extensive trolley systems had yielded) in favor of larger and more powerful individually operated vehicles and a few light-rail systems. With this movement, we made the correlate commitment to a vast infrastructure of roads and highways—which operates across and connects all of these rural, suburban, and urban areas. Of course, the United States is not alone in this, which makes historical and contemporary cross-cultural comparisons important. (And, as with forests, after we have cut down most in Europe and the United States, we now encourage developing nations to preserve theirs.) For example, many westerners are especially concerned with the damage that will be done when China surpasses us in automobiles per capita. In this case, as all others, empirical information is important in decision making.

Car Facts

- In New Delhi alone—one of the worst polluted cities in the world—air pollution has been causing 7,500 deaths a year, and 1.2 million people receive medical treatment for car-emission and air-pollution-related illnesses.
- China has declared the auto sector to be the chief pillar of the future economy with eight million cars produced in 2000, possibly reaching twenty-three million by 2010.

(Myers and Kent 2005, 235–36)

Important moral and political issues present themselves when considering these types of issues: on what grounds should local environmental-economic decisions involve consultation with other parties around the world who will be affected? What business do we have to urge other people not do what we have done ourselves—a point made more contentious by the fact that much deforestation, mineral extraction, industrialization, and vehicle production is generated or supported by the same capital system in Europe and the United States. (We will need to return to this issue later in the chapter in light of autonomy and distributive justice.)

8. Buildings, Houses, Lawns

The buildings that we design and construct and in which we spend such a large portion of our lives come with their own challenges and moments for ethical decision making. In places with wetter climates, reports show that "many [buildings have been] badly built, poorly insulated, and damp. Leaky flat rooms, condensation on thin walls, rooms too hot in summer and too cold in winter were typical complaints and all contributed to general ill health, and chronic respiratory problems in particular" (*Gaia Atlas* 1992, 82). Similarly, in hot, dry climates, we create building that generate enormous amounts of energy to keep occupants cool. And in cities across the nation, innovative buildings using glass and mirror have created glare and blinding problems on sunny days. What are architects ethical responsibilities in constructing buildings? (For more discussion on this, see chapter 2 and chapter 6.)

Another dimension of ethics concerning the built environment has to do with disparities in access to adequate and affordable housing and the disparities of housing for differing groups in different places. How can we better think about and build housing in terms of human rights? Is housing a right? Is affordable housing a right? What role, if any, should the government play in the provision of housing for the poor in a just society? As planner and ethicist Timothy Beatley argues:

> Housing (or shelter, as it is sometimes referred to) is one of the most basic human needs. While not usually a constitutional right, it is a moral claim frequently at the heart of many disputes about land use policy. The U.N. Declaration of Human Rights (Article 25 [1]), for example, lists housing as an important component of 'a standard of living adequate for . . . health and well-being'. In the United States many housing advocates point to the strong declaration in the 1949 Housing Act as the basis for the right:
> The Congress hereby declares that the general welfare and security of the nation and the health and living standards of its people require housing production and related community development sufficient to remedy the serious housing shortage, the elimination of substandard and other inadequate housing through the clearance of slums and blighted areas, *and the realization as soon as feasible of the goal of a decent home and a suitable living environment for every American family*, thus contributing to the development and redevelopment of communities and to the advancement of the growth, wealth, and security of the nation. [Author's emphasis.] (Beatley 1994, 74–75)

Shifts in the political economy have changed the way that the government and housing providers and advocates interpret and act upon the 1949 Housing Act. There currently are a number of governmental housing programs that each show unique ways of addressing the provision of housing for the poor. Some are tenant-based, like the Moving to Opportunity (MTO) Program,[3] or focus more on assistance to the residents themselves (e.g., rental subsidies like the Housing Voucher Program formerly known as Section 8) and some focus more on expanding the supply of affordable housing, such as the HOME program. There are also programs like the HOPE VI program, which replaces distressed public housing with new mixed-income neighborhoods (See appendix III for a fuller exploration of the ethical implications of this program), as well as other non-government programs designed to provide affordable housing such as community land trusts. In this program, people purchase their own home but the non-profit land trust owns the land underneath it to ensure that the property remains affordable for future homebuyers (it prevents people from purchasing the houses and flipping them for a profit).

And to what degree do private developers have a moral obligation to make housing affordable? There is no legal obligation on affordability in the private housing market; we can be charged whatever the market can bear. But is there an ethical dimension to this when the market squeezes out modest and low income people from decent living quarters?

Lawns

The area surrounding our housing is typically covered by a lawn—a favorite (as well as historically and economically important) feature of dwellings and other buildings in the United States, England, Australia, and many other parts of the world (especially as spread by Anglo-American influences). But, there has been considerable argument and evidence that the lawn has environmentally harmful dimensions. For example, compared to naturally occurring grasslands, the ordinary lawn has greater surface runoff, more nutrients lost in drainage water, and because of cultural practices about how to care for lawns there are also substantial pesticides and fertilizer nutrients washed into the local water supply and removed in grass clippings. Efforts to maintain lawns create more carbon dioxide output than input. As a consequence, there is less biological diversity as turf grasses and turf-adapted animals and microbes displace local species; fossil-fuel supplies are more rapidly depleted, and local air pollution and global warming are increased; municipal water supplies are more heavily used, as are municipal waste facilities; pesticides and herbicides may contaminate food chains, and even threaten human health; and runoff may disrupt the biological functions of local waters, and even cause large dead zones in deeper collection zones. (Bormann, Balmori, and Geballe 1962, esp. 90–91, 117; Jenkins 1994).

Given all these negative environmental consequences, is it ethical to continue our current practices in regard to lawns? If so, how do we perceive and respond to the larger environmental problems involved? If not, how could we better design and maintain lawns or green open spaces to achieve a healthier environment? It seems clear that our cultural preferences need to be examined, especially the aesthetic perceptions and preferences and our investment in the image and ideology that lawns (and the green) represent.

Moreover, how can we point to the environmental ramifications of such popular and widespread practices as growing and caring for lawns without seeming to pontificate? Are lawn-growers morally evil? Challenges come in consciousness-raising about the impacts of our cultural practices on the environment, being made aware of alternative strategies and making these strategies feasible and desirable. In addition, ethical choices do not simply lie with the individual consumer; there are choices also at the corporate level about what kind of fertilizers to produce and sell, and at the community and municipal level about watering practices, and the like.

9. Poverty and the Disadvantaged

Just as we cannot avoid hard decisions and responsibilities in regard to environmental crises and everyday problems we cannot ignore our responsibilities to address poverty—both as part of our general ethical duties and as an aspect inseparable from the natural and built environments and our well-being within them. So we must consider the ethical questions related to poverty and its attendant environmental issues of housing discrimination, segregation, and overcrowding, to name a few. In this short section it is our intention to raise several concerns as matters not just of social justice but environmental justice as well.

To begin, we must examine and recognize the extent to which the world's population is devastated by poverty:

> What is absolute poverty? "A condition of life so limited by malnutrition, illiteracy, disease, squalid surroundings, high infant mortality, and low life expectancy as to be beneath any reasonable definition of human decency." [This is] the classic description of absolute poverty, as defined by Robert McNamara, former president of the World Bank, in 1978 . . . In the 'boom' year of the 1980s, the number of people worldwide living in absolute poverty increased from 700 million in 1980 to about 1.2 billion by 1990. Thus, nearly a quarter of humanity lives in a state of virtual destitution.
>
> (*Gaia Atlas* 1992, 76; cf. 77–79)

Absolute poverty (when defined as having an income of less that $1 per day) afflicts 1.9 billion people—every sixth person in the world. Of those absolute poor, most are landless laborers, marginal farmers, and unskilled laborers in cities. In developed nations, we see fewer cases of absolute poverty as described by the World Bank, but still witness startling disparities in wealth and access to resources. According to the U.S. Census, the percentage of households living in poverty rose to 12.5 percent in 2003, for a total of 35.5 million Americans. The poverty standards for U.S. children are particularly bleak. According to the Economic Policy Institute the poverty rate for minors in 2006 was 21.9 percent—the highest poverty rate in the developed world (Allegretto 2006).[4]

Our short tour of environmental phenomena can then return to the where we started: the city, and specifically for our purposes here, urban poverty. Increasingly, urbanization occurs without any significant opportunities for migrants. People tend to try and live close to their source of income, as factory workers, traders, or domestic servants. Urban centers are the preferred locations for the informal settlements that permeate developing-world cities. Given half a chance, people will do their best to turn squatter camps into neighborhoods to be proud of, using informal patterns of mutual support. But often they are hindered by the authorities who don't like what they perceive as disorderly camps (*Gaia Atlas* 1992, 68; cf. 71–72, 128–131). Similar debates and reactions can be found in the U.S. in regard to poor neighborhoods and public housing.

We cannot talk about settlement patterns and their ethical implications without acknowledging that a history of "housing discrimination, residential segregation, and limited public transportation severely limit the access" of certain groups, particularly people of color, to the suburbs (Bullard 1990, 1). For African-Americans, this has created what Mindy Fullilove calls an "archipelago state" where "Black America is a many-island nation within the American nation" (Fullilove 2005, 27). First the rural South, known as the Black Belt, was home to many African-Americans after the era of slavery, but between 1910 and 1930 there was a "great migration" of one and a half million African-Americans to the major cities of the Northeast and Midwest. Then, from 1940 to the 1970s many of these same migrants moved into the inner cities (Fullilove 2005). Scholars have attested to the active creative life in the archipelago ghetto nation, but however well people got by supporting one another, these were communities created nonetheless from exclusion. To the extent that such segregation continues today, we can question the social and environmental justice of our housing practices and settlement patterns. For fuller consideration of issues related to housing the poor, see appendix III, the case study on HOPE IV.

Worldwide we are faced with dramatic housing inadequacies with one billion people living in slums—defined by poor quality of construction, insecurity of tenure, inadequate access to safe drinking water and sanitation, and overcrowding (Myers and Kent 2005, 187). Overcrowding is one of the attendant issues of urban poverty, and it is a feature of most major world cities today. In the cities of the developing world it is fact of daily life. Lagos tops all other cities with an occupancy rate of 5.8 people per room. By comparison, Indian cities average about three people per room, while North American cities have between one-half and one person per room (*Gaia Atlas* 1992, 72). "Shanties are often built on areas unfit for human habitation—on rubbish dumps, steep hillsides, areas prone to subsistence or flooding, or on polluted land. In Rio de Janeiro in 1987 hundreds of people died in favelas built on steep slopes when rainstorms washed away the bare soil on which their shacks were built" (*Gaia Atlas* 1992, 73–74).

In considering these issues related to poverty, there are many ethical questions that come to mind. To what extent do those of us in the environmental professions have a responsibility to address poverty? How can we do so?

10. Positive Positions and Contributions toward Sustainability

There are several ways to facilitate the decision making process in response to the environmental problems facing us.

- The first involves continuing to seek a more adequate definition and vision of what sustainability is (one that develops beyond the multiple definitions noted at the beginning of the chapter and that avoids many of the unnecessary dichotomies and perhaps dilemmas).
- The second consists in unknotting dichotomies and dissolving dilemmas by reconceptualizing and reclassifying where appropriate, and initiating new, alternative social constructions where possible.
- The third involves what the environmental disciplines and professions can contribute, perhaps uniquely, to solving ethical and environmental problems. This involves opening the possibilities of new perceptions (aesthetic, categorical, and ideological). Some examples of these perceptual shifts can be seen in the transformation of "swamps" to "wetlands" and their denizens going from being evil, frightening creatures of the night to friendly insect-controllers for which we built bat-houses and tourist attractions in downtown Austin). Especially important is the professional ability to create different empirical conditions and consequences by means of new modes of designing, building, and living, for example with new technology or new knowledge from past and current best practices.

We will see here that a better definition and vision of sustainability will redistribute factors, showing that the critical elements are not opposed, but actually shared. In other words, while we may have thought that the environmental decisions we must make are between doing either X or Y (either economic development or environmental protection—to which we shall return shortly), we need to recognize that each of the several real choices we have involve some different measure of all the basic factors (economic, environmental, cultural). This means that while the necessary choices are more complex and difficult than we imagined, the basic factors to consider are not so different in each of the alternatives. Again, this shows that the ethical dilemmas are not primarily factual but a matter of worldviews, values, and politics.

When we attempt to deal with dilemmas that are based on oppositions or choices that are too simplistic to admit an adequate response—such as, should we save the spotted owl and the first-growth forest or support the logging industry?—we are close to an implicit answer about what sustainability is and how we need to make decisions accordingly. As Engel and Engel argue, decisions about ecological action and sustainability are, in effect, choices between differing—and likely competing—entire life worlds, all of which also involve some version of the inseparable features: economic-physical development and environmental integrity. They also operate by way of the second strategy noted above: to unknot dichotomies and start dissolving dilemmas by reconceptualizing and reclassifying, arguing for the adoption of new, alternative social constructs. Mugerauer argues that Engel and Engel's special contribution is to explain that "what appeared as a complex polar issue—preservation and intrinsic value on one side and conservation and instrumental value on the other— dissolves before us when we see that it does not present the most basic alternatives," since "as a matter of fact, one either nurtures or harms entire eco-communities, including human members . . . the real ecological ethical choices are between paths of development that are ecologically sustainable for entire mixed communities of plants, animals, and people, and the choices for those ways of development that do not ecologically sustain whole communities of plants, animals, and people" (1996, 19–20).

What can Environmental Disciplines and Professions Uniquely Contribute to Environmental Well-Being, Decision Making, and Resolving Dilemmas?
The environmental professions and disciplines can help eliminate or reduce dilemmas by creatively eliminating (what were thought to be inevitable) harms by learning from the vernacular traditions of the places within which they are embedded and by developing new social-physical conditions through the use of innovative materials, forms, and processes, thus changing the empirical conditions and their effects by imaginative design and construction techniques. In addition, the environmental professions have a unique role in opening up new perceptual possibilities by generating new aesthetic, categorical, and ideological complexes.

What to do? Environmental and Social Focus Responsibility of Everyone, but especially the Environmental Disciplines and Professions
Arthur Versluis and Victor Papanek charge all of us with responsibility in regard to ethical environmental decisions, speaking of a spiritual need that is not necessarily identified with religion. Versluis contends:

> We each must come to terms with who we are as spiritual beings and with the natural world as a place of spiritual revelation. This is particularly true in America, where there is so little concern with the preservation of open land, where unlike Europe so far, cities are allowed to sprawl over the countryside endlessly, eating up the earth, and leaving behind gaudy, tawdry, garish, decaying commercial strips and rows of rotting apartments. American mercantilism is omnivorous and will not stop until it has consumed everything beautiful; it seems altogether evident that one cannot stop the juggernaut of the modern world. But each individual can come to understand spiritual truth, can see the world in a new way, and can become spiritually renewed, regenerated.
>
> (Versluis 1992, 136)

For his part, Papanek "calls for ethical responsibility and spiritual values in design and architecture to help us find a sustainable and harmonious way of life . . . [and contends that] all of us, not just architects, can benefit by looking at and learning from past building traditions" (1995, p.13).

Paper or Plastic? Wood or Steel?

Every day millions of people across the U.S. walk into su-
permarkets and are asked, "Paper or plastic?" In the ordinary
act of buying groceries we are faced with a basic decision
that has environmental implications. Thus, we make an impact with even simple mundane activities and choices. On a
larger scale, architects, engineers and construction managers
make more-lasting choices about which materials to use. In
making choices we can consider the embodied energy f materials. This generally refers to the amount of energy consumed
by all processes associated with the production of a product
including mining, manufacturing, and transporting materials
along with administrative functions of buildings. (*Your Home
Technical Manual*, a joint initiative of the Australian government   and   design,   and   construction   industries—
www.greenhouse.gov.au/yourhome/technical/fs31.html.   See
Thompson & Sorvig (2000) for basic, comprehensive information on embodied energy.

Wood is considered by many a good construction material
because it is a renewable resource (assuming that we are not
cutting the few remaining old-growth forests). But, deforestation causes erosion and increases in CO_2 (higher levels of
CO_2 result not only from cutting down or burning forests—
which are crucial in maintaining the balance of atmospheric
composition—but from "burning the brushland for subsistence agriculture and wood fires for cooking" which accounts
for "almost 30% of the CO_2 released into the atmosphere
each year" (Al Gore 2006, 227)

Steel production also contributes significantly to pollution,
but some contend that it is more recyclable than wood, or
even reusable if properly designed, and thus a better choice.

Clearly, good decisions require knowledge. Do some research
on either wood or steel's contribution to pollution and see to
what extent factual information helps shape your decision
about which is more recyclable—or where the issue comes
down to interpretation based on larger viewpoints.

Papanek elaborates how we can learn from traditional architecture:

> To think intelligently about vernacular architecture and environment, we must
> rid ourselves of fallacies . . . [In] trying to understand the rich tradition of ver-
> nacular architecture . . . we really can't see the subject at all unless we set aside
> . . . individual interpretations and realize that vernacular architecture is the re-
> sult of multiple causation. We would need to consider: the methodology (the
> combination of material, tool, and process), dispersion and congruence pat-
> terns, cumulative slow-paced evolution, social expectations and practices re-
> garding the environment, cultural beliefs and values, and aesthetic forms and
> symbolisms—all dynamically interactive in a network or matrix. (Papanek
> 1995, 118–138)

11. Lessons of the Vernacular

As we have seen in the course of this book, one key to resolving some environmental dilemmas is to unravel the tension between alternatives—each of which
has some desirable and some undesirable aspects—which is precisely what
makes a dilemma a dilemma. To build something in a particular location because we need the facility now, or the jobs and economic boost that will come
with it; or to not build there because it will harm the natural environment or the
people living on the site, or because it will cost too much to build there and
mitigate the likely damages. Finding alternative possibilities for designing and
building in a way that does not do such harms obviously provides a preferable
solution—an approach often more possible than initially thought if all the players, from clients to designers to contractors to maintenance staff, collaborate and
remain open to new choices (that is, the air-conditioning experts can not insist
that all HVAC (heating, ventilation, air-conditioning) solutions must involve
more air conditioning, nor the construction company that concrete is the only
material that can be considered, and so on).

Toward this end, learning to appreciate the lessons of vernacular architecture and traditional settlements can provide fresh ideas for how to conceive and
build, as well as for alternative social patterns that are useful. For example, we
can better understand how neighborhoods have worked with large numbers of
people in close proximity, or how pedestrian dynamics actually enliven places,
increasing business and safety. An especially fruitful area of transfer lies in
building and settlement form, and material and energy use; for example, passive
solar and thermal control. Wonderful examples can be found of how ventilation
by means of wind chimneys can control heat and humidity in the desert, or how
placing earthen buildings very close together enables the inner areas to be
shaded and cooler in the mid-day sun. Hassan Fathy operated at both the cultural
and material levels in planning New Gourna, a resettlement area that resulted
from dam construction and subsequent flooding of the original village in Egypt.
Though he received some criticism for creating forms that were considered by
some to be inaccurate in regard to traditional design and construction and thus

too new or not innate to the population, there was substantial community participation, including training for many in what was needed to erect their own
buildings. In addition to the insights for cultural-built and natural environmental
design—as Fathy puts it for a new attitude to rural rehabilitation—there are economic lessons here, given his ability to provide housing at an exceptionally low
cost per unit ($500 for the time) (Fathy 1973).

Lessons of the Vernacular: Forms and Materials

What can we learn from the vernacular that is useful today?
Find some cases in which the vernacular is not at all a good
idea for us today, or at least not in some of the conditions in
which it is promoted. Then, find some cases in which the
vernacular was not successful in its own time and place—we
need to stay alert so we don't become falsely nostalgic for
the good old days that never were.

What new materials, forms, technologies can be helpful to
solve environmental dilemmas? There is little point in saying
that technology is bad, since humans have become human in
large part through it. Articulate the character of appropriate
technology, to use Schumaker's wonderful phrase.

How can we do our best to avoid unintended consequences
(such as what has happened with the greening of parts of the
developing world to supply food that resulted in monocul-
tures, dependence on fertilizers, the consequent increased
consumption of oil byproducts)?

What truth is there to the claim that designers and builders
have an ethical responsibility in regard to materials and their
honest use?

The next step in Fathy's work shows how what we learn from one traditional context (here within the Middle East's hot arid climate) about the importance of local building materials, methods, and forms can be applied to the
Southwest of the United States for instance. It also shows us that success depends on an integration of social, cultural, engineering, planning, and design
factors. Ways to live in harmony with the environment, without the environmental costs of air-conditioning obviously are important as we attempt to solve
the dilemmas about the need to house the earth's growing population, to elimi-

nate the disparities between rich and poor, and to conserve energy at all levels. Hence the second volume of Fathy's research spells out for non-experts the relevant more technical aspects such as thermal conduction and resistance, radiation, thermal convection, atmospheric pressure, water vapor, cooling by evaporation, thermal gain and loss, and dynamic thermal equilibrium. (Fathy 1986).

Applying this to some of the problems we considered earlier in this chapter, we might find different answers to whether we should continue to build large cities in the Southwest's hot deserts. Reframing the question in light of the lessons of vernacular architecture and settlement patterns, instead of asking, "Should we continue to build cities that depend on non-sustainable energy consumption?" we can ask, "How could we forego air-conditioning (which not only consumes huge amounts of energy, pollutes the atmosphere with CO_2, and itself increases the heat by its very processes, instead cooling by proven passive thermal and wind controls)?" Though such questions do not solve the problems at hand, nor address other issues such as water consumption, but they do change the ideas about possibilities for innovative solutions. The shift in focus moves the questions where they most properly belong: on our perceptions of needs and desires, our valuation of nature and future generations as compared to our current habits. Do we need and want to live in the desert? If so, the question would be how to do so in a sustainable manner. The question would be whether we are prepared to make the necessary changes, to sacrifice some of the patterns of consumption and convenience, of wearing suits and ties to look correct for business purposes, of driving in cars that are literally glass and steel boxes—what could be worse in the heat?

12. New Forms and Materials

At the other end of the spectrum from vernacular resolutions to some social-environmental dilemmas, there is substantial effort to find new forms and materials to mitigate the poor living conditions in the exploding cities of today and tomorrow. In contrast to assumptions and decisions behind the failed high-rises of the post-World War II period, in which many of the poor around the world were miserably housed (exemplified by the Pruitt-Igoe housing project in St. Louis that was demolished shortly after it was constructed), there does not need to be a dilemma between urban housing and a sustainable environment. Or, at least, the dilemma may be reduced to a set of still-difficult, but manageable problems. As Ken Yeang and others are demonstrating, the green skyscraper is a viable option for urban living. There is also the emerging strategy of living buildings. The Living Building Challenge was recently put forward by the Cascadia Region Green Building Council in the Pacific Northwest. While not restricted to high-rises, it is a challenge to architects, engineers and other design professionals to employ green strategies that go beyond the LEED platinum level and generate all of a building's energy with renewable resources, and that captures and treats all of its water on site.

Given exploding urban populations and the desire to avoid the spread of sprawl and further ecological degradation, sustainable buildings, especially high-rises, with their small footprints, can eliminate some of what were assumed to be inevitable social or environmental harms associated with large urban buildings, thus in themselves constituting an ethical choice. Dramatic reduction in energy use can, in fact, be coupled with enhanced quality of environment and ways of life, especially if there is comprehensive collaboration at the beginning of the process, when decisions have the most power to set the course of events and yet the lowest cost of change (before actual construction begins). As Yeang contends, "building designers (the architects, engineers, and other specialists involved with the production of buildings) can make a significant difference and can contribute to the achievement of a sustainable future," which will directly benefit future generations and make it easier for policy makers to make good decisions. (Yeang 1999, 7).

Debates about the merits and disadvantages of tall buildings are not likely to be resolved, nor do they need to be, given the variety of local conditions and many options that should remain open to imaginative designers if they are to make the contributions of which they are capable. For example, it would be a good research project to compare the views on and approaches to urban high-rises by Yeang with that of Roaf, Crichton, and Nicol (2005, 240–268). In any case, it may be that the approach advocated by Yeang and his colleagues will fulfill the vision of Paulo Soleri, who argued in the 1960s that if we did not discipline ourselves to leave much of the natural world alone, especially by finding creative ways to live satisfactorily—even richly—in very dense high-rises, we would wind up spreading ourselves across the face of the earth, as a form of cancer that spreads everywhere—a scenario that some find already almost fully realized.

Here we again see the indispensable role of engineering, which is provided by the many specialist engineers as well as by architects and landscape architects, and the need for all decision makers, including clients and users, to become more informed about technical advances, new materials, and methods. We would claim that this is an ethical responsibility—to become ecologically educated not only to change our assumptions and expectations, but to participate responsibly and effectively in the decision making processes. An increasing number of books provide reliable guides to the basic orientation of sustainability as well as information about specific environments, materials, forms, and methods. (See for example, Roaf, Crichton, and Nicol 2005; Benyus 1997; Ball 1997; Addington and Schodek 2005; Brownell 2006).

In addition to at least partially resolving environmental dilemmas by finding new ways to design and build cities and homes, the environmental disciplines and professions exemplify ways to undo some of the dichotomies that unnecessarily generate perceptions of unavoidable harms, that exaggerate harmful consequences, and that prevent creative reframing of issues and the development of projects that can initiate positive change.

Among the most prevalent and unnecessarily troublesome dichotomies, we have already considered those between the natural and built environments, engineers and architects, formal and social aesthetics. But, perhaps the candidate for the simultaneously most false, unnecessary, and harmful dichotomy is the one perceived between economic prosperity and environmental well-being. In the first place, the differences simply do not hold. All economic development involves transformation of the natural and built environments, ranging from extraction, use, or transformation of natural resources to the facilities in which we produce, distribute, and consume the products or services generated, to the settlements that either thrive or wither as a result. All changes in the natural and built environment have actual or potential economic dimensions: materials become scarcer or more plentiful or regenerate at varying speeds, conditions for life become harsher or easier, and so on. In other words, just as choices are not to save one or another organisms in isolation, but always a choice between entire mixed communities of living beings and life worlds, so too the choices are always among multiple economic-environmental complexes, each with their own combinations of beneficial and detrimental results.

This certainly is the case in regard to saving or exploiting the environment. While many industrial corporations resist environmental regulation as too costly, the provision of the services and products necessary for environmental remediation generates profits for other companies and new kinds of jobs. The question really is one of what social-economic-environmental complexes we decide to create and sustain, and which we decide to abandon. Al Gore is among the many political and business leaders who recognize our current oversimplified and inaccurate perceptions, and who encourage us to move beyond them:

> [Another] problem in our way of thinking about global warming is our false belief that we have to choose between a healthy economy and a healthy environment . . . The implication is that this is not only a choice we have to make, but a difficult one. But, in fact, it's a false choice for two reasons. First, without a planet, we won't fully enjoy those gold bars. And, second, if we do the right thing, then we're going to create a lot of wealth, jobs, and opportunity . . . .
>
> One of the keys to solving the climate crisis involves finding ways to use the powerful force of market capitalism as an ally. And, more than anything else, that requires accurate measurements of the real consequences—positive and negative—of all the important economic choices we make. The environmental impact of economic choices has often been ignored because traditional business accounting has allowed these factors to be labeled "externalities" and routinely excluded from the balance sheet. . . . Now, however, many business leaders are finally recognizing the full effects of their choices and "price" in such factors as environment, community impact, and employee longevity by using sophisticated techniques to measure their true value.   (Gore 2006, 270–271)

13. A New Environmental Professionalism & Aesthetic

Aesthetics

As with sustainability itself, so too aesthetics and beauty have many definitions, the topology of which ranges across contested territory full of subtle and important differences in what we believe and value, and how we act. We already have considered many definitions and varieties of aesthetic elsewhere in this book. Their very names (as well as the false dichotomies we have seen) show that there is no overarching, consistent or agreed upon system of classification: formalist, social, ecological, naturalistic, sacred, modernist, and so on.

Beauty and the Beast

Beauty appears
- to be of many kinds—artistic, scientific, mathematical, ecological, erotic . . .
- to be a matter of many specific aesthetic approaches (some of which operate in several other categories)
- to be closely related to worldviews

How is beauty important in regards to our caring for the environment?

As with sustainability, there are many and contested definitions of beauty. Work out a tolerant position that accommodates a variety of modes of beauty, but that does not lapse into a radical relativism in which one just uselessly says there is no measure or who is to say?, when in fact, many phenomena, including unjustified brutality against living beings is ugly.

Compare the ideas about beauty here with those treated in the section of chapter 3 that addresses the various roles inhabited by professionals and residents.

→ refer back to issues of formalist vs. social aesthetics in chapter 3, in the section on professional roles
→ refer back to the functionalist debate in chapter 4, principles & rules, the section on truthfulness

Further, the fundamental role of perception—of whether we see something at all, or whether we immediately view it as significant or trivial, hateful or dear—makes it important for us to consider further the role of aesthetics in our individual sets of values and touchstones, in alternative worldviews, and among competing theories and practices. As we have seen, the chief dichotomies oppose aesthetics as a specialized elite viewpoint with most people's oblivion to any significant aesthetics and the persistent contrast between formalist versus social aesthetics.

What's Beauty Got To Do With It?
Beauty affects how we see and value, not only individual phenomena and experiences, but also entire dimensions of the world, such as nature—as we began to see in chapter 1 in the section on worldviews. Not surprisingly, many who become environmental professionals, whether in design, ecology, sustainability, or something else, are especially attuned to aesthetic factors. But so too, in varying ways, are we all:

> Many ecologists move by a certain "feel" for the way we ought to live, the way we ought to handle nature . . . The aesthetic component has many different aspects. It surfaces in the concern of architects and city planners to build human habitats that go with nature rather than against it. Economist E.F. Schumacher displays it when he waxes eloquent about a "Buddhist Economics that would promote simplicity, elegance, and fine quality." The millions drawn to "the environmentalist movement" by the waste of Western cultures—the ugly signs, ugly housing, disfigured landscapes, disfigured skies—are people in aesthetic revolt . . . This is not to say their sole motivation is a vision of beauty or a repulsion by ugliness . . . It is simply to say that "ugliness" and "waste" play a part, and that they have many levels and aspects. Science also appreciates beauty, both that of nature itself and that of "elegant" solutions and equations. Finally, it may be argued that Eastern and Western aesthetics are central to religious views and practices. For instance, there is the belief that "if one achieves union with the Tao" beautiful works will follow effortlessly, "mindlessly", as they do in nature . . . Japanese aesthetics, which has both inspired and derived from Shinto and Buddhism (especially Zen), is unthinkable apart from this orientation to nature. (Carmody 1983, 50-52)

Recent scholarship and research has urged a return to a more holistic understanding of organism-environment relationships than the post-enlightenment era's almost exclusive emphasis on vision. As Victor Papanek explains,

> Our understanding and appreciation of a design or building has been seriously handicapped by concentrating almost entirely on our sense of sight; [but] we might regain the joy of reading the fabric of a building through all our senses, and [a sense of] why some buildings make us feel good . . . of building to human scale in relation to town and community planning . . . (1995, 13)

That is,

> It is clear that we do not aesthetically appreciate simply with our five senses, but rather with an important part of our whole emotional and psychological

selves. Consequently, what and how we aesthetically appreciate cannot but play a role in the shaping of our emotional and psychological being. This in turn helps to determine what we think and do, and think it correct for ourselves and others to think and do. In short, our aesthetic appreciation is a significant factor in shaping and forming our ethical views. (Carlson 1975, 67)

The varying approaches to aesthetics return us to the major worldviews considered in chapter 1 that substantially shape or make coherent our interpretations and measures that we use to make decisions and to act. In addition to considering alternative aesthetics by referring back to worldviews, we can see that there is a range of aesthetic positions that can be considered a progression from the brutally functional to social, and from formal to ecological—a process, perhaps, of tentatively putting dimensions back together.

→ You may want to return to chapter 1 to review the major worldviews

---

Question: The Aesthetics of Nature

- To what extent do you think there is merit in acknowledging the independent value and beauty of nature?

- How would we arrive at an appropriate aesthetic of nature?

- Would it not be important to develop a method of design that learns from nature, whether or not we think of it as bio-mimicry?

The aesthetics of nature can be seen as distinct from humanly made artifacts and art works; as such, it poses interesting questions of relationship and valuation that are addressed differently by the major worldviews—theocentric, anthropocentric, and ecocentric. Some theories hold that, in contrast to humanly produced art works, the natural world is beautiful in itself. "According to this view, the natural environment, insofar as it is untouched by humans, has mainly positive qualities: it is, for example graceful, delicate, intense, unified, and orderly, rather than bland, dull, insipid, incoherent, and chaotic. All virgin nature, in short, is essentially aesthetically good. The appropriate or correct aesthetic appreciation of the natural world is basically positive and negative aesthetic judgments have little or no place." Such a view can derive from beliefs that natural phenomena are prior to and independent of humans (naturalism) or because of the belief that "the natural world is designed, created, and maintained by an all-knowing and all-powerful God (theism)." (Carlson 1975, 72, 81; cf. 72–101).

In contrast, some landscape ecologists and landscape architects question the viability of viewing nature as utterly pristine or apart from human settlement—that in fact this perpetuates a false dichotomy between humanity and nature that makes addressing environmental problems especially challenging (see also chapter 1 for more on this issue, along with Nassauer 1997; Spirn 1984).

Allen Carlson points out that "in addition to being historically important, the landscape model gives us at least initial guidelines as to what to appreciate in nature and how," but that at the same time it confounds things. As Ronald Rees argues in relation to the romantic movement: "in this respect the romantic movement was a mixed blessing. In certain phases of its development it stimulated the movement for the protection of nature, but in its picturesque phase it simply confirmed our anthropocentricism by suggesting that nature exists to please as well as to serve us. Our ethics, if the word can be used to describe our attitudes and behavior toward the environment, have lagged behind our aesthetics. It is an unfortunate lapse that allows us to abuse our local environments and venerate the Alps and Rockies." (Carlson 1975, 46; Rees 1975, 312)

Since the term aesthetics names a facet of our cultural-historical perceptions, experiences, and desires, we again find that beauty is inseparable from economic and functional aspects of objects and places, which themselves are deeply social and political. Historically differing landscapes and cityscapes often present viable alternative visions precisely because they often contain (and may preserve) a complex of valued dimensions for a certain quality of life. Hence the appeal of the traditional—advocated in differing ways by figures ranging from Christopher Alexander to new urbanism, each contending they can solve some of our environmental-social quandaries.

As noted in chapter 2, the environmental professions are about placemaking and they call for a unique ethics that embraces this unique place-based ontology. While this is especially true for landscape design, it is no less so for architecture, planning, appropriate construction and engineering. Papanek makes the argument in regard to what might be called the aesthetics of site:

> The received view explains the selection of a site through the interplay of four determinants: distance from markets, raw material sources, situation within a transportation net and available labor. The aesthetic factor—closeness to concerts, sports, theatres, conviviality appealing to the senses—is usually ignored. This fifth possible determinant of location, the aesthetic parameter, is not just equal in strength to any of the other four but can be stronger than all combined . . . The aesthetics of site have been overlooked, since modern location theory originated at a time during the 19th century when virtually all cities, towns and villages possessed it to such an extent that the aesthetic assets of each were cancelled out by the beauty of the others. (1995, 108)

In a parallel way (that also develops themes introduced in chapter 2 concerning professional roles and contending aesthetics), Wasserman and colleagues emphasize the inseparability of the social-environmental-aesthetic dimensions of the environmental design professions:

> Contemporary architecture is a social-design enterprise. Reason and creative invention are applied to environmental problems. It is enmeshed in social-economic-political-cultural circumstances . . . Insofar as architecture is rooted in the social and cultural, it is the physical manifestation of the prevailing mores of the time in which it is/was built, bearing a testimony to its era. Architecture's human dimension: its communal nature; its aspiration to mark ritual, myth, cosmos, capital, or power; its protection against the elements; and its intention to make changes in the world for continued, presumably "enhanced," "improved," and/or "better," inhabitation make architecture an intrinsically ethical enterprise.   (Wasserman, Sullivan, and Palermo 2000, 37)

A New Design Responsibility – A New Ethical and Ecological Aesthetic
Our considerations of sustainability and the ways we might reconceptualize matters as a means to make progress in decision making have led us not only to a clearer sense of what the deeper issues are, but back to the fundamentally—and inescapably—ethical character of the environmental professions and disciplines. Questions of sustainability are environmental questions, social-political questions, aesthetic questions, and questions of reflection upon the responsibilities inherent in all design and practice.

Finally, even while our more sophisticated definitions, classifications, and new alternative constructs help in clarifying what needs to be decided and provide an orientation in the decision making processes themselves, the conceptual finally needs to be integrated with the opening of new perceptual possibilities, in the creation of new actualities through design and construction. The reflection, in other words, needs to end in responsibility enacted and discharged through practice.

The ethical trail leads, then, to a call for a new design responsibility to be discharged through a new aesthetic and mode of practice. Again, Papanek is a strong voice in regard to this vocation:

> Ecology and the environmental equilibrium are the basic underpinnings of all human life on earth; there can be neither life nor human culture without it. Design is concerned with the development of products, tools, machines, artifacts and other devices, and this activity has a profound and direct influence on ecol-

ogy. The design response must be positive and unifying. Design must be the bridge between human needs, culture, and ecology.

He goes on to enumerate how the designer must deal with questions raised in the processes of "potentially ecologically dangerous phases" involving production and pollution: choosing materials, the manufacturing process, packaging the product, the finished product, transporting the product, and waste (1995, 29–32).

This approach entails a new aesthetic that will be ecologically responsible and, according to Papanek, involves several ethical points:

1. The sustainability of life on this planet—not only for humankind but for all our fellow species—is paramount.

2. Sustainability can be helped or hindered by design. The impact of petrol-powered automobiles on the environment, wars, foreign policy, economics, morals, and jobs is profound enough to serve as a chilling example.

3. Ethical design must also be environmentally sound and ecologically benign. It needs to be human in scale, humane, and embedded in social responsibility.

4. Such design requires the help of governments, industry, entrepreneurs and laws, and the support of ordinary people through local groups and individual decisions to shop intelligently and invest ethically.

5. Designers and architects all seem to be waiting for some fresh style or direction that will provide new meaning and new forms for the objects we create, based more on real requirements than on an arbitrary invented style.

6. All objects, tools, graphics and dwellings must work toward the needs of the end-user on a more basic level than mere appearance, flamboyant gesture, or semiotic statements. Nevertheless, the lack of any spiritual basis for design will make ethical and environmental considerations mere well-intentioned afterthoughts.

7. Design, when nourished by a deep spiritual concern for the planet, environment, and people, results in a moral and ethical viewpoint. Starting from this point of departure will provide the new forms and expressions—the new aesthetic—we are all desperately trying to find.

(Papanek 1995, 235)

Even if we have made substantial progress in understanding what is required in good environmental decision making for professionals, and have found some useful strategies, we cannot forget the fundamental ethical concern with the rights of others and our obligations to care for them, in part by bringing benefit to them, by not allowing harm to come to them, by respecting their autonomy, and by promoting justice. We already saw this in all the major ethical theories and in the principles and rules that develop from those theories, and, in this chapter, in the proposed deeper definition of sustainability.

14. Environmental and Social Justice

Environmental Justice: The Crossroads of Equity Issues

The environmental justice movement (also known as environmental equity) addresses the inequity particularly associated with hazardous-waste sites located in areas inhabited by racial minorities or the poor (Agyeman and Evans 1996).

Environmental justice includes:
Procedural equity: the fairness with which rules, regulations, and assessments are made and reinforced; unequal protection arises from unscientific, secretive and non-democratic behaviors.

Social equity: the way sociological factors such as race, ethnicity, class, culture, and political power influence environmental decision making practices so that certain groups seem to be systematically disadvantaged in terms of, for example, living in the most polluted neighborhoods (or countries).

Geographic equity: the way in which the location of communities and their proximity to non-desirable land uses, such as toxic-waste incinerating plants, landfills, and sewage works, is not randomly configured, but located in the most environmentally disadvantaged areas (Bullard ethic of care),

Inter-generational equity: the way that environmental choices and conditions made today will impact future generations.

Inter-species equity: concerns balancing human needs with ecosystem survival and the needs of nonhuman species.

Environmental justice may be defined as the sum of the interactions of these dimensions of equity (Haughton 1996). In 1992, the Bush administration created the U.S. Office of Environmental Justice, and in 1994 President Clinton ordered every federal department and agency to "make achieving environmental justice part of its mission." By 1997, at least seven states had passed environmental justice laws, and many more are considering them (*Economist* 1997; Roseland 1998, 134).

Because decisions concerning sustainability are decisions concerning entire mixed communities, they are fundamentally questions of distributive justice especially because the principle of autonomy requires full active participation— if not more strongly final decision making and consent—of those involved in the lifeworld in question. Disparities in environmental quality and decision making processes are among the major challenges facing environmental ethics.

It would seem that an adequate ethical response to serious environmental dilemmas would have to include provision for those in danger of becoming (or continuing to be) disadvantaged as a consequence of the decisions that we make, especially if that same group is excluded from the decision process. Two concerns emerge, then: to identify and include those who are unjustly treated and to find ways to increase the self-determination and informed consent of those adversely affected.

Two major groups immediately come to mind as unusually impacted by environmental decisions that have significant harmful outcomes and that just as often do not have a voice in making those decisions:

1. the local inhabitants of lifeworlds that are controlled by political, economic, or other power relations such that the entire mixed community within which they live is damaged as are their lives in this bio cultural environment

2. the marginalized within any given society, such as the poor or racial-ethnic-religious minorities.

To focus on the second group in order to begin a dialogue, consider the relationships between poverty, pollution, and disease and sub-standard environmental conditions. As we noted above in looking at urban squatters, the world's cities continue to grow rapidly, in part because there is the perception that prospects for a better life, for sharing some part of the riches that circulate, are better in urban places. Not only are many marginalized groups without adequate housing, or without housing at all, but they live in this condition in the midst of the development that brings opportunity and prosperity to others. Clearly here we have cases of environmental and economic injustice by any normal measure.

The history of squatter settlements is a story of confrontations: between illegal settlers, governments, and urban authorities and private landlords. Authorities tend to consider squatter settlements to be unsightly, and one way of eradicating the problem is to bulldoze them. They are often built on land earmarked for development, so most developing world cities have a history of forced evictions. In Seoul, for instance, between 1983–1988, more than 700,000 people had to give up their often well-built homes to urban redevelopment projects connected with the Olympic Games. Often squatters are forced out of their homes and moved to remote locations. However, given the chance, people drift back to the original location to rebuild their homes in the city (*Gaia Atlas* 1992, 74).

Further issues of both social and environmental justice arise when considering the living conditions of the poor in the U.S. In terms of environmental justice, there is a body of research showing trends of higher environmental pollution in low-income communities of color. One of the best-known studies of this is Bullard's (1990) book, *Dumping in Dixie*. Here, Bullard examines "the environment-development dialectic, residence-production conflict, and residual impact of the de facto industrial policy" (i.e., "any job is better than no job") on the region's ecology: in the Southeastern U.S. Bullard documents intensified land use conflicts and industrial expansion in low-income communities, noting that while poor white communities are also affected, the 1983 U.S. General Accounting Office (GAO) study of hazardous-waste landfill siting in the region shows a disproportionate number of such landfills in Black communities. Again, if we are to live in a just society, how can we understand and address these trends?

Then, too, those with scant resources have little choice but to occupy the least desirable areas, as we see in the discussion of the racial discrimination and environmental injustice as described both in Bullard's *Dumping in Dixie* and in Fullilove's *Root Shock*. In cities, these undesirable areas usually include industrial sites, areas with high crime, areas close to heavily used transportation or other infrastructure systems, and related places. To cite a report of conditions so typical we often lose our sense of empathy:

> Factories are usually located in or close to cities and it is the poorest areas, particularly in developing-world cities that are the worst affected by pollution, since communities grow up around the factories as people flock to them for work. These settlements are in constant danger from air pollution, since they are invariably located downwind of the chimneys; whereas the rich can buy their way into upwind areas. Polluted air flows freely into squatter homes and vegetation that helps to filter air is usually absent. Water may have to be collected from sources close to factory outfall pipes and soil may be contaminated with lead, mercury, and chlorinated compounds. Diarrhea, skin diseases, tuberculosis, bronchial problems, emphysema, and many other diseases are commonplace (*Gaia Atlas* 1992, 96; cf. pp. 97–101)

Worldwide, 1.2 billion people lacked access to safe drinking water in 1990—a figure that remained the same through 2000 (Myers and Kent 2005, 132). According to the United Nation's Environmental Program, half the world's hospital beds are occupied by people suffering from water-borne diseases.

There are increasing numbers of studies that combine first-rate science with environmental justice issues; however, there continues to be a lack of remedial action, in large part due to continuing resistance to allocating responsibility—and quite possibly the continuation of institutionalized racism. Even though recent complexity and self-organization theory have demonstrated conclusively that complex environmental and urban phenomena—including the health problems being discussed here—arise from the interactions of numerous factors, substantial elements within private and public sector power structures insist that since the single, linear cause can not be found [and in fact it does not exist], no one is responsible and thus no one need take remedial action. We also live in a time that does not press governments to assume such social tasks. (Among the many good studies on this matter, see Gail Sandlin, 2008).

Environmental Justice—Organizations & Publications

The following are a few of the organizations and publications
that focus on the concept of environmental justice and the problems connected with it:

- Society for Ecofeminism, Environmental Ethics, and Social Ecology

Many groups and publications concerned with environmental
ethics in general also attend to environmental justice. From
among the growing number, especially note:

- International Society for Environmental Ethics
- International Association for Environmental Philosophy
- *Environmental Ethics*
- *Ethics and the Environment*
- *Environmental Values, Ethics, and the Environment*
- Worldviews: Environment, Culture, and Religion

---

15. Who Decides?—Toward Collaboration, Compassion, and Care

As we press further into what is involved in ethical decision making, we enter a
realm that is more and more inconvenient and impractical in that more and more
groups need to be included, many of whom are injured parties whose rights need
to be respected. But this is not easy: even if it is a laudable ideal, it is very difficult to organize and see through large-scale participatory projects. At times, it
seems much easier to have the experts arrive at solutions (as was desired in the
age of progressivism, but is not so popular now with public skepticism about
technical expertise and the desire of power groups to bypass or control ostensi-
bly impartial professionals). But, we must do this to be ethical and to balance
that ethical responsibility with pragmatic practice. Indeed, that the latter might
seem to weigh more heavily as important environmental decisions are usually
considered to be political rather than ethical issues. Indeed, it is in the realm of
politics that society works through the dynamics of power and control, of what
is acceptable as the appropriate manner of decision making. But all of this is still
fundamentally about ethics as well.

Politically, beyond the problems of exposure to unhealthy, dangerous, and
demoralizing phenomena, the poor and other marginalized groups have been
regularly excluded from the decision making processes that shape their environments and thus their lives. The point is put sharply by architect-planner John

R. Short in his analysis of contemporary urban structures and experiences
(which attempts to recognize both individual and structural features):

> Poverty is not simply low income, it is an inability to influence outcomes on a
> regular and meaningful way. The poor are the alienated of the city both in their
> feeling of powerlessness and their sense of engagement from the wider society.
> When poverty is more the product of personal characteristics, the result is the
> individual poor . . . [and] our concern should be to lessen their suffering and
> provide opportunities for the creation and maintenance of self-respect. [Or
> when it is a matter of] whole groups of citizens, the result is an underclass, . . .
> the structured poor, the outcome of economic, class, and racial-ethnic struc-
> tures. (Short, 54–55)

> → On the social dimension of environmental ethics compare to chapter
> 2, the sections on diversity, representation

Participation in the Urban Landscape (*Socio-cultural Issues*)
Given these realities—especially that the disenfranchised are among those making critical environmental decisions even though the outcome of such processes
impact them in disproportionately negative ways—we might come to believe
that there is little hope for ethically appropriate social or economic improvement
in the condition of the poor and disenfranchised. Yet, as futurist and sustainability analyst Mark Roseland argues, even amidst our discouraging failure there
remains an opening for positive action:

> The traditional approach to public demand for greater participation has been
> described as "decide, educate, announce, defend," otherwise know as DEAD.
> Collaborative processes are an alternative which can lead to better communica-
> tion and understanding. Quite different perspectives can find common ground
> and agree to recommendations regarding particularly difficult issues. This does
> not necessarily mean that everyone comes to full agreement, but rather that
> there is no substantial disagreement: participants can live with the outcome . . .
>
> Stakeholders often demand genuinely cooperative decision making, if not
> outright control over decision making. In response, formal recognition has been
> provided at some levels of government through legislation legitimizing public
> participation initiatives . . . Truly meaningful participation requires that all con-
> cerned and affective stakeholders are provided the information and resources
> they require to influence and contribute to the decision making process, and
> that planning and decision making processes must be designed and imple-
> mented to foster comprehensive stakeholder participation. The issues of who
> participates, when they participate and how they participate are critical to
> achieving fairness, efficiency, and stability in decision making.
>
> The essential difference between conventional and collaborative, or
> "shared decision making," is the level of true collaboration and involvement of
> those not traditionally involved in decision making (Crowfoot and Wondolleck
> 1990). Specifically, shared decision making involves planning *with* stake-
> holders rather than *for* stakeholders. Shared decision making processes depend
> on the explicit recognition that all stakeholder values and interests are legiti-
> mate.   (Roseland 1998, pp. 182-183)

Note too that although Roseland's vocabulary differs from our more formal presentations of ethical principles and rules, clearly he is addressing the same ideas about autonomy, informed consent, and honesty.

→ for an complex actual situation about which to exercise questions about participation and marginalization, see the box on Hydro-Quebec in this chapter and the full case with exercises in appendix III.

In Today's Post-modern World, the Only Motive for Ethical Behavior Is Likely to be Compassion-Care.
How can hope for better, more ethical decisions and outcomes be affirmed, given the bleak picture of environmental conditions, the systemic exclusion of some people from the decision making process, and the difficulty of finding solutions to our simplest problems? How can we overcome indifference and the lack of resources that block inclusion or remediation of harms from the beginning? How do we overcome the powerful economic and political forces that actively seek to exploit both the environment and its inhabitants, despite the resulting immanent threats not only to those who are being controlled, but to those directing events?

This stage of reflection is no time for a falsely projected happy ending. Not only are the inseparable human and environmental conditions in severe distress, but in our post-modern era there is little belief in shared truths to which we might turn as a basis for understanding and action. Nor do we have local, much less universal, agreement that there are human rights and what they might be.

Do we have to fall back, then, on the most basic, the most pragmatic measures—such as avoiding global monetary losses as forecast by economists and the insurance industry, or even the warnings that wars will result from the massive population displacements to come—in order to move ourselves to a state of attentive concern and action? Certainly many leaders of the scientific, political, and business communities concerned with the fate of the earth and its peoples have already included these pragmatic dimensions in their declamations.

In the end we must continue to question and examine the way we live, think and act. We believe that ethical concern depends not on economic or other self-directed gain alone, but on compassion—the heart of the ethic of care. This is ultimately what it means to be an ethical practitioner and an ethical person, to be socially responsive as a fellow member of the global environment.

Mugerauer, following ethicists such as Werner Marx and Alasdair MacIntyre, argues that "we form an initial impression of compassion, and an impulse to action following from that compassion, by confronting our own mortality. When we vividly realize that we are mortal, we come to the basic insight that we are not self-sufficient . . . If we become compassionate toward people, we do not face the mutually exclusive questions of whether we should be compassionate for this or that group of people, or for the animals, or for the plants of an ecosystem. To be compassionate is to be compassionate for all members of a given, whole life-world" (1996, 24-25).

→ Also see the section on wisdom and virtue at the end of
  chapter 4, continuing the reflections of the ethic of care.

What Are We Prepared To Do When Dilemmas Remain?

> If necessary, when faced with an environmental dilemma
> am I—are we—prepared to:
> - Find a way to make a trade-off?
> - Share the burden?
> - Compromise in order to come to a truce on mutually
>   standing differences?
> - Yield, in the name of an overall resolution?
> - Make a sacrifice?

Obviously, not all dilemmas can be dissolved. This is especially the case when the decisions to be made by multiple parties involve conflicting core values where either we agree to a hierarchy, but not on who should give way, or where we can not find a common ground at all. When we can not reframe the problems into terms that all parties—including the environment—can live with, we come to the point where conflict remains. If it is not to escalate into violence, some action will be necessary. What are we prepared to do to maintain ethical responsibility, and to be as caring as we are able? Are we prepared to yield in the name of a solution rather than insist on the dilemma? Finally, who we are, how we think, act, and feel, is up to us, however much we are shaped by our socio-cultural condition. It is up to us to try to step out of that particular condition and interrogate our practices, as citizens and human beings.

In the end, it is not just a matter of who we are willing to see in the mirror, but who we see reflected in our fellow human beings—and in all cohabitants of the earth.

Notes

1. Our thanks to Debra Guenther of Mithun Partners, Inc., in Seattle, and MLA student Eric Berg for their clarification on the Sustainable Sites Initiative. Both have served on the committee for the development of this initiative.

2. See the many international websites that are issuing reports on the global climate, some of which are listed in appendix I. For example, there is the *Fourth Report of the intergovernmental Panel on Climate Change*, just released as we finish this book, on the IPCC website: www.ipcc.ch.

3. According to the U.S. Dept of Housing and Urban Development, the MTO is a 10-year research demonstration that combines tenant based rental assistance with housing counseling to help very low-income families move from poverty-stricken urban areas to low-poverty neighborhoods.

4. U.S. Census data highlighted here were reported in "Income, Poverty and Health Insurance Coverage in the U.S.: 2003." Available online at www.census.gov/hhes/www/html.

The childhood poverty data appear in Allegretto 2006, "U.S. Government does Relatively Little to Lessen Child Poverty Rates" in Economic Policy Institution's *Economic Snapshot*, July 19 2006, available online at www.epinet.org/content.cfm/webfeatures_snapshots_20060719.

The poverty line is an absolute measure of need first developed in the 1960s and set at approximately three times the annual cost of a nutritional diet. It varies by funding source and other factors. For more details see U.S. Census Bureau www.census.gov/hhes/www/poverty/povdef/html.

Chapter Six

Professional Codes and Beyond

Now that we have considered personal ethical yardsticks, shared worldviews, the challenges of place-based and environmental professions, and reflexive practice, we can turn to the formal codes of ethics that govern these professions. In doing so, we can examine how the codes build upon theory-based principles and rules and where they still leave critical ethical decision-making issues for individual practitioners to interpret and apply to different situations.

Note that this chapter differs from the others in respect to the large number of questions that occur within the text of the body of this chapter. While all chapters have questions throughout, as well as focal exercises at the end, this chapter has questions that should be directly engaged throughout because many readers will be prepared by experience or inclined by interest to consider in detail many issues related directly to specific environmental professions and disciplines.

Ethical Codes of Conduct

Each of the environmental professions discussed in this book has its own formalized code of ethics to which members must adhere. These codes are created and upheld by the professional organizations for each field of practice. For architects, they are put forward by the American Institute of Architects (AIA), for planners, the codes are governed by the American Planning Association (APA), for landscape architecture it is the American Society of Landscape Architects (ASLA), for engineering the codes are defined by the National Society of Professional Engineers (NSPE) and the Construction Management Association of American (CMAA) regulates codes for construction management.

→ Exercises to connect the codes to Principles and Rules of Chapter Three and the Theories of Chapter Four

→ The Codes are found in Appendix II (as are the web sites for them)

Together, the codes of ethics for all of these professions focus on the obligations, duties and responsibilities of members (note, the language of obligation and duty is quite deontological). The codes are usually organized according to the constituents to whom one is obligated, for example, the public, colleagues, and so on. For most professions, ethical codes usually carry broadly stated principles, then more specific ethical standards that are goals to which members should aspire, and finally explicit rules of conduct, the violation of which is subject to investigation, possible charges, and other enforcement procedures. Over time, each of these professions has adopted new codes and adapted existing ones to address contemporary concerns.

While they may be organized in somewhat different ways, and involve different degrees of specificity, there are important common threads in the codes for the various professions examined here. For example, all codes have some rule about whistle-blowing or what to do when encountering illegal conduct, or discovering fraudulent activities or claims, particularly if they will adversely affect the safety of the public. Similarly, across the codes there are rules about full disclosure, confidentiality, conflicts of interest, and public safety, as well as obligations to maintain skill levels, articulated in terms of professional development, continuing education, competency, integrity, truthfulness, and contributions to the advancement of practice (note that the terminology here derives from the larger principles and rules, such as integrity and veracity, that have been treated in an earlier chapter). First, let's take a brief look at the codes of each of these fields of practice to understand better how the governing organizations of each profession frame ethical concerns. We will then explore the implications of these codes and the questions that they raise.

Architecture

The AIA codes are among the most thorough, and they flesh out a great deal of detail. The codes are divided into canons that cluster around four broad obligations: to the public, to the client, to the profession, and to colleagues. Within each of these canons are specific ethical standards and accompanying rules. It is the rules themselves that are paramount, as it is mandatory to comply with them, and violating them is grounds for disciplinary action by the AIA. Attached to some rules are commentaries to help clarify or elaborate on the intent of a rule. However, the commentaries themselves are not considered part of the code; they are merely to help those seeking guidance in how to conform to the codes or enforce the codes.

The first cluster of ethical standards fall under "general obligations," and they address the maintenance and advancement of knowledge and skill, standards of excellence, the respect for and conservation of natural and cultural heritage, upholding human rights, and promoting allied arts and industries. Interestingly, under the standard of "advancing knowledge and skill" is a rule to "demonstrate a consistent pattern of reasonable care and competence." What is meant by care is unclear here but it seems more synonymous with carefulness than the kind of care articulated in the theories about ethic of care that we discuss in chapter 4. Under the standard for human rights is a rule about non-discrimination on the basis of race, religion, gender, national origin, age, disability, or sexual orientation.

AIA Rules Regarding Obligations to the Public
The second canon concerns obligations to the public. Here we see rules regarding upholding the law, prohibiting payments or gifts to public officials (although campaign contributions are permissible), prohibiting fraud or "wanton disregard for the rights of others," and what to do when encountering violations of the law or regulations (i.e., when to whistle-blow). The code delineates several acceptable options: to inform the client or employer, to refuse to consent to the problematic decision, or to report the decision to a public official responsible for enforcing the regulation. What is interesting is that the commentary explains that this rule extends only to violations of the building laws that threaten public safety, and that the obligation under this rule applies only to the safety of the finished project. This suggests that there are no explicit obligations, at least within the AIA codes for ensuring safety before the building is complete. This is likely because there are distinct rules for the construction management and engineering professions that would cover the construction phase and because of current practices concerning risk assumption and liability. So this omission is more a matter of defining where one profession's obligations begin and another's ends. The rules in this canon can be summarized as:

- Don't knowingly violate the law
- Don't offer gifts or payments to public officials to influence their judgment
- Don't accept gifts or payments when serving in a public capacity
- Don't engage in fraud or wanton disregard of others
- When encountering a situation where a law or regulation is violated and will materially adversely affect public safety; either advise against it, refuse to consent, or report the decision to a public official or building inspector
- Don't counsel or assist in fraudulent or illegal activity
- Disclose if you are being compensated for public statements regarding architecture.

AIA Rules Regarding Obligations to the Client
This set of rules focuses on the nature of the professional's relationship to the client and the concern for maintaining professionalism and a positive working relationship with clients. The main concerns here involve being properly qualified, following laws and regulations, not misleading clients and being impartial in judgment. In this cluster of rules we see echoes of virtue ethics and concepts from positive psychology in the idea of the practice of excellence and maintaining integrity. The specific rules are as follows:

- Take into account laws and regulations in providing professional service
- Perform professional services only when you, together with appropriate consultants, are qualified
- Don't materially alter the scope and objectives of the work without a client's consent
- Don't render services if your professional judgment could be affected by your responsibilities to another project or person
- Render decisions impartially when serving as a judge of contract performance or as an interpreter of contract documents
- Don't recklessly mislead clients about the results that can be achieved through your services
- Don't knowingly disclose information that will have an adverse affect on clients (confidentiality)

AIA Rules Regarding Obligations to the Profession
- This particular set of rules cluster around obligations to file complaints against colleagues who are violating the ethical codes (whistle-blowing), and issues of libel, slander and making false statements of material facts. Principles of truthfulness are pivotal to this set of rules. It is noteworthy that filing complaints against colleagues who are violating some code of ethics is considered an obligation or duty; it is not an ethical option to remain silent and not report the violation. Interestingly, the code includes a qualifier that you are protected from libel or slander if you make the complaint "in good faith" so here there is recognition of the importance of intentionality. The rules in this cluster can be summarized as follows: You must file a complaint if you discover another architect has violated the code of ethics
- Don't sign or seal professional work for which you don't have responsible control
- Don't willingly make false statements of material facts
- Don't make misleading or false statements about your qualifications
- Make sure that those you supervise conform to code of ethics

AIA Rules Regarding Obligations to Colleagues
This set of rules focuses on issue of what we commonly call fair play and giving credit where it is due, since these rules focus on propriety (what is proper) regarding proprietorship (who owns what):
- Recognize and respect the contributions of employees/employers/business colleagues
- When leaving a firm, don't take project materials without permission
- Don't unreasonably withhold permission for an employee to take their work with them when they leave a firm.

The AIA enforces twenty-four rules of conduct in all. The National Council of Architectural Registration Board also has a set of rules that focus on competence, conflict of interest, full disclosure and compliance with the law.

Landscape Architecture

The American Society of Landscape Architects (ASLA) has two codes: one for professional ethics and one distinctly focusing on environmental ethics. According to the ASLA, both the profession as a whole and the professional code of ethics were "built on the foundation of several principles—dedication to the public health, safety, and welfare and recognition and protection of the land and its resources." Given the particular focus of landscape architecture on ecosystems and environmental health (among other concerns), it is perhaps not surprising but heartening to see a distinct focus on the land and other natural resources in a unique set of ethical codes. We will now take a closer look at each of these two codes.

ASLA Code of Professional Ethics

Like the codes of the other professional organizations examined here, these codes are also organized into two broad canons, each of which contains ethical standards, or goals that members of the profession should strive to meet. The first canon is about professional responsibilities, while the second is about member responsibilities. Within each canon, under many of the ethical standards, there appear particular rules. In addition to the two canons, there is a separate set of rules of procedures for filing and resolving complaints.

The first canon on Professional Responsibilities includes statements about obeying the laws governing practice and business affairs, and conducting one's duties with honesty, dignity, and integrity. There are also rules about full disclosure of relevant information to clients, the public, and other interested parties as well as regulations about protecting the interests of clients and the public through competent performance, and obligation to participate in continuing education, educational research, and development and dissemination of technical information. Full disclosure is important and assumed to be ethical because it operates on the principle of respect for persons and their autonomy. It assumes that clients and others involved in the project have the right to full information about the project and the choices that are made in the design—and probably construction—process.

In the second canon, the codes focus on Member Responsibilities which include upholding the ethical standards of the ASLA code of environmental ethics and ensuring that they and other members adhere to the code of professional ethics and the constitution and bylaws of the ASLA (so matters of whistle-blowing are discussed here). Under this set of responsibilities, members are also encouraged to serve on elected or appointed boards, committees and commissions dealing with the arts, environmental and land-use issues.

Listed separately from the above sets of responsibilities is a set of rules for filing complaints. Interestingly, the rules state that anonymous complaints will be disregarded, suggesting a requirement for a more rigorous kind of accountability that anonymity can sometimes circumvent. If a violation has been determined to have occurred, sanctions against the perpetrator range from letters of admonition, letters of censure, and probationary suspension of membership to expulsion from the society.

ASLA Code of Environmental Ethics

Within the ASLA code of environmental ethics, there are four fundamental tenets: (1) the health and well-being of biological systems and their integrity are essential to sustain human well-being; (2) future generations have a right to the same environmental assets and ecological aesthetics; (3) long-term economic survival has a dependence upon the natural environment; and (4) environmental stewardship is essential to maintain a healthy environment and a quality of life for the earth. To address these main principles or tenets, there are ethical standards for the profession's approach to the physical and, more specifically, natural environment.

According to this Code of Environmental Ethics, landscape architects and members of the ASLA have an ethical obligation to uphold the following ethical standards:

- Support and facilitate the environmental public policy statements of the Society. (There are fifteen policy statements on issues ranging from the planning and management of coastal zones, public parks, open space preservation, rural landscapes, historic sites, appropriate use of vegetation, wetlands, water-resource management, principles of land use planning and wildlife habitat protection.) (See appendix II for the actual codes.)
- Act responsibly in the design, planning, management, and policy decisions affecting the health of the natural systems.
- Respect historic preservation and ecological management in the design process.
- Develop and specify products, materials, technologies, and techniques that conserve resources and foster landscape regeneration.
- Seek constant improvement in our knowledge, abilities, and skills; in our educational institutions; and in our professional practice and organizations.
- Actively engage in shaping decisions, attitudes, and values that support public health and welfare, environmental respect, and landscape regeneration.

This Code of Environmental Ethics is totally unlike the other professional codes we have reviewed in its attention to the well-being and even rights of non-human living entities and the landscape overall. As noted below, the code of the National Society of Professional Engineers includes attention to sustainability, but it is broadly stated.

Planning

The American Planning Association's Code of Ethics includes what it calls aspirational principles that constitute the ideals to which planners are meant to be committed. These are broken down into different areas of responsibilities—

overall responsibilities to the public, responsibilities to clients and employers, and to the profession and colleagues. (It is interesting that these are termed "responsibilities" as compared to the AIA's "obligations" or the ASLA ethical "standards," which one has an obligation to uphold). These subtle shifts in language reflect different attitudes toward professional ethics and how ethics is understood. All can be considered essentially duty-based, but each term can connote different degrees of restrictiveness.

Responsibilities to the Public
The principles pertaining to planners' overall responsibilities to the public begin with the following statement: "Our primary obligation is to serve the public interest and we, therefore, owe our allegiance to a conscientiously attained concept of the public interest that is formulated through continuous and open debate." Additional obligations to the public are then delineated, such as "being conscious of the rights of others," having "special concern for the long-range consequences of present actions," "seeking social justice by working to expand choice and opportunity for all persons," dealing fairly with all participants in the planning process, paying "special attention to the interrelatedness of decisions." All of these principles address politically contentious social and process issues, and the public nature of the profession. It is noteworthy and unique that these are explicitly incorporated into the code of ethics. There are, in fact, specific rules regarding participatory process, ("We shall give people the opportunity to have a meaningful impact on the development of plans and programs that may affect them. This is noteworthy because participation should be broad enough to include those who lack formal organization or influence.") Participation is not spotlighted in the codes of ethics for the other professions addressed in this book.

Responsibilities to Clients and Employers
The aspirational principles dealing with responsibilities to clients and employers begin with a general statement that planners "owe diligent, creative, and competent performance of the work we do in pursuit of our client or employer's interest. Such performance, however, shall always be consistent with our faithful service to the public interest." There are three specific responsibilities listed in this section of the codes, stating that planners shall (1) exercise independent professional judgment on behalf of our clients and employers; (2) accept client/employer decisions unless it is illegal or inconsistent with the primary obligation to the public interest; and (3) avoid a conflict of interest or even the appearance of a conflict of interest in accepting assignments from clients or employers.

Responsibilities to the Profession and Colleagues
Finally, responsibilities to the profession and colleagues address protecting and enhancing the integrity of the profession, educating the public about planning issues and their relevance to everyday life, and sharing the results of experience

and research to contribute to the body of knowledge of the field. It is interesting that among the responsibilities listed in this realm is to examine the applicability of theory, research, practice, methods to each particular situation and to "not accept the applicability of a customary solution without first establishing its appropriateness to the situation." This explicit directive to be sensitive to context and the uniqueness of each situation is noteworthy. While some might argue that this should be assumed, apparently the governing body of the planning profession felt it important to explicitly state this—which is not the case in the other codes of ethics. Such a statement speaks not only of the context-sensitive nature of the profession, but of a more social constructionist approach to practice. This is further evidenced in the *Planning Code of Ethics* in an overview statement that precedes the principles: "As the basic values of society can come into competition with each other, so can the aspirational principles we espouse under this Code. An ethical judgment often requires a conscientious balancing, based on the facts and context of a particular situation and on he precepts of the entire Code."

Because many of the principles are considered aspirational, any allegation that someone has failed to achieve them cannot be the subject of a misconduct charge or be a cause for disciplinary action. They are merely precepts for ways of behaving that are considered ideal or exemplary. In that regard, these code are looser than some other codes that make the violation of such principles a point for disciplinary action.

It is the second section of the planning code of ethics that contains the actual rules of conduct to which planners are held accountable. There are twenty-five rules of conduct in all. Interestingly, they all state what one ought not to do, for example: not engage in illegal activities, not use the power of the office to seek special advantages, not take credit for other people's work, not deliberately conducte any wrongful act, not sell services to influence decisions by improper means and so on. If anyone violates any of these rules, that person can be charged with misconduct and shall have the responsibility of responding to and co-operating with the investigation and enforcement procedures. If found to be blameworthy by the AICP Ethics Committee, that person shall be subject to the imposition of sanctions that may include loss of certification.

The third and final section of the planning code of ethics contains procedural provisions. This section describes the way that one can obtain an advisory ruling, and details how a charge of misconduct can be filed, and how charges shall be investigated, prosecuted, and adjudicated.

Engineering

Like other codes of professional ethics, those of the National Society of Professional Engineers include several broadly stated fundamental canons to which engineers should adhere, such as holding paramount the health, safety, and welfare of the public, performing services only in one's area of competence, issuing public statements only in an objective and truthful manner, acting as faithful agents or trustees for each employer or client, avoiding deceptive acts, and acting in a manner that will enhance the honor, reputation, and usefulness of the profession. Each one of these canons has particular rules attached to it. In addition, there are professional obligations listed that include such issues as being guided in all relations by the highest standards of honest and integrity. As is the case with the other professional codes, themes of truthfulness, confidentiality, and the public interest are prominent:

- At all times strive to serve the public interest.
- Avoid all conduct or practice that deceives the public.
- Do not disclose confidential information without consent.
- Do not be influenced by conflicting interest.
- Do not attempt to obtain employment or advancement by untruthfully criticizing other engineers or by other questionable methods.
- Do not attempt to injure the professional reputation, prospects, practice, or employment of other engineers.
- Accept personal responsibility for professional activities (provided, however, engineers may seek indemnification for services arising out of their practice for other than gross negligence, where the interests cannot otherwise be protected).
- Give credit for engineering work to whom credit is due, and recognize the proprietary interests of others.

Truthfulness versus Confidentiality

The code of ethics for engineers requires professionals to be truthful. At the same time, engineers must also keep confidences. Can you see any ways in which these directives may come into conflict? For example, what if . . . ?

Interestingly there was some revision to the NSPE code in 2006 to clarify and include sustainable development. The list of professional obligations includes a statement that "engineers shall strive to adhere to the principles of sustainable development in order to protect the environment for future generations." Sustainable development is later defined in the code as "the challenge of meeting human needs for natural resources, industrial products, energy, food, transportation, shelter, and effective waste management while conserving and protecting environmental quality and the natural-resource base essential for future development." Such additions suggest that sustainability is formally considered an imperative for the engineering profession.

Some clarifications of competitive bidding were provided in revisions in January 2006 to correct misunderstandings of a U.S. Supreme Court decision of 1978 that declared that competitive bidding is not required. In fact, any engineer or firm can refuse to a bid for services, clients are required to seek bids, all current laws governing bids are being upheld, and state and local chapters can seek legislation on selection and negotiation procedures by public agencies (That this was revised as recently as Jan 2006 suggests that at least some of the misunderstandings were relatively recent—another point worthy of further investigation).

Construction Management

The Construction Management Association of America (CMAA) has recently updated its code and adopted new definitions of industry roles. Key changes include expanding the scope of the code to program management as well as construction management, reflecting a growing recognition that program management is a vital service for construction owners. The new code also clarifies that subscribers include both individuals and corporations, and provide simpler language on conflicts of interest. Moreover, the CMAA board of directors adopted the new code in recognition that "developments in the construction industry have led to uncertainty about the proper roles of project participants," so it released a new set of industry definitions to address this issue. The code is briefer than those of some of the other professions examined in this book. It essentially comprises ten statements regarding:

1. *Client Service.* Serving clients with honesty, integrity, candor, and objectivity, and providing services with competence, reasonable care, skill and diligence consistent with the interests of the client and the applicable standard of care.

2. *Representation of Qualifications and Availability.* This rule relates to truthfully and accurately representing one's qualifications, accepting assignments for which one is qualified, and assigning staff to projects in accordance with their qualifications.

3. *Standards of Practice.* Furnishing services in a manner consistent with the established and accepted standards of the profession and with the laws and regulations that govern its practice.

4. *Fair Competition.* Representing project experience accurately to prospective clients and only offering services and staff that one is capable of offering. Included here are statements about engaging in fair competition for assignments.

5. *Conflicts of Interest.* Endeavoring to avoid conflicts of interest; and disclosing conflicts which in one's opinion may impair objectivity or integrity.

6. *Fair Compensation.* Negotiating fairly and openly with clients regarding compensation, and charging fees and expenses that are reasonable and commensurate with the services provided and responsibilities and risks assumed.

7. Release of Information. Only making statements that are truthful, keeping information and records confidential when appropriate, and protecting the proprietary interests of clients and colleagues.

8. Public Welfare. Not discriminating in the performance of services on the basis of race, religion, national origin, age, disability, or sexual orientation, or knowingly violating any law, statute, or regulation in the performance of professional services.

9. Professional Development. Continuing to develop professional knowledge and competency, and contributing to the advancement of practice by fostering research and education and by encouraging fellow practitioners.

10. Integrity of the Profession. Avoiding actions that promote self-interest at the expense of the profession, and upholding the standards of the construction management profession with honor and dignity.

Questioning the Codes

As you consider the codes as summarized earlier in this chapter, and as they appear in full in appendix II, reflect on the following questions:

1. Are the codes adequate for ethical decision-making or do they specify only minimal obligations?
2. Are the codes more than self-protection?
3. Are the critical terms empty of content?—Aren't clearer definitions possible?
4. Can the professions be value neutral?
   - If so, what are their ethical obligations?
   - If not, should they take on big social issues? How could that be done without imposing their values?
5. Doesn't being moral finally require moving beyond rules and regulations to ethics?

Beyond the Codes: Critiques and Questions on the way to Collaborative Decision-Making

By their nature, codes of ethics are broadly stated so that they might apply to a full array of situations. This seems to be both a blessing and a curse. While this may be necessary for broad applicability, it also leaves the codes open to varying interpretations. Ways to interpret the codes can actually present a dilemma unto itself. Across the professional codes of conduct explored here, there is an emphasis on embracing the spirit and the letter of the law. But we must ask ourselves: is ethical decision-making simply about adhering to these codes? Is one behaving ethically if one is not breaking any of the rules put forward in the codes? In other words, are the codes enough or do they simply impose moral minimums on practice? Are there are ethical dimensions that go beyond the obligatory? What can the codes tell us about the decisions we must to make in everyday practice? Considering what else there is to ethics beyond professional codes of conduct calls us to address issues of professional silos and ponder whether and how we might move toward more collaborative decision-making. Certainly a large part of what is necessary lies in finding ways to recognize real differences without reducing them to stereotypes, which, in turn, requires that we genuinely understand the identities, roles, and proper interests and responsibilities of the major stakeholders in environmental projects.

The following sections of this chapter raise a series of critical questions concerning the codes.

1. Are the Codes Adequate for Ethical Decision Making or Do They Stipulate Only Minimal Obligations?

In a certain way, the codes of ethics impose the moral minimums; they offer what, at minimum, must be honored to maintain an ethical practice. Certainly, rules and codes are necessary for maintaining ethical standards, but they often do not provide sufficient guidance for navigating the complexities of the projects in which practitioners engage. Perhaps by their nature, the codes cannot do more without losing more general applicability to the variety of circumstances in which practitioners might find themselves. However, we can ask whether some principles have been privileged over others. What, for example, can professional codes tell us about negotiating relationships among multiple stakeholders, or about how to handle our own positionality in relation to other participants? How do we address power differentials among participants or road-blocking by an antagonistic stakeholder?

As we noted earlier, many of the codes are framed in terms of obligations. However, to decide that we have an obligation does not mean that it should be codified into a rule or that we should monitor everyone's performance based on it. But we do have to consider how we can encourage "fidelity to our obligations." Does one only act unethically if there is a rule against it? (Markie, 1994) For example, is it only unethical to pay to win a bid on a construction project because there is a law against it?

Moreover, some of the codes focus on what we ought not do (don't give gifts to public officials, don't take project materials without permission) rather than on what we ought to do. This is quite different than statements of what one ought to do: (tell the truth, be fair). In addition, when there are ethical decisions to be made about what to do, there first is a decision about whether or not to act at all. We note that the codes do not move us into the sphere of positive ethical concern or proactive reflection; when reviewing the codes overall, we see a notable absence of the ethic of care among the principles governing codes of conduct. (There is some mention of care in the codes for construction management in the discussion of standards of reasonable care that are applicable to clients; but it appears that what constitutes reasonable care in this context is something closer to conscientiousness or non-sloppy work. This is quite different from an ethical principle that guides action by having us consider our relationships to others and whether we are acting in a caring manner.) As was noted in chapter 2 and further discussed in chapter 4, the ethic of care focuses on commitment to others as a way to maintain integrity. It emphasizes empathy and relationships rather than objective decisions. It does not privilege impartiality or see morality as a constraint that limits our pursuits, rather it considers morality as enabling effective engagement. Given all the limitations that are involved, it is not surprising that critiques and debates about the codes of ethics abound. But these debates are quite instructive and cause us to consider the ethical dimensions of practice more closely.

2. Have the Codes[1] Evolved Beyond Professional Self-Protection?

During the turbulent social revolutions of the 1960s and 1970s, distinguished planner and scholar Peter Marcuse raised the question of whether planning ethics were mere self-protection or could be something more: planning ethics could logically go beyond narrow attention to client-serving, guild-serving, guild-related roles of planners to examine their real effect on the social, economic, and political systems in which the planners' activities take place. Professional ethics could logically deal with issues of power and act directly to further values such as equity and democracy. Indeed, professional ethics might even logically support movement toward structural change and new power relationships where planning's own tools and historical analysis shows them to be needed. (Marcuse 1976, 20)

This is a compelling argument; so we can ask: Have the ethical guidelines of planning changed since then? Should they have? If so, how? If not, why not? How—practically—could planners deal aggressively with the issues of power and "act directly to further values such as equity and democracy." (Is it correct to assume that planners would not be imposing their personal views is they furthered these values, which seemingly have been decided upon and repeatedly affirmed by the American people?)

Victor Papanek, a renowned designer and educator (and one of Frank Lloyd Wright's most successful students, explored "the connection between the spiritual in design and the intent of the designer. But there still remains the question of design ethics." He continues:

- Before we can honestly address this question, we must first eliminate the red herring of "professional ethics" or "professional codes of conduct." These are generally rules that some trade group or professional organization has drawn up to further its own fortunes and eliminate competition between members. They also usually protect the group, or its members, from public scrutiny and criticism. To evaluate whether the ethical rules of a group are really more than a self-protection racket is fairly easy. All we have to do is ask some simple questions:

- Is the code of ethics simply self-serving?
- Does the code of conduct really protect the public?
- Is this code truly regulative, that is, do the members comply with it, and can the public make its own judgments about the compliance of the members?
- Are these rules clear and specific about the possible pitfalls inherent in the particular profession or work performed by its members?
- Can non-members observe and judge compliance with the rules by members, and is it enforceable?
- Is this code of ethics, as well as the group or association, so constructed as to anticipate future changes, and therefore willing to teach, learn, and inform its membership as well as the public.
- Can the professional leadership of such professional organizations be made aware that, due to the modern media, we are living in an increasingly transparent society, in which secret deals, whitewashing and stone walling will no longer work?

(1995, pp. 69–70)

For an informative narrative of professional architectural codes and canons (NCARB and AIA), see Wasserman, Sullivan, and Palermo (2000, 106–117), who do a good job explaining the impact that court action in the mid-1970s had on all the professions' codes when it was ruled that the directives for self-regulation of members amounted to a violation of fair competition. For example, they explain how judicial action against the AIA in 1975 coincided with negative public perceptions: "The code appeared to clients to be a set of rules that were established to protect the architect in the competitive business world" (p. 16).

"Noble sounding words can become . . .
a comfortable substitute for hard thinking."
(Florman 1987)

---

3. Are the Crucial Terms in Ethics Codes "Empty" of Content? Is It Possible to Give Clearer Definitions? Some time ago, William H. Lucy (1988) examined the first five principles of the code of ethics for the planning profession among thirteen new principles added in 1987 to deal with some of the most difficult subjects in the field and reflect some political values of the profession in however broad a manner (the current planning code is found in appendix II). The subject matter of each principle is stated in one sentence, which, Lucy argues, runs the risk of trivializing significant issues. Let's look more closely at the particular principles Lucy examines and the questions he asks of them:

❑ *Serve the public interest*—what does this mean? First, it assumes one might know what the public interest is? Is it an accumulation of individual wants? Who has the right to judge these?

❑ *Support citizen participation in planning*—when should this happen? This is often interpreted as the public's ability to review and comment on proposals, but does not clarify or require opportunities for people to initiate proposals. Moreover, participation usually does not come from a representative sample of the population, rather it often reflects narrow self interests.

❑ *Recognize the comprehensive and long-range nature of planning*—Lucy argues that this contradicts the second principle of participation because public interest is continually modified, and long-term planning requires more stability.

❑ *Expand choice and opportunity for all persons*—what does this mean? What constitutes choice and opportunity? and who determines that?

❑ Facilitate coordination through the planning process

Overall, regarding those five principles dealing with planning processes and political values, Lucy contends, that the principles often contradict one another, and sometimes address issues that they should not or that involve improperly drawn conclusions. Though he believes "the public interest [must be more than] an accumulation of individual wants [and thus] is a major task of political philosophy . . . essential to the future of the planning profession and to the nation," he finds what is proposed to be so abstract and all-encompassing that it eliminates any basis for discussion (Lucy 1988, 147).

Read the APA code in appendix II and then consider Lucy's criticism of the planning codes. Do you think he is justified in this criticism? Have things changed since the late 1980s? How would you articulate the planner's obligations differently—better? (It would help to review chapter 3 on principles and rules and chapter 4 on theories to give a full response).

What is the "Public Interest?"

What does or should it mean to say that professionals must serve the public interest?

How can the public interest be determined?

How do we know whether we are truly serving the public, especially in today's diverse, multicultural society?

→ See Sandercock (2003) for a stimulating, if controversial presentation of planning's obligations in our globalized, pluralistic era.

Florman speaks critically of the engineering code of ethics' pledges to protect the public interest, or to make technology humane, arguing that it is easy to say that one strives to achieve this, but it is much more challenging to aptly implement it—or even understand it practical implications:

It is oh so easy to mouth clichés, for example to pledge to protect the public interest, as the various codes of engineering ethics do. But such a pledge is only a
beginning and hardly that. The real questions remain: *What* is the public interest, and *how* is it to be served? It is all very well for scholars to opine that an
"optimum technology" is one that "is directed toward the highest possible human goals" or to proclaim that "engineers should make technology more humane." But it is frivolous to suggest that these goals—and the means to attain
them—can be readily discerned by good-hearted individuals. . . noble sounding
words can become a soporific, a comfortable substitute for hard thinking, and so
work against the cause they claim to serve.

Having made this point, the quest for engineering ethics becomes all the
more challenging. How is it possible to move beyond platitudes? . . . Where will
it all end? . . . Certainly a code with real meaning and teeth is beyond the realm
of possibility. When *Chemical Engineering* presented its readers with a number
of "Perplexing Problems in Engineering Ethics," the letters in response were
dramatically divided and philosophically diverse. Such an experiment is enough
to indicate that the prospect of achieving homogeneity seems unrealistic—and,
some would say, undesirable. . . Nevertheless, the thrashing about, the impas-
sioned and often silly debates, the search for virtues that nobody can define—
these sharpen our wit and enrich our spirit. . . In engineering it is often the process rather than the product that captures our interests. Nowhere is this more true
than in the field of engineering ethics. (1987, 80–84)

Codes = Platitudes?

Are the codes just really platitudes, as Florman argues?
Is it possible to state a code of ethics broadly so that it
may apply to various situations and still be meaningful,
or are codes always, by default, going to be platitudi-
nous?

---

*4. Can the Professions be Value Neutral? Is Truth Objective or Is It Always
Situated?*

The basic argument here is between the traditional view that holds that truth, especially scientific knowledge, is value-free and objective, and the post-modern
or post-structuralist position that knowledge is a matter of continuous contextual
or situated interpretation. The latter view, which has gained increased momentum over the past few decades, holds that all knowledge is a result of finite human beings trying to understand complex reality from within their unavoidable
limitations of space, time, resources, and ability.

In addition to considering the source of our value and belief systems and
how and why those change or remain stable through life, we need to reflect on
the sources of our understanding and the relationship they bear on our deci-

sions—a matter clearly connected to our roles in life. For example, it has long been held that scientists and professionals should be "value neutral" if they are to obtain objective knowledge and to apply their technical expertise to achieve the goals of their clients and society. Following the positivist model of the natural sciences, professional attempt to collect all available data, generalize from particular observation to general theory, laws, and models, and test these by comparing them to reality. The adoption of systems analysis, operation research, and mathematical modeling incorporates not only vast amounts of information about natural and social processes, but also goals and images, all in a continually self-adjusting, self-improving manner (Mugerauer 1990, Faludi 1973, Friedman 1967).

The post-modern or post-structuralist position generated during the 1970s and 1980s—based on studies of the history, sociology, and theory of science—argued that scientific knowledge has never been objective and neutral. This newer position contended that, like all other human projects, the generation of knowledge is a matter of merely conventional practices. If so, from this it would follow that the technologies and professions have been unwarrently imposing their methods on society. Scientific statements would need to be seen "in the particularity of their occurrence" (Foucault 1972, 1973) and practices would need to be understood in terms of the situatedness of those attempting to know and act in the existential conditions within which they found themselves. The argument is that recognizing the situatedness of knowledge would result in a more genuinely empirical procedure because it would recognize local differences and multiple discursive formations. Because of this it would be possible to be both critical and yet open to exchange, which would nurture collective decision-making and change (Baudrillard, 1975, p. 119; Mugerauer, 1990, p. 17; Foucault, 1972, 1973; Rosenau, 1992).)

In contrast, the classic objectivist view has been especially influential in engineering, where we find Samuel Florman once again to be a major authority in articulating the issues of the profession, including explicitly dealing with the tension a professionally neutral approach can create. In response to the regular calls for engineers or large engineering societies to take political positions—a phenomenon common to all professions—he differentiates objective professional knowledge and ethical obligations from individual, purely personal beliefs:

Perhaps it matters whether we are talking about the individual or personal level. Many have argued that the personal is political and that both inextricably involve ethics; that taking a position is ethical but trying to be value-free is both impossible and even unethical. Some maintain that it is one thing to take a stand on an issue as an individual but another for an entire profession (or professional organization) to take a formal stand on an issue. For example, if some advocacy group rallying around an environmental problem or social-justice issue approached a professional organization to see if it would endorse the group's effort to stop over-fishing or to boycott a certain company whose manufacturing processes were polluting in a low-income community. When it comes to this organization level, taking a stand on an issue as a group of professionals becomes decidedly more complicated. And what of individual differences within the organization?

Professional Ethics & Personal Morality

Engineering ethicist Samuel Florman provocatively argues:

In the end, one's stance on any issue is based upon personal morality. Naturally, one may endorse a shared standard of virtue, whether religious or otherwise. But we dare not define "good" engineering by the precepts of any particular religious, philosophical, or political group. We may jointly pledge to work on behalf of the "public welfare," but our ideas about exactly what that welfare is, and how it is to be pursued, are mostly individual, not profession-wide. (1996, 156)

Engineering ethics is not, or should not be, a medium for expressing one's personal opinions about life [about issues such as] protecting the environment versus exploiting our resources, [or whether] we should use pesticides that save lives at the risk of doing damage in the food chain, drill for oil offshore at the risk of polluting our beaches, build a dam or protect an endangered species—These are essentially political issues, matters of choice for society. . . Engineers do not have the responsibility, much less the right, to establish goals for society. Although they have an obligation to lead, like most professionals, they have an even greater obligation to serve. (1987, 95; 1996, 154–155)

- What is your reaction to this argument?
- Should professional ethics—for engineering or any of the other environmental profession—be separated from such large social concerns?
- Do political issues really stand outside of ethics?
- Does taking a stand on an issue like offshore drilling conflict with professional ethics?
- Or is the opposite true?

4-a. If Professionals Can Be Value Neutral, What Are Their Ethical Obligations?
Supposing you do believe that professionals can, and should be, value neutral. Then what is the ethical obligation of the professional? Florman proposes that we emphasize professional competence and conscientiousness as the most realistic way to do good, as this is the ultimate obligation of the professional. While he articulates this concern as it arises in engineering, similar debates have ap-

peared in architecture, landscape architecture and planning. In any of the professions, really, there are countless discussions about professional duties and obligations. Interestingly, there is less written about the professional's rights, which suggests that the professional, as one in a position of power, does not need as much protection as the general public or audience that the given professional serves. So professional ethics are more concerned about the duties of professionals as providers of a service. And this is why ethics are often put in terms of impartiality and fairness in the provisions of services. One could also argue that just selecting a given profession is a matter of value judgment—in addition to disposition or personal skills and interests.

4-b. If Professionals Can Not Be Value Neutral—If Value Engagement Is Unavoidable—Is It Required? Can One Do Professional Work Without Imposing One's Values on Society? Is it Possible for Professionals to Actually Take On Much Less Be Responsible for—the Underlying, Societal Issues? Individually?
As a profession? Suppose value preference is unavoidable; even so, would it be required or merely optional for professionals to engage in efforts to change the decision process and improve environmental outcomes? How likely is it that they would do so? How would changes in the process or improvement to outcomes actually happen? In reference to matters of land use, environmentalist and futurist Mark Roseland argues we need to ensure that land use planning integrates various environmental, social, and economic objectives rather than simply balancing these objectives. For Roseland, land use decisions require changes in attitudes, institutional structures, and behavior. But these cannot be imposed. No single agency has a sufficiently comprehensive mandate, and resistance to change, especially if perceived as coming from the outside, is often quite strong. Further, professionals' ability to take on large issues such as environmental dilemmas ultimately requires the willing cooperation of community members and the public at large, the mobilization of which would seem beyond the power of any one professional group, much less individual. The pivotal issue, then, would be for professionals to use their expertise to convince others of the value of their concerns. In the case of land use planning:

> Realistically this willingness must rest on more or less self-interested motivations as well as broader enlightenment. The usually recognized motivations in land use decision-making include desire for increased property value, concern about liability and litigation, reliance on good public image, fear of health effects or job loss, worry about crime, and hope for new commercial or professional or social opportunities. . . Advances in planning therefore must be linked to concurrent, broader changes in social attitudes and values that are democratic, community oriented and environmentally responsible. (Roseland 1997, 34–35)

5. Doesn't Being Moral Finally Require Moving Beyond Rules and Regulations to Ethics?

In examining professional ethics, we inevitably confront larger social issues (social ethics, if you will). There are many insightful writings on the role of a professional in society, and the ethical implications of that role. For example, Flores (1988) notes that professionalism involves a complex set of role characteristics involving specialized knowledge and training, dedication to public services, and some autonomous decision-making authority. Along with this role come expectations of integrity, hence the aforementioned focus in the professional codes on duties and obligations as opposed to rights. These are the normative aspects of professionalism, and the various codes of ethics have been established accordingly. Ethical codes are essential to help maintain integrity in the professions, to articulate aspirations and expectations of members of professional societies and organizations, and to protect the public at large from any misconduct—unwitting or otherwise. Here the emphasis is not so much on how to *act* as opposed to how one should *be* (Flores, 1988). This is not to say that the codes are unnecessary but that professional ethics, out of necessity, will venture beyond the codes and rules.

It is not that being moral means merely observing rules of conduct. Otherwise, professionalism is reduced to rule-governed behavior involving the mechanical application of codes. Rather, professionalism contains another critical dimension—an idealized way of being that contributes to the realization of what is central to the profession and for the good of society.

(Flores, 1988)

In our society, professions are organized into formal associations and societies, each with their own policies and rules that govern the conduct of individual professionals. The development of these policies and rules reflects that society's beliefs and the aspirations of their professions. To some degree, these are recast as moral imperatives. As you continue reading through the chapter, keep thinking about the role of the codes and how to turn a universalistic, largely negative and coercive authority—the regulatory system—into a positive stimulus for achieving highly differentiated environments that inform and liberate (Ventre 1990, 60–61).

Who Makes the Decisions? Group Processes, Participation, and Roles

The fact that there are so many individuals and different groups involved in environmental decision-making in any given case means that there inevitably will be miscommunications. As Habermas (1979) has shown in his critical communication studies, some of these miscommunications are accidental and some are structural. For example, a passing noise outside our building that interrupts an important meeting may not be predictable, but we know there will be distractions, some of which we can plan how to deal with (the same goes for those resulting from individuals' idiosyncrasies). More seriously, the very specialization that legitimately drives knowledge and successful practice within professions, much less among different ones, causes meaning to shift when we move across disciplinary boundaries: we do not share the same vocabulary, assumptions, or expectations in regard to implications (Forester 1982, Albrecht and Lim 1986). Any important term, such as sustainability, or environment has different denotations, connotations, and value associations.

Given the diverse agendas and goals of often contending individuals and groups, it is not surprising that environmental decisions are full of tensions and oppositions. Further, in regard to our core issues, what are perceived to be dichotomies among these differing groups and factors are often the very source of the dilemmas that projects generate. Thus, by understanding the different players and by finding ways to undo false or unnecessary dichotomies (as well as recognizing and facing up to those that stand in principle or fact), we can go a long way toward dissolving many dilemmas. Such an accomplishment obviously would be a key to successful collaboration and resolutions that can satisfy diverse parties. A necessary first step here is becoming clearer on the processes and on the identities of the stakeholders involved.

1. Many Stakeholders

Who makes the decisions concerning complex environmental issues? In any significant project, a great many people are involved and there are numerous questions and issues that unfold, requiring decisions to be made along the way. Naturally, there are often substantial differences among the parties involved in an environmental issue. Here it is important to think about who is involved, and what their special characteristics and identities are if we are to appreciate their particular viewpoints and concerns, and understand why collaborative participation by all is necessary.

Who Makes Land Use Decisions?

Individuals faced with ethical judgments about land use
- Landowners and landholders
- Builders and land developers
- Public land-users (outdoor recreationists: e.g. off road vehicle enthusiasts, hunters, campers, birders, hikers, among others)
- Citizens and representatives of particular community interests
- Elected or appointed officials (members of a city council, planning commissioners, parks and recreation managers, sewer and street managers, and others)
- Land-use professionals and resource managers
- Banks and lending institutions
- Homeowners and renters
- Environmental and conservation groups (local, regional, and national)

(Beatley, 1994, p. 7; cf. pp.6-7)

For a simple comparison, The University of Washington's College of Architecture and Urban Planning Institute for Collaborative Building has identified the following list of players or stakeholders (each with up to a dozen sub-categories) as part of the decision making process:
- Owners
- Financiers
- Property agents
- Community
- Constructors
- Design, engineering, and consulting professionals
- Labor force
- Regulators
- Policy makers
- Services
- Suppliers and manufacturers
- Utility providers
- Media and publications
- Professional associations
- Educators

How do these lists compare?
How does the identification of different stakeholders influence the way we understand a project and its ethical imperatives?

To begin to be more concrete and focus on specific professions and problems, consider Timothy Beatley's list of those involved in land use decisions (his book is especially to be commended to political and governmental figures involved in public land-use policy making) and the list from the University of Washington's Institute for Collaborative Building. These lists are a good beginning, but we obviously can expand the set of professionals to include all those we are engaging in this book. Are there others who you think should especially be added to the preceding lists?

One of the major problems in ethical environmental decision-making involves the relationships among the relevant professionals and other decision makers, clients, and the public, as well as among the various professionals themselves. Of course, the relationship between the professionals and the client or public already is complex enough. For example, in evaluating existing or possible future environmental impacts of a proposed project, the analysis of the current conditions (soil contamination, erosion, contaminant levels in the water, vegetation continuity in relation to bird populations, urban storm-water drainage and runoff, traffic impact, noise pollution, and so on) may depend on more than a dozen specialized scientists and engineers. All of these specialists have to be trusted to provide correct information and to explicitly call our attention to the range of uncertainty or alternative ways to interpret the data, and to make the information understandable. In the case of construction projects, the technical expertise involved in such issues as site alternatives and orientations, building-envelope and roof configurations, HVAC systems, cladding and interior materials, construction timeline, etc.—all of which are dynamically interactive with each other— usually is beyond the capacity of the client or users to understand directly. There is also a gap between experts and laypeople in the ability to visualize new strategies and designs: compared to the population in general, designers have an extraordinary capacity to imagine what a three-dimensional space will look like and how it is likely to be experienced when there is not so much as a drawing yet made. Even with graphics of various kinds (plans, perspectives, blueprints), it often is difficult for non-professionals to interpret and visualize the intended end result. This difference in ability to visualize contributes to the professional's disproportionate expertise in environmental matters, and is a special factor in their responsibility to provide the intelligible information necessary for others to make decisions.

→ For further discussion regarding the ethics behind sharing knowledge and making it comprehensible, see the section on informed consent in chapter 3

In the case of professionals, while there obviously will be a higher degree of mutual understanding about technical matters among different professions, often there are significant differences, or even barriers, to communication due to their different roles and perspectives (Habermas 1979, Forester 1982, Albrecht and Lim 1986). Realms of expertise, ranging from background knowledge and assumptions when coming to a project to methodology and preferred procedures, are becoming increasingly specialized and narrowed as result. Thus not only might the engineers, designers, and contractors see things differently, but sub-specialist groups within each profession may not speak the same language beyond a certain point. Then there are the fracture lines that have historically plagued the professions (often deliberately cultivated, unfortunately) in which differences, such as those of learning and action styles, are exaggerated. For example, there seems to be some truth to the perception or experience that many engineers and many designers see things differently from one another—hence the tensions between the Corps of Engineers, landscape architects, urban ecologists, and environmentalists, as we have seen when it comes to deciding on what to do for flood control on the Mississippi or in the region around New Orleans.

Not the least of the differences involves the very serious, but often unspoken, issue of who really is in charge. Historically (for several millennia) the architect has been the master coordinator of all the specialized crafts and trades as well as the authority on the design itself. Since the early twentieth century, however, much of the power of decision-making has passed to the engineers, not only in terms of form and materials, but also of economic analysis and control. At the same time, most owners (or developers) are quite certain that they are the bosses, with all the others hired only to do what they want.

While solving these problems of collaboration and cooperation is far beyond the practical realm of having to make specific environmental decisions, we need to be aware of these issues in each particular case, and to continue the efforts already underway in education, organizational management, project assessment and planning to create a new realm of collaboration.

→ On the issue of "who is in charge?" see the case of Rincon Center in Appendix III.

2. Who Should Decide?

Consider the issue of who actually decides in comparison to that of who should decide—that is, who has an ethical right to participate, whose rights should be part of the collaborative decision making process and need to be respected by others. The following argument confronts the American emphasis on individualism as part of the problem. This is akin to the exercise in chapter 1 about privatism versus a civic attitude. Evaluate the claims below regarding the case of building construction and discuss:

In attempting to extract clear and unequivocal values from a project, there is a tendency to portray the process of building development as both linear and unproblematic and to view the attitudes and intentions of individuals as remaining static throughout the process, thereby informing and shaping the decision-making process in a direct, even deterministic way. This emphasis on the importance of individual agency tends to see the way to achieve more sustainable buildings as a problem of convincing key decision-makers and other autonomous individuals involved in the process of the importance of the issues. As Guy and Shove suggest, "the vocabulary is typically individualized," and the challenge is to change the perceptions, attitudes, opinions and motivations of designers (2000, 63). Furthermore, the motivation for tackling a problem comes from our moral obligation and our self-interest in enhancing the resource base and its life (Trudgill 1990, 105). This emphasis on the role and importance of the individual tends to reinforce a set of attitudes already prevalent in architectural discourse, where there is a long tradition of attributing the results of complex development processes typically involving hundreds of people to an individual creator—usually a single architect (Guy and Moore 2005, 27).

Identifying Legitimate Stakeholders

Traditionally, the owners of projects—in capitalist countries, those who contract and pay for them, either the private sector or the government—control the decisions and manage the built environments that result.

But what about the users? What about the taxpayers who pay for public projects? To what extent should they be involved in the decision-making?

What about those whose lives are impacted by the projects—a critical issue in cases of environmental harm?

How can a decision-making process respect those who have a legitimate ethical right to participate and yet firmly exclude others who do not have such legal or moral rights, yet who would like to block projects?

→These questions also ask "Who is the client?" To find out more about this tangled problem see chapter 3 on principles and rules, especially the sections on autonomy, informed consent, and justice.

The above argument not only raises the issue of the proper roles of individual and communal parties in the decision making process, but also makes the important point that the process is a continuing one that does not end, and often becomes more complex as it continues (as we considered in regard to wicked problems in chapter 2)

How can we adequately take the different dynamics of public and private organizational processes into account? There is a good argument (for example from the behavior analysts at Carnegie-Mellon University) that organizations are "not homogeneous and unitary with single goals; rather they are coalitions of sub-groups, each with their own partial goals, imperfectly rationalized in terms of general goals. Thus they proceed not in a rational mode, but rather via a series of compromises. In this regard, public non-profit organizations behave much like private, profit ones." Among the most important features of decision-making, in both such organizations, are the following:

1. Quasi-resolution of conflict. Conflicts (between the different goals of the sub-groups) are never really resolved.

2. Avoidance of uncertainty. Uncertainty is often more than stakeholders and organizations are capable of handling.

3. Probabilistic search. Faced with a pressing problem, organizations will find a fairly immediate solution, even though these can be simple-minded and biased by the training, experience and goals of the participants.

4. Organizational learning. Goals may be adapted in light of experience; the organization may change its attention rules; and it may change the order in which alternatives are considered in light of previous successes and failures. (adopted from Hall, 1981, pp. 208-11).

3. Particular Stakeholders and Diversity among Professionals. Identities and Roles, Differences and Commonalities

In considering major stakeholders of a project (policy-makers, the public), we want to give fair characterizations of each group or category and to open discussion to understand their genuine differences and commonalities—in order to move toward a fuller participatory model in decision making. Contributing to these goals, the material here gives us an excellent opportunity to continue to dissolving environmental and decision process dilemmas by undoing unnecessary and false dichotomies and stereotypes, including: the supposed engineer-designers dichotomy, the policy-maker–public dichotomy, and the view that "science must be reductive." In all of these cases, it is crucial to be honest and to acknowledge characteristics and differences where they exist; but, this must be done without generalizations that project or assume that all members of a group or class are identical in this or that respect, or without utilizing and continuing stereotypes that distort the empirical complexity and variety of people and situations.

Scientists have Exceptional Power:
Science and technology have enormous power today. In part this is evident in the fact that many scientific theories have passed into popular thought, even emerging as valuations and measures that we use unconsciously as part of our world views, such as the "survival of the fittest" (as we saw in chapter 1). So, before considering the differences that appear within scientific practices, knowledge, and ethical obligations, we should start by pausing to acknowledge this power and to become open to questioning its limitations and alternatives. Discussing the relation of science and spiritual traditions and outlooks, the Dalai Lama says:

The idea of the "survival of the fittest" has been misused to condone, and in some cases to justify, excesses of human greed and individualism and to ignore ethical models for relating to our fellow human beings in a more compassionate spirit. Thus, irrespective of our conceptions of science, given that science today occupies such an important seat of authority in human society, it is extremely important for those in the profession to be aware of their power and to appreciate their responsibility. (The Dalai Lama 2005, 115)

How could an appreciation of science's power and appropriate ways to socially integrate it be increased among both scientists and non-scientists?

Engineers and Contractors:

To begin, it seems that professionals tend to have a clear idea of who they are and what they are about. Engineers and Contractors range from those who are entirely pragmatic to those who see themselves as visionaries for a utopian future. Some focus on professional conscientiousness while others emphasize their responsibility for social reform. We see these differences, for instance, in the origins of American planning with engineers and health professionals who operated with the twin motives of rational scientific knowledge and the social improvement of appalling urban conditions in nineteenth century industrialization.

Matters are not simple in this varied and complex field, given the great diversity among engineers and contractors. In regard to the professions and environmental problems, legitimate concerns, complaints, and calls for change do need to be specific. But, the failure to recognize differences among members and approaches of any professional group is likely to cause resentment among the innocent members of the group who are laboring hard and long to accomplish just what is called for. Perhaps this statement by the Prince of Wales, who is very dedicated to sustainability and environmental education, may be an example of such a generalization that aggravates some of the parties:

Engineers are crucial to the solution of these [climate change] problems, but it might be that the problems could be avoided in the first place if the education and training of engineers were to include a bit more about the globe's essential life-support systems. It is after all these systems that ensure the habitability of our planet as it spins in the vast spaces of the universe. (Prince Philip, 2000)

What important differences within engineering knowledge and practice are omitted here? What dimensions of the complaint are valid? How would they be rectified?

Planners:

Planners are highly diverse. It should be relatively easy to describe the core identity of planners since it often is noted that over the past hundred and fifty years, planning emerged as a profession born out of the twin roots of science and the urge for social reform. Yet, the history of the last century or so and current attitudes make the question a problematic one. A "proper" role for planners has been to envision the way society and the built environment might be, as seen in the idea of the garden city proposed by Ebenezer Howard or Corbusier in urbanism. Yet there also has been a populist resistance to official planning, as in the case of Jane Jacobs, who argued in her influential *The Death and Life of Great American Cities* that "the city is not a work of art," but instead needs to incrementally facilitate residents' everyday movements. Partly as the result of the often unhappy results of urban renewal and the transportation woes of metropolitan areas (not to mention the disillusionment with science, technology, and political leadership after two world wars and Viet Nam), the public has nowhere near as much trust in experts as there was in the age of progressivism. A major aspect of resolving environmental dilemmas involves finding a way for planners and the public to develop mutual trust and work fruitfully together.

Designers:
The immediate complication to specifying the identity and role of designers is the great variety of design professions that are involved in the environment (as with engineers and planners too), including: architects, landscape architects and other landscape professionals, interior designers, product-industrial designers, and others. Here, we will consider only architectural and landscape architectural designers (omitting the important urban designers, product-industrial designers, and others only because of lack of space). Overall, however, as Roaf, Crichton, and Nicol (2005) point out, it is crucial to consider the entire cast of players. They ask: "What about the basic concerns of the designing professions, in terms perhaps of their 'wider responsibility to conserve and enhance the quality of the environment and its natural resources or even the interests of their clients'."

Landscape Architects:
Not surprisingly, ecologically-oriented designers and landscape architects call for an emplaced ethics, as advocated in the first part of this chapter. Within the landscape architecture profession there is a wide variety of practitioners and practices. Some landscape architects work on high-end private projects like residential landscape design, and some specialize in golf courses, while others work on public projects such as urban parks or environmental restoration and phytoremediation projects. Still others work on cultural landscapes preservation or therapeutic garden design. Despite these differences in specialty areas (and in attendant values), most landscape architects would agree that in projects involving ecological processes (say, using strategies for cleaning and managing storm water on site or developing green roofs) there is great utility and value in sit- specific and even incremental strategies. This is particularly true for practitioners who seek innovative design solutions for environmental problems like polluted storm water run-off, the heat-island effect or the endangerment of species habitat in urban or developing areas. In such cases, modest and site specific strategies are often considered usually more feasible and preferable than global strategies for several reasons:

The problems may be world-wide, yet they will yield only to decentralized, to human-scale and local interventions. This is partly due to the fact that we are still unable to assess the impact of what we do as designers and as consumers— only if our intrusions are modest in scale are the chances of major miscalcula- tions reassuringly remote. Most architects and designers—especially young in- dustrial designers—feel that high technology is bound to disturb the ecological balance even more profoundly. (Papanek 2000, 25)

This goes along with the landscape ecology perspective advocated by such scholars as Anne Spirn and Joan Iverson Nassauer. As discussed elsewhere in this book, there is a strong focus among landscape architects who are particu- larly interested in ecological design, who seek to design with nature in mind, and who call for an interdisciplinary approach to landscape architecture which looks the landscape in a holistic manner, seeking to understand patterns and in- tegrated systems.

Within landscape architecture, there is a great deal of discussion about in- terdisciplinary collaboration and the tensions that this can sometimes cause. Just as there are tensions between architects and engineers (as described below), there are sometimes tensions between architects and landscape architects on a project. Much of this tension is couched in the nature of the professions having different foci and values. Some have argued that architects see the landscape as a blank canvas, and, partly as a response to that, we have books like *The Space Between the Buildings* which emphasize how the landscape is more than a back- drop for architecture.

Architects:

As is the case in landscape architecture, in addition to individual differences, there are diverse major types of architects and designers, which also means even greater variety apart from the basic approaches. Clearly there is not agreement in this profession about what design should be or aspire toward, nor about what is the desired model for success. But, because most architects pay attention to some contextual elements or dimensions, differences among them often, though not always, reflect differences in the emphasis placed on environmental factors. (The major exceptions involve aesthetic formalists and those modernists who seek to defamiliarize us in principle, both of whom insist on the autonomy of art and architecture.) At the least, we contend that design must accommodate: cli- matic and geological features; materials and the laws of physics and chemistry that go with them; social customs, uses and expectations (including economics and politics-power relations); forms and shapes (and, with historical change, the building typologies that combine form and social custom).

Designers may emphasize one aspect over others, but rarely does this make sense without seeing how the central aspect of a design combines with the other elements. For example, often formalist views are identified with modernist ar- chitecture. While this is generally a fair assessment, obviously form is part of any design and the term "form" can not be co-opted by only one viewpoint. Moreover, as we will see shortly, the original European founders of modernism had a radical social agenda to accompany, even drive, their use of rather pure forms, so that initial and continuing tradition is at odds with what we have come to consider formalism (i.e., a more purely aesthetic approach that is generally not interested in social function as advocated by left-of-center politics). In short, we need to be more thoughtful and careful about the labels we use and how we generalize. What follows is meant to be only a sample of the variety of features that architects address to begin to reflect the complex and subtle distinctions over which members of the profession wrangle—points to be especially kept in mind when we approach and work to dissolve common but sloppy dichotomies involving architects as if there were only one band of them.

To start, however, with some of the most common perceptions—before complicating or undoing some of them, we need to consider the two dominant perspectives in architecture. Some architects, such as John Ruskin, have emphasized their moral responsibility to improve society; in a similar vein, the modernist Walter Gropius contended that architecture was a key to dramatic, even utopian, social reform. Given the difference between Ruskin's and Gropius' aesthetic and practice, we see that both forms and materials could vary wildly across even those with the same type of social conviction. In contrast, in the twentieth century, a more purely formal-geometric aesthetic developed out of the work of the early European modernists. This shift partly resulted from the fact that much of their pioneering work was done in the United States, where patrons were corporations and the wealthy elite (the latter, of course, also sponsored the villas and government projects realized in Europe). At first, and still for some such as Richard Meier, formalist architecture in its modern mode is characterized by a purist geometry, though recently it has been carried onward by deconstructivism.

> The Modern Movement's intentions in the first half of the 20th century . . . to address social projects . . . sweep aside class restrictions, make a more egalitarian society—Whatever its naiveté viewed in hindsight, this was an ethical stance. Even though after the Museum of Modern Art exhibition of 1931 the aesthetic of modernism was usurped as an object of connoisseurship and adopted by the modern corporation (exactly the opposite of its original objectives), many of its intentions continue to have ethical merit (Twombly, 1996, p. 299) (For reliable and useful accounts of these developments, see especially Twombly 1996, Rowe 1994.)

It appears that what was advocated and known about architecture at one time was both developed more exclusively along the non-modernist trajectory and simultaneously forgotten or ignored by the heirs of modernist formalism. Modernists Le Corbusier, Ludwig Mies van der Rohe, and Sigfried Giedion employed a moral language to explain architecture because they proposed to design a new social world. The idea was that architecture could combine the admirable clarity and honesty of contemporary engineering's buildings, and especially machines, with a higher spiritual purpose—to begin a cultural revolution that would provide a morally and physically healthy environment for workers in the new industrial world. (see Le Corbusier, *Towards a New Architecture*; see also David Watkin 2001, 37–61). However, the early ideals of the founders concerning what Taut's called healthy socialism in the machine age society were soon lost—and today remain largely forgotten even in the architectural community—as high modernism separated ideas about formal expression and functionalism and shifted to a formalist aesthetics. These issues of the actual, possible, and desired relationships of forms, materials, and uses, or of social and aesthetic goals is a complex tangle, as can be seen by even these few references given here:

→ To explore more fully the critical and continuing debate between the social and aesthetic branches of modernist designers, see exercises 3.b and 3.c at the end of this chapter.

→ This debate also involves the definition of and an ethical position on the use of materials. See chapter 4, the section on truthfulness and exercises 5.2.a and 5.2.b

→ For a case in which the architect describes himself as an esthete but still explicitly discusses how he takes all the other elements seriously, and assumes the architect must negotiate with those holding opposite viewpoints, see the case of Rincon Center, San Francisco in appendix III.

Importantly, however, the contrast between the two poles (formalistic design and design for social reform/change) soon becomes blurred as we consider the work of architects such as Glenn Murcutt (with numerous modest-sized buildings), T. R. Hamzah and Yeang (Menara Mesiniaga, Malaysia), Hellmuth, Obata, and Kassabaum (Edificio Malecon, Buenos Aires), and some of the projects of Norman Foster and Partners (with large structures like Swiss Re Headquarters, London), of Richard Rogers Partnership (DaimlerChrysler Headquarters, Berlin), and of Santiago Calatrava. These architects have combined technical engineering, industrial materials, and strong formal dimensions of design to create high-style, high-performance designs that are often, in fact, cited as exemplary in regard to sustainability. Here we find a very promising approach to undoing the dichotomy and move forward, even within the modernist aesthetic.

Of course, there are many different architectural positions, and these have direct ethical implications. Here are just a few representative views that advocate and practice a social or spiritual basis for design—more are presented in chapter 5 where we broaden beyond architecture proper to explicitly treat environmental design and sustainability in their diverse modes.

Karsten Harries, in his well-received *The Ethical Function of Architecture*, contends that the ethical status of architecture is related to its most powerful social dimensions:

Should architecture not continue to help us find our place and way in an ever more disorienting world? In this sense, I shall speak of the ethical function of architecture. "Ethical" derives from "ethos". By a person's ethos we mean his or her character, nature, or disposition. Similarly we speak of a community's ethos, referring to the spirit that presides over its activities. "Ethos" here means the way human beings exist in the world: their way of dwelling. By the ethical function of architecture I mean its task to help articulate a common ethos. (2000, 4)

Many architects vehemently contend that specific designs for buildings and communities are indispensable to achieve desired (or recover now lost) forms of traditional community life and the associated civic virtues. One of the best architectural ethicists, Philip Bess, makes such a civic argument:

Neo-traditionalists seek, or should seek, to help create new neighborhoods and towns that encourage a participatory common life that is, for the most part, freely chosen. Here, individual lives of learning, piety, filial affection and obligation, respect for others, pursuit of excellence, and the competitive creation of wealth can be pursued largely in practices sustained by families, the workplace, religious institutions, schools, libraries, and other political and voluntary associations; these pursuits can take place in a beautiful, multi-centered, pedestrian-scaled physical environment of background buildings, monumental buildings, and public spaces conducive to the common good, in which automobiles are conveniences rather than necessities. In this scenario, neo-traditionalist town plans would be meritorious in part for their aesthetic and sound environmental attributes. More valuable would be their ability to strengthen the communal practices and institutions that currently exist, but in a weakened and fragmented state, in contemporary cities and suburbs. (1993, 81)

Finally, in one of his influential books on design education and practice Victor Papanek contends that we can and need to recognize the spiritual dimensions of design, broadly conceived (i.e. not necessarily religious):

It is the intent of the designer as well as the intended use of the designed object that can yield spiritual value. The questions that must be asked are:
   ❑   Will the design significantly aid the sustainability of the environment?
   ❑   Can it make life easier for some group that has been marginalized by society?
   ❑   Can it ease pain?
   ❑   Will it help those who are poor, disenfranchised or suffering?
   ❑   Will it save energy or—better still—help to gain renewable energies?
   ❑   Can it save irreplaceable resources?
A positive answer to these or similar questions does not make the design visibly spiritual. But the performance of such services to our fellow humans and the planet will help us inwardly. It will nourish our soul and help it to grow. That's where spiritual values enter design. (1995, 54)

→ For more on the topic of varieties of aesthetics and their relationships to social goals, environmental design, and sustainability, see chapter 5

→ These issues are inseparable from the question "Who is the Client?" The one who pays, the users, the public, future generations, or . . . ? For more on this issue see chapter 3, principles and rules, the sections on autonomy, informed consent, beneficence, and non-maleficence

Policy-Makers:
Without entering into politics—the extension of ethics, as has been understood since Plato and Aristotle—we can at least begin to consider the complexity of information and competing agendas and goals that policy-makers have to deal with. As sustainability researchers and architects Guy and Moore appreciate:

> Despite a number of success stories and growing recognition of the multiple benefits of energy-efficient housing, it cannot be denied that many local policies to promote sustainable building fail to live up to expectations. Criticism is leveled in particular at the relatively low rates of technology dissemination . . . Local policy-makers are well aware of this implementation gap between policy objectives and operational achievements. . . [The three main barriers], it is widely held, relate essentially to a lack of information among key actors about the technological options, inadequate financial incentives for actors to adopt sustainable technologies and market forces that favor short-term cost-saving for the developer over long-term benefits for the user of a building. (2005, 75–77)

What can environmental professionals do to support public-policy makers and public employees in their attempts to achieve greater sustainability?

The Public:
Suppose we start again and ask afresh, "Who should be involved in environmental decisions?" The most generous view is obvious: everyone affected by the decision. This can be an empowering experience for all participants:

> Empowerment is a simple concept; it implies giving more power to individuals over the compass of their lives through better administrative structures and improved social arrangements. It should be possible to set mutually acceptable limits to individual empowerment that do not infringe on the rights of others. Engagement implies the involvement of people in all the various activities of their public life and a democratization in the way we arrive at social goals. (Short 1989, 76)

But, as we know, enacting such an ideal is not always achievable in all circumstances. Nor would it even be desirable to everyone—after all, we need to be realistic about the way power operates. In regard to the ethical obligations of environmental professionals, we can specifically ask, "Given both the importance and difficulties of public empowerment and engagement, versus letting the professionals do it all, what degree of public participation is realistic? Or desired?"

Throughout this book, we considered the various ways that not only professionals, but all of us, are involved in decision making concerning environmental dilemmas. We also dealt with sectors of the public as we went along, especially in the case material in chapter 5 and the appendices to follow. To attend to the poor and disenfranchised, because they often bear the brunt of environmental problems and normally are not included in the decision making process, we regularly include them in our explicit discussion and case material.

→ See especially the section on the poor and disempowered above in this chapter, the parallel sections in chapter 5, and the cases of HOPE VI and Hydro-Quebec in appendix III.

The goal of this chapter was to present the most important dimensions of decision making from the perspective of the environmental professions. Here, the intent is to discuss the major problems and to introduce the cast of characters involved in dealing with environmental dilemmas—including making explicit the values and beliefs that underlie differences, and acknowledging and directly addressing conflict. But, as is clear, the chapter does not come to a resolution of the issues, nor do we think it should. Rather, we need to continue to develop and clarify the ethical dimensions of the place-based professions, to work on dissolving dilemmas by re-examining worldviews and reframing dilemmas in a way that can undo some of the most aggravating dichotomies, and by applying our ideas in depth to environmental issues.

What's Next?

You can work to untangle two of the most professionally stressful—and deeply interconnected—dichotomies by doing the exercises below, the first of which focuses on the perception of differences between engineers-contractors and architects-designers. The second exercise develops the dichotomy discussed above, between formalist and socially-oriented design approaches and aesthetics.

Exercises for Chapter Six: Real Differences and False Dichotomies

As we noted in chapter 1, dilemmas that are kept in the theoretical or abstract realm can remain interminable—unable to really be solved—if disconnected from the phenomena from which they arise. In the case of environmental ethics, this means that the codes (just as we will see with the principles and rules) need to be understood in light of specific situations in which one has to make a decision (Harding, 1985). By considering specific cases (such as those we offer in this book) and deciding how to act in particular circumstances, we can grapple more readily with the principles, interpreting them in ways that can guide what one considers right conduct.

Doing the exercises here goes a long way to practicing how to dissolve two dichotomies at once, and would be a big step toward eliminating many possible dilemmas in environmental decisions. Note that the supposed dichotomy between engineer/contractor and architect/designer is significantly rooted in the dichotomy between formalist and socially-oriented approaches that we considered in the sphere of architecture/design. If one is not an aesthetic formalist (modern, deconstructivist, or otherwise) there is not much basis for the engineer-contractor versus architect-designer contrast, since the latter is based on the perceived difference between emphasizing the practical and the formalistically aesthetic.

Beyond Dichotomies and Stereotypes

Exercise 6.1 Engineers-Contractors vs. Architects-Designers

What was said earlier in this chapter about the variety of architectural/design positions and the obvious dangers of most generalizations needs to be taken just as much to heart when we encounter the supposed dichotomy between engineers/contractors and architects/designers. In both cases, we do need to recognize honestly that there are differences that characterize some architects and some engineers (at least in some phases of their work), but we can do so without emphasizing differences to the point of generating or perpetuating dualisms. If we were to ignore shared characteristics, we would miss the richness and variety of what can be understand as belonging to an archetype (a form which itself never appears, but is manifest in countless specific manifestations across different times and cultures), such as the warrior or the wise old woman. Indeed, to simplify and over-generalize results in the exact opposite: the flat, mono-dimensional stereotype that reduces complex realities to less than they are.

To note some of the real differences to be dealt with when they appear (especially in their most insistent versions), the architectural and construction professions have been slow in coming to agree on the proper documents needed to pass from designer to contractors: there is a long and troubled history to the situation in which there is little agreement between what the architectural establishment deems to be the proper documents, which the designer is responsible for and needs to convey, and what the contracting establishment considers due in order to move to the next stage of construction. Or, there would appear to be some—some, but not more than that—truth to the characterization of engineers and contractors emphasizing functionality, cost, schedules, and other pragmatic dimensions, whereas architects/designers would emphasize and develop their ideas more on the basis of aesthetics or possible cultural impact and symbolic importance. Hence, we should not be surprised to hear that: "Studies confirm the perception that "architects are perceived as more "artistic" that engineers and more preoccupied with design and form"" (Roaf, Crichton, and Nicol 2005,

321). Does this tell us about the architects and engineers, or does it tell us something about research assumptions and methodologies or both?

What are your views about the differences between some engineers-contractors and some architects-designers? What kinds of conflicts are those genuine differences likely to generate in perceptions of the environment and environmental problems? Can you suggest ways to lessen the conflicts that tend to result from those differences in attitude, valuation, and practice? What other information, definitions or categories can you bring to bear to further dissolve the differences for those who would like to do so? How would you recommend proceeding when you (or some of the other stakeholders) need to work cooperatively with professionals who are not interested in deemphasizing the differences (for example, because they honestly see doing so as an abandonment of a core identity, role, or responsibility, or for other reasons)?

Exercise 6.2   Modernism Design and Aesthetics: Socially Oriented or Formalist?

Obviously, not all design needs to be modernist. But since the approach remains very influential in many schools of architecture and in professional practice, everyone has to deal with the debate about the relationship of aesthetics and social emphasis in order to understand architects and to work with them successfully.

Interpretation of the past and of remaining possibilities continues to be the source of lively disagreements in architecture. What "really" happened in the course of the twentieth century development of design theory and practice and what should be going on today? Think it through—perhaps even reading more on the topic—and try to come to a fuller understanding of the attitudes, values, and work out your own view on modernism and come to at least a preliminary personal position on what design viewpoint you hold—either socially oriented or formalist modernist, or one of the other positions treated here (including the spiritually or environmentally oriented as treated in chapter 5.

On the one hand, the distinguished architectural historian and theorist Christian Norberg-Schultz explains that while the Bauhaus positively "freed us from copying obsolete form" through its free experiments and artistic activities, in order that "education in this field should above all be founded upon an understanding of the nature of the architectural totality," which at the least means that its methods still "ought to be supplemented and developed on the basis of a better understanding of psychological and sociological factors." In regard to issues such as the relation of form and function, "any closer scrutiny of the last hundred years shows that the new architecture is not a result of the wish for *l'art pour l'art*, but has sprung from the strivings of idealistic individuals to make man's [sic] environment better" (1965, 19).[2]

In contrast to the view that architecture, finally, is *not,* a matter of a purely formalist aesthetic since its proper aesthetic inherently includes the social or moral, the authors of one of the most respected architecture ethics texts argue the contrary—that architecture has value as a sphere of autonomous artistic objects:

> When architecture asserts itself as such, beyond its role as artistic production it has no compelling moral force. That is, it is no longer architecture which by definition has a conceptual purpose, but an art object, which has aesthetic "purposiveness without purpose" as its inherent object. (Wasserman et al 2000, 87)

If considered, then, in their most polar forms, the non-autonomous and autonomous approaches to design sharply contrast, as does the criticism of each side by the other. For example, from an ecological point of view, the cultural construction of the conditions under which the avant-garde generates buildings in a high culture, formalist mode needs to be criticized because it does not simultaneously provide for efficient and comfortable use or concern itself with high-performance (as would be part of sustainability) (Salingaros 2003; Roaf, Crichton, and Nicol 2005, 322–27). Here is a statement of the apparently most obvious clash of the intuitively discernable opposing positions.

The Modern Development of Aesthetic Formalism:

In modern aesthetics (as with Kant): art is seen as inherently valuable for the unity and beauty of its form, rather than instrumentally valuable as a practical means to accomplish something else. Here, because of its functional dimension, architecture is seen as less purely aesthetic than painting or music.

With the creation of non-representational art by the early part of the twentieth century, a movement developed to appreciate art for arts sake.

As part of this movement, many great modernist architects—such as Le Corbusier—carefully shaped their public identity as "artists" and their architectural creations as "art," in contrast to mere building. While many modernists held that great aesthetic form is inseparable from function—as in the famous dictum form follows function—thus attempting to fuse the two dimensions, holding the formal and social in tension, others detached them, shunning the pragmatic limitations of utility, budget, and client desires. A case in point is Philip Johnson, who mocked Ruskin, telling students at Harvard in 1954, "Its got to be clear that serving the client is one thing and the art of architecture is another" (cited in Short 1989, 37)

So, how do you interpret the story? Does either position describe your own viewpoint? And, here is the main professional ethics question: If you are either a formalist or socially oriented modernist, how will you work with those who hold the opposite position, as well as all the other professionals, clients, and users who hold entirely other views? Or, if you are not a modernist of either stripe, how will you work with the formalists or socially-oriented modernists who have very strong—and still powerful positions within the profession and education—convictions about what the design, treatment of materials, and so on should be like?

Exercise 6.3—Aesthetics and Individualism: Pressing Deeper into the Core of the Formalist Aesthetic (and the Issue of Privatism versus the Civic View of Chapter One)

A strong claim is made by one of the genuine heirs to the tradition of high-design in America—that the great works of the twentiety century by Wright, Le Corbusier, Mies van der Rohe, Aalto, and others all have one striking feature in common.

> They are all individualistic and idiosyncratic statements; the buildings . . . make explicit gestures that are only tenuously linked to their purpose. Through several centuries one view of architectural ideology has been heard more loudly than others. It is the concept of "artistic individualism," which finds particular buildings important, or evaluates general progress in architecture on a personal basis—usually of style, fashion, fad, decoration, embellishment or ornamentation embodied in specific buildings and developed from architect to architect through history. This traditional theory . . . considers a building significant or unimportant according to how much it incorporates the "idea of ideas" of its individual designer. The history of architecture then is seen as the interaction of such significant ideas, developed in buildings. This concept of architecture has only recently shown signs of losing its significance. (Papanek 1995, 134–35)

Remember that we do need to honestly face and learn to deal with deeply held positions insofar as they continue to operate and impact projects. How can those who would wholeheartedly support the approach Papanek identifies and those who oppose it (for example, as one of the sources of our disagreements) come to some mutual accommodation?—after all, they typically do need to work together.

Notes

1.An exceptional reference book to all professional codes, not just those of the built environment, is *Codes of Professional Responsibility*, Third Edition, Rena A. Gorlin, editor, Washington, D. C.: Bureau of National Affairs, 1994.

2. In Enlightenment aesthetic theory, such as Kant's and Schopenhauer's, because of its practical requirements, architecture was considered to be less a pure fine art (such as music, for example); thus at that time it would not have been considered in terms of art for art's sake—a position that changed with early twentieth century aesthetic formalism).

Consider the issue of who actually decides in comparison to that of who should decide—that is, who has an ethical right to participate, whose rights should be part of the collaborative decision making process and respected by others. The following argument confronts the American emphasis on individualism as part of the problem. This is akin to the exercise in chapter 1 about privatism versus a civic attitude. Evaluate the claims below regarding the case of building construction and discuss:

In attempting to extract clear and unequivocal values from a project there is a tendency to portray the process of building development as both linear and unproblematic and to view the attitudes and intentions of individuals as remaining static throughout the process, thereby informing and shaping the decision-making process in a direct, even deterministic way. This emphasis on the importance of individual agency tends to see the way to achieve more sustainable buildings as a problem of convincing key decision-makers and other autonomous individuals involved in the process of the importance of the issues. As Guy and Shove suggest, "the vocabulary is typically individualized," and the challenge is to change the perceptions, attitudes, opinions and motivations of designers (2000, 63). Furthermore, the motivation for tackling a problem comes from our moral obligation and our self-interest in enhancing the resource base and its life (Trudgill 1990, 105). This emphasis on the role and importance of the individual tends to reinforce a set of attitudes already prevalent in architectural discourse, where there is a long tradition of attributing the results of complex development processes typically involving hundreds of people to an individual creator—usually a single architect (Guy and Moore 2005, 27).

Appendixes

Appendix I: Websites

A. Global Climate Reports and Analyses

As might be expected, this is a vast and rapidly expanding area.
Perhaps the most important site is that of the
> Intergovernmental Panel on Climate Change,
> which has just issued its fourth report
> http://www.ipcc.ch/SPM2feb07.pdf

Among the other most useful introductory sites are:

> Data on climate-related disasters per continent,
> http://www.un.ep.org/geo2000/english/figures.html

> Dobson units and ozone thickness measurement,
> http://theozonehole.com

> English report on threat of climate change,
> http://news.bbc.co.uk/1/hi/sci/tech/3381425.stm

> Energy consumption by region,
> http://www.unep.org/geo2000/english/figures.html

> Insurance payments for natural disasters,
> www.munichre.com/pdf/topics_e.pdf

> On the Kyoto Protocol,
> http://unfccc.int/index.html
> http:unfcc.int/resource/kpstate.pdf
> http:unfcc.int/resource/kpthermo.html

> Worldwide Institute, State of the World Report 2005,
> http://www.worldwatch.org/pubs/sow/2005

B. Professional Organizations and Codes

AIA
American Institute of Architects,
Code of Ethics and Professional Conduct,
http://www.aia.org/ethics.html

APA
American Planning Association,
American Institute of City Planners,
AICP Code of Ethics and Professional Conduct,
http://www.planning.org/ethics/conduct.html

ASLA
American Society of Landscape Architects,
Code of Professional Ethics,
http://www.asla.org/about/codepro.htm,

Code of Environmental ethics,
http://www.asla.org/profpractice

CMAA
Construction Management Association of America,
http://www.cmaanet.org/ethics.php>

NCARB
National Council of Architectural Registration Boards,
Rules of Conduct,
http://www.ncarb.org

NSPE
National Society of Professional Engineers,
Code of Ethics for Engineers,
http://www.nspe.org/ethics/eh1-code.asp,
http://www.nspe.org/pf-home.asp

Appendix II: Professional Codes

AIA
American Institute of Architects
Code of Ethics and Professional Conduct

APA
American Planning Association–
American Institute of City Planners
AICP Code of Ethics and Professional Conduct

ASLA
American Society of Landscape Architects
Code of Professional Ethics
Code of Environmental Ethics

CMAA
Construction Management Association of America
Code of Professional Ethics for the Construction Manager

NSPE
National Society of Professional Engineers
Code of Ethics for Engineers

THE AMERICAN INSTITUTE
OF ARCHITECTS

2004 Code of Ethics & Professional Conduct

Preamble

Members of The American Institute of Architects are dedicated to the highest standards of professionalism, integrity, and competence. This Code of Ethics and Professional Conduct states guidelines for the conduct of Members in fulfilling those obligations. The Code is arranged in three tiers of statements: Canons, Ethical Standards, and Rules of Conduct:

- Canons are broad principles of conduct.
- Ethical Standards (E.S.) are more specific goals toward which Members should aspire in professional performance and behavior.
- Rules of Conduct (Rule) are mandatory; violation of a Rule is grounds for disciplinary action by the Institute. Rules of Conduct, in some instances, implement more than one Canon or Ethical Standard.

The Code applies to the professional activities of all classes of Members, wherever they occur. It addresses responsibilities to the public, which the profession serves and enriches; to the clients and users of architecture and in the building industries, who help to shape the built environment; and to the art and science of architecture, that continuum of knowledge and creation which is the heritage and legacy of the profession.

Commentary is provided for some of the Rules of Conduct. That commentary is meant to clarify or elaborate the intent of the rule. The commentary is not part of the Code. Enforcement will be determined by application of the Rules of Conduct alone; the commentary will assist those seeking to conform their conduct to the Code and those charged with its enforcement.

Statement in Compliance With Antitrust Law

The following practices are not, in themselves, unethical, unprofessional, or contrary to any policy of The American Institute of Architects or any of its components:

(1) submitting, at any time, competitive bids or price quotations, including in circumstances where price is the sole or principal consideration in the selection of an architect;
(2) providing discounts; or
(3) providing free services.

Individual architects or architecture firms, acting alone and not on behalf of the Institute or any of its components, are free to decide for themselves whether or not to engage in any of these practices. Antitrust law permits the Institute, its components, or Members to advocate legislative or other government policies or actions relating to these practices. Finally, architects should continue to consult with state laws or regulations governing the practice of architecture.

CANON I

General Obligations

Members should maintain and advance their knowledge of the art and science of architecture, respect the body of architectural accomplishment, contribute to its growth, thoughtfully consider the social and environmental impact of their professional activities, and exercise learned and uncompromised professional judgment.

E.S. 1.1 Knowledge and Skill: Members should strive to improve their professional knowledge and skill.

Rule 1.101 In practicing architecture, Members shall demonstrate a

consistent pattern of reasonable care and competence, and shall apply the technical knowledge and skill which is ordinarily applied by architects of good standing practicing in the same locality.

Commentary: By requiring a "consistent pattern" of adherence to the common law standard of competence, this rule allows for discipline of a Member who more than infrequently does not achieve that standard. Isolated instances of minor lapses would not provide the basis for discipline.

E.S. 1.2 Standards of Excellence: Members should continually seek to raise the standards of aesthetic excellence, architectural

education, research, training, and practice.

E.S. 1.3 Natural and Cultural Heritage: Members should respect and help conserve their natural and cultural heritage while striving to improve the environment and the quality of life within it.

E.S. 1.4 Human Rights: Members should uphold human rights in all their professional endeavors.

Rule 1.401 Members shall not discriminate in their professional activities on the basis of race, religion, gender, national origin, age, disability, or sexual orientation.

2004 CODE OF ETHICS AND PROFESSIONAL CONDUCT

E.S. 1.5 Allied Arts & Industries: Members should promote allied arts and contribute to the knowledge and capability of the building industries as a whole.

CANON II

Obligations to the Public

Members should embrace the spirit and letter of the law governing their professional affairs and should promote and serve the public interest in their personal and professional activities.

E.S. 2.1 Conduct: Members should uphold the law in the conduct of their professional activities.

Rule 2.101 Members shall not, in the conduct of their professional practice, knowingly violate the law.
Commentary: The violation of any law, local, state or federal, occurring in the conduct of a Member's professional practice, is made the basis for discipline by this rule. This includes the federal Copyright Act, which prohibits copying architectural works without the permission of the copyright owner. Allegations of violations of this rule must be based on an independent finding of a violation of the law by a court of competent jurisdiction or an administrative or regulatory body.

Rule 2.102 Members shall neither offer nor make any payment or gift to a public official with the intent of influencing the official's judgment in connection with an existing or prospective project in which the Members are interested.
Commentary: This rule does not prohibit campaign contributions made in conformity with applicable campaign financing laws.

Rule 2.103 Members serving in a public capacity shall not accept payments or gifts which are intended to influence their judgment.

Rule 2.104 Members shall not engage in conduct involving fraud or wanton disregard of the rights of others.
Commentary: This rule addresses serious misconduct whether or not related to a Member's professional practice. When an alleged violation of this rule is based on a violation of a law, or of fraud, then its proof must be based on an independent finding of a violation of the law or a finding of fraud by a court of competent jurisdiction or an administrative or regulatory body.

Rule 2.105 If, in the course of their work on a project, the Members become aware of a decision taken by their employer or client which violates any law or regulation and which will, in the Members' judgment, materially affect adversely the safety to the public of the finished project, the Members shall:
(a) advise their employer or client against the decision,
(b) refuse to consent to the decision, and
(c) report the decision to the local building inspector or other public official charged with the enforcement of the applicable laws and regulations, unless the Members are able to cause the matter to be satisfactorily resolved by other means.
Commentary: This rule extends only to violations of the building laws that threaten the public safety. The obligation under this rule applies only to the safety of the finished project, an obligation coextensive with the usual undertaking of an architect.

Rule 2.106 Members shall not counsel or assist a client in conduct that the architect knows, or reasonably should know, is fraudulent or illegal.

E.S. 2.2 Public Interest Services: Members should render public interest professional services and encourage their employees to render such services.

E.S. 2.3 Civic Responsibility: Members should be involved in civic activities as citizens and professionals, and should strive to improve public appreciation and understanding of architecture and the functions and responsibilities of architects.

Rule 2.301 Members making public statements on architectural issues shall disclose when they are being compensated for making such statements or when they have an economic interest in the issue.

CANON III

Obligations to the Client

Members should serve their clients competently and in a professional manner, and should exercise unprejudiced and unbiased judgment when performing all professional services.

E.S. 3.1 Competence: Members should serve their clients in a timely and competent manner.

Rule 3.101 In performing professional services, Members shall take into account applicable laws and regulations. Members may rely on the advice of other qualified persons as to the intent and meaning of such regulations.

Rule 3.102 Members shall undertake to perform professional services only when they, together with those whom they may engage as consultants, are qualified by education, training, or experience in the specific technical areas involved.
Commentary: This rule is meant to ensure that Members not undertake projects that are beyond their professional capacity. Members venturing into areas that require expertise they do not possess may obtain that expertise by additional education, training, or through the retention of consultants with the necessary expertise.

Rule 3.103 Members shall not materially alter the scope or objectives of a project without the client's consent.

E.S. 3.2 Conflict of Interest: Members should avoid conflicts of interest in their professional practices and fully disclose all unavoidable conflicts as they arise.

2004 CODE OF ETHICS AND PROFESSIONAL CONDUCT

Rule 3.201 A Member shall not render professional services if the Member's professional judgment could be affected by responsibilities to another project or person, or by the Member's own interests, unless all those who rely on the Member's judgment consent after full disclosure.

Commentary: This rule is intended to embrace the full range of situations that may present a Member with a conflict between his interests or responsibilities and the interest of others. Those who are entitled to disclosure may include a client, owner, employer, contractor, or others who rely on or are affected by the Member's professional decisions. A Member who cannot appropriately communicate about a conflict directly with an affected person must take steps to ensure that disclosure is made by other means.

Rule 3.202 When acting by agreement of the parties as the independent interpreter of building contract documents and the judge of contract performance, Members shall render decisions impartially.

Commentary: This rule applies when the Member, though paid by the owner and owing the owner loyalty, is nonetheless required to act with impartiality in fulfilling the architect's professional responsibilities.

E.S. 3.3 Candor and Truthfulness: Members should be candid and truthful in their professional communications and keep their clients reasonably informed about the clients' projects.

Rule 3.301 Members shall not intentionally or recklessly mislead existing or prospective clients about the results that can be achieved through the use of the Members' services, nor shall the Members state that they can achieve results by means that violate applicable law or this Code.

Commentary: This rule is meant to preclude dishonest, reckless, or illegal representations by a Member either in the course of soliciting a client or during performance.

E.S. 3.4 Confidentiality: Members should safeguard the trust placed in them by their clients.

Rule 3.401 Members shall not knowingly disclose information that would adversely affect their client or that they have been asked to maintain in confidence, except as otherwise allowed or required by this Code or applicable law.

Commentary: To encourage the full and open exchange of information necessary for a successful professional relationship, Members must recognize and respect the sensitive nature of confidential client communications. Because the law does not recognize an architect-client privilege, however, the rule permits a Member to reveal a confidence when a failure to do so would be unlawful or contrary to another ethical duty imposed by this Code.

CANON IV

Obligations to the Profession

Members should uphold the integrity and dignity of the profession.

E.S. 4.1 Honesty and Fairness: Members should pursue their professional activities with honesty and fairness.

Rule 4.101 Members having substantial information which leads to a reasonable belief that another Member has committed a violation of this Code which raises a serious question as to that Member's honesty, trustworthiness, or fitness as a Member, shall file a complaint with the National Ethics Council.

Commentary: Often, only an architect can recognize that the behavior of another architect poses a serious question as to that other's professional integrity. In those circumstances, the duty to the professional's calling requires that a complaint be filed. In most jurisdictions, a complaint that invokes professional standards is protected from a libel or slander action if the complaint was made in good faith. If in doubt, a Member should seek counsel before reporting on another under this rule.

Rule 4.102 Members shall not sign or seal drawings, specifications, reports, or other professional work for which they do not have responsible control.

Commentary: Responsible control means the degree of knowledge and supervision ordinarily required by the professional standard of care. With respect to the work of licensed consultants, Members may sign or seal such work if they have reviewed it, coordinated its preparation, or intend to be responsible for its adequacy.

Rule 4.103 Members speaking in their professional capacity shall not knowingly make false statements of material fact.

Commentary: This rule applies in all professional contexts, including applications for licensure and AIA membership.

E.S. 4.2 Dignity and Integrity: Members should strive, through their actions, to promote the dignity and integrity of the profession, and to ensure that their representatives and employees conform their conduct to this Code.

Rule 4.201 Members shall not make misleading, deceptive, or false statements or claims about their professional qualifications, experience, or performance and shall accurately state the scope and nature of their responsibilities in connection with work for which they are claiming credit.

Commentary: This rule is meant to prevent Members from claiming or implying credit for work which they did not do, misleading others, and denying other participants in a project their proper share of credit.

Rule 4.202 Members shall make reasonable efforts to ensure that those over whom they have supervisory authority conform their conduct to this Code.

Commentary: What constitutes "reasonable efforts" under this rule is a common sense matter. As it makes sense to ensure that those over whom the architect exercises supervision be made generally aware of the Code, it can also make sense to bring a particular provision to the attention of a particular employee when a situation is present which might give rise to violation.

2004 CODE OF ETHICS AND PROFESSIONAL CONDUCT

CANON V

Obligations to Colleagues

Members should respect the rights and acknowledge the professional aspirations and contributions of their colleagues.

E.S. 5.1 Professional Environment: Members should provide their associates and employees with a suitable working environment, compensate them fairly, and facilitate their professional development.

E.S. 5.2 Intern and Professional Development: Members should recognize and fulfill their obligation to nurture fellow professionals as they progress through all stages of their career, beginning with professional education in the academy, progressing through internship and continuing throughout their career.

E.S. 5.3 Professional Recognition: Members should build their professional reputation on the merits of their own service and performance and should recognize and give credit to others for the professional work they have performed.

Rule 5.301   Members shall recognize and respect the professional contributions of their employees, employers, professional colleagues, and business associates.

Rule 5.302   Members leaving a firm shall not, without the permission of their employer or partner, take designs, drawings, data, reports, notes, or other materials relating to the firm's work, whether or not performed by the Member.

Rule 5.303   A Member shall not unreasonably withhold permission from a departing employee or partner to take copies of designs, drawings, data, reports, notes, or other materials relating to work performed by the employee or partner that are not confidential.

Commentary: A Member may impose reasonable conditions, such as the payment of copying costs, on the right of departing persons to take copies of their work.

RULES OF APPLICATION, ENFORCEMENT, AND AMENDMENT

Application
The Code of Ethics and Professional Conduct applies to the professional activities of all members of the AIA.

Enforcement
The Bylaws of the Institute state procedures for the enforcement of the Code of Ethics and Professional Conduct. Such procedures provide that:

(1) Enforcement of the Code is administered through a National Ethics Council, appointed by the AIA Board of Directors.

(2) Formal charges are filed directly with the National Ethics Council by Members, components, or anyone directly aggrieved by the conduct of the Members.

(3) Penalties that may be imposed by the National Ethics Council are:
    (a) Admonition
    (b) Censure
    (c) Suspension of membership for a period of time
    (d) Termination of membership

(4) Appeal procedures are available.

(5) All proceedings are confidential, as is the imposition of an admonishment; however, all other penalties shall be made public.

Enforcement of Rules 4.101 and 4.202 refer to and support enforcement of other Rules. A violation of Rules 4.101 or 4.202 cannot be established without proof of a pertinent violation of at least one other Rule.

Amendment
The Code of Ethics and Professional Conduct may be amended by the convention of the Institute under the same procedures as are necessary to amend the Institute's Bylaws. The Code may also be amended by the AIA Board of Directors upon a two-thirds vote of the entire Board.

2004 Edition. This copy of the Code of Ethics is current as of September 2004. Contact the General Counsel's Office for further information at (202) 626-7311.

APA
American Planning Association–
American Institute of City Planners
AICP Code of Ethics and Professional Conduct

Adopted March 19, 2005
Effective June 1, 2005

The Executive Director of APA/AICP is the Ethics Officer as referenced in the following.

We, professional planners, who are members of the American Institute of Certified Planners, subscribe to our Institute's Code of Ethics and Professional Conduct. Our Code is divided into three sections:

Section A contains a statement of aspirational principles that constitute the ideals to which we are committed. We shall strive to act in accordance with our stated principles. However, an allegation that we failed to achieve our aspirational principles cannot be the subject of a misconduct charge or be a cause for disciplinary action.

Section B contains rules of conduct to which we are held accountable. If we violate any of these rules, we can be the object of a charge of misconduct and shall have the responsibility of responding to and cooperating with the investigation and enforcement procedures. If we are found to be blameworthy by the AICP Ethics Committee, we shall be subject to the imposition of sanctions that may include loss of our certification.

Section C contains the procedural provisions of the Code. It (1) describes the way that one may obtain either a formal or informal advisory ruling, and (2) details how a charge of misconduct can be filed, and how charges are investigated, prosecuted, and adjudicated.

The principles to which we subscribe in Sections A and B of the Code derive from the special responsibility of our profession to serve the public interest with compassion for the welfare of all people and, as professionals, to our obligation to act with high integrity.

As the basic values of society can come into competition with each other, so can the aspirational principles we espouse under this Code. An ethical judgment often requires a conscientious balancing, based on the facts and context of a particular situation and on the precepts of the entire Code.

As Certified Planners, all of us are also members of the American Planning Association and share in the goal of building better, more inclusive communities. We want the public to be aware of the principles by which we practice our profession in the quest of that goal. We sincerely hope that the public will respect the commitments we make to our employers and clients, our fellow professionals, and all other persons whose interests we affect.

A: Principles to Which We Aspire

1. Our Overall Responsibility to the Public
Our primary obligation is to serve the public interest and we, therefore, owe our allegiance to a conscientiously attained concept of the public interest that is formulated through continuous and open debate. We shall achieve high standards of professional integrity, proficiency, and knowledge. To comply with our obligation to the public, we aspire to the following principles:

a) We shall always be conscious of the rights of others.
b) We shall have special concern for the long-range consequences of present actions.
c) We shall pay special attention to the interrelatedness of decisions.
d) We shall provide timely, adequate, clear, and accurate information on planning issues to all affected persons and to governmental decision makers.
e) We shall give people the opportunity to have a meaningful impact on the development of plans and programs that may affect them. Participation should be broad enough to include those who lack formal organization or influence.
f) We shall seek social justice by working to expand choice and opportunity for all persons, recognizing a special responsibility to plan for the needs of the disadvantaged and to promote racial and economic integration. We shall urge the alteration of policies, institutions, and decisions that oppose such needs.
g) We shall promote excellence of design and endeavor to conserve and preserve the integrity and heritage of the natural and built environment.
h) We shall deal fairly with all participants in the planning process. Those of us who are public officials or employees shall also deal evenhandedly with all planning process participants.

2. Our Responsibility to Our Clients and Employers
We owe diligent, creative, and competent performance of the work we do in pursuit of our client or employer's interest. Such performance, however, shall always be consistent with our faithful service to the public interest.
a) We shall exercise independent professional judgment on behalf of our clients and employers.
b) We shall accept the decisions of our client or employer concerning the objectives and nature of the professional services we perform unless the course of action is illegal or plainly inconsistent with our primary obligation to the public interest.

c) We shall avoid a conflict of interest or even the appearance of a conflict of interest in accepting assignments from clients or employers.

3. Our Responsibility to Our Profession and Colleagues
We shall contribute to the development of, and respect for, our profession by improving knowledge and techniques, making work relevant to solutions of community problems, and increasing public understanding of planning activities.
a) We shall protect and enhance the integrity of our profession.
b) We shall educate the public about planning issues and their relevance to our everyday lives.
c) We shall describe and comment on the work and views of other professionals in a fair and professional manner.
d) We shall share the results of experience and research that contribute to the body of planning knowledge.
e) We shall examine the applicability of planning theories, methods, research and practice and standards to the facts and analysis of each particular situation and shall not accept the applicability of a customary solution without first establishing its appropriateness to the situation.
f) We shall contribute time and resources to the professional development of students, interns, beginning professionals, and other colleagues.
g) We shall increase the opportunities for members of underrepresented groups to become professional planners and help them advance in the profession.
h) We shall continue to enhance our professional education and training.
i) We shall systematically and critically analyze ethical issues in the practice of planning.
j) We shall contribute time and effort to groups lacking in adequate planning resources and to voluntary professional activities.

B: Our Rules of Conduct

We adhere to the following Rules of Conduct, and we understand that our Institute will enforce compliance with them. If we fail to adhere to

these Rules, we could receive sanctions, the ultimate being the loss of our certification:
1. We shall not deliberately or with reckless indifference fail to provide adequate, timely, clear and accurate information on planning issues.
2. We shall not accept an assignment from a client or employer when the services to be performed involve conduct that we know to be illegal or in violation of these rules.
3. We shall not accept an assignment from a client or employer to publicly advocate a position on a planning issue that is indistinguishably adverse to a position we publicly advocated for a previous client or employer within the past

three years unless (1) we determine in good faith after consultation with other qualified professionals that our change of position will not cause present detriment to our previous client or employer, and (2) we make full written disclosure of the conflict to our current client or employer and receive written permission to proceed with the assignment.

4. We shall not, as salaried employees, undertake other employment in planning or a related profession, whether or not for pay, without having made full written disclosure to the employer who furnishes our salary and having received subsequent written permission to undertake additional employment, unless our employer has a written policy which expressly dispenses with a need to obtain such consent.

5. We shall not, as public officials or employees; accept from anyone other than our public employer any compensation, commission, rebate, or other advantage that may be perceived as related to our public office or employment.

6. We shall not perform work on a project for a client or employer if, in addition to the agreed upon compensation from our client or employer, there is a possibility for direct personal or financial gain to us, our family members, or persons living in our household, unless our client or employer, after full written disclosure from us, consents in writing to the arrangement.

7. We shall not use to our personal advantage, nor that of a subsequent client or employer, information gained in a professional relationship that the client or employer has requested be held inviolate or that we should recognize as confidential because its disclosure could result in embarrassment or other detriment to the client or employer. Nor shall we disclose such confidential information except when (1) required by process of law, or (2) required to prevent a clear violation of law, or (3) required to prevent a substantial injury to the public. Disclosure pursuant to (2) and (3) shall not be made until after we have verified the facts and issues involved and, when practicable, exhausted efforts to obtain reconsideration of the matter and have sought separate opinions on the issue from other qualified professionals employed by our client or employer.

8. We shall not, as public officials or employees, engage in private communications with planning process participants if the discussions relate to a matter over which we have authority to make a binding, final determination if such private communications are prohibited by law or by agency rules, procedures, or custom.

9. We shall not engage in private discussions with decision makers in the planning process in any manner prohibited by law or by agency rules, procedures, or custom.

10. We shall neither deliberately, nor with reckless indifference, misrepresent the qualifications, views and findings of other professionals.

11. We shall not solicit prospective clients or employment through use of false or misleading claims, harassment, or duress.

12. We shall not misstate our education, experience, training, or any other facts which are relevant to our professional qualifications.

13. We shall not sell, or offer to sell, services by stating or implying an ability to influence decisions by improper means.

14. We shall not use the power of any office to seek or obtain a special advantage that is not a matter of public knowledge or is not in the public interest.

15. We shall not accept work beyond our professional competence unless the client or employer understands and agrees that such work will be performed by another professional competent to perform the work and acceptable to the client or employer.

16. We shall not accept work for a fee, or pro bono, that we know cannot be performed with the promptness required by the prospective client, or that is required by the circumstances of the assignment.

17. We shall not use the product of others' efforts to seek professional recognition or acclaim intended for producers of original work.

18. We shall not direct or coerce other professionals to make analyses or reach findings not supported by available evidence.

19. We shall not fail to disclose the interests of our client or employer when participating in the planning process. Nor shall we participate in an effort to conceal the true interests of our client or employer.

20. We shall not unlawfully discriminate against another person.

21. We shall not withhold cooperation or information from the AICP Ethics Officer or the AICP Ethics Committee if a charge of ethical misconduct has been filed against us.

22. We shall not retaliate or threaten retaliation against a person who has filed a charge of ethical misconduct against us or another planner, or who is cooperating in the Ethics Officer's investigation of an ethics charge.

23. We shall not use the threat of filing an ethics charge in order to gain, or attempt to gain, an advantage in dealings with another planner.

24. We shall not file a frivolous charge of ethical misconduct against another planner.

25. We shall neither deliberately, nor with reckless indifference, commit any wrongful act, whether or not specified in the Rules of Conduct, that reflects adversely on our professional fitness.

C: Our Code Procedures

1. Introduction

In brief, our Code Procedures (1) describe the way that one may obtain either a formal or informal advisory ethics ruling, and (2) detail how a charge of misconduct can be filed, and how charges are investigated, prosecuted, and adjudicated.

2. Informal Advice

All of us are encouraged to seek informal ethics advice from the Ethics Officer. Informal advice is not given in writing and is not binding on AICP, but the AICP Ethics Committee shall take it into consideration in the event a charge of misconduct is later filed against us concerning the conduct in question. If we ask the Ethics Officer for informal advice and do not receive a response within 21 calendar days of our request, we should notify the Chair of the Ethics Committee that we are awaiting a response.

3. Formal Advice

Only the Ethics Officer is authorized to give formal advice on the propriety of a planner's proposed conduct. Formal advice is binding on AICP and any of us who can demonstrate that we followed such advice shall have a defense to any charge of misconduct. The advice will be issued to us in writing signed by the Ethics Officer. The written advice shall not include names or places without the written consent of all persons to be named. Requests for formal advice must be in writing and must contain sufficient details, real or hypothetical, to permit a definitive opinion. The Ethics Officer has the discretion to issue or not issue formal advice. The Ethics Officer will not issue formal advice if he or she determines that the request deals with past conduct that should be the subject of a charge of misconduct. The Ethics Officer will respond to requests for formal advice within 21 days of receipt and will docket the requests in a log that will be distributed on a quarterly basis to the Chair of the AICP Ethics Committee. If the Ethics Officer fails to furnish us with a timely response we should notify the Chair of the AICP Ethics Committee that we are awaiting a response.

4. Published Formal Advisory Rulings

The Ethics Officer shall transmit a copy of all formal advice to the AICP Ethics Committee. The Committee, from time to time, will determine if the formal advice provides guidance to the interpretation of the Code and should be published as a formal advisory ruling. Also, the Ethics Committee has the authority to draft and publish formal advisory rulings when it determines that guidance to interpretation of the Code is needed or desirable.

5. Filing a Charge of Misconduct
Any person, whether or not an AICP member, may file a charge of misconduct against a Certified Planner. A charge of misconduct shall be made in a letter sent to the AICP Ethics Officer. The letter may be signed or it may be anonymous. The person filing the charge is urged to maintain confidentiality to the extent practicable. The person filing the charge should not send a copy of the charge to the Certified Planner identified in the letter or

to any other person. The letter shall accurately identify the Certified Planner against whom the charge is being made and describe the conduct that allegedly violated the provisions of the Rules of Conduct. The person filing a charge should also cite all provisions of the Rules of Conduct that have allegedly been violated. However, a charge will not be dismissed if the Ethics Officer is able to determine from the facts stated in the letter that certain Rules of Conduct may have been violated. The letter reciting the charge should be accompanied by all relevant documentation available to the person filing the charge. While anonymously filed charges are permitted, anonymous filers will not receive notification of the disposition of the charge. Anonymous filers may furnish a postal address in the event the Ethics Officer needs to reach them for an inquiry.

6. Receipt of Charge by Ethics Officer

The Ethics Officer shall maintain a log of all letters containing charges of misconduct filed against Certified Planners upon their receipt and shall transmit a quarterly report of such correspondence to the Chair of the Ethics Committee. Within two weeks of receipt of a charge, the Ethics Officer shall prepare a cover letter and transmit the charge and all attached documentation to the named Certified Planner, who shall be now referred to as "the Respondent." The Ethics Officer's cover letter shall indicate whether the Ethics Officer expects the Respondent to file a "preliminary response" or whether the Ethics Officer is summarily dismissing the charge because it is clearly without merit. A copy of the cover letter will also be sent to the Charging Party, if identified. If the cover letter summarily dismisses the charge, it shall be sent to an identifiable Charging Party by receipted Certified Mail. The Charging Party will have the right to appeal the summary dismissal as provided in Section 11. After the Ethics Officer has received a charge, the Charging Party may withdraw it only with the permission of the Ethics Officer. After receiving a charge, the Ethics Officer shall have a duty to keep an identified Charging Party informed of its status. If an identified Charging Party has not received a status report from the Ethics Officer for 60 calendar days, the Charging Party should notify the Chair of the AICP Ethics Committee of the lapse.

7. Right of Counsel

A planner who receives a charge of misconduct under a cover letter requesting a preliminary response should understand that if he or she desires legal representation, it would be advisable to obtain such representation at the earliest point in the procedure. However, a planner who elects to proceed at first without legal representation will not be precluded from engaging such representation at any later point in the procedure.

8. Preliminary Responses to a Charge of Misconduct

If the Ethics Officer requests a preliminary response, the Respondent shall be allowed 30 calendar days from receipt of the Ethics Officer's letter to send the response to the Ethics Officer. The Ethics Officer will grant an extension of time, not to exceed 15 calendar days, if the request for the extension is made within the 30 day period. Failure to make a timely preliminary response constitutes a failure to cooperate with the Ethics Officer's investigation of the charge. A preliminary response should include documentation, the names, addresses and telephone numbers of witnesses, and all of the facts and arguments that counter the charge. Because the motivation of the person who filed the charge is irrelevant, the Respondent should not discuss it. The Ethics Officer will send a copy of the preliminary response to the Charging Party, if identified, and allow the Charging Party 15 calendar days from the date of receipt to respond.

9. Conducting an Investigation

After review of the preliminary response from the Respondent and any counter to that response furnished by an identified Charging Party, or if no timely preliminary response is received, the Ethics Officer shall decide whether an investigation is appropriate. If the Ethics Officer determines that an investigation should be conducted, he or she may designate a member of the AICP staff or AICP counsel to conduct the investigation. The Respondent must cooperate in the investigation and encourage others with relevant information, whether favorable or unfavorable, to cooperate. Neither the Ethics Officer , nor designee, will make credibility findings to resolve differing witness versions of facts in dispute.

10. Dismissal of Charge or Issuance of Complaint

If, with or without an investigation, the charge appears to be without merit, the Ethics Officer shall dismiss it in a letter, giving a full explanation of the reasons. The dismissal letter shall be sent to the Respondent and the Charging Party by receipted Certified Mail. If, however, the Ethics Officer's investigation indicates that a Complaint is warranted, the Ethics Officer shall draft a Complaint and send it to the Respondent by receipted Certified Mail, with a copy to the Charging Party. The Complaint shall consist of numbered paragraphs containing recitations of alleged facts. Following the fact paragraphs, there shall be numbered paragraphs of alleged violations, which shall cite provisions of the Rules of Conduct that the Ethics Officer believes are implicated. The allegations in the Complaint shall be based on the results of the Ethics Officer's investigation of the charge and may be additional to, or different from, those allegations initially relied upon by the Charging Party. The Ethics Officer shall maintain a log of all dismissals and shall transmit the log on a quarterly basis to the Chair of the Ethics Committee.

11. Appeal of Dismissal of Charge

Identified Charging Parties who are notified of the dismissal of their ethics charges shall have 30 calendar days from the date of the receipt of their dismissal letters to file an appeal with the Ethics Committee. The appeal shall be sent to the Ethics Officer who shall record it in a log and transmit it within 21 calendar days to the Ethics Committee. The Ethics Committee shall either affirm or reverse the dismissal. If the dismissal is reversed, the Ethics Committee shall either direct the Ethics Officer to conduct a further investigation and review the charge again, or issue a Complaint based on the materials before the Committee. The Ethics Officer shall notify the Charging Party and the Respondent of the Ethics Committee's determination.

12. Answering a Complaint

The Respondent shall have 30 calendar days from receipt of a Complaint in which to file an Answer. An extension not to exceed 15 calendar days will be granted if the request is made within the 30 day period. In furnishing an Answer, the Respondent is expected to cooperate in good faith. General denials are unacceptable. The Answer must specifically admit or deny each of the fact allegations in the Complaint. It is acceptable to deny a fact allegation on the ground that the planner is unable to verify its correctness, but that explanation should be stated as the reason for denial. The failure of a Respondent to make a timely denial of any fact alleged in the Complaint shall be deemed an admission of such fact. The Ethics Officer may amend a Complaint to delete any disputed fact, whether or not material to the issues. The Ethics Officer also may amend a Complaint to restate fact allegations by verifying and adopting the Respondent's version of what occurred. The Ethics Officer shall send the Complaint or Amended Complaint and the Respondent's Answer to the Ethics Committee with a copy to an identified Charging Party. The Ethics Officer shall also inform the Ethics Committee if there are any disputed material facts based on a comparison of the documents.

13. Conducting a Hearing

a) If the Ethics Officer notifies the Ethics Committee that material facts are in dispute or if the Ethics Committee, on its own, finds that to be the case, the Chair of the Committee shall designate a "Hearing Official" from among the membership of the Committee. At this point in the process, the Ethics Officer, either personally or through a designated AICP staff member or AICP counsel, shall continue to serve as both Investigator-Prosecutor and as the Clerk serving the Ethics Committee, the Hearing Official and the Respondent. In carrying out clerical functions, the Ethics Officer, or designee, may discuss with the Ethics Committee and the Hearing Official the procedural arrangements for the hearing. Until the Ethics Committee decides the case, however, the Ethics Officer or designee shall not discuss the merits of the case with any member of the Committee unless the Respondent is present or is afforded an equal opportunity to address the Committee member.

b) The Ethics Officer shall transmit a "Notice of Hearing" to the Respondent, the Hearing Official and an identified Charging Party. The hearing shall normally be conducted in the vicinity where the alleged misconduct occurred. The Notice will contain a list of all disputed material facts that need to be resolved. The hearing will be confined to resolution of those facts. There shall be no requirement that formal rules of evidence be observed.

c) The Ethics Officer will have the burden of proving, by a preponderance of the evidence, that misconduct occurred. The Ethics Officer may present witness testimony and any other evidence relevant to demonstrating the existence of each disputed material fact. The Respondent will then be given the opportunity to present witness testimony and any other evidence relevant to controvert the testimony and other evidence submitted by the Ethics Officer. The Ethics Officer may then be given an opportunity to present additional witness testimony and other evidence in rebuttal. All witnesses who testify for the Ethics Officer or the Respondent shall be subject to cross-examination by the other party. The Hearing Official shall make an electronic recording of the hearing and shall make copies of the recording available to the Ethics Officer and the Respondent.

d) At least 30 calendar days before the hearing, the Ethics Officer and the Respondent shall exchange lists of proposed witnesses who will testify, and copies of all exhibits that will be introduced, at the hearing. There shall be no other discovery and no pre-hearing motions. All witnesses must testify in person at the hearing unless arrangements can be made by agreement between the Respondent and the Ethics Officer prior to the hearing, or by ruling of the Hearing Official during the hearing, to have an unavailable witness's testimony submitted in a video recording that permits the Hearing Official to observe the demeanor of the witness. No unavailable witness's testimony shall be admissible unless the opposing party was offered a meaningful opportunity to cross-examine the witness. The hearing shall not be open to the public. The Hearing Official shall have the discretion to hold open the hearing to accept recorded video testimony of unavailable witnesses. The Respondent will be responsible for the expense of bringing his or her witnesses to the hearing or to have their testimony video recorded. Following the closing of the hearing, the Hearing Official shall make findings only as to the disputed material facts and transmit the findings to the full Ethics Committee, the Ethics Officer, and the

Respondent. The Hearing Official, prior to issuing findings, may request that the parties submit proposed findings of fact for his or her consideration.

14. Deciding the Case

The Ethics Committee (including the Hearing Official member of the Committee) shall resolve the ethics matter by reviewing the documentation that sets out the facts that were not in dispute, any fact findings that were required to be made by a Hearing Official, and any arguments submitted to it by the Respondent and the Ethics Officer. The Ethics Officer shall give 45 calendar days notice to the Respondent of the date of the Ethics Committee meeting during which the matter will be resolved. The Ethics Officer and the Respondent shall have 21 calendar days to submit memoranda stating their positions. The Ethics Officer shall transmit the memoranda to the Ethics Committee no later than 15 calendar days prior to the scheduled meeting. If the Committee determines that the Rules of Conduct have not been violated, it shall dismiss the Complaint and direct the Ethics Officer to notify the Respondent and an identified Charging Party. If the Ethics Committee determines that the Ethics Officer has demonstrated that the Rules of Conduct have been violated, it shall also determine the appropriate sanction, which shall either be a reprimand, suspension, or expulsion. The Ethics Committee shall direct the Ethics Officer to notify the Respondent and an identified Charging Party of its action and to draft a formal explanation of its decision and the discipline chosen. Upon approval of the Ethics Committee, the explanation and discipline chosen shall be published and titled "Opinion of the AICP Ethics Committee." The determination of the AICP Ethics Committee shall be final.

15. Settlement of Charges

a) Prior to issuance of a Complaint, the Ethics Officer may negotiate a settlement between the Respondent and an identified Charging Party if the Ethics Officer determines that the Charging Party has been personally aggrieved by the alleged misconduct of the Respondent and a private resolution between the two would not be viewed as compromising Code principles. If a settlement is reached under such circumstances, the Charging Party will be allowed to withdraw the charge of misconduct.

b) Also prior to issuance of a Complaint, the Ethics Officer may enter into a proposed settlement agreement without the participation of an identified Charging Party. However, in such circumstances, the proposed settlement agreement shall be contingent upon the approval of the Ethics Committee. An identified Charging Party will be given notice and an opportunity to be heard by the Ethics Committee before it votes to approve or disapprove the proposed pre-Complaint settlement.

c) After issuance of a Complaint by the Ethics Officer, a settlement can be negotiated solely between the Ethics Officer and the Respondent, subject to the approval of the Ethics Committee without input from an identified Charging Party.

16. Resignations and Lapses of Membership

If an AICP member who is the subject of a Charge of Misconduct resigns or allows membership to lapse prior to a final determination of the Charge (and any Complaint that may have issued), the ethics matter will be held in abeyance subject to being revived if the individual applies for reinstatement of membership within two years. If such former member, however, fails to apply for reinstatement within two years, the individual shall not be permitted to reapply for certification for a period of 10 years from the date of resignation or lapse of membership. If the Ethics Officer receives a Charge of Misconduct against a former member, the Ethics Officer shall make an effort to locate and advise the former member of the filing of the Charge and this Rule of Procedure.

17 . Annual Report of Ethics Officer
Prior to January 31 of each calendar year the Ethics Officer shall publish an Annual Report of all ethics activity during the preceding calendar year to the AICP Ethics Committee and the AICP Commission. The AICP Commission shall make the Annual Report available to the membership.

American Society of Landscape Architects
ASLA Code of Professional Ethics

Preamble

The profession of landscape architecture, so named in 1867, was built on the foundation of several principles—dedication to the public health, safety, and welfare and recognition and protection of the land and its resources. These principles form the foundation of the American Society of Landscape Architects (ASLA) Code of Professional Ethics (the Code) as well.

The Code applies to the professional activities of all ASLA professional members, i.e., Full Members, Associate Members, and International Members (herein, referred to simply as Members), and contains important principles relating to the duties of Members to clients, employers, and employees and to other Members of the Society.

The Code is arranged so that each Canon contains Ethical Standards—essentially goals that Members should strive to meet. Some of the Ethical Standards contain objective Rules. Violation of Rules might subject an ASLA Member to a complaint, while violation of Ethical Standards will not. Therefore, the word "should" is used in the Ethical Standards and "shall" is used in the Rules.

The policies established by the Board of Trustees relative to environmental stewardship, quality of life, and professional affairs are summarized in the ASLA Code of Environmental Ethics. Members should make every effort to enhance, respect, and restore the life-sustaining integrity of the landscape and seek environmentally positive, financially sound, and sustainable solutions to land use, development, and management opportunities.

Canon 1. Professional Responsibility

ES1.1 Members should understand and honestly obey laws governing their professional practice and business affairs and conduct their professional duties within the art and science of landscape architecture and their professional Society with honesty, dignity, and integrity.

R1.101 Members shall deal with other Members, clients, employers, employees, and the public with honesty, dignity, and integrity in all actions and communications of any kind.

R1.102 Members shall not violate the law in the conduct of their professional practice, including any federal, state, or local laws and particularly laws and regulations in the areas of antitrust, employment, environmental and land-use planning, and those governing professional practice.

R1.103 Members shall not give, lend, or promise anything of value to any public official or representative of a prospective client in order to influence the

judgment or actions in the letting of a contract of that official or representative of a prospective client.

Commentary: However, the provision of pro bono services will not violate this Rule.

R1.104 Members on full-time government employment shall not accept private practice work with anyone doing business with their agency or with whom the Member has any government contact on matters involving applications for grants, contracts, or planning and zoning actions. In the case of private practitioners elected or appointed to government positions or others doing business or having alliances with those doing business with their board, council, or agency, they must disqualify and absent themselves during any discussion of these matters.

R1.105 Members shall recognize the contributions of others engaged in the planning, design, and construction of the physical environment and shall give them appropriate recognition and due credit for professional work and shall not maliciously injure or attempt to injure the reputation, prospects, practice, or employment position of those persons so engaged. Credit shall be given to the design firm of record for the use of all project documents, plans, photographs, sketches, reports, or other work products developed while under the management of the design firm of record. Use of others' work for any purpose shall accurately specify the role of the individual in the execution of the design firm of record's work.

Commentary: Members representing views opposed to another Member's views shall keep the discussion on an issue-oriented, professional level.

R1.106 Members shall not mislead through advertising or other means existing or prospective clients about the result that can be achieved through use of the Member's services or state that they can achieve results by means that violate the Code or the law.
Commentary: So long as they are not misleading, advertisements in any medium are permitted by the Code.

R1.107 Members shall not accept compensation for their services on a project from more than one party unless all parties agree to the circumstances in writing.

R1.108 Members shall not misrepresent or knowingly permit the misrepresentation of their professional qualifications, capabilities, and experience to clients, employers, or the public or be a party to any exaggerated, misleading, deceptive, or false statements or claims by the firms, agencies, or organizations that employ them.

Commentary: Members shall not take credit for work performed under the direction of a former employer beyond the limits of their personal involvement and shall give credit to the performing firm. Employers should give departing employees access to work that they performed, reproduced at cost, and a description of the employee's involvement in the work should be noted on each product and acknowledged by the employer.

R1.109 Members shall not reveal information obtained in the course of their professional activities that they have been asked to maintain in confidence or that could affect the interests of another adversely. Unique exceptions: to stop an act that creates harm; a significant risk to the public health, safety, and welfare that cannot otherwise be prevented; to establish claims or defense on behalf of Members; or in order to comply with applicable law, regulations, or with the Code.

R1.110 Members shall not copy or reproduce the copyrighted works of others without prior written approval by the author of the copyrighted work.

R1.111 Members shall not seek to void awarded contracts for a specific scope of service held by another Member.
Commentary: This shall not prohibit competition for the original or subsequent contracts or prohibit a client from employing several Members to provide the same scope of service.

R1.112 Members shall not seek to obtain contracts, awards, or other financial gain relating to projects or programs for which they may be serving in an advisory or critical capacity.
Commentary: This does not prevent a Member from seeking an award or contract for a project over which the Member has no influence or role in its selection, approval, or supervision or any other role that could constitute a conflict of interest.

ES1.2 Members should seek to make full disclosure of relevant information to the clients, public, and other interested parties who rely on their advice and professional work product.

R1.201 Members making public statements on landscape architectural issues shall disclose compensation other than fee and their role and any economic interest in a project.

R1.202 Members shall make full disclosure during the solicitation and conduct of a project of the roles and professional status of all project team members and consultants, including professional degrees, state licenses, professional liability insurance coverage, and any other potential material limits to qualifications.

R1.203 Members shall make full disclosure to the client or employer of any financial or other interest that bears on the service or project.

R1.204 Members shall convey to their clients their capacity to produce the work, their availability during normal working hours, and their ability to provide other construction or supervisory services.

ES1.3 Members should endeavor to protect the interests of their clients and the public through competent performance of their work and participate in continuing education, educational research, and development and dissemination of technical information relating to planning, design, construction, and management of the physical environment.

R1.301 Members shall undertake to perform professional services only when education, training, or experience in the specific technical areas involved qualifies them, together with those persons whom they may engage as consultants.

R1.302 Members shall not sign or seal drawings, specifications, reports, or other professional work for which they do not have direct professional knowledge or direct supervisory control.

R1.303 Members shall continually seek to raise the standards of aesthetic, ecological, and cultural excellence through compliance with applicable state requirements for continuing professional education.

R1.304 Public discussion of controversial projects and issues shall be conducted on a professional level and shall be based on issue-oriented, factual analysis.

Canon 2. Member Responsibilities

ES2.1 Members should understand and endeavor to uphold the Ethical Standards of the ASLA Code of Environmental Ethics.

ES2.2 Members should work to ensure that they, their employees or subordinates, and other Members adhere to the Code of Professional Ethics and the Constitution and Bylaws of the American Society of Landscape Architects.

R2.201 Members having information that leads to a reasonable belief that another Member has committed a violation of the Code shall report such information.

Commentary: Often a landscape architect can recognize that the behavior of another poses a serious question as to the other's professional integrity. It is the duty of the professional to bring the matter to the attention of the ASLA Ethics Committee; which action, if done in good faith, is in some jurisdictions protected from libel or slander action. If in doubt, the Member reporting under this Rule should seek counsel prior to making such a report.

R2.202 The seal or logo of the American Society of Landscape Architects shall be used only as specified in the ASLA Bylaws.

R2.203 Members shall adhere to the specific, applicable terms of the ASLA Bylaws regarding use of references to ASLA membership. Members are encouraged to use the appropriate ASLA designation after their names.

ES2.3 Members are encouraged to serve on elected or appointed boards, committees, or commissions dealing with the arts and environmental and land-use issues.

R2.301 Members who are elected or appointed to review boards, committees, and commissions shall seek to avoid conflicts of interest and the appearance of conflicts of interest and shall comply with local rules and policies with regard to conflict of interest. Members serving on such boards, committees, and commissions shall disqualify themselves in accordance with rules of ethics and this Code and shall not be present when discussion is held relative to an action in which they have an interest. A Member shall make full disclosure and request disqualification on any issue that could involve a potential conflict of interest.

Rules of Procedure for Filing and Resolution of a Complaint

The Code applies to the professional activities of all ASLA professional members (herein, referred to as Members).

Anyone directly aggrieved by the conduct of a Member may file a complaint along with supporting documentation with the ASLA Ethics Committee (the Committee) within one (1) year of the alleged violation. The Committee may extend the time limit if deemed equitable under the particular circumstances.

Complaints shall be made only for alleged violations (hereafter, referred to as violations) of the Rules and may not be made for violations of the Ethical Standards of the Code. Complaints shall be made against an individual Member or Members and not against firms, associations, or other bodies. Anonymous complaints will be disregarded.

The complaint shall be submitted in writing to the Ethics Committee at ASLA national headquarters and shall include the following:

▪ The name, address, phone number, fax number, and e-mail address of the complainant.

▪ The name, address, phone number, fax number, and e-mail address of the respondent.

▪ The circumstances giving rise to the complaint, including dates of violations, supporting information and exhibits, and references to the Rules violated. The complaint shall contain all relevant information, including any third-party statements or exhibits that the Committee would need to make a fair determination; the resolution of the complaint will rely solely on the written record.

▪ A list of pending actions against the respondent, or against the complainant by the respondent, in relation to the complaint, such as lawsuits, alternative dispute resolution procedures, or professional licensing board or other regulatory proceedings.

If the complaint is being filed more than one (1) year after the violation, the submission shall include the reasons why the filing is late and why an extension of the filing requirements should be granted.

The complainant, by filing the complaint, agrees to confidentiality with regard to the complaint and shall avoid public disclosure or discussion of the complaint. A breach of confidentiality may result in the complaint being dismissed.

The Committee will determine whether the information received, if true, violates the Code.

On acceptance of the complaint by the Committee, the complainant shall be informed that the complaint is accepted and the respondent shall be provided with a copy of the complaint. The respondent shall have sixty (60) days to reply to the complaint. The response shall be submitted in writing to the Ethics Committee at ASLA national headquarters and shall include the following:

● Admittance or denial of the complaint. If the respondent admits to the complaint, actions taken to become compliant with the Code.

● Factual information in defense of the complaint, including supporting information and exhibits. The response shall contain all relevant information, including any third-party statements or exhibits that the Committee would need to make a fair determination; the resolution of the complaint will rely solely on the written record.

• A list of pending actions against the complainant, or against the respondent by the complainant, in relation to the complaint, such as lawsuits, alternative dispute resolution procedures, or professional licensing board or other regulatory proceedings, and any reasons why the resolution of the complaint should be deferred.

If no response is received within sixty (60) days, notice shall be given to the respondent and an additional ten (10) days shall be given for a reply. Failure to respond or an unresponsive reply may result in the complaint being resolved in favor of the complainant.

The respondent shall keep the complaint confidential and avoid public disclosure or discussion of the complaint. A breach of confidentiality may result in the complaint being resolved in favor of the complainant.

The Committee will provide the complainant with a copy of the reply. The complainant shall have thirty (30) days from the date of the Committee's transmittal of the reply to the complainant to rebut the reply. Copies of the rebuttal shall be provided to the Committee, which will provide a copy to the respondent. The respondent shall have thirty (30) days from the date of the Committee's transmittal of the rebuttal to the respondent to reply to the rebuttal. The Committee will provide a copy of the reply to the complainant.

On acceptance of the complaint and response, and receipt of a rebuttal and reply if filed, the Committee will consider the complaint, issue findings, and make a determination. The Committee may determine that no violation occurred. If the Committee determines that a violation has occurred, it shall:

1. Issue a confidential Letter of Admonition. This action shall be binding unless appealed to the Executive Committee, which will review all information submitted by the parties and render a binding and final decision within sixty (60) days of receipt of the appeal that (1) upholds the Committee's action or (2) retracts the Committee's action and dismisses the complaint.

2. Or, refer the matter to the Executive Committee with a recommendation to issue a Letter of Censure. The Executive Committee will review all information submitted by the parties and (1) accept the recommendation of the Committee and issue a Letter of Censure, or (2) dismiss the complaint, or (3) increase the recommended sanction against the respondent, or (4) refer the matter back to the Committee to issue a confidential Letter of Admonition. The action of the Executive Committee shall be binding unless appealed to the Board of Trustees, which will review all information submitted by the parties and render a binding and final decision.

3. Or, refer the matter to the Executive Committee with a recommendation for Probationary Suspension of Membership. The Executive Committee will review all information submitted by the parties and (1) accept the recommendation of the Committee and specify a Probationary Suspension of Membership, or (2) dismiss the complaint, or (3) increase the recommended sanction against the respondent, or (4) reduce the recommended sanction against the respondent. During a suspension, the former Member shall be prohibited from using an ASLA designation. The action of the Executive Committee shall be binding unless appealed to the Board of Trustees, which will review all information submitted by the parties and render a binding and final decision.

4. Or, refer the matter to the Executive Committee with a recommendation for Expulsion from the Society. The Executive Committee will review all information submitted by the parties and (1) accept the recommendation of the Committee and expel the respondent from the Society, or (2) dismiss the complaint, or (3) reduce the recommended sanction against the respondent. Expulsion from the Society shall be a permanent termination of membership and all privileges of membership and a forfeiture of dues paid and all connection with the national Society and any applicable chapter. The action of the Executive Committee shall be binding unless appealed to the Board of Trustees, which will review all information submitted by the parties and render a binding and final decision.

Notice of a decision shall be provided to both the complainant and the respondent.

The respondent may appeal as provided above; such appeal shall be made within sixty (60) days of the date of notice of a decision. The complainant may appeal only a dismissal of the complaint; such appeal shall be made within sixty (60) days of the date of notice of a dismissal.

Appeals to the Board of Trustees shall be entrusted to a subcommittee of the board composed of a chair and four (4) members appointed by the president on a case-by-case basis. The chair and subcommittee members shall be duly elected, currently serving chapter trustees representing chapters other than the one or ones from which the complaint arises. Trustees shall decline appointment if there is any question as to their impartiality and resign from the subcommittee if such question arises after appointment.

Resolution of appeals will be based solely on the written record. The subcommittee of the Board of Trustees will review all information submitted by the parties and render a binding and final decision within sixty (60) days of receipt of the appeal that (1) upholds the Executive Committee's action, or (2) retracts the Executive Committee's action and dismisses the complaint, or (3) increases the sanction against the respondent, or (4) reduces the sanction against the respondent.

Official notice of Censure, Probationary Suspension, or Expulsion will be published in the Society's newsletter, *Landscape Architecture News Digest (LAND)*, if a decision is not appealed within sixty (60) days of the date of notice to the complainant and the respondent or following notice to the complainant and the respondent of a binding and final decision by the appointed subcommittee of the Board of Trustees.

Adopted by the Board of Trustees: April 2, 1995
Amended by the Board of Trustees: October 1, 1998; April 17, 1999; September 10, 1999; April 21, 2001; November 2, 2001; May 6, 2006.

ASLA Code of Environmental Ethics

Preamble

Members of the American Society of Landscape Architects should make every effort within our sphere of influence to enhance, respect, and restore the life-sustaining integrity of the landscape for all living things.

Members should work with clients, review and approval agencies, and local, regional, national, and global governing authorities to educate about, encourage, and seek approval of environmentally positive, financially sound, and sustainable solutions to land-use, development, and management opportunities.

The following tenets are the basis of the ASLA Code of Environmental Ethics:

- The health and well-being of biological systems and their integrity are essential to sustain human well-being.
- Future generations have a right to the same environmental assets and ecological aesthetics.
- Long-term economic survival has a dependence upon the natural environment.
- Environmental stewardship is essential to maintain a healthy environment and a quality of life for the earth.

Ethical Standards

As landscape architects and members of ASLA, we have an ethical obligation to:

ES1 Support and facilitate the environmental public policy statements of the Society, a synopsis of which follows:

ES1.1 The coastal zone and its resources should be preserved, developed, and used in a carefully planned, regulated, and responsibly managed manner.

ES1.2 Parks and public areas throughout the world should be created, expanded, and managed for the well-being of the populations and resources of this planet.

ES1.3 Public lands should be maintained and administered in a manner promoting ecosystem health, while recognizing special issues relating to stewardship and long-term sustainability inherent in wildland environments.

ES1.4 State, regional, and local governments should continue to build on the strong nationwide legacy of parks and other protected public areas to preserve lands of significance for future generations and provide safe and healthful outdoor recreational opportunities for all citizens, while conserving landscape character and natural, historic, and cultural resources.

ES1.5 Open space preservation should be incorporated into every planning effort, from the regional to the site level.

ES1.6 The rural landscape is a limited resource that is vital to the well-being of the earth's life forms; the rural landscape's essential qualities should be conserved as the competing needs of a growing population are met.

ES1.7 Historic sites, districts, and cultural landscapes should be identified, inventoried, evaluated, classified, protected, and enhanced to ensure that they are available for the education and enjoyment of this and future generations.

ES1.8 The appropriate use of vegetation in the built environment is a major influence on the quality of life in a healthy environment; re-created indigenous plant communities or representative communities should be integrated into the built environment with attention given to appropriate species selection and the creation of a suitable growing environment.

ES1.9 The character and condition of the visual environments is as important as that of natural, historic, and cultural resources and should be maintained and enhanced and safeguarded from actions that degrade or destroy critical scenic resources.

ES1.10 Water resources should be equitably allocated, available water supplies should be efficiently used, all forms of water pollution should be eliminated, and land use should conserve and protect water resources and related ecosystems to sustain a high-quality standard of living and the maintenance of the quality of ecosystems.

ES1.11 Wetlands are essential to the quality of life and the well-being of the earth's ecosystems; wetland resources should be protected, conserved, and enhanced and site-specific development and management efforts should allow for compatible land use, while preserving the ongoing functions of wetland resources.

ES1.12 The natural and cultural elements of waterways and their corridors should be protected through the systems of national, state, and local designation of rivers and greenways to ensure their integrity and use by this and future generations.

ES1.13 The principles of land-use planning and design and the principles of wildlife habitat protection should be integrated to promote the enhancement, protection, and management of landscapes that promote wildlife.

ES1.14 Transgenic plants should not be used until the best available science indicates there will be no adverse environmental effects caused by their use.

ES1.15 Non-native invasive species adversely impact the ecological function of natural systems worldwide. Non-native invasive species should not be introduced where those species could contribute to the degradation of the environment and long-term maintenance and management programs should be established to control or remove non-native invasive species from land and water.

ES2 Act responsibly in the design, planning, management, and policy decisions affecting the health of the natural systems.

ES2.1 In developing design, planning, management, and policy, identify and invoke stakeholders—both communities and individuals—in helping to make decisions that affect their lives and future; ensure that they have appropriate access to relevant information, presented in an understandable form, and create opportunities for them to contribute to solutions.

ES3 Respect historic preservation and ecological management in the design process.

ES3.1 Strive to maintain, conserve, or re-establish the integrity and diversity of biological systems and their functions. Restore degraded ecosystems. Use indigenous and compatible materials and plants in the creation of habitat for indigenous species of animals.

ES4 Develop and specify products, materials, technologies, and techniques that conserve resources and foster landscape regeneration.

ES5 Seek constant improvement in our knowledge, abilities, and skills; in our educational institutions; and in our professional practice and organizations.

ES6 Actively engage in shaping decisions, attitudes, and values that support public health and welfare, environmental respect, and landscape regeneration.

Adopted by the Board of Trustees: October 27, 2000
Amended by the Board of Trustees: April 16, 2003; May 6, 2006.

CMAA
Construction Management Association of America
Code of Professional Ethics for the Construction Manager

Since 1982, the Construction Management Association of America (CMAA) has taken a leadership role in regard to critical issues impacting the construction and program management industry, including the setting of ethical standards of practice for the Professional Construction Manager.

The Board of Directors of CMAA has adopted the following Code of Professional Ethics of the Construction Manager (CODE) which apply to CMAA members in performance of their services as Construction and Program Managers. This Code applies to the individuals and to organizations who are members of CMAA.

All members of the Construction Management Association of America commit to conduct themselves and their practice of Construction and Program Management in accordance with the Code of Professional Ethics of the Construction Manager.

As a professional engaged in the business of providing construction and program management services, and as a member of CMAA, I agree to conduct myself and my business in accordance with the following:

1. **Client Service.** I will serve my clients with honesty, integrity, candor, and objectivity. I will provide my services with competence, using reasonable care, skill and diligence consistent with the interests of my client and the applicable standard of care.
2. **Representation of Qualifications and Availability.** I will only accept assignments for which I am qualified by my education, training, professional experience and technical competence, and I will assign staff to projects in accordance with their qualifications and commensurate with the services to be provided, and I will only make representations concerning my qualifications and availability which are truthful and accurate.
3. **Standards of Practice.** I will furnish my services in a manner consistent with the established and accepted standards of the profession and with the laws and regulations which govern its practice.
4. **Fair Competition.** I will represent my project experience accurately to my prospective clients and offer services and staff that I am capable of delivering. I will develop my professional reputation on the basis of my direct experience and service provided, and I will only engage in fair competition for assignments.
5. **Conflicts of Interest.** I will endeavor to avoid conflicts of interest; and will disclose conflicts which in my opinion may impair my objectivity or integrity.

6. **Fair Compensation.** I will negotiate fairly and openly with my clients in establishing a basis for compensation, and I will charge fees and expenses that are reasonable and commensurate with the services to be provided and the responsibilities and risks to be assumed.

7. **Release of Information.** I will only make statements that are truthful, and I will keep information and records confidential when appropriate and protect the proprietary interests of my clients and professional colleagues.

8. **Public Welfare.** I will not discriminate in the performance of my Services on the basis of race, religion, national origin, age, disability, or sexual orientation. I will not knowingly violate any law, statute, or regulation in the performance of my professional services.

9. **Professional Development.** I will continue to develop my professional knowledge and competency as Construction Manager, and I will contribute to the advancement of the construction and program management practice as a profession by fostering research and education and through the encouragement of fellow practitioners.

10. **Integrity of the Profession.** I will avoid actions which promote my own self-interest at the expense of the profession, and I will uphold the standards of the construction management profession with honor and dignity.

NSPE
National Society of Professional Engineers
Code of Ethics for Engineers

Code of Ethics for Engineers

Preamble

Engineering is an important and learned profession. As members of this profession, engineers are expected to exhibit the highest standards of honesty and integrity. Engineering has a direct and vital impact on the quality of life for all people. Accordingly, the services provided by engineers require honesty, impartiality, fairness, and equity, and must be dedicated to the protection of the public health, safety, and welfare. Engineers must perform under a standard of professional behavior that requires adherence to the highest principles of ethical conduct.

I. Fundamental Canons

Engineers, in the fulfillment of their professional duties, shall

1. Hold paramount the safety, health, and welfare of the public.
2. Perform services only in areas of their competence.
3. Issue public statements only in an objective and truthful manner.
4. Act for each employer or client as faithful agents or trustees.
5. Avoid deceptive acts.
6. Conduct themselves honorably, responsibly, ethically, and lawfully so as to enhance the honor, reputation, and usefulness of the profession.

II. Rules of Practice

1. Engineers shall hold paramount the safety, health, and welfare of the public.

a. If engineers' judgment is overruled under circumstances that endanger life or property, they shall notify their employer or client and such other authority as may be appropriate.

b. Engineers shall approve only those engineering documents that are in conformity with applicable standards.

c. Engineers shall not reveal facts, data, or information without the prior consent of the client or employer except as authorized or required by law or this Code.

d. Engineers shall not permit the use of their name or associate in business ventures with any person or firm that they believe is engaged in fraudulent or dishonest enterprise.

e. Engineers shall not aid or abet the unlawful practice of engineering by a person or firm.

f. Engineers having knowledge of any alleged violation of this Code shall report thereon to appropriate professional bodies and, when relevant, also to public authorities, and cooperate with the proper authorities in furnishing such information or assistance as may be required.

2. Engineers shall perform services only in the areas of their competence.

a. Engineers shall undertake assignments only when qualified by education or experience in the specific technical fields involved.

b. Engineers shall not affix their signatures to any plans or documents dealing with subject matter in which they lack competence, nor to any plan or document not prepared under their direction and control.

c. Engineers may accept assignments and assume responsibility for coordination of an entire project and sign and seal the engineering documents for the entire project, provided that each technical segment is signed and sealed only by the qualified engineers who prepared the segment.

3. Engineers shall issue public statements only in an objective and truthful manner.

a. Engineers shall be objective and truthful in professional reports, statements, or testimony. They shall include all relevant and pertinent information in such reports, statements, or testimony, which should bear the date indicating when it was current.

b. Engineers may express publicly technical opinions that are founded upon knowledge of the facts and competence in the subject matter.

c. Engineers shall issue no statements, criticisms, or arguments on technical matters that are inspired or paid for by interested parties, unless they have prefaced their comments by explicitly identifying the interested parties on whose behalf they are speaking, and by revealing the existence of any interest the engineers may have in the matters.

4. Engineers shall act for each employer or client as faithful agents or trustees.

a. Engineers shall disclose all known or potential conflicts of interest that could influence or appear to influence their judgment or the quality of their services.

b. Engineers shall not accept compensation, financial or otherwise, from more than one party for services on the same project, or for services pertaining to the same project, unless the circumstances are fully disclosed and agreed to by all interested parties.

c. Engineers shall not solicit or accept financial or other valuable consideration, directly or indirectly, from outside agents in connection with the work for which they are responsible.

d. Engineers in public service as members, advisors, or employees of a governmental or quasi-governmental body or department shall not participate in decisions with respect to services solicited or provided by them or their organizations in private or public engineering practice.

e. Engineers shall not solicit or accept a contract from a governmental body on which a principal or officer of their organization serves as a member.

5. Engineers shall avoid deceptive acts.

a. Engineers shall not falsify their qualifications or permit misrepresentation of their or their associates' qualifications. They shall not misrepresent or exaggerate their responsibility in or for the subject matter of prior assignments. Brochures or other presentations incident to the solicitation of employment shall not misrepresent pertinent facts concerning employers, employees, associates, joint venturers, or past accomplishments.

b. Engineers shall not offer, give, solicit, or receive, either directly or indirectly, any contribution to influence the award of a contract by public authority, or which may be reasonably construed by the public as having the effect or intent of influencing the awarding of a contract. They shall not offer any gift or other valuable consideration in order to secure work. They shall not pay a commission, percentage, or brokerage fee in order to secure work, except to a bona fide employee or bona fide established commercial or marketing agencies retained by them.

III. Professional Obligations

1. Engineers shall be guided in all their relations by the highest standards of honesty and integrity.

a. Engineers shall acknowledge their errors and shall not distort or alter the facts.

b. Engineers shall advise their clients or employers when they believe a project will not be successful.

c. Engineers shall not accept outside employment to the detriment of their regular work or interest. Before accepting any outside engineering employment, they will notify their employers.

d. Engineers shall not attempt to attract an engineer from another employer by false or misleading pretenses.

e. Engineers shall not promote their own interest at the expense of the dignity and integrity of the profession.

2. Engineers shall at all times strive to serve the public interest.

a. Engineers shall seek opportunities to participate in civic affairs; career guidance for youths; and work for the advancement of the safety, health, and well-being of their community.

b. Engineers shall not complete, sign, or seal plans and/or specifications that are not in conformity with applicable engineering standards. If the client or employer insists on such unprofessional conduct, they shall notify the proper authorities and withdraw from further service on the project.

c. Engineers shall endeavor to extend public knowledge and appreciation of engineering and its achievements.

d. Engineers shall strive to adhere to the principles of sustainable development1 in order to protect the environment for future generations.

3. Engineers shall avoid all conduct or practice that deceives the public.

a. Engineers shall avoid the use of statements containing a material misrepresentation of fact or omitting a material fact.

b. Consistent with the foregoing, engineers may advertise for recruitment of personnel.

c. Consistent with the foregoing, engineers may prepare articles for the lay or technical press, but such articles shall not imply credit to the author for work performed by others.

4. Engineers shall not disclose, without consent, confidential information concerning the business affairs or technical processes of any present or former client or employer, or public body on which they serve.

a. Engineers shall not, without the consent of all interested parties, promote or arrange for new employment or practice in connection with a specific project for which the engineer has gained particular and specialized knowledge.

b. Engineers shall not, without the consent of all interested parties, participate in or represent an adversary interest in connection with a specific project or proceeding in which the engineer has gained particular specialized knowledge on behalf of a former client or employer.

5. Engineers shall not be influenced in their professional duties by conflicting interests.

a. Engineers shall not accept financial or other considerations, including free engineering designs, from material or equipment suppliers for specifying their product.

b. Engineers shall not accept commissions or allowances, directly or indirectly, from contractors or other parties dealing with clients or employers of the engineer in connection with work for which the engineer is responsible.

6. Engineers shall not attempt to obtain employment or advancement or professional engagements by untruthfully criticizing other engineers, or by other improper or questionable methods.

a. Engineers shall not request, propose, or accept a commission on a contingent basis under circumstances in which their judgment may be compromised.

b. Engineers in salaried positions shall accept part-time engineering work only to the extent consistent with policies of the employer and in accordance with ethical considerations.

c. Engineers shall not, without consent, use equipment, supplies, laboratory, or office facilities of an employer to carry on outside private practice.

7. Engineers shall not attempt to injure, maliciously or falsely, directly or indirectly, the professional reputation, prospects, practice, or employment of other engineers. Engineers who believe others are guilty of unethical or illegal practice shall present such information to the proper authority for action.

a. Engineers in private practice shall not review the work of another engineer for the same client, except with the knowledge of such engineer, or unless the connection of such engineer with the work has been terminated.

b. Engineers in governmental, industrial, or educational employ are entitled to review and evaluate the work of other engineers when so required by their employment duties.

c. Engineers in sales or industrial employ are entitled to make engineering comparisons of represented products with products of other suppliers.

8. Engineers shall accept personal responsibility for their professional activities, provided, however, that engineers may seek indemnification for services arising out of their practice for other than gross negligence, where the engineer's interests cannot otherwise be protected.

a. Engineers shall conform with state registration laws in the practice of engineering.

b. Engineers shall not use association with a nonengineer, a corporation, or partnership as a "cloak" for unethical acts.

9. Engineers shall give credit for engineering work to those to whom credit is due, and will recognize the proprietary interests of others.

a. Engineers shall, whenever possible, name the person or persons who may be individually responsible for designs, inventions, writings, or other accomplishments.

b. Engineers using designs supplied by a client recognize that the designs remain the property of the client and may not be duplicated by the engineer for others without express permission.

c. Engineers, before undertaking work for others in connection with which the engineer may make improvements, plans, designs, inventions, or other records that may justify copyrights or patents, should enter into a positive agreement regarding ownership.

d. Engineers' designs, data, records, and notes referring exclusively to an employer's work are the employer's property. The employer should indemnify the engineer for use of the information for any purpose other than the original purpose.

e. Engineers shall continue their professional development throughout their careers and should keep current in their specialty fields by engaging in professional practice, participating in continuing education courses, reading in the technical literature, and attending professional meetings and seminars.

Footnote 1 "Sustainable development" is the challenge of meeting human needs for natural resources, industrial products, energy, food, transportation, shelter, and effective waste management while conserving and protecting environmental quality and the natural resource base essential for future development.

As Revised January 2006

"By order of the United States District Court for the District of Columbia, former Section 11(c) of the NSPE Code of Ethics prohibiting competitive bidding, and all policy statements, opinions, rulings or other guidelines interpreting its scope, have been rescinded as unlawfully interfering with the legal right of engineers, protected under the antitrust laws, to provide price information to prospective clients; accordingly, nothing contained in the NSPE Code of Ethics, policy statements, opinions, rulings or other guidelines prohibits the submission of price quotations or competitive bids for engineering services at any time or in any amount."

Statement by NSPE Executive Committee

In order to correct misunderstandings which have been indicated in some instances since the issuance of the Supreme Court decision and the entry of the Final Judgment, it is noted that in its decision of April 25, 1978, the Supreme Court of the United States declared: "The Sherman Act does not require competitive bidding."

It is further noted that as made clear in the Supreme Court decision:

1. Engineers and firms may individually refuse to bid for engineering services.
2. Clients are not required to seek bids for engineering services.
3. Federal, state, and local laws governing procedures to procure engineering services are not affected, and remain in full force and effect.
4. State societies and local chapters are free to actively and aggressively seek legislation for professional selection and negotiation procedures by public agencies.
5. State registration board rules of professional conduct, including rules prohibiting competitive bidding for engineering services, are not affected and remain in full force and effect. State registration boards with authority to adopt rules of professional conduct may adopt rules governing procedures to obtain engineering services.
6. As noted by the Supreme Court, "nothing in the judgment prevents NSPE and its members from attempting to influence governmental action . . ."

Note: In regard to the question of application of the Code to corporations vis-a-vis real persons, business form or type should not negate nor influence conformance of individuals to the Code. The Code deals with professional services, which services must be performed by real persons. Real persons in turn establish and implement policies within business structures. The Code is clearly written to apply to the Engineer, and it is incumbent on members of NSPE to endeavor to live up to its provisions. This applies to all pertinent sections of the Code.

1420 King Street
Alexandria, Virginia 22314-2794
703/684-2800 • Fax:703/836-4875
www.nspe.org
Publication date as revised: January 2006 • Publication #1102

Appendix III—Cases

Case 1: Engineers, Architects, and Safety

Here we present two cases that raise issues of responsibility to clients and the public, informed consent, non-disclosure, honesty-veracity, loyalty, confidentiality, beneficence, and non-maleficence. See where you stand on these issues as you read through the cases. We suggested not reading report 5 before this point.

Exercise 1.A The Repaired Flaw: Extra Safe or Deceptive?

The architecture firm of West and East, Inc. had its proposal for a new hotel in Atlanta, to be built for Hyatt Regency Inc., approved last summer and the contract negotiations went exceptionally well. During the initial phases of construction, you (a consulting architect) and an engineering colleague discover that on three of the first eight floors put up so far, small cracks are appearing in the floor slabs where the elevator shafts join the parking garage. You do an initial investigation and determine that though there does not immediately appear to be any compromise of building integrity, there also is no obvious reason for the cracks. Thus, you cannot make a final recommendation of the course of action, since you do not know the real cause or situation.

You report the cracks to East and West, Inc. Its people are concerned for several reasons. First, the building obviously has to be safe. In addition, however, they are in the midst of a lawsuit over a previous project in which a hospital waiting-room ceiling collapsed during a minor earthquake in California, though they had guaranteed that it complied with all regulations and codes. They want to be responsible for a good building, and also do not want to do any further damage to their reputation and profits.

They respond to your report by deciding to add a series of new, additional columns—triple-reinforced—in the critical areas. This will cost more and may not be necessary or a fully targeted response to the specific problem, but there seems no doubt that this portion of the building will stand to eternity with this

301

precaution. With this massive reinforcement, there is no way the elevator-parking garage interface will fail.

In a meeting the next week with the hotel management team, East and West, Inc. cover the project progress, mentioning a slight delay, but not elaborating on the details, much less the cause or basic problem. (East and West, Inc. decided to eat the cost and not have the additional costs of repair figured into the reports and billing submitted.) They reason that there is no point in unnecessarily alarming the client; plus, since the new construction is hyper-safe and comes with no additional cost, there is no need to bring up the potentially delicate issue. They have instructed you and your engineer colleague not to discuss the matter if it should come up. Since you are their employee, they remind you that they make the final decisions about your recommendations and that in public you need to defer to the team spokesman.

Another week later, the hotel management team again meets with East and West, Inc. They are concerned with the current costs and ask pointedly if there is any way that costs can be reduced. They have so many hotels under construction around the country, that they are having a cash-flow problem and would like to have a savings of even one or two percent. They have noticed the unusually massive construction in the area under repair (two of the three floors that initially had cracks have been redone, with one to go; and presumably to be continued on all eight floors, though that has not yet been finally decided) and ask whether such elaborate work is really necessary or whether it might be scaled back, and if so, how much could be saved. East and West, Inc. note that the work is necessary, but that it will not result in costs higher than the original bid. As usual, you are present as part of the East and West, Inc team. The hotel manager, who has worked with you on other projects, looks your way and asks if you agree or have anything to add about how costs could be reduced.

Questions:
Is the firm of East and West, Inc. acting ethically here?
What, if anything, should you say in response to the hotel manager's last question?

Exercise 1.B Engineers' Judgment, Risk, and Non-Maleficence

Keeping the major ethical theories in mind and thinking about the non-mechanical character of ethical judgments, read the following professional reflection and discuss whether and how evaluations such as these made by engineers can be impartial and fair without being either overly subjective or objective:

> As a civil engineer working in the construction industry, I have encountered designers whose work entails unnecessary expense. The design engineer is a

sort of god—the project specifications are sometimes referred to as the bible and doubtless it is tempting to specify, regardless of cost, the most exacting methods and the most expensive equipment. Engineers who follow such a course, heedless of their clients' best interest, are usually winnowed out by the exigencies of the marketplace. More subtle—and more insidious—is the influence of inspectors, those engineers who are charged with verifying that contractors comply with plans and specifications. It is absolutely essential that these inspector-engineers be totally honest and vigilant. Quality control depends upon them, to say nothing of public safety. But it is also important for inspectors to be reasonable in interpreting contract documents. Since in erecting a building there is no such thing as perfection, what deviation from the ideal is permissible? How level is level? How smooth is smooth? Tolerances can be spelled out numerically; but there invariably comes a point where common sense, traditional practice, and pragmatism enter the picture.

(Florman 1987, 142–43)

Case 2. Becoming—and Staying—a Planner

It is important to do this exercise incrementally. The whole point is to work through a wicked problem, that is, one that unfolds as you go along. Reading the case all the way through will not allow you to do the exercise. Rather, you need to read until you are faced with a question and decision; only after you have answered, does it make sense to go on.

The Situation

You have just completed your degree and have a great job in the small city where you grew up. While you moved away for school, you have long wanted to live and work back there. Plus, you really needed this job as you are a single parent with three children in school and no other means of support.

It is only your third month on the job, but you have come to know that the director of planning requires all employees to follow his policy directives quite closely. While he allows times for discussion and disagreement, once the official position is set, failure to implement the program as prescribed can lead to termination. This is not idle rumor; a few staff have been fired in the past because they failed to comply with, or tried to circumvent, official positions.

The current project you're working on involves considering rezoning a large parcel of land adjacent to a beach and near a bird sanctuary and a coral reef that lies around a point. The parcel in question is owned by the city and currently zoned as miscellaneous open space (the zoning is looser on the edge of town). The space is informally used as a park by some of the locals. Though it is not formally part of the nearby protected area, since it is undeveloped, it has functioned as a barrier to help protect that area.

You voice your concerns about the environmental impacts to the director, but he makes it clear that this project is a top priority with city officials and state politicians as it will create a substantial number of jobs, increase tax revenue, and increase surrounding real estate values in an economically stagnant area. There is a lot of pressure to develop this area. The project itself is part of a regional economic development plan.

Not only that, but the local residents have come out strongly in favor of the project. You know some of these community members and grew up with them. Most have lived in the area their entire lives, but lately they have suffered from a languishing economy. Many families worked in a manufacturing plant that recently closed down. So they have come to town meetings to voice their support of the project as a way of creating new revenues and jobs. They want to see the community get back on its feet economically, and want to bring new vitality to the area.

The project would be a public-private partnership venture to create a resort community with mixed use (condos, time-sharing villas, restaurants, marina, water sports, etc.) with a 50-year ground lease. This would require the rezoning of the area adjacent to the sanctuary and coral reef.

1. Stop. Consider this First Situation and Question.

You personally are very ecologically minded, and having grown up in the area, you are knowledgeable about the fragility and importance of the local ecosystem. You see that the project's commercial success will hinge on the use of the beach and water by residents and tourists, and you know this will infringe upon the protected area. You voice your concerns in the staff meetings, but the director makes it clear that this is a top-priority project.

You understand the concerns of the local residents, but you are still worried about the impact on the preserve. You try to explain this, but they don't seem to understand.

What do you do?

Continue only after you have thought about the issue and made a decision as to what to do. It would be especially helpful if a group could discuss the case, with each person contributing and giving a viewpoint.

2. Next: Consider the Second Situation and Question

Suppose you have decided to continue at your job and set some personal-values and differences aside on this project. While at work on the project, you discover that the marina franchise to be included in the plan (both because it was a low bidder and because it is owned by the governor's executive assistant's son-in-law) has violated environmental law in the past (they were charged with illegal dumping on a project ten years ago). They also plan to make accommodations for the use of power boats. You take this up with your director, but he says there will be no change in the directions to proceed.

What do you do now?

Again, continue only after you have thought about the issue and made a decision as to what to do.

3. Next: Consider the Third Situation and Question

Two weeks later, over lunch with a friend and colleague who is the legal counsel for city planning, your friend voices concern over a proposal she is researching. While checking on allowable expenditures of federal funds for Community Development Block Grants and Job Training Funds to be used in a pending public-private economic development grant, she has become aware of certain problems. (Though your friend does not know it, you quickly realize that her project is the same one on which you are working.) While a certain amount of discretion is allowed to the state and local government agencies in the matter of expenditures, the project as proposed will not actually utilize funds directly as required for low-income training. It will, in fact, use fifty percent of those funds to train non-eligible college students in management training slots. And while jobs and tax revenues will be generated, the plan calls for the resort to be exclusive and amenities will not be available to the public.

What do you do now?

Case 3. Hydro-Quebec

Here is a complex, real case that emerged recently out of Canada.
- Part A presents the case material—excerpts from journalists and others
- Part B contains the exercises and questions for you to consider.

The case study examines the ethical implications surrounding the James Bay Power Project in Northern Quebec, Canada, one of the last major undeveloped hydroelectric sites in North America. It highlights sensitive and highly charged issues at play in such projects—how it will alter a huge land area including culturally-based land uses, economic vitality, sensitive habitat for at risk species, and local ways of life. As you will see, there are many layers of issues and ethical decisions. Like many such power projects around the world, this one is entangled in controversy. The following articles lay out the situation as it unfolds.

Case 3.A—Case Material
1. The James Bay Power Project, *Canadian Geographic*, Feb/March 1990
2. Creating a New Way of Life, *MacLean's*, May, 1990—2 stories
3. Realpolitik in Arctic Quebec, *Arctic Circle*, Sept/Oct 1991
4. Rupert River Surrendered, *Ottertooth*, February, 2002
5. Cree Approve New Agreement with Quebec, *Environmental News Service*, Feb., 2000

Report 1. The James Bay Power Project
Canadian Geographic (Feb/March 1990)
"The environmental cost of reshaping the geography of northern Quebec."
By Peter Gorrie

With its waters now diverted to the La Grande River, this section of the once mighty Eastmain has been reduced to a trickle. The same fate awaits the Rupert River where natives have fished for centuries. The doubling of the flow of the La Grande forced residents of Fort George, situated on an island in the river's mouth, to abandon their community and set up the new town of Chisasibi.

Little is known about the effects of a radically altered terrain on migrating caribou. Another concern is whether increased river flows will reduce the number of ice-free channels where beluga whales winter in James Bay.

HYDRO-QUEBEC sums up its corporate attitude about the massive James Bay hydro-electric project on the cover of one of its glossy pamphlets:
La Grande Riviere: A Development In Accord With Its Environment.

The booklet's proclamation is part of a series of messages aimed at convincing the public that more than $40 billion worth of powerhouses, dikes, transmission lines, roads, towns, and airports can be inserted harmoniously into an unspoiled northern wilderness.

For the past 19 years it has been a relatively trouble-free selling job as the provincial Crown corporation - with enthusiastic backing from Premier Robert Bourassa and most Quebeckers - announced plans to harness the power of 20 rivers flowing into James and Hudson bays, then built the first phase of the project. For much of the 1980s there was almost no debate, as an economic recession cut energy demands and further phases were put on hold.

Demand for electrical power is again strong and the giant utility has relaunched an ambitious 15-year plan to complete the development. As it does, it is also facing renewed questions about environmental and economic costs and the possibility that, for the first time, the huge project will be examined at public hearings.

Hydro-Quebec insists the development is essential and will not cause unacceptable damage. One of its reports concluded that in the first phase remedial measures . . . have generally achieved their objectives, and other studies offer assurances that remaining phases are environmentally acceptable.

Premier Bourassa made his views on the project patently clear in a 1985 book, Power From The North: Quebec is a vast hydro-electric plant in the bud, and every day, millions of potential kilowatt hours flow downhill and out to sea. What a waste!

He and other supporters extol the jobs and income the project and its subsequent exports of electricity will bring Quebec. The utility has awarded billions of dollars worth of engineering and supply contracts to Quebec firms, enabling them to develop high-technology products and become international competitors. And, they say, every kilowatt of power from James Bay will cut the amount that power plants fuelled by coal, oil or nuclear energy would have to generate at greater risk to the environment.

Critics counter that the project will create few long-term jobs while taking a devastating toll on the environment. They also worry that the 9,000 local Cree and Inuit will lose their source of food, livelihood and identity.

The provincial government and Hydro-Quebec have not ignored such concerns. Most of Quebec's environmental laws were introduced after the James

Bay project was announced in an apparent attempt to minimize damage by the development. The utility set up an environment division with officers at every construction site. Its subsidiary managing the project, the *Société d'energie de la Baie James*, has a committee to advise it on environmental protection. The power company is spending hundreds of millions of dollars on impact studies and remedial measures - from creating new fish spawning grounds to landscaping tourist lookouts.

Even the New York-based National Audubon Society, which says plans for future phases should be delayed, and perhaps scrapped, acknowledged in a recent report that the province is willing to go to great lengths to reduce impacts during construction.

But all this is of little comfort to the 500,000-member Audubon Society and other critics. They complain that since James Bay is a key part of the provincial government's strategy for economic growth, environmental concerns have not been allowed to impede its progress. The province and Hydro-Quebec act on the assumption the project must proceed, and only then consider how to cope with adverse consequences.

As a result, critics contend, the utility's research is inadequate or flawed, provincial reviews are cursory, and applications to proceed with various stages have been approved before impact studies were complete. The Cree and the provincial government each has two people to review and assess studies by 400 Hydro-Quebec staff and a small army of consultants.

Native people battled the project from the outset. In 1975 - after winning an injunction in Quebec Superior Court, then losing on appeal - the Grand Council of the Cree agreed to let the project proceed in return for $225 million, some control over about 75,000 square kilometers of land and an environmental review process.

But the development, described by Bourassa as the project of the century, faces new political and legal challenges.

The Federal Court; in a case involving the Rafferty-Alameda dams in Saskatchewan, ruled last year that the federal government has a duty to review projects affecting its jurisdiction. The James Bay project falls into that category since it would affect native people as well as migratory bird breeding habitat protected by a Canada-U.S. treaty.

As well, the Cree have launched another legal challenge to try to force an extensive federal review and hearings, and the Inuit of northern Quebec recently asked the Federal Environmental Assessment Review Office for a public review.

In the northeastern United States, where Hydro-Quebec hopes to earn billions of dollars from long-term energy sales, environmentalists are demanding their governments insist on thorough impact studies before deciding whether to approve import.

In response, Hydro-Quebec officials have acknowledged that hearings might be worthwhile, and some in the utility are urging a two- or three-year delay.

The scope of the James Bay development is breathtaking. It would harness the energy of almost every drop of water in the rivers flowing through 350,000 square kilometers of northwestern Quebec - more than one-fifth of Canada's largest province.

The water would be collected in vast reservoirs behind powerhouses on the main rivers. While some would be released year-round to spin turbines and generate electricity, the system is geared more to winter when demand for power is at its peak. Then reservoir levels would drop as much as 20 meters as water is released and generating stations are pushed to capacity.

Leased year-round to spin turbines and generate electricity, the system is geared more to winter when demand for power is at its peak. Then reservoir levels would drop as much as 20 meters as water is released and generating stations are pushed to capacity.

Cascading rivers would be dammed and diverted to create the reservoirs, flooding a combined area bigger than the surface of Lake Ontario. Some rivers would be reduced to a trickle; others simply submerged.

Hydro-Quebec's latest development strategy calls for a three-stage completion of the project. If it goes ahead according to plan, by early next century it will generate up to 28,000 megawatts of power.

The project includes:

❑   La Grande. Phase One: completed in 1985 after 12 years and at a cost of about $16 billion, it includes three reservoirs and powerhouses on the La Grande River - LG2, LG3 and LG4 - with a combined production of 10,282 megawatts. In this phase, five smaller rivers were diverted into the La Grande to increase its power. Its average flow into James Bay has doubled and is four times the previous rate in winter. LG2 is now being expanded, with the addition of a 1,998-megawatt powerhouse called LG2A. This add-on will produce more power than the combined output of Quebec's single nuclear-powered generating station and its 25 plants fueled by coal or oil.

❑   La Grande, Phase Two: its centerpiece is a powerhouse, LG I, near the mouth of the river, and five more—Brisay, Eastmain I and 2, and Laforge 1 and 2 - on rivers diverted in Phase One. They are scheduled to be in operation by 1996. Work on the Brisay dam and hydro-electric station was expected to start this spring.

❑   Great Whale: north of the La Grande is the basin of the wild Great Whale River, or Grande rivière de la Baleine, which flows into Hudson Bay. This phase includes three power stations with a total capacity of 2,890 megawatts, and diversion of two other rivers. Final plans are being reviewed, but three or four reservoirs would be created on the Great Whale River by 2001.

❑   The NBR Project: the initials represent three large rivers, the Nottaway, Broadback and Rupert, which flow into the southern end of James Bay. The Nottaway and Rupert rivers are to be diverted into the Broadback where up to eight powerhouses would generate 8,700 megawatts. Hydro-Quebec's target for completion of the first powerhouse is from 1998 to 2004, depending on demand. In addition, 12 sets of transmission lines - with a combined length of more than 5,500 kilometers and nearly 12,000 towers - will carry the power to markets in southern Quebec where it would be routed to customers either in Canada or the

United States.

The scene of all this activity is a wilderness of lakes, rivers, spindly spruce and willow, lichens and peat bogs along the east side of James Bay and the southeast coast of Hudson Bay.

Hydro-Quebec reports the region is home to 39 animal species, including moose, caribou, beaver, muskrat and lynx. The cold lakes and fast-flowing rivers teem with fish. The coastline is rich habitat for fish and birds, as well as whales and seals. Those resources are a crucial source of food and income for the Cree and Inuit. As well, the coastal waters are an internationally renowned resting and breeding ground for millions of migratory birds.

As Phase One has made clear, dams, dikes, powerhouses and roads bring dramatic change. Damage to the natural environment is concentrated along the edges of water bodies, the richest habitats for plants and wildlife. Some rivers have been reduced to creeks. For example, downstream from its diversion into the La Grande, the Eastmain River's flow has been cut by 90 percent.

In these shrunken waterways, riverbeds dry up leaving stagnant pools. Exposed clay and sand are eroded by rain and melting snow, and sediment chokes the mouths of tributaries. Spawning grounds are often destroyed and species such as brook trout, which live in clear, oxygen-rich rapids, can no longer survive.

Some of these rivers are subject to periodic flooding as excess water is released from reservoirs upstream. The result is heavy erosion and the destruction of new plants struggling to establish themselves in the exposed, barren riverbeds.

To date, the main remedy has been construction of weirs, or small dams, that turn sections of these shriveled rivers into shallow lakes, with an entirely new habitat. Where weirs were considered too costly, exposed riverbeds have been planted to try to reduce erosion.

The opposite occurs in rivers that carry diverted water in a new direction. Their flow is greatly increased. For example, the Boutin now carries 15 cubic meters of water per second; when the Great Whale project is completed, the little river will have swollen to 154 cubic meters per second as it carries the water from several lakes to the reservoir behind one of the main powerhouses.

Increased flows cause erosion. The resulting sediment load is deposited in places where the river slows - including reservoirs, whose capacity is gradually reduced by silting - and at the mouth, where a delta may form. Vegetation along the shore may be destroyed, eliminating habitat for ptarmigan, Canada geese and some species of ducks. The damage is increased on fast-flowing rivers subjected to the fluctuating demands of power stations.

The new reservoirs flood rivers and submerge vast areas of forest. Shorelines become a tangled, inaccessible mess as trees and shrubs die and rot. Decaying vegetation eats up dissolved oxygen in the water and adds to the supply of nutrients, creating algae blooms. In most cases, shoreline vegetation and habitats cannot be reestablished because of changing water levels.

Major changes also occur in estuaries, whether river flows have been reduced or increased. Water temperature patterns, the length and extent of ice cover in winter, and the mixing of fresh and salt water - all are altered.

Normally, rivers run highest during the spring melt; levels are lowest in winter. The James Bay development will reverse this natural pattern. Flows will be greatest in winter - up to 10 times the normal volume - and the spring runoff will be diminished.

One result will be a change in water salinity at various sites during the year in James Bay and Hudson Bay. That could, in turn, wreak havoc on fish and mammals that require specific types of food or water conditions to prepare for migration, reproduce or survive the long, intensely cold winters. In addition, nutrients that now flow into the bays will settle instead in the reservoirs.

Scientists do not have enough information to predict the consequences. But in such a complex and fragile environment to which plants and wildlife have adapted successfully but precariously such information is essential. Over the millennia, the impact could be catastrophic.

The Audubon Society's report on James Bay cites examples of the potential damage to the bay's ecosystem. Coastal marshes and tidal flats are rich feeding grounds for many species of migratory birds, which must eat voraciously for a short time to store energy for flights to wintering areas in the southern United States and Central America.

A main source of food is a small clam that burrows in vast numbers in the mud of saltwater marshes and tidal flats. Millions of birds would have no alternative food if these feeding spots were destroyed by ice scouring or changes in salinity and temperature. Many species "would be severely threatened, possibly even to extinction," the society says.

Belugas winter in ice-free waters around islands in James Bay. The open areas appear to result from the spacing of the islands and the action of wind and tides in the channels among them. If ice patterns are affected by altered river flows, the whales could be at risk.

Hydro-Quebec says it has found only small adverse changes where the La Grande River runs into James Bay. But the Audubon Society and other critics argue those results are not reassuring because too little time has passed to assess the impact. And, they say, while individual elements of the project might not have much effect, the total development could have devastating consequences. "If the damage from an individual project is marginal, the project can be approved, even though the cumulative impact of many such projects will mean the loss of the ecosystem," the Audubon Society warned in its report.

The utility is collecting volumes of information that is not of much use but suggests the appearance of action, says Alan Penn, a geographer appointed by the Cree to Hydro-Quebec's environmental review committee. It can describe things in a broad sense, but not the processes critical at certain times of the year that determine whether species survive.

"The kind of data collection going on is not designed to focus on problems, but to provide general reassurance," Penn says. "It's what happens when you invite the developer to develop his own system of environmental monitoring."

But there is no denying one immediate and serious outcome - the release of mercury, which damages the human nervous system and can, with prolonged exposure, cause death.

Mercury is commonly found in rocks throughout the north in an insoluble form that does not affect the air and water. However, bacteria associated with decomposition of organic matter transform it into methyl mercury, which vaporizes, enters the atmosphere, then falls back into the water. From there it enters the food chain, reaching highest concentrations in fish species that prey on other fish. Local people consume large quantities of such fish - pickerel, pike-· and lake trout - which are their most reliable source of high-quality protein.

New reservoirs induce a burst of decomposition that accelerates the release of mercury. On the La Grande, levels of mercury in fish downstream from the dams climbed to six times their normal levels within months of the project's completion. A 1984 survey of Cree living in the village of Chisasibi at the river's mouth found that 64 percent of the villagers had unsafe levels of mercury in their bodies.

In time, as drowned vegetation is completely decomposed, the release of mercury should return to normal. How long that will take is not known. In studies completed up to 1981 - when Hydro-Quebec put the James Bay project on hold - the mercury problem was not even mentioned. When it was finally recognized, the utility estimated that high levels would last up to six years. But a March 1988 study carried out by the utility on the Laforge 1 power station states mercury levels would remain high for 10 to 20 years. It could be a generation. or longer before fish are safe to eat again, Penn says.

In 1987. Hydro-Quebec appointed a committee. with two Cree representatives, and gave it a 10-year budget of near $18.5 million to study the mercury hazard. To date, it has produced no practical solutions.

Decomposition can be reduced by clearing areas before they are flooded. But that is extremely expensive and poses the difficulty of disposing of the vast quantities of trees and brush. As a result, the power utility is clearing only selected areas - those that are close to power stations and other access points, and those around inlets of streams where fish spawn.

"A great deal of research needs to be done," the mercury committee concluded in its most recent report. In the meantime, it suggested weakly, native people should stop eating tainted fish and "anything that can be done to foster continuation of traditional pursuits would be much appreciated."

Decomposition has another by-product also causing concern - the release of methane, one of the greenhouse gases blamed for global warming. The amount of methane in the atmosphere is rising by one percent annually. It is produced naturally by decomposition in peat bogs, wetlands and lakes. Human activity also has made a big contribution. Large quantities of methane are generated by livestock, rice paddies, and the burning of trees and brush as forests are cleared.

Nigel Roulet, a scientist at York University in Toronto who has studied methane production in northeastern Quebec, says precise forecasts are not yet possible. But the James Bay reservoirs could be a significant new source of manmade methane.

By itself, the project will not change the earth's climate, but every contribution adds to the greenhouse effect, Roulet says.

While some proponents point out that global warming will be much worse if the power to be generated at James Bay is produced instead by coal- or oil-burning generators, the argument ignores the potential of conservation to cut energy demand. This is the view of Brian Craik, who has been involved with the project since 1972 and currently represents the Cree in discussions with the federal government.

Ultimately, the question must be asked: Are projects of this size, which basically reshape the geography of a vast area desirable?

James Bay is one of the last major undeveloped hydroelectric sites in North America. As planned, it will account for nearly 25 percent of the continent's hydro-electric power. It will alter a huge land area in some ways that are known and others that even experts can only guess at.

So far, it has all been done without public hearings, and very little questioning.

"I'm really very upset about this," says Helene Lajambe, an economist with the Centre for Energy Policy Analysis at the University of Quebec in Montreal. "James Bay doesn't make sense for Quebec." The province is already a wasteful consumer of electricity and demand is being fuelled artificially - through ad campaigns and price breaks - to justify the project, she says.

Last year, Quebec approved construction of three aluminum smelters which it attracted, in part, by offering the huge amounts of power they need at a cost tied to the international price of aluminum. That is an unstable yardstick, and if aluminum prices drop, Hydro could lose money on the deal, Lajambe says. In addition, she argues, power projects and aluminum smelters are expensive and environmentally damaging ways to create relatively few jobs.

The utility's cut-rate price plan for industry began to unravel late last year, however, as the low water levels of its northern reservoirs drastically reduced the generating capacity of the James Bay complex and its other hydro facilities. To head off what it termed serious supply problems, Hydro-Quebec launched another campaign, this time to convince its industrial customers to switch back from electricity to oil. That promotion quickly fell afoul of federal Environment Minister Lucien Bouchard who warned that the program could jeopardize Canada's acid rain negotiations with the United States. By encouraging the increased use of oil by industry, the utility, he said, could prevent Quebec from meeting its commitment to cut acid rain-causing emissions to 600,000 tons annually this year.

Even if Hydro-Quebec sells James Bay power to the United States, Quebec will lose in the long run. The province will have put billions of dollars into developments that stimulate manufacturing and high-technology jobs elsewhere, Lajambe says. Quebec is investing its limited capital and best minds in projects "that chain us to an economy that depends even more on the production of resources. James Bay slows down the development process."

The access road to the NBR project will also open up from 12 million to 18 million cubic meters of marketable lumber, most of which would be exported, Brian Craik says. "The environment would be subsidizing not only the sale of hydro but also lumber to the United States."

Potential customers in the U.S. appear to be getting cold feet about power deals. Maine has postponed signing a contract for a small long-term purchase, and the municipal council in Burlington, Vt., concerned about the environmental impact of James Bay, recently recommended that the local utility not buy power from the project.

At a conference in Montreal last summer, American energy economists argued the northeastern states could save money if they rejected James Bay power and, instead, paid for conservation programs in Quebec and then bought the electricity those measures would free up. But Hydro-Quebec officials say the project will proceed, even without a U.S. market for the power. And they remain convinced it is environmentally sound and in the public interest.

Nevertheless, some officials are urging a delay, not because of concerns over the project's environmental consequences but because it requires a public relations campaign. And that would likely involve hearings, says Gaetan Guertin, the utility's manager of siting and impact studies. "The major conclusion we have is that maybe the public is not well prepared to react positively to these projects."

As the debate simmers, negotiations over hearings drag on and Hydro-Quebec awaits approvals while engineering work is continuing. The utility is convinced James Bay power is needed and that, even with a conservation effort, demand will grow by three or four percent annually. But none of its studies have asked: What next? James Bay is Quebec's last hydro-electric mega-project. Once it is done, the province will, like neighboring Ontario, have no major rivers left to tame. Will it then also opt for nuclear power, creating the very problems it claims to be avoiding by developing James Bay?

If public hearings are held, they will probably focus on direct impacts. Are caribou threatened? When fish are contaminated, what will local people eat? But critics suggest the debate should centre on a much bigger question: Can humans limit their appetite for power so that such mega-projects do not need to be considered? Hydro-Quebec and most other utilities assume the answer is no. Environmentalists insist it must become yes if the earth is to remain habitable. The James Bay project, they say, will not only increase the damage caused by the search for new power sources, it will also help delay the push for Hidden Box here, conservation that is likely to come only when we run out of alternatives.

Report 2-A. Changes Threaten Cree Traditions

This next article, also from a Canadian magazine, highlights the ways in which the Hydro-Quebec project has posed challenges for Cree people seeking to maintain their native traditions.

CREATING A NEW WAY OF LIFE

On a chilly day early this month, a brisk west wind from James Bay brought midafternoon snowflurries to the Cree village of Chisasibi. There, in a house equipped with a microwave oven, a color television, a stereo and other modern appliances, 74-year-old Joseph Rupert was .sitting at his kitchen table, talking about the annual goose hunt. Rupert said that he planned to spend the rest of the month camped on the east shore of James Bay, about 50 km north of Chisasibi, 1,000 km north of Montreal, with his son and several of his nine grandchildren. If the geese are plentiful, Rupert and his son will bring back enough fowl to feed the family through the summer. But even though hunting, trapping and fishing continue to be cornerstones of the Cree economy, band leaders are striving to create more manufacturing and service jobs because hydroelectric development and an increasing population are growing threats to the traditional Indian lifestyle. Said Billy Diamond, chief of the Waskaganish band: "We need business and employment opportunities for our young people."

Creating job opportunities for the next generation is a challenge, because 50 per cent of the approximately 9,700 James Bay Cree are under 21. And according to federal government statistics, the unemployment rate among tribe members aged 15 to 21 is now 55 per cent. The nine Cree bands have responded by developing a regional airline, Air Creebec, to serve northwestern Quebec and northeastern Ontario, and by launching their own construction company to build housing. As well, Diamond's Waskaganish band runs a canoe-manufacturing company and a barge operation. Said the chief: "I'm your typical corporate Indian."

The largest and most ambitious of the ventures is the airline. Tribal leaders launched it in 1982, with an investment of $12.5 million that they received from Ottawa and Quebec in return for relinquishing claims to 70,000 square miles of land for the first phase of the James Bay hydroelectric project. Air Creebec now employs 300 people and brings in $30 million a year in revenues, compared with $10 million during its first year of operation. This year, projected operating profits are $3 million.

Most of the other Cree ventures are based in individual communities. In 1985, Diamond's band entered into a joint venture with Toronto-based Yamaha Motor Canada Ltd. and its Japanese counterpart to manufacture 23-foot fibre-glass canoes at a factory in Waskaganish, on the southeast coast of James Bay. The new company, which is called Cree Yamaha Motors Ltd., has sold boats to Inuit fishermen in the Arctic and sportsmen in Atlantic Canada, Diamond said. But he acknowledged that it is difficult to convince other Cree to switch from the traditional wooden fishing boats.

Interest: Besides canoes, Diamond said that Cree Yamaha will also manufacture a 37-foot diesel-powered boat capable of carrying 75,000 lb. of cargo. Diamond said that the company has orders for seven of the boats, which will sell for $200,000 apiece. The

Waskaganish Cree also continuing interest in a commercial shipping company called Moosonee Transportation Ltd., which is based in Moosonee, Ont., on the southwest coast of James Bay. The company carries fuel, food and other goods to communities on both sides of the bay during the summer months.

Still, such traditional occupations as fishing and trapping remain the primary forms of employment for many Cree. The 1975 James Bay and Northern Quebec Agreement, under which the Cree gave up parts of their territory for hydroelectric development, created an income-security program. Under the system, the Quebec government subsidizes individual Cree who spend a certain number of days each year hunting, trapping and fishing. Norman Hawkins, a Montreal chartered accountant, said that, as of March 31, 1989, more than 1,200 families received a total of $12.1 million in income-security payments. Added Samuel Tapiatic, deputy chief of the Chisasibi band: "We don't hunt for sport. It's a way of life for us."

The Cree who still follow the traditional way of life usually spend six months a year trapping beaver and other animals. May is devoted to the goose hunt. But that way of life is under threat from the hydroelectric developments that have flooded thousands of square miles of hunting and trapping territory. Rupert contends that by building dams and reservoirs on La Grande River, Hydro Quebec has eliminated what was once a major route to trapping and hunting grounds in the interior. "We are losing our traditional way of life because of the land they flooded," he added. For his part, Diamond claimed that the diminished land base leaves no room for any additional Cree hunters or trappers. As a result, the next generation may be more preoccupied with balance sheets than traplines.

D' ARCY JENISH in Chisasi, *MACLEAN'S* / MAY21, 1990, p. 55.

→ In light of what you have learned from this article about likely impacts of the Hydro-Quebec project on Cree traditions, what ethical concerns does this raise for you?

Report 2-B. Update on the situation

Yet another magazine article highlights some of the ecological impacts of Hydro-Quebec. See how the facts outlined in the article below influence your reaction to the Hydro-Quebec project.

Artificially swollen rivers will carry more sediment, which could lead to the creation of deltas at their mouths. That sediment buildup could then destroy the rich beds of sea grass that are the main food source of migrating ducks and geese along the James Bay coast.
•   As the demand for electricity rises and falls, the volume of water needed to drive Hydro Quebec's turbines does the same. As a consequence, the water levels in the reservoirs rise and fall too, with the result that their shorelines have become barren and will remain that way because vegetation, also an animal food source, will not have a chance to become firmly rooted.

- The volume of fresh water flowing into James Bay during the winter months, when the demand for power peaks, will be up to 10 times the normal amount. That, says Penn, will play havoc with fish and mammals that have adapted to a saltwater habitat.
- Even the beluga whales that winter in open water among offshore islands in James Bay could be endangered, experts say, for two reasons: the cows are accustomed to nursing their calves in spring in the freshwater runoff that will not occur in. Rivers harnessed by the project, and, second, more fresh water in winter could lead to more ice where the whales swim.

Of all the conservation and environmental objections to increasing James Bay's generating capacity, the most vigorous and widely publicized has been put forward by the 600,000 member Audubon Society. In a 1989 report, it urged Hydro Quebec to make expansion conditional on the outcome of far more detailed environmental impact studies than have been done so far. Said Jennifer Hansell, a 25-year-old Audubon environmental policy analyst: An argument we put forward is that Quebec doesn't need to build new power plants to meet its energy needs. She added, If they were more energy-efficient, they would have enough for their own needs and have enough left over for export.

The report said that further massive changes in water flow could jeopardize even polar bears and James Bay's 61,000 ringed seals. It also expressed concern for the millions of migrating waterfowl and shorebirds that feed and breed on the bay's tidal flats and salt marshes. Said Hansell: The entire population of some species depends on James Bay. If we are concerned about our own survival, we should realize that birds are the most sensitive to environmental change and are the first to go. Said Penn: There is a definite potential in the long term for the alteration and, probably, impoverishment of waterfowl habitat. The environmental studies undertaken up to now by Hydro Quebec, said Penn, are not designed to focus on problems, but to provide general reassurance. It's what happens when you invite the developer to create his own system of environmental monitoring.

Habitat: Spokesmen for other environment agencies have also criticized the Quebec utility. Said Daniel Green, co-president of the Montreal-based Victory over Pollution Society: For years, we have had to accept this paternalistic attitude of "Trust us, we know what's best," but no more. Hydro Quebec is finally going to have to answer some tough questions. Declared Jan Beyea, the Audubon Society's senior staff scientist: In terms of wildlife and habitat James Bay is the northern equivalent of the destruction of the tropical rain forests.

For his part, Hydro Quebec's Drouin said that the enterprise had been undertaken with concern for the environment and is truly one of the seven wonders of the world. With the preservation of such a vast area at stake, long, painstaking-and perhaps costly-environmental hearings will clearly be needed to determine the future of Quebec's northern wilderness.

RAE CORELLI with TASHA DIAMANT in Toronto and D'ARCY JENISH in Chisasibi, *MACLEAN's* / May 21, 1990, p. 56.

The following article highlights complex relations of different groups to Hydro-Quebec in terms of both environmental damage and impact on native peoples.

Report 3. Realpolitik in Arctic Quebec, *Arctic Circle*, Sept/Oct 1991

"Why Makivik Corporation Won't Fight This Time"

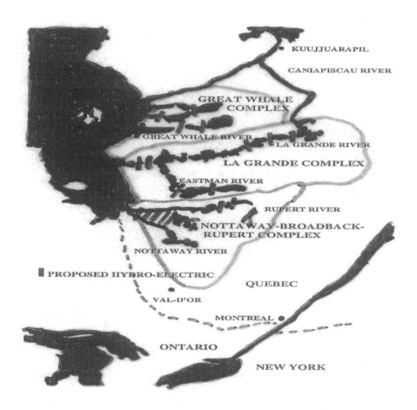

Makivik Corporation owes its very existence to confrontation with Hydro-Quebec, but these days the two companies look more like partners than adversaries. Makivik and Hydro-Quebec are negotiating compensation for the Inuit of Nunavik (Arctic Quebec) stemming from the planned construction of the Great Whale hydro-electric project. That has angered the Cree of the James Bay region and numerous environmental and human rights organizations who want the project to be cancelled because they believe it will lead to massive environmental damage and spell the end of a way of life for native people.

Makivik Corporation was formed in 1978, under the leadership of Charlie Watt, then president of the Northern Quebec Inuit Association, after Nunavik Inuit and Cree obtained a court injunction halting construction of the first phase of the James Bay hydroelectric development (the La Grande project). Negotiations ultimately led to the James Bay and Northern Quebec Agreement (JBNQA), signed by the Inuit of Northern Quebec, the Cree of James Bay, the federal government, the Quebec government, Hydro-Quebec, the James Bay Energy Corporation and the James Bay Development Corporation. At the time, many people in the Inuit communities of Salluuit, Ivujivik, and Povungnituk refused to accept the terms of the James Bay Agreement and tried to challenge it in court. Some of those same dissidents are now opposed to Makivik's conciliatory position on the Great Whale project.

The 455-page JBNQA extinguished aboriginal title to most of the land traditionally used and occupied by the Inuit, Cree and Naskapi of Northern Quebec. In return, the Inuit were given $9 million in compensation and promises relating to everything from better housing and health care to the building of airports and the establishment of a regional police force. Makivik Corporation was created to administer the money for the Inuit of Nunavik. The JBNQA gave the Cree similar promises and $125 million in compensation.

Sixteen years after the signing of the Landmark James Bay Agreement, Makivik President Charlie Watt says the Inuit are being wise in repeating what they did in the 1970s: negotiating with Hydro-Quebec for a compensation package of economic benefits. As for the environmental concerns, Watt says construction of the Great Whale project is inevitable, so negotiation—not confrontation—is the best way to protect Inuit interests.

Dubbed Mega-Watt by his critics, the Makivik leader hopes to bargain for the creation of a regional vocational training school, the establishment of training and career counseling programs for Inuit, and the preferential use of Inuit workers and businesses on Hydro-Quebec procurement and construction contracts. The two sides will also discuss an economic development fund for the Inuit of Nunavik, and the monitoring of pollutants, especially mercury that will likely be released into the environment as a result of flooding caused by the project. There is also speculation that a revenue-sharing agreement between Makivik and Hydro-Quebec is on the table.

Eighty percent of the seventy-six delegates at Makivik's annual general meeting in Kuujjuaq in March approved a memorandum of understanding that sets out the items being negotiated by Makivik and Hydro-Quebec. But the approval has been heavily criticized by opponents of the negotiations. They object to the fact that the contents of the memorandum are being kept secret, and they say it was approved unfairly and behind closed doors. The memorandum was only accepted by the Makivik delegates after an intense debate that raged for hours in a hot, airless Kuujjiuaq school gymnasium. It went on until midnight on March 20 and for several more hours the next morning. Reporters were excluded, but through the windows of the gym they could see delegates apparently denouncing the idea of negotiating with Hydro-Quebec, followed by cheering and clapping. The chairman of the assembly, Makivik Vice President Zebedee Nungak, defended the idea of keeping the debate behind closed doors because he said it would allow for a more free and open discussion. He also said it would not be a good idea for Makivik to reveal its negotiating strategy to Hydro-Quebec. At the end of the day, Mary Simon, a member of the Kativik Environmental Quality Commission (an Inuit-controlled body set up under the JBNQA), ended up in a heated discussion with Charlie Watt. The Makivik Executive was also severely criticized by some delegates for beginning negotiations with Hydro-Quebec before seeking their approval.

Sappa Fleming, the Inuit mayor of Kuujjuarapil (also called Wha-pamagoostui, Great Whale River and Poste de la Raleirae), is resolutely opposed to any negotiation between Makivik and Hydro-Quebec. His counter-resolution, which called Makivik to withdraw from all talks on the Great Whale project and to reassess the whole idea of negotiating with Hydro-Quebec, was never discussed at the Makivik meeting. Some delegates said the resolution died without discussion because it hadn't been properly tabled. Others called it a ploy by the Makivik Executive to get its own way. Fleming accuses Watt of not listening to the people of Kuujjuarapik. The soft-spoken mayor says people like Wall are making decisions that will destroy a traditional way of life, and they are doing it from big-city offices a thousand kilometers from Nunavik. The Makivik Executive responded by circulating a memo describing how it had informed Inuit in Nunavik about the issue. The memo cited the mandate Makivik had been given at the previous year's annual meeting to enter into the negotiations with Hydro-Quebec. Those talks in turn led to the memorandum of understanding debated this year. The officers also reminded delegates that Makivik had held four meetings with the Kativik Regional Government as well as a field trip during which the Makivik Executive visited all fourteen Nunaviik communities to discuss the issue.

Makivik's mandate to negotiate is by no means unconditional. Delegates insisted that the Kativik Environmental Quality Commission conduct a proper and complete environmental and social impact assessment of the Great Whale project and that Makivik take proper account of the potential cumulative environmental and social impacts of the project. The resolution also notes that Makivik is opposed to the Quebec government's strategy of dividing its environmental assessment of the project into two parts, one for roads, airstrips and other related infrastructure, and the other for the project itself. But the resolution does not contain any language directly opposing the construction of the Great Whale project.

The approval of negotiations with Hydro-Quebec has pitted Makivik against virtually every other concerned interest group, including other Inuit organizations, the Cree, human rights groups, and high-profile environmental organizations like the National Audubon Society, the Sierra Club, the Northeast

Alliance to Protect James Bay and the James Bay and Northern Quebec Task Force.

A statement issued last November by the Inuit Circumpolar Conference, an international organization representing Inuit in Canada, Alaska, Greenland and, on an ex officio basis the Soviet Union, says:

The proposed Great Whale mega-project raises some of the most important ecological and social questions of our time. Should the project proceed as planned, thousands of square miles of traditional aboriginal territory will be flooded. Hundreds of miles of levees and dikes will be built. Likely impacts include destruction of essential wildlife habitats, marine mammals and migratory birds. Important traplines will be drowned. It is also anticipated that mercury contamination will destroy significant quantities of fish. Contaminated fish will be a serious threat to the health of indigenous peoples who rely heavily on this resource.

And further on: "At stake is more than the integrity of the environment and wildlife in and around Northern Quebec. At stake is also the distinct identity, values and practices of the aboriginal peoples concerned."

Unlike the Inuit, who are divided on the question of whether or not Makivik should negotiate with Hydro-Quebec, the James Bay Cree are unequivocal in their opposition to the Great Whale project. They say no to the project and no to any negotiations with Hydro-Quebec. Bill Namagoose, executive director of the Grand Council of the Crees, says his people will never trade their birthright for money.

The $13-billion Great Whale project will affect more than 4,300 square kilometers of black spruce forest on the eastern coast of Hudson Bay, land the Cree have occupied and used for centuries. The complex will consist of five dams and 133 dikes, and will flood an area the size of Prince Edward Island. One of the five dams to be built is near the mouth of the Great Whale River, where the half-Cree, half-Inuit community of Kuujjuarapik is located. The Cree are also very concerned about a proposed 500-kilometre road to connect the hydro-project, and the town of Kutijjuarapik, with the outside world to the south. Many believe the road will bring a stream of drugs, alcohol and social problems into the region, Cree leaders say there was a big increase in alcohol and drug abuse in the 1970s when a road was built to connect the La Grande project to southern Quebec. Violet Pachanos, chief of Chisasibi, says interdiction became virtually impossible once drug dealers were able to drive in from Val d'Or.

Cree leaders, now looked upon by many as masters of the public relations game, invited American environmentalists to join them at their Grand Council general assembly last year in Kuujjuarapik. Jim Higgins, an environmentalist with the Vermont Coalition to Save James Bay, was one of those who attended. He says more and more Americans are questioning the need to develop Northern Quebec as a source of cheap electricity for the United States. The public relations efforts of the Cree are paying off closer to home as well. Late last year an Angus Reid poll showed that 72 percent of Quebecers object to starting work on any plan of the Great Whale project before environmental assessments have been done.

The Cree are quick to criticize Makivik's position on Great Whale. Last year Grand Chief Matthew Coon Come angrily denounced Makivik, accusing it of refusing to consult its Inuit constituents and displaying a level of arrogance more characteristic of the Quebec government. The Cree say Makivik is practicing corporate government and that Watt is trading away a traditional way of life for a few dollars, money that will never compensate for the environmental and social devastation that will be caused by the Great Whale project. Coon Come says most of the land that will be affected by the project is Cree land, not Inuit, and that is why Makivik is so eager to negotiate with Hydro-Quebec. He believes the main support for negotiation comes from Inuit communities that won't be affected by the development.

Roben Brunelle, Vice-president of Indian and Inuit affairs for Hydro-Quebec, thinks the Cree have a credibility problem of their own. He says the Cree have been awarded $50 million in tendered contracts for work on the existing La Grande project, and he says they can't be very strongly opposed to hydroelectric development if they are willing to work on the project and accept money from Hydro-Quebec. But by accepting work on the La Grande development, the Cree are only benefiting from something [that has been rightfully their resource and from a] decision that at least one of the Cree signatories to the James Bay Agreement says he regrets. If anything, that former decision has strengthened their resolve against the as yet unstarted Great Whale project.

As of mid-August, the Cree were pursuing major litigation files against the proposed Whale project, including two in the Federal Court of Canada, two in Quebec Superior Court, and one each with the National Energy Board and the Access to Information Commission. In one of these cases begun in May 1989 in the Federal Court of Canada, the Cree are seeking an injunction to stop the project. They want the court to rule on their title and jurisdiction over traditional Cree land, on breaches of the James Bay Agreement, and on the responsibility of the federal government to carry out an environmental assessment of the project. Although more than two years old, this proceeding is still considered by lawyers representing the Cree to be at a preliminary stage.

The Cree have refused to participate in any public hearings on the environmental impact of the project as long as it is in two phases, Makivik and the Cree agree on this point and have launched a joint action in Quebec Superior Court in Montreal to force Hydro-Quebec to conduct a single environmental assessment. (Hearings are scheduled for September 16-20.) Notwithstanding the objections of Makivik and the Cree, the Inuit-controlled Kativik Environmental Quality Commission is conducting public consultations, on behalf of Nunavik Inuit, on the project's first phase. The commission has until September 12 to present its findings to Quebec's Environment

Minister. It has assessed Hydro-Quebec's five-volume environmental impact study on infrastructure relating to the Great Whale project and is holding meetings in Nunaviik communities to gauge public reaction to it. This has angered the Cree, several hundred of whom recently prevented Hydro-Quebec officials and members of the Kativik commission from holding a public meeting in Kuujjuarapik.

In August 1990, the National Energy Board (NEB) issued a decision approving the export of electricity under two Hydro-Quebec contracts with American customers: a 450 megawatt deal with Vermont and a 1,000 megawatt agreement with the New York Power Authority. There were conditions attached to the NEB approval, however. They stipulated that any facilities built to generate the electricity for these contracts must undergo federal environmental review. Hydro-Quebec and the Quebec government appealed the ruling on two points. They claimed the electricity being exported would come from Quebec's existing supply, and they felt the NEB was acting beyond its mandate in addressing environmental issues other than those relating to the actual export of the power. On July 9 of this year the Federal Court agreed with Quebec's position and ruled that the conditions must be dropped. At the time this article was written, the Cree had not yet decided whether they would appeal this decision to the Supreme Court of Canada. Delays caused by these legal wranglings could easily play havoc with Hydro-Quebec's schedule for Great Whale, which calls for electricity exports to begin in 1996.

Charlie Watt thinks Cree opposition to the Great Whale project is a red herring. The wily Liberal senator has gone so far as to suggest that they have adopted their hard-line approach as a tactic to improve their bargaining position with Hydro-Quebec. And Watt is equally cynical about Sappa Fleming and other dissident Inuit leaders, questioning whether they really represent their communities. He points out that delegates to this year's Makivik general assembly re-elected him for another three-year term with a healthy majority, effectively endorsing his views. He won more than twice the combined vote of his two opponents and was victorious in Kuujjuarapik. Many delegates said they support him because he has a clear position and a plan of action, unlike others who just want to stop talking with Hydro-Quebec.

Watt has promised to express the concerns of the Hudson Bay communities in negotiations with Hydro-Quebec. He notes that the negotiating committee includes four members from Kuujjuarapik and insists that Makivik will not sign a deal with Hydro-Quebec unless the power utility meets the conditions set out in the memorandum of understanding. This will have to be taken on faith, however, because a provision of the memorandum bars either Makivik or Hydro-Quebec from releasing information about an agreement without the consent of both parties. Any final agreement between Makivik and Hydro-Quebec must be ratified by a vote of the Inuit of Nunavik, but Makivik's critics believe the ratification will be rammed through in the same manner as the memorandum of understanding that was passed at their general assembly.

Watt's real agenda is the lining of Makivik pockets for the benefit of its elite, his critics say. Their fears were hardly allayed by the revelation that Hydro-Quebec has agreed to pay Makivik up to $1.5 million in compensation for expenses incurred in the negotiations. Of this total, more than half a million dollars will be used to pay the salaries of Makivik's negotiators and consultants: another $544,000 will pay for their transportation, lodging and food. But the negotiations are important to Nunavik Inuit, says Watt, who sees Makivik as the engine powering the Inuit drive for economic and political self-sufficiency.

Makivik is one of the wealthiest native organizations in the country, with a net worth of about $150 million. It owns a string of businesses, including First Air, a regional commercial airline with scheduled flights between Boston, major cities in eastern Canada and points across the Arctic. Apparently Watt doesn't want to stop there; recently he has been eyeing the Montreal-based Canada Steamship Lines.

Negotiations with Hydro-Quebec over compensation for the Great Whale project are complicated somewhat by other negotiations between the Inuit and the Province of Quebec. Talks aimed at the creation of a new Inuit self-government body in Nunavik are moving forward. On June 27, Inuit and Quebec government negotiators signed a framework agreement that will eventually lead to an autonomous governance structure in the region. (In that agreement, Inuit negotiators displayed a conciliatory attitude different from that of many southern Indian groups. They agreed, for example, to the principle that their new government's powers may be delegated to them by the province, rather than insisting on an inherent right to self-government.) Watt argues that new powers will be weakened if the Inuit can't afford to pay for them. Without money to pay for programs, Watt says, the Inuit of Nunavik would no be no more than a bunch of native people on our knees waiting for the next government handout. He says Makivik is trying to ensure that Nunavik Inuit will be able to afford to set up their own justice system, a health and social service system, and a marine infrastructure program. He also wants control over federal manpower transfers.

Senator Watt is not the only politician who has made the connection between hydro-electric power, economic power and political power. Quebec Premier Robert Bourassa sees the Great Whale project as an important step in achieving economic independence for his province. Bourassa wants to convince his American customers that hydro-electric power is a clean, cost-effective alternative to nuclear generators and the burning of fossil fuels. Hydro-Quebec is using a subtle campaign to support this image in the U.S. The utility is holding backroom meetings with customers such as Vermont Senator Jim Jeffords, who has been wined and dined by Hydro-Quebec development. Hydro-Quebec has also taken out advertisements in U.S. publications. One ad, headlined A Message to Our

Vermont Friends from Hydro-Quebec refers to the fact that Quebec has been selling hydro-electric power to Vermont for decades, something Hydro calls symbolic of the strong cultural and economic bonds between our people. It refers to hydro-electric power as a gift from nature, and says the JBNQA and other accords recognize the need to protect the native culture and way of life.

According to Vermont environmentalist Jim Higgins, Hydro-Quebec's tactics are a major problem for opponents of the Great Whale project. He and his allies have launched major publicity campaigns of their own to convince U.S. voters and politicians that hydro-electricity is not a clean alternative source of power. The ads also stress the social impacts of such development. Campaigns by environmentalists and the Cree, like last year's canoe trip into New York City, seem to be changing public opinion in their favor south of the border. This August, New York City mayor David Dinkins expressed concern about native rights and the environment of Northern Quebec, and proposed that contracts with Hydro-Quebec be delayed. New York State governor Mario Cuomo has said the contracts are in jeopardy and could be cancelled altogether.

While Kuujjuarapik mayor Sappa Fleming may not like the fact that decisions affecting the people of Arctic Quebec are being made by Makivik executives in offices in Montreal, his campaign against the Great Whale project may be given its greatest boost yet by decisions made even further from Nunaviki—in boardrooms and legislatures in Vermont, New York and Washington. If contracts between the Americans and Hydro-Quebec are rescinded, and the Great Whale project is cancelled, the environment of that part of Arctic Quebec may yet be saved. What would such a future hold for Charlie Watt, Makivik Corporation and the Inuit of Nunavik? That depends on who you ask.

Stephen Puddicombe is a CBC radio reporter based in Iqaluit

Report 4. Rupert River Surrendered, Ottertooth

3/12/2003
www.ottertooth.com/Reports/Rupert/News/rupertsurrender.htm
Environmental assessment a "waste of time," says environment group,

Rupert Reverence "agrees with the general directorship of Hydro-Quebec on at least one point: the environmental-impact evaluation process is a waste of time and a waste of public money. For different reasons, of course."

"We have good reasons to doubt the worth of all this process. Remember that no hydro-electric project has ever been stopped in Quebec by the public consultation process. Also remember that the environmental evaluation process provided for in the James Bay Agreement only provides recommendations." The Minister of the Environment—and the National Assembly—are in no way bound by these recommendations when a decision is to be made concerning the realization or not of Hydro-Quebec's projects. Already, by a clause in the Cree-Quebec Agreement, the Grand Council of the Cree has consented not to publicly oppose the undertaking of the projects. The Quebec government gains important sums in revenue from the sale of hydroelectricity outside Quebec. Smaller scale projects (the Hertel-des Cantons line project, for example) have already been approved by the National Assembly despite unfavorable public opinion and court judgments.

Exercises: Hydro-Quebec

Exercise 1. General questions

- Does it really seem that any significant development of the environment or generation of power is going to negatively impact one or another group? If so, how do we decide which? What do you think could be done about it?
- How would it be possible to discuss a trade off or common measure between a groups' ways of life and economic benefit?
- Without falling victim to the danger of losing all your principles by compromising, is there no way to avoid dissolving the dualistic thinking that lies behind the opposition of the categories of environmental protection and economic development?
- How does the problem of distributive justice play out in the Hydro-Quebec case?
- How wide is the sphere of responsibility in this case? Do we need to include the rights of and duties to Canadians only? North Americas? A Global population?
- Do you believe that there is any way in our current culture to seriously consider whether it makes sense to consider the rights of the natural environment, and not only those of humans?

Exercise 2. Hydro-Quebec Case Disposition

The following exercise can be done in conjunction with principles and rules of chapter 3. The basic exercise should be done after reading reports 1-4 above, but *definitely before reading* Report 5 below (*Environment News Service*, February 5, 2002, "Cree Approve New Agreement with Quebec").

Though this exercise can be done alone, it is much more interesting and generative of insights if a group or class divides up to assume the various roles. That way, one or more people can think through the issue from a particular perspective and work out which principles and rules would apply in regard to how they would be treated under various scenarios. Work out the details of the situation and the twists and turns of the decision making required for you to make a recommendation as to what should be done.

Read reports 1–4 (but not 5) and answer the following:

1) Whose Interests are Involved (and What are They)?
Identify all of the involved parties, and the arguments and evidence (both explicit and implicit) about how their well-being would be impacted under the most likely major scenairo(s). In the Hydro-Quebec case, the parties would involve at least:

- Premier Robert Bourassa and the government
- Hydro-Quebec as a corporation
- The James Bay Cree (with Grand Chief Ted Moses)
- Makivik
- Waskaganith Band (Chief Billy Dismond)
- Samultapratic-Chisasibi Band
- The Inuit of northern Quebec
- Northeastern States and residents who would receive power
- Environmental groups in Canada and United States (e.g., Audubon Society)
- The fish, birds, mammals of the region?
- The environment itself?

2) What Values, Principles, Rules, and Codes are the Most Relevant to the Case?
Be sure to make clear which apply and how, given the details of the case. This needs to be done for all of the involved parties. Try to be explicit about how definitions and distinctions, assumptions and implications, and the actual details of the case bear on the matter.

3) What do You Recommend as the Course of Action to be Taken?
This does not ask for something simple, such as Just have everybody vote to build the dam or not. It asks for a measured response about what to do, given all the possibilities. Here, at least keep notes on the alternatives you consider, but certainly be clear and precise about your decision-recommendation.

4) What are the Main Considerations in Favor of Your Position?
Explicitly work out and present, for each of the main considerations, how your position is justified. Be explicit in presenting reasons, arguments, empirical features or evidence, principles, rules, and so on, both abstract and from the details of the case, to support your decision.

5) What are the Main Considerations Against Your Recommendation? How or Why are they Outweighed or Overcome?

Explicitly work out each of the main considerations that need to be taken into account and that indicate that your recommendation is not justified or that it is inadequate. Be explicit in presenting reasons, arguments, empirical features or evidence, principles, rules, and so on, to show that these considerations are finally overcome in your decision.

Now that you have finished the above portion of the exercises, you might read report 5 below to consider what happened next. The reason we suggested not reading report 5 before this point is because of the common mistaken assumption that if we had more facts we would know what the right answer would be to an environmental dilemma. But, it turns out that all we learn is what a next stage outcome appeared to be, which is not at all the same as finding out what might be better or worse. Consider what knowing a next stage in a dilemma means to your understanding and judgment in light of what was discussed in chapters 4 and 5 about the relevance of consequences for the merit of a particular decision (a point contested by Utilitarianism which is strongly consequentialist, and deontology, which is not, and also by natural law). And, remember, knowing what is in one more report does not settle whether that specific consequence is good or bad. Surely that remains a matter of contention among the differing parties.

Report 5. Environment News Service, February 5, 2002
3/12/2003 <http://forests.org/articles/reader.asp?linkid=7338

"Cree Approve New Agreement with Quebec"

NEMASKA, Quebec, Canada, February 5, 2002 (ENS) - In secret ballot referendums held among the Cree which ended Sunday, close to 70 percent voted to approve an Agreement in Principle establishing a new relationship between the government of Quebec and The James Bay Crees. The agreement will allow hydropower and forestry development that had been blocked by disputes between the indigenous people and the provincial government.

"This is an historic moment for the Crees," said Grand Chief Ted Moses. "We will build our communities, find and create employment opportunities for the Crees in the development of the territory and we will build our Nation."

"This is an agreement to implement Quebec's obligations under section 28 of the [1975] James Bay and Northern Quebec Agreement while at the same time it preserves and increases the Cree rights in the agreement. It is an agreement that vindicates the long Cree campaign since 1975 to have our rights respected," Chief Moses said.

The agreement includes cash payments to the Cree of C$24 million in 2002, C$46 million the following year, then C$70 million a year for 48 years. The Cree also get more control over their community and economy, more power over logging and more Hydro-Quebec jobs.

"We will receive from Quebec payments in order for us to properly carry out these responsibilities in accordance with priorities and means which we, the Cree, deem appropriate for our own development," said Chief Moses when the Agreement in Principle was signed last October.

In return, the Cree have promised to drop C$3.6 billion in environmental law-suits against the government.

The Cree also agreed to accept hydropower installations along the Eastman River and Rupert River, subject to environmental approval.

The agreement will allow Hydro-Quebec to build its planned C$3.8-billion Eastmain and Rupert hydroelectric projects, part of the controversial James Bay power development plan. The projects will generate 1,200 megawatts of electricity when they are completed in 10 years.

The Cree position concerning hydropower has changed since the 1990s when a Cree campaign managed to keep the province of Quebec from building the Great Whale River hydro-electric project as the second phase of its plan, first announced in 1971, to dam and divert almost every major river running into James and Hudson Bays.

That effort by the Cree included an eight million dollar lawsuit and an information campaign aimed at power customers in New England [that also was spread by the media to neighboring states].

The traditional territory of the James Bay Cree Nation is in boreal, sub-arctic Canada. It has been adversely affected by hydroelectric mega-projects involving river diversions and river basin reengineering since the 1970s, according to the Cree submission to the World Commission on Dams in November 2000. [This information also was disseminated by the tribal leaders.]

"We have been dispossessed, displaced and environmentally, culturally, economically and socially devastated by large hydro-development projects, initiated and built in our traditional lands by the state-owned electricity corporations Hydro-Quebec and Manitoba Hydro respectively, against our wishes and without our consent," the Cree said.

The governments of Canada, Quebec and Manitoba "have benefited from over 20 years of multi-billion dollar revenues at our expense," the Cree said, and they have not "adequately mitigated, remediated or compensated us as peoples for the profound and ongoing injuries and losses we have suffered."

"Deprived of adequate lands and resources, we now endure mass poverty and unemployment, ill health including epidemics of infectious disease and suicide, and crises of hopelessness and despair," they said.

This new agreement offers hope for a new relationship between the province of Quebec and the Cree Nation, said Chief Moses.

The agreement settles forestry disputes between Quebec and the Cree. The Quebec forestry regime will apply in Northern Quebec, but major adaptations will be made to this regime to ensure the protection of the Cree traditional way of life.

A joint Cree-Quebec Forestry Board will review forestry regulations and forestry plans for Cree territory and provide recommendations to conciliate forestry activities with the Cree traditional uses of the territory and the protection of the natural environment. "We will also be closely involved in all aspects of forestry planning and management through meaningful and results-oriented consultation processes at the community level," Chief Moses said.

No other agreement entered into between the Crees and any government has been subjected to referendum processes involving the Cree Nation as a whole.

The whole process involved two tours of the communities by the Cree leaders during which the people debated the issues more than at any time in recent Cree history. At the end of this, the Cree leadership listened to the demands of the Cree people and sought political confirmation through referendum processes of the decision to proceed or not with this new agreement.

"A substantial portion of the Cree People have obviously supported and endorsed the position taken by the majority of their leaders in favor of the new agreement," Chief Moses said Sunday.

Chief Moses and Quebec Premier Bernard Landry are to meet Thursday for a formal signing. The pact is based on an agreement in principle reached last October 23.

Exercise 3—Native American Views on Hydro-Projects

Compare the views of other native peoples on hydroelectric power projects and dams with those covered in the Hydro-Quebec case by reading James W. Ransom's essay, "The Waters," in Haudenosaunee [Six Nations-Iroquois] Environmental Task Force, *Words That Come Before All Else: Environmental Philosophies of the Haudenosaunee*, 1995, 25–43.

Case 4. Rincon Center, San Francisco

Case Materials:
- ❏   Description of project, players and their roles, and major events.
- ❏   6 Exercises

The project story is drawn from Douglas Frantz, *From the Ground Up: The Business of Building in the Age of Money* (1991); all page references are to that book.

Description of the Project

Rincon Center is a San Francisco mixed-use project (apartments, offices, shops, restaurants), built from 1984-89, two blocks from the Ferry Terminal. It was developed as part of the then-hot real estate development South of Market.

The project incorporates and somewhat preserves a historic older five-story building that had been a post office, utilizing its refurbished lobby and twenty-seven restored murals (and receiving substantial tax credits for doing so).

The major form for the Center is a tower, with retail and restaurants, six stories of office space, and twenty-four stories of residential (320 rentals, including some very expensive penthouse units). The centerpiece and unifying element was to be a dramatic atrium, with an eighty-five-foot waterfall, to be added with significant structural modifications.

The Major Players and their Basic Relations are:
- ❏   *Michael Blumenthal*, developer-speculator, overextended financially (p. 21), who takes on two partners
- ❏   *1. Poo Quong Chin*, president of Chin and Hensolt Engineering (structural engineers), thus part owner and structural engineer
- ❏   *2. Ron Tutor*, president of Tutor-Saliba Corporation, a major construction and engineering firm-contractor, thus also an owner-partner
- ❏   *Randy Verrue*, western division manager of Perini Land and Develop ment Co. & Construction (pp. 12, 84), who said: "The developer's job is to give direction to the architect. . . . We give the project as much definition as we can and then have the creative geniuses go to work" (p. 69).

Given the new reality of architect as showman (p. 34), Verrue rejected the design firms of SOM, which wanted too much control (pp. 36–7) and HOK, because of an unresolved legal issue involving that firm, Pirini, and Alemeda County (p. 38). Instead *Verrue* hires:

❑   *Scott Johnson* as chief architect. Johnson, a graduate of Harvard's GSD
      (Graduate School of Design) and now heading the firm of William
      Pereira Associates (which earlier had done the bold Transamerica
      building in San Francisco), says of himself: I am an esthete (70). *John-
      son* brings from his firm:
❑   *Edmund Einy, Craig Jameson,* and *Chuck Grein.*
❑   *Jay Mancini, who* later replaces Verrue as the lead developer's repre-
      sentative on the project (73).
❑   *Harry Topping,* an MBA with degrees in architecture and architecture
      history (pp. 96–7), hired by Mancini as an assistant.
❑   *Dennis Oh,* an engineer from Chin & Hensolt (p. 88). (Refer back to
❑   *Poo Quong Chin,* above.)
❑   *Bob Mayer,* a former architect with an MBA from Stanford and a vice-
      president with Citibank, the *project's financier,* along with
      Perini Land.

Some of the Major Events

Johnson is unhappy that the Planning Commission decides that the two towers
planned for Rincon Center must have identical tops—which he feels is improper
because it is stipulated by the non-architectural commission president, overrid-
ing his design and judgment on the matter—also emphasizing that the final decisions were not to be his (pp. 104–105).

Johnson considers himself aligned with the artistic rather than engineering
dimension of the profession:

> Architecture is for me an art. It has more to do with art than with physics or me-
> chanical engineering. Often architects with this philosophy are put down by com-
> petitors as just artists. Prospective clients are warned that the artists can't create truly
> lasting, functional buildings, that they are too self-indulgent and unable to design a
> workable structure. That is nonsense. The mind is not divisive. You need to know
> material to know what it can do. In a sense, an artist must be more knowledgeable
> about mechanics and materials because he is testing them, pushing them to their lim-
> its, creating new and revolutionary designs, rather than relying on what has been ac-
> complished a hundred times before by the cookie cutter school of architecture. (pp.
> 50–51)

To stay on schedule, the project was fast-tracked, and to stay on their tight
budget Ron Tutor intended to save $5 million or more by building the new tow-
ers out of concrete (pp. 93) [for details on this critical issue of the use of concrete and skyscrapers, pp. 93–95—see below]. At a meeting, we are told: He assumed the structure would be concrete. After all, he was an owner in addition to
being the general contractor. And Tutor was a concrete man, so he also would
provide the concrete work for Rincon Center. But the meeting adjourned without
a final decision (p. 95).

Mancini knew that Randy Verrue dearly loved the elegance of Citicorp Center, its forty-one stories wrapped in a skin of glass and creamy white pre-cast concrete, with sleek corners. Large surfaces of the new building and its towers were to be covered with pre-cast concrete panels, and Verrue had often said he would like to replicate the color of Citicorp Center. Standard non-premium concrete has gray cement in it, so its color is gray and often less uniform, panel to panel. To achieve the white that Verrue wanted, white cement would have to be added to the concrete mix at a cost of $200,000 or more. Tutor proposed a major saving by not only eliminating the white but by replacing the pre-cast concrete with less expensive, thin, concretelike panels (called GFRC—gypsum fiber reinforced concrete) on the exterior cladding. He did not put a figure on the switch, but it probably would cut half a million or more. (p. 150).

Because the atrium lobby needed to be an exciting attraction (p. 77), and the developer's attitude was the bigger the better (p. 79); Johnson hired Dianna Wong as a senior designer to work on the atrium (p. 79); they shared the idea of strong vertical walls and extensive use of glass. (p. 80) with a patterned granite floor (p. 82). Mancini wanted a water fountain in the center of the atrium to focus attention.

In early 1986, the focus of Scott Johnson's frustrations on Rincon was the atrium. Jay Mancini and Harry Topping were dissatisfied with his design and with Halcyon's plans for the retail layout. [To get another opinion, they replaced Halcyon with] Bob Carey, the president of Urban Centre Developments, a prosperous retail consulting firm across the bay in Oakland . . . Carey had recently finished plans aimed at enlivening the retail space at Rockefeller Center, a credential that Mancini found particularly impressive. . . .

Unlike Mancini, Scott Johnson was not particularly impressed with Carey or his background. . . . Mancini had long objected to the modern look of the atrium. . . . He felt Johnson's design was too cold. . . . Mancini said to Topping one day after a trip to Los Angeles, "The metal and glass might go well in San Diego, but it would be a bust in San Francisco" . . . In part, the final shape of the atrium at Rincon Center was the result of a market study [which] predicted that the shortage of retail space would increase sharply over the next fifteen years . . . Scott Johnson distains the use of the word compromise in describing the circumstances he faced in designing the atrium. "To most people, in an artistic way, compromise is de facto a negative term," he says. "I think, for complex projects in cities today, the design process has to accommodate participation." His job, as he perceives it, is to listen to the client (and, in other instances, to public agencies) and try to allow his architecture to grow out of their needs while still retaining the qualities he believes are essential to good design and function. So when Carey's new ideas for the atrium [replacing his interior storefronts with wooden ones] were adopted by Mancini and Topping, Johnson had figured that he had to listen carefully and make use of them.

The most difficult change for him to make was eliminating the glass curtain wall, which he thought brought zest and excitement to the atrium. [To do so would respond to Mancini's desire to replace it with] stone to evoke the feeling he'd had from looking at pictures of shopping arcades in Europe. [When] it became clear that the budget had no room for material that expensive, Johnson came up with the idea of substituting panels of gypsum board, which would be heavily rusticated and painted to give the illusion of depth and richness. . . . Mancini and Topping both reacted positively to the changes [and to Johnson's idea] of an illuminated water fountain in the center of the atrium]. For Johnson, the Rincon atrium perfectly fitted his definition of what a contemporary architect does. The world no longer was a place where an architect could design a building in the solitude of his studio and impose it on the public or the owner. . . . So then, the practice of designing a building to respond to the broad demand of its owners need not seem extraordinary. The trick in the case of a project as complicated as Rincon, a project with as many influences as Rincon, was finding a way of doing so that retained, or even enhanced, the elegance and usefulness of Scott Johnson's original conception . . .

During excavation, it became clear that the seemingly minor soil movements on the site could not easily be controlled when within three weeks the wooden sheeting lining the excavation had been pushed in about five inches from the edges of the pits. The hole was slowly collapsing. So the work of soil engineer, Mike Majchrzak, was supplemented with more focal attention from structural engineers.

The entire foundation structure for the new building had to be redesigned to incorporate stronger elements and more concrete than originally planned. Costs were mounting. . . . Mancini predicted that the failure of the shoring and related problems would add $6 million or more to the final cost of the project. (pp. 149–93)

→ Note, we will eventually return to the issue of concrete, as another dimension with complex ramifications.

Design disputes continued:

one such was over the material that would be used for the storefronts in the atrium. This long-standing dispute centered on Scott Johnson's plan for metal and glass facades; Jay Mancini had favored wood all along. Now, in the summer of 1987, Richard Altoona, another consultant hired by Mancini, had sided with Bob Carey, both agreeing with Mancini that at least half of the storefronts should be done in wood to create the rich atmosphere the developers wanted. Mancini finally selected solid cherry, [which] indeed gave a rich look, but was also an expensive one, which added to the bulging budget . . . Another design dispute had concerned the atrium floor. Randy Verrue had wanted granite, but Mancini had convinced him that marble was the only material that would make it look right. . . . Verrue had agreed to marble, but the strained construction budget would not handle the cost. Instead, they had decided to use a less expensive agglomerate of crushed marble. (pp. 222, 229)

The atrium walls "evoke the warmth and grandeur of sandstone, but that is one of many illusions necessitated by budget limitations on Rincon Center. The atrium walls are gypsum board, also known as drywall, that have been artfully painted and cut to look like limestone. Similarly, some of the round columns defining the eating area in the atrium appear to be red granite but are merely hollow columns with a faux finish applied by a team of painters. Small screened openings in their bases help ventilate the atrium" (p. 8).

Decisions Regarding use of Concrete

Remember, in order to stay on schedule on a project that was fast-tracked, and to stay on its tight budget, Ron Tutor intended to "save $5 million or more by building the new towers out of concrete" (p. 93). "He assumed the structure would be concrete. After all, he was an owner in addition to being the general contractor. And Tutor was a concrete man, so he also would provide the concrete work for Rincon Center. But the meeting adjourned without a final decision" (p. 95; for details on concrete and skyscrapers, see pp. 93–5).

Though most skyscrapers are built with steel H-beams, steel girders welded to them as the building rises, they also can be constructed with concrete structural elements. Concrete has the advantage of having a high compression strength, that is of being able to stand up to the compression resulting from the massive weight of the building's materials (concrete actually has greater compression strength than steel, but is substantially heavier). On the other hand, steel not only has good compression strength, but "a higher tension strength than concrete"— the ability to resist the stress from a building's normal movement in the wind. To compensate for its innate rigidity, concrete is reinforced; that is, steel bars (rebar) are placed inside the concrete elements in order to provide a greater amount of elasticity (more than adequate, for example, for a seventy-story building). Concrete also is substantially less expensive than steel, which is why it is used in highways, bridges, and sports stadiums, though the more rebar needed, the more expensive the approach (1991, pp. 93–5).

In 1985, Harry Topping, Mancini, Randy Verrue, Dennis Oh, and Ron Tutor were discussing construction material. "Some of the engineering experts in Perini Corporation's San Francisco construction office favored steel for Rincon. They had worked with it more often and felt it was more predictable. But Tutor was insisting on concrete and, since he was a partner and not just the contractor, and since the project was being led by the firm's development arm, the engineers never challenged Tutor." Mancini and Verrue did raise the issue, and though "Dennis Oh had reservations, he kept them to himself because he assumed that Tutor knew what he was talking about. Only Topping, not yet on the job, pushed the issue"—to all of whom Tutor more than vigorously insisted on concrete. Rather than postpone the decision until an "outside engineering firm could compare the cost and speed of steel with concrete," which "would have taken two or three weeks and cost $10,000 while Rincon was on a tight budget and a fast track" (missing the planned-on "deadline would cost a couple of million dollars because the tax credit (for the historic preservation of the old post office) was being cut from 25 percent to 20 percent. . . . Besides, nobody really wanted to make Ron Tutor angry" (pp. 95–7). (Verrue came to regret the choice.)

"In the summer of 1985, a geotechnical engineer named Michael Praszker had been hired to conduct a series of tests aimed at determining whether the pilings and soil would sustain the weight. . . . The three strength tests resulted in charts that demonstrated that pilings were capable of withstanding significant additional weight" (pp. 137–39).

As the building changed, "more walls would be strengthened (by applying another four to six inches of concrete, sprayed on through a pressurized system called "shot-crete," and the new concrete would be tied into the old walls using steel rebar) and more columns would receive steel cladding" (p. 141). But the engineers from Chin and Hensolt wanted to build fourteen new concrete walls to make up for the weakness in the core of the building caused by the removing of beams [to accommodate the enlarged empty atrium space, opened up at the top for a skylight], and that was going to cost more. The proposed walls were called shear walls. Shear is a destructive force that results from lateral movement; as its name suggests, it is the tendency for material to split (or shear) apart. . . . Chen and Hensolt had written a letter to Mancini pointing out the need for new walls [reinforced by] Dennis Oh, the project manager for Chen and Hensolt . . .—the additional costs were $276,000."

The concrete was being poured for the columns, beams, floors—"Ron Tutor had promised the developers that he could complete two floors a week, right up to the top of the towers. In Tutor's experience, this did not seem to be an unreasonable timetable." As often happens in innovative, complex projects "when it came time to transfer the theory to the practice, delays were considerable and unexpected by the general contractor": "it wasn't long until [Tutor's figures] had been reversed and he was completing one floor every two weeks. Delays were not the only problem. The building was requiring more concrete than Tutor had expected" (pp. 214–18).

"A skeptic about concrete from the start, Harry Topping believed that the delays were inevitable because it was such a "low-tech" construction method. . . . Topping and Mancini did not have even a glimmer of how far out of line costs were getting on the project at this point because there was no one really keeping an eye on day-to-day expenditures . . . Rincon's developers were relying on Ron Tutor to keep costs down, since he was not only the general contractor but a part owner. It had seemed like a good idea at the time" (p. 219). Verrue and Mancini figured that since "here our partners were the structural engineer and the contractor," we presumed that Chin and Tutor "were going to have a sharp eye on costs" (p. 219). "The final cost of the construction . . . had been set at $63.8 million . . . Tutor's last estimate of the construction costs had come in at $65 million" (p. 220). "If the concrete money ran out before the work was done, Bob Mayer envisioned a major fight between the developers and Tutor. At that point, the people with the most financial risk would be Citibank, [which] was funding the construction along with a million a month out of Perini's pocket" (p. 221) . . . "Each month, as the concrete [cash] draw grew and the building did not keep pace, Mayer raised the issue with Tutor. Each time he was told not to worry. The columns and girders get narrower as the building goes up because there is less weight to support, the contractor said, so we will be using less concrete" (p. 221).

A former architect with an MBA from Stanford, Bob Mayer, the vice president with Citibank working with the developers, "did not like the use of concrete as the main construction material. He had spent long enough as an architect to suspect that concrete was not right for the project. He felt that it would be too slow and possibly too costly. But Verrue had assured him that Tutor had promised to bring the building in on time and under budget. And Perini's track record was indeed reassuring to Mayer. The company had never gone seriously over budget on any project Citibank had financed. Mayer figured they know what they were doing when it came to choosing the building material and estimating the costs." (p. 118)

When "the regular monthly meeting for Rincon Center at Citibank was held on December 2, Ron Tutor wanted more money for concrete and rebar. If his request was approved, 90 percent of the two budgets would be spent. Yet Ben Wang had told Bob Mayer that the towers were only up ten stories. Wang's estimate was that the job was only 50 percent complete, so far as the concrete and rebar were concerned. So Mayer refused to loan the project more money for concrete. His intent never was to stop the project. . . . But he needed to draw attention to the problem with the concrete and rebar so that a solution would be devised. The earlier assurances from the developers had not been sufficient, as the current problems proved. . . . A few days after Mayer's drastic action, Tutor submitted a huge change order to Randy Verrue." He wanted $3 million more for the concrete and rebar budgets. He blamed the overruns on changes in the design of the building since the GMP had been signed and on over-designing in the concrete columns and girders. None of it was his fault, Tutor said, so he would not pay the costs.

Verrue faced a crisis. Approve the change order and he would have to persuade Mayer to unfreeze the concrete budget or Perini would foot the bill for the extra costs. Demand that Tutor honor the GMP and the contractor could shut the job down and mothball the project until a court settled the dispute (p. 236). . . . In the meantime, whether awaiting a court decision or getting out new bids, Perini would still face interest costs in excess of $40,000 a day. . . . "No matter what the contract says, the practical matter is that you don't stop construction," said Verrue (p. 237). The Perini executives back in Framingham agreed with Verrue: Tom Steele said later: . . . "You have to make a decision about what is the most practical way to proceed with respect to your dispute with the contractor. . . . We felt that the most rational economic decision was to get the project done." . . . Practical considerations almost always override legal ones (p. 237).

The contract with Tutor would be renegotiated and, in the meantime, Citibank agreed to free up additional money so work could continue. In February, Tutor came over to Verrue's office and sat down with Verrue, Mancini, and John Costello. Verrue's assistants were trying to explain the magnitude of the financial problems to him and Tutor kept interrupting to denigrate Costello and Mancini. His language was extremely harsh and personal. While Randy Verrue is tough and frequently uses strong language, he does not swear in public. He refused to sit quietly as Tutor berated his staff, so he stood up at the conference table and said simply and loudly, "This meeting is over." With that, he walked out of the room, followed by the surprised Mancini and Costello. (pp. 237–38).

"The building was beginning to look more like a $74 million job than a $64 million one. After three weeks without a settlement, Verrue decided that they needed a mediator to help resolve the dispute. . . . By the middle of March, a letter of understanding was negotiated that amounted to a cost-plus contract for Tutor-Salbina. The developers would pay the entire cost of construction and Tutor would receive a flat fee—$2 million rather than $2.5 million, to be paid in two $1 million installments, one and two years after the completion of the project (p. 239). The episode contributed to the sense shared by many people associated with the project that Rincon Center's new buildings never should have been built out of concrete. The design demands for a concrete building in a seismic area erased the cost advantages over steel. The complicated nature of the construction slowed a process that was probably never going to go as fast as Ron Tutor had expected. Scott Johnson believed that Tutor had underestimated the complexity and costs because he was unaccustomed to building this sort of premium mixed-use project."

"For all his detractors, there was validity to Tutor's claims. Design changes [including those of upper level apartments] had affected the construction schedule. The ductile-frame system required more concrete and steel rebar than anyone had anticipated. If he was unaccustomed to dealing with a project of this complexity, so too were the architect and the developers." (For even more on concrete see pp. 214–21, 235–36, 252.)

Explicit focus on Who Decides?

Collaboration and final decision by owner(s):
"Mancini liked to compare the decision making on Rincon Center to his days as a liberal arts student at Lawrence College in Appleton, Wisconsin. He described it in terms of an academic exercise in which he listened to the arguments and opinions of Harry Topping, the architects, and the growing ranks of consultants. Then, he said, he would dissect the argument and come up with the right answer. . . . Few others involved in the project were willing to put such a positive gloss on the way decisions were made at Rincon. Scott Johnson, in particular, had grown critical of Mancini's methods. While Johnson applauded group decisions intellectually, he felt strongly that there was not always a "right" decision for every dilemma. . . . "What you do," said Johnson, "is weigh this thing and that thing carefully and apply the best experience and data available. . . . But, in the end you have to trust instinct and talent and art and a little mystery." Mystery eluded Jay Mancini. He saw the building as a product. . . . He was the "captain of the team" and he often compared the job to his days as an officer leading a Marine reconnaissance platoon in Vietnam. [But, the pressures were great: as he said,] "I wasn't able to predict events, much less control them"(pp. 229–31).

Still, as project manager, Jay Mancini offered this assessment: "Its my building. Not [the architect's]. I have to live with it. So, I'll make the final decisions" (p. 267).

Exercises

Exercise 1.

Analyze the situation of the Rincon Center development, trying to be honest about the personality traits and professional roles of the players and at the same time working to see which stereotypes might be revised—candidates for which include owners-developers in relation to the rest of the professional team; the architect in relation to the engineer; the aesthetic and pragmatic dimensions of the architect.

Exercise 2.

Suppose a general agreement develops to set aside the usual relations and contractual approach in order to pragmatically get the project completed. Do you think that this is possible—or could be successful? At what price?

Exercise 3.

Think through these questions concerning conflict of interest. It could be argued that there are conflicts of interest on behalf of Tutor and perhaps others with multiple roles. Try to sort out, Who really is the client? On behalf of whose good are the team obligated to act—all the owners? To whom does the team owe ultimate loyalty? Note that those involved seemed to assume the opposite: not only that there was no conflict of interest, but that the multiple roles would make the project better, more manageable. To what extent did that turn out to be true or false?

Exercise 4.

The Architect's views on aesthetics and the honesty of materials play a role in this case (issues especially connected to the issues raised in chapters 3 and 4, especially the responsibility for veracity-truthfulness). The problems to discuss concern two major worries: failing to see an ethical problem when there is one; imagining there is an ethical problem or dilemma when there is not.

Question: Is the problem of honesty in regard to aesthetics and honesty of materials still relevant today?
In the case of Rincon Center, a series of decisions are made about materials and the way the interior will look. On the one hand, this may be interpreted as a matter of adjusting the vision of the architect with that of the developers (and their consultants) and of dealing with costs. On the other hand, the process and decisions involve situations that historically have been considered ethically important to many architectural traditions: that there needs to be an honesty in use of materials, not deception. Is that set of concerns simply a feature of past architectural cultures and perspectives, so that, if it is no longer operative, there is no ethical problem here at all? Or is the issue a contemporary ethical question (though it may or may not be the case that it appears in the Rincon Center)?

Exercise 5.

In regard to the use of concrete, is there a violation of the responsibility to allow for informed consent in this project? Does Tutor frustrate the requisite respect for autonomy by pushing too hard? In your judgment, is there a problem in regard to not giving truthful information or bullying participants toward a less than free, predetermined answer?

Exercise 6.

At a more complex level: Given the importance of trust, respect, and reputation in a community and clearly in the small world of big building projects, do any of the players significantly fulfill the ethical responsibility to listen, to act so as to prevent problems and do good things without having a crisis to avert. Does anyone rise to the level of virtuous action here?

Exercise 7.

Two analyses incorporate material from Rincon Center in arguing (a) that to avoid injustice when approving design projects we need explicit and pluralistic controls, and (b) to reduce the harmful environmental impact of property development professionals need to be more ethical. Consider what additional perspectives these two studies bring to treatments of decision making, justice, and nonmaleficence: Simon Guy, Environmental Innovation and the Property Business and James Mayo, Justice Issues on Project Approval (http://books.google.com/books/ucpress?vid=ISBN9780520083998.

Case 5.   Proposition 933, State of Washington (2006)

Issues involved:
- ❑ Public-private dichotomy—property rights/takings
- ❑ Individual bundles of values
- ❑ Comparative worldviews
- ❑ Principles and rules

Exercise 1.

Even without the extensive case material, it is useful to debate ethical issues in general.

Consider the following scenario: An individual property owner owns a fifty-acre parcel of riverfront land and wishes to construct a new family home just a few feet from the banks of the river. While large floods are rare on this river, the proposed site for the house falls within the established hundred-year flood zone. Upon requesting a building permit from the county planning office, the property owner is told that she will not be permitted to locate the structure in the flood zone. Although the property owner has sufficient land lying outside the flood zone on which to construct the house, she very much desires the riverfront location because of the view and other recreational amenities offered by the site. In appealing the denial of her building permit, the property owner argues that she and her family understand the risks of living in the floodplain and that the government has no right to prevent her from taking such risks. In short, she accuses the county of being paternalistic, in overruling the personal risk-taking judgments of individuals. (Beatley 1994, 155–56)

What is your position regarding this case? Question: In this case, is the county in fact acting paternalistically?

Exercise 2. An even larger question

Given the effect that many individuals' actions have on others (including indirect impacts such as insurance and tax rates, demand for materials, and so on), what is the proper balance between individual freedom of choice and government restrictions to protect the public from negative effects?

The Case Itself: Initiative 933

Base Information/Case Material

In the fall of 2006, the voters of the State of Washington were asked to decide whether to pass or defeat Ballot Initiative 933, titled Property Fairness Initiative, that, according to one analysis, appear[ed] to be based on a simple premise: If regulations imposed by Washington State or local governments restrict the use or development of private property, the loss of value to the owner should be reflected in a policy of "pay or waive." Government should either compensate the owner for damages or waive the regulation that imposes the restriction. (Northwest Center for Livable Communities 2006, 1). There were various economic and legal arguments for and against passage, but here, of course, we want to focus on the ethical issues.

Environmental Impact:
"The largest single impact of I-933 would be to critical areas that are protected to prevent flooding and protect fish, wildlife and groundwater. In the near-term, I-933 compensation claims on timberland with critical areas could total $3.1 billion and farmland with critical areas could be $3.2 billion" (p. 3).

Political Factors:
"Public opinion surveys and the ability of I-933 advocates to get the measure on the ballot suggests that many citizens support reasonable remedies to help landowners whose property values are affected by regulations. But using a sweeping and overly general approach to help one set of aggrieved people, the initiative would have the unintended consequence of creating another, larger set of aggrieved people.

If land use laws cannot be waived, there would be a newly aggrieved group of non-benefited taxpayers responsible for paying I-933's costs of compensation.

If land use laws were waived, the list of aggrieved people would include property owners suffering a loss of value as possibly undesirable development arrives on neighboring property. It would include communities that see their character and quality of life damaged by unrestricted development. It would also include a large group of land developers with the type of proposals that normally receive routine approval but would now be backlogged by the processing of I-933 compensation claims.

A truly fair remedy would safeguard current values as well as compensate losses created by restrictions. This means protecting property owners against neighboring, inappropriate uses and shielding communities threatened by overdevelopment.

Fairness also means accounting for "windfalls"—the value added by regulation—as well as "wipeouts," or losses from regulation. Failure to make this calculation is one reason huge compensation costs from I-933 could fall on the general taxpayer (pp. 3–4).

["Critical area ordinances required under the Growth Management Act (GMA) are promulgated by each county in five broad categories: fish and wildlife habitat conservation areas, wetlands, geologic hazard areas, aquifer recharge areas" (p. 42; cf. pp. 53-55)] . . .

"Most critical area ordinances adopted under the authority of the Growth Management Act contain a procedure that allows the local government to modify regulations under certain circumstances. Although there is no specific statutory authorization for "reasonable use" regulations, local governments have adopted this procedure to avoid constitutional takings claims. The procedure has not been challenged legally, so there has been no determination whether this practice complies with the GMA.

The intent of reasonable use is to secure some degree of sufficient use for a property owner who has been deprived of all use. As written, the procedure generally allows for the least intrusive uses with the least impact to critical areas. Typically, reasonable-use procedures have been applied only to allow single-family dwellings. Some jurisdictions establish specific maximum sizes for structures (p. 11).

"Land use regulation (i.e. zoning) was first established to protect single-family neighborhoods from incompatible and nuisance uses. These restrictions and controls served to protect health and safety. Over time, land use regulations have broadened in scope. Today, the authority for them often rests more on protecting general welfare than on health and safety. The broadening of authority and the intrusion it creates now imposes what some consider too great a burden on individual landowners. However, I-933 proposes to redress these inequalities in a way that would likely remove the predictability of zoning and could require the return to pre-zoning nuisance laws. Compatibility of use may no longer be determined by general land use regulations" (p. 16).

Also, note the following:

"The final item [of qualified areas of restriction], property line setbacks, illustrates a broadening of land use regulation beyond direct impacts on public health and safety to provide broad "public benefit" by protecting endangered fish and wildlife populations and watersheds from erosion and siltation, preserving open space and rural character, and generally enhancing environmental sustainability.

"A common element in achieving these goals is 'buffering' of farm and resource lands, setting aside part of the land base for economic production. The property rights movement has asked at what point the general public should compensate affected landowners for restrictions that serve a public benefit rather than protect against immediate threats to public health and safety. . . ."

Another "key issue is the role of the local permit process to delay, restrict or prevent landowners from constructing new housing or adding to existing housing and other personal use facilities on their property. This issue has provided vivid anecdotal examples that have been used in campaigns to make the case for property rights reform" (p. 55).

If Washington farm and forest land-owners follow the pattern of Oregon land-owners in response to Oregon Measure 37, we can anticipate significant numbers of requests to change land use designation in order to permit non-farm and non-forest land uses. As discussed above, in Oregon most claims seek to have land rezoned [to urban uses, particularly] for residential development (p. 35; cf. p. 17).

To encourage continued production of agricultural products or timber, lands that are currently used for non-commercial timber production or agriculture are granted lower taxation levels than if they were in urban uses. Washington State allows qualified landowners to enroll in several programs that grant "current-use" taxation status (p. 29).

As basic information, however, analysis revealed that, economically: In the near term, I-933 could cost taxpayers nearly $8 billion—more than $1,000 per resident—to pay expected compensation claims. . . . Virtually every county would likely be faced with claims, yet none have tax revenue source in place for paying them (p. 2).

Legal Factors:

"Though described as establishing a "pay or waive" system, I-933 does not have the power to permit waivers under three of the most relevant state laws—the Growth Management Act, the State Environmental Policy Act, and Shoreline Management Act. As drafted, the Initiative does not legally amend these laws, and the laws do not permit waivers" (p. 2).

The report proposes instead a "Collaborative Process and Individual Equity," including transfer development rights programs (pp. 56–59).

Exercise 3. Whose rights?

Apply what you have learned about untangling the issue of "Who is the client?" to answer the question: How do we sort out which competing rights of which groups have ethical priorities to in regard to property rights? Specifically, how can we find some pattern for weighting or prioritizing people's concerns and rights that might be socially and ethically helpful in this area that is almost perennially a problem?

Exercise 4. In regard to the Ethic of Care

Consider: In contrast to what might be termed the legalistic approach of deontology, utilitarianism, and natural law, all of which emphasize arguments and evidence (clearly a heritage of emphasis on judgment), the ethic of care advocates a different, more holistic approach that focuses attention on the emotional component and our relationships with others, as well as that of cognition. This seems a good match for such emotionally volatile issues as property rights. Explore: How would an ethic of care approach these issues? Remember to take into account the complex relation of justice (thought to be a major dimension, though variously defined, in the property rights debates) and care.

Exercise 5. Ethics Proper Versus Our Bundles of Values and World Views.

In chapter 1 we saw how most of us have a bundle of beliefs, values, and attitudes on which we act in everyday life, without usually undertaking a formal deliberation about a course of action. For example, people commonly cite maxims, such as you are free to do what you want as long as it doesn't hurt anyone.

Similarly, we saw how most of us have a coherent worldview, even if we are not explicitly aware of it, or, even if we are, how we normally operate with it as a tacit basis for value preference and decision making. In contrast, as we have shown, the four major theories involve much more explicit reflection and, often, extensive social dialogue, if not debate. Read and collect accounts in the popular press about legislative property issues of which Proposition 933 is an example. Then, describe and analyze them in terms of whether they are examples of response from the standpoint of personal bundles of beliefs, of a worldview shared with others in the community, or something more like an ethics proper. What is your evaluation of which, if any, of the three approaches makes more of a contribution to a socially useful advance in decision making?

Case 6. HOPE VI

Public Housing and Neighborhood Revitalization

Current public housing policy and the HOPE VI program in particular raise critical ethical issues related to architecture, planning, engineering (social and physical) as well as policies on housing and poverty. Designed to revitalize what the government considers severely distressed public housing, the HOPE VI program (Housing Opportunities for People Everywhere) has demolished tens of thousands of public housing units nation-wide and has rebuilt public housing sites as mixed income communities. HOPE VI is a grant program administered by the U.S. Department of Housing and Urban Development (HUD) that aims to disperse pockets of poverty and transform sites of severely distressed public housing into new mixed-income housing developments. To do this, public housing units are either rehabilitated or demolished, necessitating the relocation of thousands of low-income households across the country (Manzo, Kleit, and Couch, 2008). On these former public housing sites, combinations of market-rate and subsidized housing are erected to accommodate a mix of subsidized renters, subsidized homeowners, and the introduction of market-rate homeowners into previously poverty-concentrated areas. The result is the privatization of a portion of formerly publicly-owned land and the conversion of traditional unit-based subsidies to tenant-based subsidies in privately owned housing stock. Over the first ten years of the program, HOPE VI has relocated 56,221 households nationwide (McCarty, 2005). Relocated households have legal protections under the Uniform Relocation Act (URA)[1] that mandates their receipt of comparable housing. Even if a move off-site is only temporary, residents still must relocate as the current housing is demolished. Given the large-scale relocation of entire communities that HOPE VI redevelopment requires, it is critical to understand the impact of the program on the thousands of poor families that it displaces.

The HOPE VI program has become very controversial. On the one hand, some public housing stock is indeed deteriorating and given the failure to fund a growing backlog of public housing modernization needs, the HOPE VI program offers one of the few funding opportunities for local housing authorities to revitalize their properties. Indeed, the House-passed 2007 funding bill would result in the deepest shortfall in public-housing operating subsidies in more than twenty-five years—these funds enable local housing authorities to maintain developments, pay utility bills and keep rents affordable.[1]

There are many complex ethical issues involved in the HOPE VI program—particularly regarding the displacement of some of the most vulnerable households in the nation. Beliefs about poverty, its sources, and effects (e.g., the contagion effect) and the government's role in the provision of housing are at the core of the controversy around the HOPE VI program in housing-policy circles.

What are the trade-offs in demolishing this public housing versus rehabilitating it? How can housing policies, particularly the funding of modernization and capital improvements, better support strategies that wouldn't require the dismantling of entire communities?

Moreover, there is evidence that nationwide there is a net loss of public housing units through the HOPE VI program. Do we or the government have a moral duty to maintain the same number of housing units? As Susan Popken from the Urban Institute stated before the U.S. Senate in 2007, since the HOPE VI program provides individual Housing Authorities (HA) with considerable latitude in how they carry out the redevelopment, particularly in determining relocation and re-occupancy procedures, there are a number of significant choices and dilemmas that HA staff face when implementing this program. For example, there are dilemmas around the choice of whether to pursue a HOPE VI grant in the first place, as well as how to proceed with the redevelopment and relocation of current residents. Regarding relocation, there are choices that must be made about whether or not to provide one-for-one replacement of public-subsidized housing units on site or elsewhere (a policy once required by HUD at the outset of the program, but no longer required), whether people can stay on-site during the redevelopment, and policies on the process of residents' return to the site (i.e., developing criteria for who can return and under what conditions). Housing Authorities have developed different strategies for all of these issues, and they vary from one HA to another. For example, some may develop a lottery system for returning residents.

Hope VI and Resident Participation.
Other ethical issues arise regarding the participatory dimension of the program. HUD requires that current residents participate in the planning of the redevelopment, in both the development of a new master plan and in discussions of the relocation process. In other words, HUD mandates citizen participation. This is part of a larger trend toward more normative, institutionalized participation noted by Hester (1999) and Francis (1997). Here also we see many different strategies for how to address participation across HOPE VI sites. Some HAs take great pains to foster resident involvement, holding series of public meetings, widely advertising them among residents, providing informational flyers in the languages spoken by residents, even providing food and translators for the meetings. But one must consider the nature of participation in this context.

HUD specifies that the goal of ascertaining the level of participation is to ensure greater accountability and integrity in the provision of assistance, which is indeed laudable. But in operationalizing this goal, participants must meet what HUD calls a threshold requirements in order for a HOPE VI application to be considered for funding.[2] The Housing Authority must also provide plans for continued outreach and involvement. HUD then evaluates the nature, extent, and quality of the outreach and involvement using a rating factor system. A total of three points can be given for resident and community involvement, one point for each of the following three factors: (1) evidence of regular and significant communication with affected residents and members of the surrounding community —including the provision of a forum where residents can contribute recommendations and opinions; (2) a description of the efforts to make available appropriate communications about HOPE VI to residents; and (3) a description of plans to provide affected residents with reasonable training on the principles of development, technical assistance and capacity-building so that residents may participate meaningfully in the development and implementation process (HUD NOFA, October, 2003). HUD also requires that these meetings be ADA accessible, and that daycare, transportation and interpreters be provided where needed.

In another section of the NOFA, which addresses the Suddenness of the approach the Housing Authority applying for a HOPE VI grant can receive points if it has held five or more public planning sessions leading to residence acceptance of the plan. One could see this as a demonstration of the care and effort HUD has put into ensuring that the process is inclusive, and indeed there is a genuine interest among many Housing Authority staff to include residents and have them understand the redevelopment. However, in the context of this point system, participation is demonstrated by signatures on attendance sheets and photos of residents sitting in meetings at the community gymnasium. Much of what constitutes participation is left totally open: What is regular and significant communication? What is reasonable training? This is left to common sense among politicians, policymakers and other government agents. Moreover, what about the experience of the residents? If participation is about empowerment[3] of community members, of claiming a stake in one's life, one's environment, and one's future, is this possible within the context of HOPE VI?

There is a whole host of questions that can be asked here: While participation as a principle is undoubtedly desirable, can it be mandated? What are the implications of mandated participation? Mandated participation seems to defeat the purpose of participation as conceived by radical planners and community organizers decades ago. According to scholars and practitioners who engage in participatory work (Sanoff, Hester, Francis) it is meant, in its most engaged form, to be transformative, aiming for paradigmatic changes in traditional practice by dismantling reliance on the expert exclusively and by exploring the emic perspective.

To be fair, HUD does include the idea of capacity building in its discussion of participation, but this degree of participation arguably extends beyond what HAs are capable of, given the nature and role of this governmental agency as part of the neo-liberal regulatory regime (Peck, 2001; Crump, 2002). Vale (2002) in his work with HOPE VI projects in Boston, has argued that HAs managing HOPE VI projects have taken the simplest interpretation of participation—using much the same design, policy, and management strategies as usual—just add people and stir.

Housing Authorities already do much of the decision making before the public meetings ever take place, and thus the decisions in which the public are involved are not very significant. Moreover, although residents are required to participate, they are not given any third-party rights (their participation does not include any real power, veto or otherwise). This raises the most difficult questions of all: What is the point of participation in HOPE VI? Does it create false hope? Is non-participation worse? Participation is problematic because the bottom line in HOPE VI projects is that residents are displaced, mostly involuntarily, yet their input is sought in the development of a community to which they may not be able to return. Indeed, given that residents housing is being demolished, their willing participation in the redevelopment necessitates their departure.

HOPE VI is confounded by the disenfranchisement of this particularly resident group, the unparalleled level of centralized control that exists in public housing, the stigma of poverty, and a history of overlooking individual human agency among public housing residents (Vale 1997). So it is necessary to interrogate a second dimension of participation—one that includes how residents negotiate different messages about the redevelopment and how they choose to make sense of what an HA tells them. Essentially, these are the negotiated dynamics that involve residents' sense of agency—an active process of bargaining that occurs both within the minds of residents, and between residents and the HA.

Another complication regarding HOPE VI sites is that the redevelopment provides opportunities not only for the provision of new construction not plagued by disrepair, mold/mildew, worn out appliances and materials, but it allows for the development of new open-space plans incorporating more ecologically sound strategies for things like on-site storm-water management, incorporating more native plants or including community gardens on site. In fact, some HOPE VI sites, particularly in the Pacific Northwest, have become national models for incorporating these strategies in the master plan. But can these things be done without the massive demolition of existing housing?

There are also ethical issues raised in the evaluation of HOPE VI projects. HUD requires that the redevelopment of each HOPE VI site be evaluated by an independent entity. Tashiro (2006) points out that the relative power (or lack thereof) of various stakeholders, increased reliance of privatization, and even the nesting of the specifics of Hope VI projects within larger frameworks of insufficient funding for public housing creates a tension between advocacy and evaluation. She argues that to not experience discomfort in this milieu is not only problematic, but perhaps unethical, and that in order to practice ethically we must engage in a critical interrogation of the underlying ideological perspectives and assumptions of the Hope VI program.

Tashiro traces ethical dilemmas to the influence of the political environment, with its devaluation of the concept of public good, and a market ideology that has decreased investment in public housing and increased privatization (profit-based housing) into what she deems should be public services. There are issues regarding turnover of HA staff, changes to their organizational structure, neighborhood context, the diffusion of responsibility that often accompanies the presence of multiple stakeholders (residents, Housing Authorities, developers, city agencies, etc.) that create individual site-based dilemmas that evaluators, and perhaps all parties, face. (Tashiro, 2006).

There are also critical questions about how evaluators position themselves in the larger projects. Whether and how it is possible to remain neutral, and if one feels they cannot be neutral, then how does one decide where their loyalties lie? Evaluators are hired by the Housing Authorities. Does critiquing their strategies or the HOPE VI program in general mean biting the hand that feeds you? How do you navigate a sense of loyalty to the HA that hired you, and the residents with whom you might sympathize or for whom you might wish to advocate, particularly if they do not want to leave?

For some guidance in ethical decision making in this context, Tashiro goes to the American Evaluation Society's guidelines on Responsibilities for General and Public Welfare, which articulates that evaluators have a responsibility for general and public welfare, not only immediate operations and outcomes of the evaluation, but also the broad assumptions, implications, and potential side effects. (American Evaluation Association, 2004, as quoted in Tashiro, 2006). Advocacy is not partisanship.

Addressing the ethics of evaluation, Schwandt (2005) argues that evaluators should examine the implicit and embedded assumptions and values that structure how service providers relate to those whom they serve. Schwandt further asserts that evaluation should engage in moral criticism of underlying principles where warranted.

Exercises. What would you do?

The Hope VI program arises many ethical questions. Consider role playing in this scenario. If you were heading a local Housing Authority and you were faced with a decision to apply for federal funds to revitalize your housing site, would you? Now, put yourself in the place of a resident: you are poor, struggling to make ends meet. You have two kids in the local school. You were recently laid off but you live in public housing so your rent was adjusted to accommodate this. You wake up one day to find a notice under your door that your community is being redeveloped—your housing will be demolished and they want input at the next meeting. Then how would you feel? Finally, imagine you are the architect or landscape architect on the project. Your firm was just hired by the local housing authority to work on the master plan for their new HOPE VI project. You are excited to work for an affordable housing provider. You go to your first community meeting and you are overwhelmed with questions from worried residents. Now how do you feel?

As you can see from this exercise, the project feels very different from the different stakeholders' perspectives, and your choices about what is right might vary in each role.

Notes

1. The Uniform Relocation Assistance and Real Property Acquisition Policies Act of 1970 (URA), as amended, has as a goal the fair and equitable treatment of persons displaced as a direct result of programs or projects undertaken by a Federal agency or with Federal financial assistance . . . to ensure that such persons shall not suffer disproportionate injuries as a result of programs and projects designed for the benefit of the public as a whole (42USC4621). One of the requirements is that the displaced person be able to obtain a comparable replacement dwelling. (42USC4624) See www.access. gpo.gov/uscode/title42/chapter61_subchapterii_.html.

2. On the one hand, this can be seen as a positive commitment of HUD to ensure the consideration and satisfaction of the public housing residents affected by the project, but it also means that HAs must demonstrate plans for participation before it happens. However, participation and people's reactions can be unpredictable. Perhaps more importantly, calling for pre-project plans for participation results in an emphasis on more superficial evidence of participation—numbers of meetings and attendees signatures.

3. Empowerment has become another buzzword—something that elites magnanimously give to those less fortunate. We must continually ask ourselves: What does it actually mean? Through what processes does empowerment happen?

Appendix IV
Theories of Sustainability: Environmental Ethics, Mixed-Communities, and Compassion

Bob Mugerauer

Introduction

If we are going to talk about sustainability, we confront a welter of meanings and contending theories. At the same time, sustainability, however defined, involves issues of moral agents and their responsibilities in regard to fellow humans, other life forms, and the natural environment. Hence, environmental ethics, and issues of competing communities needs also to be considered. As a first step, we need to clarify the terms in which the issue is posed and to try to understand the topography of the basic problems. That is, the necessary beginning is not to explain what environmental ethics would amount to, whether sustainability is possible or not, or how to solve environmental problems through specific sustainable practices. Rather, we need to begin with an intellectual geography so that we can come to an agreement about what is debated or contested and arrive at some shared terms.

Ethics

As a first point, I want to discuss briefly the character of ethics. Ethics is not simply opinion, nor is it purely identical with all possible bases for choices about values. After all, there are many ways to choose what to do in the world. We might have a god who, we believe, tells or shows us directly what to do. Or, we might act in some way that is purely traditional, that we do not think through or necessarily question or challenge. In such cases, we act according to the customs of our cultural environment.

Ethics is different from such practices, however, because ethics amounts to principled judgments and actions. Such heretically justified, legitimized judgment and action is necessary in a pluralistic world because we do not share a belief in one [or any] god or one tradition where that god or set of beliefs and customs would indicate what we all should do. That we do not share a set of religious or political beliefs or a set of values is obvious if we look at our conventions concerning major moral issues today. Is abortion right or wrong? Is homosexuality something that should be socially permitted or socially sanctioned? What shall we do about the relation of the wholeness of the environment and our need for economic growth and development? Clearly we do not have agreement on these issues.

If we cannot agree on these things by virtue of religious or traditional values, then certainly we live in a world where the only possible alternatives are either reasoned judgment, involving discussion and some decision to be enacted or violence and force wielded against each other. Of course in the absence of principled judgment and action, we do become violent toward one another, trying to impose our views about what we find acceptable. The alternative to imposed power is found in the universal human ability to reason, a capacity that enables us to understand reality and to make some decisions about it. For all the cultural, historical, ethnic, and gender differences among us, we nonetheless share a rationality that enables us to give reasons for our positions and thus arrive at grounded decisions.

In ethics, understood as this legitimized series of understandings and judgments, there are four basic principles that are relevant to our discussion of environmental ethics and sustainability. These four principles are agreed upon by many theorists no matter what their particular bent (utilitarians, deontologists, natural law people). So there is good evidence to think that as a result of the discussions and analyses of the last 2500 years, we now at least can have a basically sound justification for what we do if we act in accord with these four principles.

According to the first principle, autonomy, persons have the right to make decisions about their own courses of action, decisions about their own lives. This is, of course, a fundamental principle in ethical thought (and not simply in Western culture): if persons were not seen as being free and able to decide things, able to be responsible for their own actions, then we wouldn't have, or need, an ethics in the first place to guide responsible choices and behavior. The idea of autonomy essentially comes down to respecting another's responsible choices even if we disagree with these.

The second basic principle is beneficence which means that one has an obligation to do good [bene]. One has an obligation to help other people in terms of their fundamental dimensions and needs as embodied, social beings. Closely connected with doing good on behalf of others we find the third principle, non-maleficence: that we shall not do or allow harm to come to others. Maleficence or harm would include a broad spectrum of phenomena, not only obvious bodily or physical harm, but also harm to a person's reputation, property, or liberty. For professionals, such as planners and architects, non-maleficence includes the responsibility to guard against negligence, indifference, and obliviousness to new ideas or information that might result in harm. Thus, we are responsible for keeping up to date on the latest research findings. If you are in an environmental discipline, for instance, you need to stay current with determinations of what is toxic or what is not because a failure to do that could cause or allow harm to those for whom you're responsible. We see the pairing of beneficence and non-maleficence in the Hippocratic Oath, that doctors used to take, which said that doctors would both do good and not allow harm to come to their patients. And the same would hold today as a principled basis for planners' actions towards their clients and the public.

The fourth principle, which is more complex and to which we will return, is justice. Obviously there are many definitions of justice, a problem in itself that we have to face in dealing with our relationships to other members of our society or to other societies, and even to the relationships of different societies to the natural environment. Justice sometimes is defined fairly straightforwardly or intuitively as a sense of what is fair or what is equitable. Alternatively, justice is defined as that to which reasonable, rational people would agree if they had a choice about how their lives would be governed. Here, without debating all the alternatives or the fine points, we at least can see that the fundamental principle is that individuals, social sub-groups, and whole societies that have the right to self-determination--because they are autonomous—also are due justice (the right not to be treated unfairly, unless they should freely agree to it).

Sustainability

To move on, sustainability obviously is a vague term. One of the problems and the reason for a phrase I used in the introduction, "whether we're sustaining the unsustainable," is that sustainability already has become a buzz word and a marketing tool through which we promote our particular projects. Here sustainability becomes part of an image to generate and manipulate our production and consumption patterns. Such use of the concept and image of sustainability may be a mere posturing to persuade people to become sympathetic, to buy a product, to assume that the manufacturer or sponsor using the word "sustainability" is somehow good and to be trusted and supported. Certainly we see that products labeled "green," "environmentally friendly," and "eco-sensitive" increasingly are saleable in today's markets. Where sustain-ability is part of this green marketing strategy, it is open to, and in fact often is, abused. At least, and perhaps without being cynical, we have to be really critical about what sustainability really means.

It is also possible that sustainability might be, in fact, a pious hope. That is especially the case for many in the prosperous world of Europe and the Americas, where we have incredible over-consumption. I am certainly a case in point: my car, my home, my life pattern uses up materials and energy at a rate that is not justifiable, that is not sustainable. But often times, and I am guilty here too, sustainability is taken by people to mean "let us do what we need to, so that in the future and indefinitely, we can continue to consume at the same rate at which we are currently consuming." Certainly that is not what sustainability would mean or involve. In this sort of case, the term again is abused.

I also would like to point out, as Professor Peter Coltman has noted on several occasions, that sustainability is not the same as self-sufficiency. To be self-sufficient means that one provides for one's own needs. But that is certainly not the case for any part of American society today. We certainly are not self- sufficient at a local scale, because, as part of international, even global, networks of production, consumption, and ecological impact, what we do in a given place affects the possibilities for sustainability of other dimensions of our particular locality, of the larger bioregion within which we live, and also of national and even international realms. (When we come to the next section and ask about the scale at which a society would be sustainable— at a local, regional, national, or global scale, sustainability certainly will not appear as a local issue.)

Since we are not able to provide for our own needs at a purely local scale in a world of systems, the question of whether we are acting sustainability cannot be decided at that small scale either. Thus, the question of whether our ways of life are sustainable—the heart of what I take sustainability to be about—that is, of whether we can develop patterns that do not compromise the ways of life that might be chosen, has to be answered at the large scale. I would contend that the regional scale is the smallest at which sustainability is intelligible, and that it actually requires a trans-regional scale to operate successfully in ethical disputes among neighbors and involving resource-use across the planet. The question, then, asks about the ways we might act together across the planet so as to live in a decent but modest way and also provide the same possibilities we have had for future generations, so they can to continue to develop their own freely chosen ways of life.

This point brings us closer to the question of what sustainability would really mean, especially in relation to values, beliefs, and motives. To clarify this, I want to look at the question of sustainability in relation to current practices, values and beliefs. As I've noted, currently we understand sustainability as a certain attitude towards the earth and its prospect, which entails that we need to change the over-consumption and destruction of our natural resource base so that we not only currently change our consumptive practices, but modify these with a lasting impact. We often articulate this in terms of the Native American idea of practicing life so that the tenth generation to come will have the same possibilities as we.

As I pointed out earlier, there certainly is reason to be suspect or criticize many who use the term, "sustainability." But if we take seriously that we may be able to actually transform current values, beliefs, and practices into a new way of behaving, then sustainability may be possible. If that were the case, then sustainability would raise the question of how we could grow with some kind of equity.

Despite all the forecasts and bad news about what happens with an exploding human population, even given our efforts at modifying our own growth with birth control, clearly the world is still growing. That fact leads me to believe that, practically, we are not going to reduce the global population. As a consequence, humans will not consume less and less. The problem will remain one of finding some way to grow. Again, we arrive at another version of the basic question, "What is a legitimate way to grow and develop, with some equity?" which also asks how we can bring the ethical principles of autonomy (or self determination) and justice into the question of sustainability.

Are Conservation and Preservation [the] Alternatives?

One way to think about the issue is in terms of resource conservation. Obviously, as the world conservation strategy points out, an initial saving that also has a lasting impact can occur if we do save the fundamental resources that we are now overly-consuming. But, behind the idea of resource conservation there seem to be several conflicts, and I say "seems to be" because we assume that there are polarities here. I want to examine those more closely and, in fact, argue that they are not completely the case. In the argument that follows, I am especially going to make use of what J. Ronald and Joan Gibb Engel argue in the Introduction to their wonderful book, *Ethics of Environment and Development: Global Challenge, International Response*, (1990). As Engel and Engel and the authors in this volume point out (and as many others have argued also), it is important to clarify the real conflicts and issues beyond what merely appears to be the case. Consider three examples of what appears to be the case.

It appears that we have a polarity where resource or environmental preservation is opposite and in contest with the conservation attitude that actually is a kind of developmental outlook. In fact, if we look at the conservation movement as Pinchot and the progressives in America first articulated it, conservation basically has meant saving or preserving things so that we could develop them according to American patterns, practices, and habits. In that sense, we have developed forestry or range conservation so that we can continue to log the forests of the Midwest and the Pacific Northwest or graze the western states to keep the development of America going. Here, conservation clearly amounts to seeing nature as a resource to be used for development. And, in the normal understanding, the opposite position is that of resource preservation, where we want to preserve or to set things aside and not use them. As an example, we might cite the Nature Conservancy that purchases land and holds it by setting up preserves.

Usually, we juxtapose these two positions. We consider that preserving the land and holding it so it's not really used is a distinct and separate position that provides the alternative to conserving the land so we can keep growing crops and cattle on it, so that we can keep producing from the mines and from the forests, in short, so that we can constantly have a stock of resources for future development. Conservation-preservation seems like a polarity.

On reflection, it seems that this first polarity depends on another, deeper polarity: that between intrinsic value and instrumental value. It would appear that the conservation movement that wants to develop our natural resources would appreciate those resources purely because of their instrumental value. The forests or the ore in the mountain would be valuable for what they can be used to achieve, because of some kind of utilitarian sense that the determination of what is good or valuable is a matter of its use. This is an instrumentalist or consequentialist position. Here the forest would not be seen as having inherent value in itself, but would be valuable for, for example, the wood that could be used to build homes for people. As an opposite to instrumental value, there would again appear the idea of intrinsic value in which nature would have value in itself. Sometimes this is the view connected with, or at least attributed to, deep ecology: that the natural world or environment itself has rights because it has intrinsic value.

When we argue issues such as whether trees or endangered species have rights, or when we ponder—just as, for humans—whether natural ecosystems have value that doesn't have to be justified in terms of human-centered uses (that is, whether ecology is or should be based upon a naturalism rather than a humanism), we really are pondering the issue of intrinsic value. The extrinsic (use) versus intrinsic value (a binary) may not be the ultimate distinction, but certainly it appears that the resource-preservation movement recognizes and depends on the idea of intrinsic value, whereas the conservation development movement would depend on and be based upon the idea of instrumental or use value. We have seen these kinds of dilemmas when we try and listen to the justifications for our great social projects. Why should we enter space and explore it? Some people would argue that we should because it is intrinsically worthwhile. Human beings simply are curious beings, explorers by nature who somehow find the resources to have adventures, to discover what is unknown. Others, though, employ the idea of instrumental value to justify expenditure, arguing that we should have a space program so that we could have new and profitable production in space. In a gravity-free environment, we could make more perfect ball bearings, a very useful project.

The same argument applies in environmental issues, such as those concerning the rain forests. Many would argue that the life forms themselves, whole ecosystems, are intrinsically valuable and need to be understood and protected for their own sake. Others argue more pragmatically, more instrumentally, that there are wonderful undiscovered medicines here. The cure for your grandchild's rare disease may be in a species that's being exterminated at this very moment. This last argument would hold that the rain forest and its life forms would be valuable because of their use value for human life.

Distributive Justice

Over the last decade I have come to believe that matters and our alternatives are not so simple. While it is correct that the resource-preservation movement is responding to the idea of intrinsic value, and while the conservation development movement is responding to the idea of instrumental value, agreeing with the Engels here, I contend that the issue is much deeper. I think that sustainability really has to do with the difference between ecological integrity and the idea of distributive justice in and between generations. Environments are constituted by complexly interrelated, interdependent ecological systems. The members of these ecological systems (whether living or atmospheric or geological dimensions), have a very complex integrity that's not really understood and only recently has begun to be appreciated by human beings. So, on the one hand, we need to recognize, respect, and try to nurture and promote ecological integrity.

Distinct from this recognition and respect for ecological integrity is another issue that has to do with justice. One dimension of justice is what is called distributive justice, the idea that there are both benefits and costs associated with the manner in which we distribute and use goods. The idea of distributive justice is that both the costs (or burdens) and the benefits associated with our providing and using resources need to be fairly or equitably or legitimately spread across different societies; and, within societies, equitably spread among diverse members or groups of a given generation and, equitably, across generations. This understanding is very helpful when we come back to talking about sustainability. What we're really saying in terms of justice is that sustainability is an issue of distributive justice between today's generations and future generations. In other words, "How are the uses, the benefits, of the resources shared equitably between those alive today and those who are going to be alive in the future?"

Similarly, we are concerned with the question of what the costs are, that is, about how to give up luxury, bear the burden of environmental destruction, and cope with the disease that comes with environmental degradation. What should be the distribution of these negative dimensions among different societies or sub-groups of a given society in today's world and between today's societies and those to come in the future? What appeared as a complex polar issue before—preservation and intrinsic value on the one side and conservation and instrumental value on the other side—dissolves before us when we see that it does not present the most basic alternatives. The basic issue comes down to two more complex issues: how (a) to respect the ecological integrity of complex systems around the world and (b) simultaneously, have a system of adequately distributive justice for the benefits and harms of environmental resources among societies existing today and then between today's societies and societies in the future.

In other words, we do have a conflict; but, it is not the conflict that we might have suspected before. It is not simply the conflict between polarized groups of people who disagree. I am convinced that this substantially advances the argument about conservation versus preservation or intrinsic versus extrinsic value, because it indicates that the real moral dilemma is not represented in the contest between no-growth and pro-growth contingencies. There is a set of more fundamental issues with which people all across the spectrum must deal, and for which we need to find some shared social answer. The real question for all of us, no matter whether we're preservationists, conservationists, deep ecologists or whatever, is how to act with environmental responsibility and also with social justice among communities today and between communities today and those of the future. We have not only clarified some of the issues, but moved to a deeper level of understanding.

By beginning with the previous issues of conservation and preservation and of extrinsic and extrinsic values, we have moved on to find the more fundamental issue of the moral rights and obligations among and between generations of peoples in regard to the ecosystems and natural orders themselves. It is important to note that this shift is non-reductive. We have not reduced the issue of environmental responsibility to the issue of intrinsic versus instrumental value. We are trying to argue how we can, at one and the same time, with one and the same action, have social justice, act in terms of beneficence and non-maleficence, respect the autonomy of different social groups, and responsibly nurture the ecological integrity of the natural systems themselves. Here we have arrived at a position where we can consider a "final" alternative approach to the idea of sustainability and to these environmental issues.

As Joan and Ron Engels and the authors in their collection of essays point out, the Ottawa conference on conservation and development made five major points to which we need attend. These points are made especially clear by Peter Jacobs and David Monroe in their publication, "Conservation with Equity: Strategies for Sustainable Development," published in 1987: (1) we need an integration of conservation and development; that agrees with what I've just finished arguing; (2) We need to satisfy basic human needs; (3) we need to achieve equity and human justice—that is what I have argued above in terms of distributive justice; (4) We need to provide for social self-determination and cultural diversity; that is what I am arguing in the basic principle of autonomy; (5) We need the maintenance of ecological integrity, which is what I am calling the dimension of ecological integrity and environmental responsibility.

In short, the points I have considered above in this essay can be seen as part of a larger movement that is being supported by recent ethical-environmental thinking about how we are going to move into the future. What that means is that we hopefully have made enough progress in working through these issues that we can move beyond confusing phrases and see that arguments can be made concerning sustainability that do not have to do simply with polarized groups within a given society or community. If so, we may have a glimpse of a more profound, complex, and broader reality in which we participate and that is the site of our shared human problem. Here we would start to see that sustainability begins to mean something such as, in the Engels' words, "activity that nourishes and perpetuates the fulfillment of the whole community of life on earth." That is very important. The key phrase is "the whole community of life on earth."

Mixed Communities

It seems to me that the step forward made by the Engels and their colleagues is critical because it indicates that we have a normative understanding of what sustainable development means. To be specific, in this line of thought, life on earth is understood always in terms of individuals always already in community—a basic phenomenon that, for the most part, has been overlooked in environmental and ethical thinking. In other words, a feature of all living things on earth is that these living beings appear as individuals in communities. This is obvious in the case of animals. Animals are brought into various collective forms, whether those of ants or bees, dolphins or wolves. They live within a vast collective system where the individual members of the group have specialized tasks and they function as a whole, not only to give birth to, but to nourish the young so that the whole group survives. It is even more obvious in the case of the higher mammals, where a long period of protection of the young is undertaken, and where social grooming and other interaction takes place. It clearly is the case that human beings would not become persons if we did not have community lives. To be born as a human is to be born, perhaps of all the mammals, from the beginning the most unable to act independently for a long period in our lives.

So much communal nurturing needs to be given to human children that baby foxes, squirrels, and kittens all are able to become independent and move about in the world in a way that approximates their norms of adult animal life far before human infants are able to do so. The human infant needs not only to have the biological and psychological protection of the community, it needs to learn language. It needs to be taught how to act and behave, so that we only become full human agents, full persons insofar as we're born into, nurtured by, and remain part of the human community. From this point of view the argument is that any living being has its life not as an individual, atomic, or discrete being but as a member of a community, that is, within an already shared ecology.

No individual or sub-group of humans or animals is truly independent in the world. What really exists are interdependent communities that operate across all levels. In a given geological and vegetative realm, we find particular sets of plants, varieties of animals, and people. Across the globe, there are interlocking ecosystems or eco-communities that involve many different individuals in community. Since these mixed communities made of plants, animals, and people all show their interdependency, then the interdependency is necessary for the life of all these beings to work. Note, the humans in a given area cannot be who they are, cannot live the lives that are connected with their identities apart from the patterns of the animals in that area, apart from the types of plants, apart from the climate, atmosphere and other conditions that nurture and preserve these plants and animals.

In other words, one cannot "like," which is a fairly weak word, or respect a particular kind of living being without also respecting the entire complex environment in which and because of which it becomes and lives as it does. "Like" is a bad word to use because we tend to express mere preference such as "Oh, I like the Indians in the upper reaches of Guatemala," or, "I like the picturesque life of people along the Pacific Rim." We need to transcend that sense of personal preference, of merely liking something, and pass over to a kind of understanding and appreciation of it and its life-world. At this deeper level, then, the claim is that it does not make sense to say that I understand and appreciate the way of life of a given group of people on earth but that I do not appreciate and respect the animal life around them, the plant life around them, the full, mixed community that supports them. Such a separation is logically inconsistent. If either we or they disrespect that plant and animal communities within which they have their way of life and their identity, their way of life and identity is in danger of disappearing. As a practical matter as well as a theoretical fact, one either nurtures or harms entire eco-communities, including human members. You cannot change the way of human life without changing the plant and animal milieu, nor can you change the plant and animal environment without changing the human way of life.

As a consequence, the Engels argue, I think convincingly, that the real ecological ethical choices are between paths of development that are ecologically sustainable for entire mixed communities of plants, animals and people, and the choices for those ways of development that do no ecologically sustain whole communities of plants, animals and people. This is important because it helps us realize that we cannot ask whether we like, prefer, or choose to act on behalf of and respect a certain group of people in the Amazon and then independently or later decide whether we should develop Amazonian ecotourism or some kind of mining or forestry, or whether we should replace the rain forest with ranches to grow cattle for the beef in our restaurants or encourage local people to gather nuts from which they can craft and sell buttons and carvings to replace ivory. Those are not detachable choices. Nor are they obviously ours to make.

Our first questions about sustainability reveal themselves to be questions about what other peoples themselves have to say about their own positions. If we are to respect their autonomy, they have the right to say how it is that they want their identities to be. There are current patterns to their lives with animals and plants; if those now are what they choose to sustain, then the entire ecosystem, of which they are one integrated aspect, needs to be respected. If we take the principle of autonomy seriously, and if they choose to change their identity and thus change the way they are related to animal and plant life, we would need to recognize that right and allow them to do so. Again, it is not a question of whether we are in control; it is a question of whether they are legitimately justified in carrying out that course of action, their own course of action. Of course, this means we cannot be manipulative. We really need to listen to and respect what other peoples have to say about their ways of life and the environments that are part of that way of life.

Though we would not be making choices about the mixed communities of plants, animals, and people for those other peoples, all of us, or all involved, do still have to deal with the other issue of distributive justice. Is social justice occurring among communities? Even if a community decides, in the name of autonomy, to undertake a certain course of action, that notion would not be ethical if it causes damage or allows harm to come to the way of life to another mixed community of plants, animals and people. For example, citizens in the U.S. might say that our identity involves the incredible consumption of rare woods and hamburgers which depends on wood and beef from Brazil, which requires the rain forest to be cleared so that it can be logged and so that the cattle ranches can be run. But we could not argue that our autonomous preference for this way of life justifies destroying interdependent Amazonian communities because the principle of justice would be violated. We would not share the costs and harms to the environment equally with the eco-communities that include the people of the Brazilian milieu. In this case, the principle of justice would override our autonomy and not allow us to destroy those ecosystems.

But, as can be seen, neither autonomy or beneficence and non-maleficence or justice are so simply bounded. The complex social and ethical question is how we can have interdependent mixed communities of plants, animals and people with social justice in each community, social justice among communities at a given time on the earth, and then social justice between those communities that exist now and the ones of the future—all the while being environmentally responsible for the plant and animal and atmospheric dimensions that are mutually constitutive with human cultures. In our analysis, we have come to see that there is not an opposition between environmental responsibility and social justice; rather, the two coincide. One is not able to act justly toward a society while harming the environment of that society, because the society only exists, only has its character or identity, insofar as the complete mixed community in which it participates is respected. This more sophisticated, holistic view of environment-mixed community relationships indicates that the fundamental issue is one of social, distributive justice among groups and across generations.

The Engels and their colleagues, then, have made a major contribution to clarifying the issue and bringing the question of sustainability to a more profound level. But, translating our principled ideas into principled actions involves one final issue.

Action and Compassion

If, as we saw at the beginning, there is a superficial and unacceptable attitude in which sustainability is taken to mean maintaining our current patterns of consumption—which amount to an attempt to sustain our way of unsustainable life—if we now begin to see that a substantial change is necessary, the pragmatic problem becomes one of how such a change could come about, especially if we respect the principle of autonomy where we do not force our views on others. If we are not naive, it would seem that any move from ethical judgment as an intellectual practice to ethical action requires not only principles and logic, but motives. What would motivate people to respect mixed communities, their own and those of others, those of the future? What would motivate people to actually change their consumptive practices? How could we change from current consumptive values, beliefs, and practices to these alternative and sustainable ones?

The German theorist Werner Marx in *Towards A Phenomenological Ethics: Ethos and the Life-World*, suggests that there is only one workable motive in today's postmodern world. He believes that in today's pluralistic society traditional transcendent sources of value and even rationality are challenged. In other words, we no longer believe there is any traditional, shared justification that would indicate to us a common course of action. We do not believe that there are transcendent religious beings or philosophical ideas that motivate us to act in one way in our society. In the post-structuralist world, even human reason is challenged: the belief is put forward that cultures and time periods are so radically relative that there is no shared rationality that would enable us to come to a reasoned legitimized course of action. In this context, Werner Marx argues, that the only real motivation to practical change would be compassion: compassion, a feeling with, a fellow feeling.

He argues that we should not expect or seek a new intellectual movement, but work instead to promote feelings of compassion for other peoples in their life-worlds, that is, as they un-self-critically go about their projects immersed in complex and integrated natural and social environments. Marx suggests that we form an initial impression of compassion, and an impulse to action following from that compassion, by confronting our own mortality. When we vividly realize that we are mortal, we come to the basic insight that we are not self- sufficient. For instance, if we have an accident in which we are hurt and helpless, we immediately cry for help. Here, we recognize that we are not able to do things in the usual manner; that, in fact, our independence is incredibly fragile. We depend upon the kindness and support of others. We depend on the complex integrations of our social constructions with sets of natural systems and phenomena which constitute our viable life-worlds.

Usually, these natural systems are taken for granted, as are the social systems. Thus, we do not appreciate them or give thanks for the operating interdependencies, the provisions and resources that are made available to us. Against such inattention, a thoughtful life involves confronting our mortality, confronting our limitations, and finitude. If we become aware of how limited we are and realize our need for other people, then, Marx hopes, we might become compassionate and attentive to the things other people need. We might, in the Engels' terms, realize how all members of a mixed community need each other to maintain their current identities. This new position would include a reflective appreciation of the ways in which people need the animals and plants that belong to their shared mixed communities.

In sum: if we become compassionate toward a people, we do not face the mutually exclusive questions of whether we should be compassionate for those people, or for the animals, or for the plants of the ecosystem. To be compassionate is to be compassionate for all the members of a given, whole life-world. If we can recognize our common finitude and common dependence, we can come to realize how fragile these ecosystems or mixed communities are and become able to maintain, nurture, and keep these delicate mixed communities in balance. By developing compassion for lifeworlds (for the people, the animals, the natural environmental features), our conduct to these disparate worlds on the face of the earth would dramatically change.

If this is possible, and with Werner Marx I hope that it is, our feeling of compassion could put into action, could bring about as an effective change, the ideas considered earlier. We would be enacting social and distributive justice on behalf of entire mixed communities and between communities. Thus, we have a fuller understanding of sustainability and of our responsibility: sustainability promotes entire lifeworlds—which means the inseparable communities of people, animals, plants, soils, and other natural elements that constitute environments—which exist today and that may come in the future.

Back to the /EarthWorks/ Table of Contents
www.utexas.edu/depts/grg/eworks/eworks.html

---

credit the authors and source. The URL for this page is
www.utexas.edu/depts/grg/eworks/proceedings/engeo/mugerauer/
mughtml.html/.

Received March 20, 1996.
Published March 21, 1996.
File converted to HTML by SLC.

Bibliography

Abramson, Daniel B., Lynne C. Manzo, and Jeffrey Hou. "From Ethnic Enclave to Multi-ethnic Translocal Community: Contested Identities and Community Planning in Seattle's Chinatown-International District." *Journal of Architectural and Planning Research* 23, no. 4 (Winter 2006): 341–364.

Addington, D. Michelle, and Daniel Schodek. *Smart Materials and Technologies for the Architecture and Design Professions.* Burlington, Mass.: Architectural Press, 2005.

Adler, Mortimer. *Aristotle for Everybody.* New York: Bantam Books, 1978.

Afrasiabi, Kaveh L. "Towards an Islamic Ecotheology." *Hamdard Islamicus* 18, no 1. (1995): 33–50.

Agyeman, Julian. *Sustainable Communities and the Challenge of Environmental Justice.* New York: NYU Press, 2005.

Albrecht, Johann G., and Gill-Chin Lim. "A Search for Alternative Planning Theory: Use of Critical Theory." *Journal of Architectural and Planning Research* 3 (1986): 117–131.

Allegretto, Sylvia A. "U.S. Government does Relatively Little to Lessen Child Poverty Rates." *Economic Snapshots*, Economic Policy Institute, July 19, 2006. www.epinet.org/content.cfm/webfeatures_snapshots_20060719.

American Evaluation Association. *Guiding Principles for Evaluators.* Fairhaven MA: AEA, 2004. www.eval.org/publications/guidingprinciples.asp.

Aristotle. *Ethics: The Nicomachean Ethics.* Translated by J. A. K. Thomson. New York: Penguin Books, 1976.

Arnstein, Sherry R. "A Ladder of Citizen Participation." *Journal of the American Institute of Planners* 35, no. 4 (July 1969): 216–24.

Ashley, Benedict M., and Kevin D. O'Rourke. *Health Care Ethics.* St. Louis MO: Catholic Health Association of the United States, 1982.

Badiou, Alain. *Saint Paul: The Foundation of Universalism.* Translated by Ray Brassier. Palo Alto, Calif: University of Stanford Press, 2003.

Baier, Annette. "The Need for More than Justice." In *Justice and Care: Essential Readings in Feminist Ethics*, edited by Virginia Held. Boulder, Col.: Westview Press, 1995.

Ball, Philip. *Made to Measure: New Materials for the 21st Century.* Princeton, N.J.: Princeton University Press, 1997.

Barnes, Jonathan. Introduction and bibliography to *Ethics: The Nicomachean Ethics* by Aristotle. New York: Penguin Books, 1976.

Barry, Brian. *Political Argument: A Reissue with a New Introduction.* Berkeley and Los Angeles: University of California Press, 1990.

Basso, Keith. "Stalking with Stories." Pp. 95–116 in *On Nature: Nature, Landscape, and Natural History*, edited by Daniel Halpern. San Francisco: North Point Press, 1987.

Baudrillard, Jean. *The Mirror of Production.* St. Louis: Telos Press, 1975.

Baxter, William F.. *People or Penguins: The Case for Optimal Pollution.* New York: Columbia University Press, 1974.

Bayles, Michael D., and Kenneth Henley, eds. *Right Conduct: Theories and Applications.* New York: Random House, 1983.

Beauchamp, Tom L., and James E. Childress. *Principles of Biomedical Ethics.* New York: Oxford University Press, 1983.

Beatley, Timothy. *Ethical Land Use: Principles of Policy and Planning.* Baltimore: Johns Hopkins University Press, 1994.

Benyus, Janine M. *Biomimicry: Innovation Inspired by Nature.* New York: William Morrow, 1997.

Berkowitz, Marvin W. "Four Perspectives on Moral Argumentation." Pp. 1–23 in *Moral Dilemmas: Philosophical Issues in the Development of Moral Reasoning*, edited by Carol Gibb Harding. Chicago: Precedent Publishing, 1985.

Bess, Philip. "Communitarianism and Emotivism: Two Rival Views of Ethics in Architecture." *Inland Architect* 5/6 (May/June 1993): 74–83.

Bormann, F. Herbert, Diana Balmori, and Gordon T. Geballe. *Redesigning the American Lawn: A Search for Environmental Harmony.* New Haven, Conn.: Yale University Press, 1962.

Brand, Ralf G. *Co-Evolution Toward Sustainable Development: Neither Smart Technologies nor Heroic Choices.* PhD dissertation, University of Texas at Austin. Ann Arbor, Mich.: UMI Books, 2003.

Brownell, Blaine, ed. *Transmaterial: A Catalog of Materials that Redefine our Physical Environment.* Princeton: Princeton Architectural Press, 2006.

Brundtland, Gro Harlem, ed. *Our Common Future: The World Commission on Environment and Development.* Oxford: Oxford University Press, 1987.

Bullard, Robert D. *Dumping in Dixie: Race, Class, and Environmental Quality.* Boulder. Col.: Westview Press, 1990.

———, ed. *Confronting Environmental Racism: Voices from the Grassroots.* Boston: South End Press, 1993.

———, ed. *The Quest for Environmental Justice: Human Rights and the Politics of Pollution.* San Francisco: Sierra Club Books, 2005.

Callicott, J. Baird. *In Defense of the Land Ethic: Essays in Environmental Philosophy.* Albany, N.Y.: SUNY Press, 1989.

Callicott, J. Baird, and Roger T. Ames, eds. *Nature in Asian Traditions of Thought: Essays in Environmental Philosophy.* Albany, N.Y.: SUNY Press, 1989.

Cameron, John. "Place, belonging, and ecopolitics: Learning our way towards the place-responsive society." *Ecopolitics: Thought & Action* 1, no. 2 (2001): 18–34.

———. "Educating for Place Responsiveness: An Australian Perspective on Ethical Practice." *Ethics, Place and Environment* 6, no. 2 (June 2003): 99–115.

———. "Some Implications of Malpas' *Place and Experience* for Place, Ethics, and Education." *Environmental and Architectural Phenomenology Newsletter* 15, no. 1 (2004): 5–9.

Card, Claudia. "Intimacy and Responsibility: What Lesbians Do." Pp. 77–94 in *At the Boundaries of Law: Feminism and Legal Theory*, edited by Martha A. Fineman and Nancy S. Thomadsen. New York: Routledge, 1991.

Carlson, Allen. *Aesthetics and the Environment: The Appreciation of Nature, Art, and Architecture.* New York: Routledge, 2002.

Carmody, John. *Ecology and Religion: Toward a New Christian Theology of Nature.* New York: Paulist Press, 1983.

Castree, Noel. "A Post-environmental Ethics?" *Ethics, Place and Environment* 6, no. 1 (March 2003): 3–12.

Cheah, Pheng. *Inhuman Conditions: On Cosmopolitanism and Human Rights.* Cambridge,, Mass: Harvard University Press, 2006.

Cheney, Jim. "Postmodern Environmental Ethics: Ethics as Bioregional Narrative." Pp. 23–42 in *Postmodern Environmental Ethics*, edited by Max Oelschlaeger. Albany, N.Y.: SUNY Press, 1995.

Code, Lorraine. *Rhetorical Spaces: Essays in Gendered Location.* New York: Routledge, 1995.

Conklin, Jeffrey E. *Dialogue Mapping: Building Shared Understanding of Wicked Problems.* New York: John Wiley & Sons, 2001.

Corsellis, Tom and Antonella Vitale. *Transitional Settlement: Displaced Populations.* Oxford: Oxfam Publishing, 2005.

Collingham, John. 2000. "Partiality, distance, and moral obligation." *Ethics, Place and Environment* 3, no. 3 (October 2000): 309–13.

Cox, Kevin, Chris Kauffman, Jason Hart, Adrea Lund, and Becky Wagner. "Human Impacts on the Ecology of the Southwestern United States." Richmond IN: Earlham College, 2005. http://www.earlham.edu/~biol/desert/impacts.htm (accessed April 20, 2007).

Crump, Jeff R., "Deconcentration by demolition: Public housing, poverty, and urban policy." *Environment and Planning D: Society and Space* 20, no. 5 (2002): 581–96.

The Dalai Lama. *The Universe in a Single Atom: The Convergence of Science and Spirituality.* New York: Morgan Road Books, 2005.

Davidoff, Paul. "Advocacy and Pluralism in Planning." *Journal of the American Institute of Planners* 31, no. 4 (1965): 331–338.

Deeken, Alfons. *Process and Permanence in Ethics: Max Scheler's Moral Philosophy.* New York: Paulist Press, 1974.

Deloria, Vine, Jr. "Sacred Lands and Religious Freedom." *Native American Rights Fund Legal Review* 16, no. 2 (Summer 1991): 1–6.

Deutsche, R. *Evictions: Art and Spatial Politics.* Cambridge, Mass.: MIT Press, 1996.

Devine-Wright, Patrick, and Evanthia Lyons. "Remembering Pasts and Representing Places: The Construction of National Identity in Ireland." *Journal of Environmental Psychology* 17, no. 1 (March 1997): 33–45.

Dewey, John. *How We Think: A Restatement of the Relation of Reflective Thinking to the Educative Process.* Boston: Heath and Co., 1933.

Dietrich, William. "The Big Squeeze: Shaping the region's destiny in the face of increasing density." In *Pacific Northwest* magazine, *Seattle Times*, December 8, 2002, 16.

Dodge, Jim. *Living by Life: Some Bioregional Theory and Practice.* Belmont, Cal.: Wadsworth Publishing, 1992.

Dovey, Kimberly George. "Architectural Ethics: A Dozen Dilemmas." *Practices* 2 (Spring 1993): 26–33.

Doyal, Len, and Ian Gough. *A Theory of Human Need.* New York: Guilford Press, 1991.

Dramstad, Wenche E., James D. Olson, and Richard T. Forman. *Landscape Ecology Principles in Landscape Architecture and Land Use Planning.* Washington, D.C.: Island Press, 1996.

Drengson, Alan R. *Beyond Environmental Crisis: From Technocrat to Planetary Person.* New York: Peter Lang Publishing, 1989.

Dubrow, Gail. (2002). "Deru Kugi Wa Utareru or the Nail That Sticks up Gets Hit: The Architecture of Japanese American Identity, 1885-1942; the Rural Environment." *Journal of Planning Education and Research* 19(4) (2002): 319–333.

Edelstein, Michael R. *Contaminated Communities: Coping with Residential Toxic Exposure.* Boulder, Col.: Westview Press, 2004.

Edwards, Brian, and Paul Hyett, *Rough Guide to Sustainability.* London: RIBA Publications, 2001.

Engel, J. Ronald, and Joan Gibb Engel, eds. *Ethics of Environment and Development: Global Challenge, International Response.* Tucson AZ: University of Arizona Press, 1990.

Engel, J. Ronald, and Julie Denny-Hughes, eds. *Advancing Ethics for Living Sustainably:* Report of the IUCN workshop, April 1993, Indiana Dunes National Lakeshore, USA. Sacramento, Calif.: International Center for the Environment and Public Policy, 1993.

Fakhry, Majid. *Ethical Theories in Islam.* Leiden, Netherlands: E. J. Brill, 1991.

Faludi, Andreas, ed. *A Reader in Planning Theory.* Oxford: Pergamon Press, 1973.

Fathy, Hassan. *Architecture for the Poor: An Experiment in Rural Egypt.* Chicago: University of Chicago Press, 1973.

————. *Natural Energy and Vernacular Architecture: Principles and Examples with Reference to Hot Arid Climates.* Chicago: University of Chicago Press, 1986.

Fleddermann, C. B. *Engineering Ethics.* Upper Saddle River, NJ: Prentice Hall, 1999.

Flora, Cornelia Butler, Jan L. Flora, Jacqueline Spears, and Louis E. Swanson. *Rural Communities: Legacy and Change.* Boulder, Calif.: Westview Press, 1992.

Flores, Albert, ed. *Professional Ideals.* Belmont, Calif: Wadsworth Publishing, 1988.

Florman, Samuel C. *The Civilized Engineer.* New York: St. Martin's Press, 1987.

————. *The Introspective Engineer.* New York: St. Martin's Press, 1996.

Flyvbjerg, Bent, Nils Bruzelius, and Werner Rothengatter. *Megaprojects and Risk: An Anatomy of Ambition.* Cambridge: Cambridge University Press, 2003.

Flyvbjerg, Bent. *Making Social Science Matter: Why Social Inquiry Fails and How it Can Succeed Again.* Cambridge: Cambridge University Press, 2001.

Foreman, Dave. *Confessions of an Eco-Warrior.* New York: Harmony Books, 1991.

Forester, John. "Planning in the Face of Power." *APA Journal* 48, no. 1 (Winter 1982): 67–80.

Foucault, Michel. The *Archeology of Knowledge & the Discourse on Language.* New York: Pantheon Press, 1972.

————. *The Order of Things: An Archaeology of the Human Sciences.* New York: Vintage Books, 1973.

Francis, Mark. "Proactive Practice: Visionary Thought and Participatory Action in Environment Design." *Places* 12, no. 1 (Spring 1998): 60–68.

Frantz, Douglas. *From the Ground Up: The Business of Building in the Age of Money.* Berkeley and Los Angeles: University of California Press, 1993.

Frankena, William K. *Ethics.* Englewood Cliffs, N.J.: Prentice Hall, 1973.

Freudenberg, William R., and Susan K. Pastor. "NIMBYs and LULUs: Stalking the syndromes." *Journal of Social Issues* 48, no. 4 (1992): 39–61.

Friedman, David. "A Conceptual Model for Analysis of Planning Behavior." *Administrative Science Quarterly* 12, no. 2 (September 1967): 345–70.

Friedman, Marilyn A. "Abraham, Socrates, and Heinz: Where are the Women? (Care and Context in Moral Reasoning)." Pp. 25–42 in *Moral Dilemmas: Philosophical Issues in the Development of Moral Reasoning,* edited by Carol Gibb Harding. Chicago: Precedent Publishing, 1985.

Fullilove, Mindy Thompson. *Root Shock: How Tearing up City Neighborhoods Hurts America, and What We can Do About It.* New York: Ballantine Books, 2005.

Gardner, Howard, Mihaly Csikszentmihalyi, and William Damon. *Good Work: When Excellence and Ethics Meet.* New York: Basic Books, 2001.

Gergen, Kenneth. *The Saturated Self: Dilemmas of Identity in Contemporary Life.* New York: Basic Books, 1991.

Ghaye, Tony. "Reflection as a catalyst for change." *Reflective Practice* 6, no. 2 (May 2005): 177–87.

Giddens, Anthony. *Modernity and Self-Identity: Self and Society in the Late Modern Age.* Stanford, Calif.: Stanford University Press, 1991.

Gifford, Robert. *Environmental Psychology: Principles and Practice.* Colville, Wash.: Optimal Books, 2002.

Gilligan, Carol. *In a Different Voice: Psychological Theory and Women's Development.* Cambridge, Mass.: Harvard University Press, 1982.

Girardet, Herbert. The Gaia Atlas of Cities: New Directions for Sustainable Urban Living. New York: Anchor-Doubleday, 1992.

Girdner, Eddie J., and Jack Smith. Killing Me Softly: Toxic Waste, Corporate Profit, and the Struggle for Environmental Justice. New York: Monthly Review Press, 2002.

Glassie, Henry. Pattern in the Material Folk Culture of the *Eastern United States.* Philadelphia, Penn: University of Pennsylvania Press, 1969.

Gore, Albert, Jr. *An Inconvenient Truth: The Planetary Emergency of Global Warming and What We Can Do About It.* Emmaus, Penn: Rodale Press, 2006.

Guy, Simon, and Steven A. Moore, eds. *Sustainable Architectures: Cultures and Natures in Europe and North America.* New York: Spon Press, 2005.

Guy, Simon, and Elizabeth Shove. *A Sociology of Energy Buildings and the Environment,* London, Routledge, 2000.

Habermas, Jürgen. *Communication and the Evolution of Society.* Edited by Thomas McCarthy. Boston: Beacon Press, 1979.

Habermas, Jürgen. *Between Facts and Norms.* Translated by W. Rehg. Cambridge, Mass.: MIT Press, 1996.

Hall, Peter. *Great Planning Disasters.* Berkeley and Los Angeles: University of California Press, 1981.

Hanssen, Bjørg Lien. "Ethics and Landscape: Values and Choices." *Ethics, Place and Environment* 4, no. 3 (October 2001): 246–52.

Hardin, Garrett. *Living within Limits: Ecology, Economics, and Population Taboos.* New York: Oxford University Press, 1993.

Harding, Carol G., ed. *Moral dilemmas: Philosophical and Psychological Issues in the Development of Moral Reasoning.* Chicago: Precedent Publishing, 1985.

Harvey, David. *The Limits to Capital.* New York: Verso Books, 1999.

Harries, Karsten. *The Ethical Function of Architecture.* Cambridge, Mass.: MIT Press, 1997.

Haudenosaunee [Six Nations Iroquois] Environmental Task Force. *Words That Come Before All Else: Environmental Philosophies of the Haudenosaunee.* Ahkwesahsne, Ontario: Native North American Traveling College, 1995.

Hayden, Dolores. "Urban landscape history: The sense of place and the politics of space." Pp. 111–13 in *Understanding Ordinary Landscapes,* edited by Paul E. Groth and Todd W. Bressi. New Haven, Conn.: Yale University Press, 1997a.

———. *The Power of Place: Urban Landscapes as Public History.* Cambridge Mass.: MIT Press, 1997b.

Heidegger, Martin. *Poetry, Language, Thought.* New York: Harper & Row, 1971a.

———. *On the Way to Language.* New York: Harper & Row, 1971b.

Held, Virginia, ed. *Justice and Care: Essential Readings in Feminist Ethics.* Boulder, Col.: Westview Press, 1995.

Hess, Karl, Jr. 1992. *Visions Upon the Land: Man and Nature on the Western Range.* (Washington, D.C.: Island Press, 1992.

Hester, Randolph T., Jr. "A refrain with a view [Participation with a View]." *Places* 12, no. 2 (January 1999): 12–25.

Hinman, Lawrence M. 1985. "Emotion, Morality, and Understanding." Pp. 57–70 in *Moral Dilemmas: Philosophical Issues in the Development of Moral Reasoning*, edited by Carol Gibb Harding. Chicago: Precedent Publishing, 1985.

Hippocrates. *The Theory and Practice of Medicine.* New York: Citadel Press, 1964.

Hourani, George F. *Reason and Tradition in Islamic Ethics.* Cambridge: Cambridge University Press, 1985.

Hovannisian, R. G., ed. *Ethics in Islam.* Malibu, Calif: Undena Publications, 1985.

Huemer, Michael. "Rawls' Problem of Stability." *Social Theory and Practice* 22, no. 3 (Fall 1996): 375–95.

Interface Inc. *Sustainability Report.* Vol. II. Atlanta, Ga.: Interface Inc, 2005. www.interfacesustainability.com/social.html.

International Union for the Conservation of Nature, Ethics Working Group. "Papers from Ethics and Covenant Workshop, January." Buenos Aires: IUCN General Assembly, 1994.

Izzi Deen, Mawil Y. "Islamic Environmental Ethics, Law, and Society." Pp. 189–98 in *Ethics of Environment and Development: Global Challenge, International Response*, edited by J. Ronald Engel and Joan Gibb Engel. Tucson, Ariz.: University of Arizona Press, 1991.

Jegen, Mary Evelyn, and Bruno V. Manno, eds. *The Earth is the Lord's: Essays on Stewardship.* New York: Paulist Press, 1978.

Johns, Christopher, and Dawn Freshwater, eds. *Transforming Nursing through Reflective Practice.* Oxford: Blackwell Science, 1998.

Jung, Carl Gustav. *A Psychological Theory of Types*, edited by Gerhard Adler and R. F. C. Hull. Vol. 6 in *Collected Works.* Princeton NJ: Princeton University Press, 1976.

Kahera, Akel Ismael. "Reading the Semiotics of a Madinah: A Discourse on the Topography of Fas." *Al-Shajarah* 4, no. 1 (1999): 75–92.

Kahera, Akel Ismael, and Omar Benmira. "Damages in Islamic Law: Maghrebi Muftis and the Built Environment (9th–15th Centuries CE)." *Islamic Law and Society* 5, no. 2 (1998): 131–64.

Kant, Immanuel. *Prolegomena to Any Future Metaphysics.* Indianapolis, Ind.: Bobbs-Merrill, 1950.

———. *Foundations of the Metaphysics of Morals.* Indianapolis: Bobbs-Merrill, 1959.

Katz, Eric. "The Call of the Wild: The Struggle Against Domination and the Technological Fix of Nature." *Environmental Ethics* 14, no. 3 (Fall 1992): 265–73.

Kealey, Daniel A. *Revisioning Environmental Ethics.* Albany, N.Y.: SUNY Press, 1990.

Kelley, Klara Bonsack, and Harris Francis. *Navajo Sacred Places.* Bloomington, Ind.: Indiana University Press, 1994.

Kemmis, Stephen, and Robin McTaggart. "Participatory action research: Communicative action and the public sphere." Pp. 559–604 in the *Sage Handbook of Qualitative Research*, edited by Norman K. Denzin and Yvonna S. Lincoln. Thousand Oaks, Calif.: Sage Publications, 2005.

King, Roger. "Critical Reflections on Biocentric Environmental Ethics: Is it an Alternative to Anthropocentricism?" Pp. 209–30 in *Space, Place, and*

Environmental Ethics, edited by Andrew Light and Jonathan M. Smith. Lanham, Md.: Rowman & Littlefield, 1997.

———. "Caring About Nature: Feminist Ethics and the Environment." *Hypatia* 6, no. 1 (Spring 1991a): 75–89.

———. "Relativism and Moral Critique." Pp. 145–64 in *The American Constitutional Experiment,* edited by David M. Speak and Creighton Peden. Lewistown, N.Y.: Edwin Mellen Press, 1991b.

Kliewer, Justin. "Morality and Architectural Ornament." Masters' thesis, Department of Architecture, University of Washington. Seattle: University of Washington, 2006.

Koertge, Noretta. "Feminist Epistemology: Stalking an Un-Dead Horse." Pp. 413–10 in *The Flight from Science and Reason,* edited by Paul Gross, Norman Levitt, and Martin Lewis. New York: New York Academy of Sciences, 1996a.

———. "Wrestling with the Social Constructor." *Annals of the New York Academy of Sciences* 775, no. 1 (June 1996b): 266–73.

Kohlberg, Lawrence. "Resolving moral conflicts within the just community." Pp. 71–97 in *Moral Dilemmas: Philosophical and Psychological Issues in the Development of Moral Reasoning,* edited by Carol Gibb Harding. Chicago: Precedent Publishing, 1985.

Kuentzel, Walter F. "Self-identity, Modernity and the Rational Actor in Leisure Research." *Journal of Leisure Research* 32, no. 1 (2000): 87–92.

Ledwith, Margaret. "Personal narratives/political lives: Personal reflection as a tool for collective change." *Reflective Practice* 6, no. 2 (May 2005): 255–262.

LeGates, Richard T., and Frederic Stout, eds. *The Development of City Planning,* 9 vols . London: Thoemmes/Routledge, 1998.

LeGates, Richard T., and Frederic Stout, eds. *The City Reader.* London: Routledge, 1996.

Leopold, Aldo. *A Sand County Almanac: With Essays on Conservation from Round River.* New York: Oxford University Press, 1966.

Lester, James P., ed. *Environmental Politics and Policy: Theories and Evidence.* Durham, N.C.: Duke University Press, 1989.

Light, Andrew, and Jonathan M. Smith, eds. *Philosophy and Geography I: Space, Place, and Environmental Ethics.* Lanham, Md.: Rowman & Littlefield, 1997.

Longino, Helen E. *Science as Social Knowledge: Values and Objectivity in Scientific Inquiry.* Princeton: Princeton University Press, 1990.

Loos, Adolf. *Spoken into the Void: Collected Essays, 1897–1900.* Translated by Jane O. Newman and John H. Smith. Cambridge, Mass.: MIT Press, 1982.

Lopes de Souza, Marcelo. "Urban Development on the Basis of Autonomy: A Politico-Philosophical and Ethical Framework for Urban Planning and Management." *Ethics, Place and Environment* 3, no. 2 (June 2000): 187–201.

Loukaitou-Sideris, A. (2002). "Regeneration of Urban Commercial Strips: Ethnicity and Space in Three Los Angeles Neighborhoods." *Journal of Planning Education and Research* 19(4) (2002): 334–350.

Low, Setha M., Dana Taplin, Suzanne Scheld, and Tracy Fisher. "Recapturing Erased Histories: Ethnicity, Design, and Cultural Representation—A Case Study of Independence National Historical Park." *Journal of Architectural and Planning Research* 19, no. 4 (2002): 282–299.

Lu, Catherine. "The One and Many Faces of Cosmopolitanism." *Journal of Political Philosophy* 8, no. 2 (June 2000): 244–267.

Lucy, William H. "APA's Ethical Principles Include Simplistic Planning Theories," *APA Journal* 54 (Spring 1988): 147–149.

McCarty, Maggie. *HOPE VI Public Housing Revitalization Program: Background, Findings, and Issues.* Domestic Social Policy Division, Department of Housing and Urban Development (HUD). Damascus, Md.: Penny Hill Press, 2005.

McConnell, Shean. "Rawlsian planning theory." Pp. 30–48 in *Planning Ethics: A Reader in Planning Theory, Practice, and Education,* edited by Sue Hendler. New Brunswick, N.J.: Center for Urban Policy Research, 1995.

Malpas, Jeffrey E. "Place and Topography: Responding to Cameron and Stefanovic." *Environmental and Architectural Phenomenology Newsletter* 15, no. 3 (Fall 2004): 8–10.

Manzo, Lynne C. "Beyond House and Haven: Toward a Revisioning of Emotional Relationships With Places." *Journal of Environmental Psychology* 23, no. 1 (March 2003): 47–61.

———. "For Better or Worse: Exploring Multiple Dimensions of Place Meaning." *Journal of Environmental Psychology* 25, no. 1 (March 2005): 67–86.

Manzo, Lynne C., and Nathan Brightbill. "Toward a Participatory Ethics." In *Participatory Action Research Approaches and Methods: Connecting People, Participation, and Place,* edited by Sara Kindon, Rachel Pain, and Michael Kesby. London: Routledge, 2007.

Manzo, Lynne C., Rachel Kleit, and Dawn Couch. "'Moving Three Times is Like Having Your House on Fire Once:' The Experience of Place and Displacement among Public Housing Residents in the Pacific Northwest." *Urban Studies*, vol. 45: 11 (2008).

Manzo, Lynne C., and Douglas D. Perkins. "Finding Common Ground: The Importance of Place Attachment to Community Participation and Development." *Journal of Planning Literature* 20, no. 4 (2006): 335–50.

Marcuse, Peter. "Professional Ethics and Beyond: Values in Planning." *Journal of the American Institute of Planners* 42, no. 3 (July 1976): 264-74.

Markie, Peter. *A Professor's Duties: Ethical Issues in College Teaching.* Lanham, Md.: Rowman & Littlefield, 1994.

Martin, Mike W. *Meaningful Work: Rethinking Professional Ethics.* New York: Oxford University Press, 2000.

Martin-Schramm, James B., and Robert L. Stivers. *Christian Environmental Ethics: A Case Method Approach.* Maryknoll, N.Y.: Orbis Books, 2003.

Massey, Doreen, and Pat Jess, eds. *A Place in the World? Places, Cultures, and Globalization.* New York: Oxford University Press, 2000.

Maturana, Humberto R., and Bernhard Poerksen. *From Being to Doing: The Origins of the Biology of Cognition.* Heidelberg, Germany: Carl Auer International, 2004.

May, Larry. *The Socially Responsive Self: Social Theory and Professional Ethics.* Chicago: University of Chicago Press, 1996.

Merchant, Carolyn. *The Death of Nature: Women, Ecology, and the Scientific Revolution.* San Francisco: Harper & Row, 1980.

———. *Radical Ecology: The Search for a Livable World.* New York: Routledge, 1992.

Meredith, Dianne. "The Bioregion as a Communitarian Micro-region (and its Limitations." *Ethics, Place and Environment* 8, no. 1 (March 2005): 83–94.

Midgley, Mary. *Animals and Why They Matter.* Athens, Ga.: University of Georgia Press, 1983.

Milbrath, Lester W. *Environmentalists: Vanguard for a New Society.* Albany, N.Y.: SUNY Press, 1984.

Mill, John Stuart. *Utilitarianism.* Indianapolis, Ind.: Hackett Publishing, 1979.

Miller, Stephen L. *Environmental Values Underlying Positions Taken Towards Environmental Issues.* PhD dissertation. Urbana, Ill.: University of Illinois, 1966.

Mitcham, Carl, and R. Shannon Duval. *Engineering Ethics.* Upper Saddle River, N.J.: Prentice Hall, 2000.

Monson, Christopher. "Practical Discourse: Learning and the Ethical Construction of Environmental Design Practice." *Ethics, Place and Environment* 8, no. 2 (June 2005): 181–200.

Moore, Steven A., and Simon Guy, eds. *Sustainable Architectures: Cultures and Natures in Europe and North America.* New York: Spon Press, 2005.

Mugerauer, Robert. "Post-Structural Planning Theory." Community and Regional Planning Program Working Paper Series. Austin, Tex.: University of Texas at Austin, 1990.

——. *Interpreting Environments: Tradition, Deconstruction, Hermeneutics.* Austin, Tex.: University of Texas Press, 1995.

——. "Theories of Sustainability: Environmental Ethics, Mixed-Communities, and Compassion." *EarthWorks* 1, no. 1 (Spring 1996): http://www.utexas.edu/depts/grg/eworks/proceedings/engco/mug arnuor/mnghtml html/ (accessed April 10, 2007).

——. "Adapting Current and Future Settlements to Global Warming." Paper presented at the Second Urban Environment and Symbiotic Design Symposium, Kobe, Japan. University of Kobe, June, 2005.

Mugerauer, Robert, and Mary Murnane. "An Anatomy of Environmental Values and Perceptions: The Basis of Conflict and Cooperation in Decision-making and Negotiations." Austin, Tex.: Mike Hogg Endowment for Urban Governance, 1992.

Myers, Norman, and Jennifer Kent, eds. *The New Atlas of Planet Management.* Berkeley and Los Angeles: University of California Press, 2005.

Naess, Arne. *Ecology, Community and Lifestyle: Outline of an Ecosophy.* Translated and edited by David Rothenberg. Cambridge: Cambridge University Press, 1990.

Nash, James A. *Loving Nature: Ecological Integrity and Christian Responsibility.* Nashville, Tenn.: Abingdon Press, 1991.

Nasr, Seyyed Hossein. *The Need for a Sacred Science.* Richmond UK: Curzon Press, 1993.

Nassauer, Joan Iverson, ed. *Placing Nature: Culture and Landscape Ecology.* Washington, D.C.: Island Press, 1997.

Newton, David E. *Environmental Justice: A Reference Handbook.* Santa Barbara, Calif.: ABC-Clio Academic, 1996.

Noddings, Nel. "Caring." Pp. 60–78 in *Justice and Care: Essential Reading in Feminist Ethics,* edited by Virginia Held. Boulder, Col.: Westview Press, 1995.

Norberg-Schultz, Christian. *Intentions in Architecture.* Cambridge, Mass.: MIT Press, 1965.

Northwest Center for Livable Communities. "The Impacts of Proposed Initiative 933 on Real Property and Land Use in Washington State." Seattle: College of Architecture and Urban Planning, University of Washington, 2006.

Norton, Bryan G. *Why Preserve Natural Variety? Studies in Moral, Political, and Legal Philosophy.* Princeton, N.J.: Princeton University Press, 1987.

——. "Why I Am not a Nonanthropocentrist: Callicott and the Failure of Monistic Inherentism." *Environmental Ethics* 17, no. 4 (Winter 1995): 341–59.

Nozick, Robert. *Anarchy, State, and Utopia.* New York: Basic Books, 1974.

Nussbaum, Martha. "The Discernment of Perception: An Aristotelian Conception of Public and Private Rationality." Pp. 54–105 in *Love's Knowledge: Essays on*

Philosophy and Literature. New York: Oxford University Press, 1990.

Oechsli, Lauren, and Eric Katz. "Moving beyond Anthropocentrism: Environmental Ethics, Development, and the Amazon." *Environmental Ethics* 15, no. 1 (Spring 1993): 49–59.

Oelschlaeger, Max. *The Idea of Wilderness: From Prehistory to the Age of Ecology.* New Haven, Conn.: Yale University Press, 1992.

Oliver, Paul, ed. *The Encyclopedia of Vernacular Architecture of the World.* 3 vols. Cambridge: Cambridge University Press, 1997.

Orr, David W. 1994. *Earth in Mind: On Education, Environment, and the Human Prospect.* Washington, D.C.: Island Press, 1994.

Pader, Ellen. "Housing Occupancy Standards: Inscribing Ethnicity and Family Relations on the Land." *Journal of Planning Education and Research* 19(4) (2002): 300–318.

Paehlke, Robert C. *Environmentalism and the Future of Progressive Politics.* New Haven, Conn.: Yale University Press, 1989.

Palen, J. John. *The Suburbs.* New York: McGraw-Hill, 1995.

Papanek, Victor. *The Green Imperative: Ecology and Ethics in Design and Architecture.* New York: Thames & Hudson, 1995.

Peck, Jamie. *Workfare States.* New York: Guilford Press, 2001.

Pello, David Naguib, and Robert J. Brulle. *Power, Justice, and the Environment: A Critical Appraisal of the Environmental Justice Movement.* Cambridge Mass.: MIT Press, 2005.

Pepper, David M. *The Roots of Modern Environmentalism.* Dover NH: London: Croom Helm Publishers, 1984.

Perkins, D. D., J. B. Hughey, and P. W.Speer, "Community psychology perspectives on social capital and community development practice." *Journal of the Community Development Society* 33, no. 1 (2002): 33–52.

Petulla, Joseph M. *American Environmentalism: Values, Tactics, Priorities.* College Station. Tex.: Texas A & M University Press, 1980.

HRH The Prince Philip. "Foreword." *Ingenia* 3 (January 2000).

Piven, Frances Fox. "Whom Does the Advocacy Planner Serve?" In *The Politics of Turmoil,* edited by R. Cloward, and F. F. Piven. New York: Vintage, 1965.

Polèse, Mario, and Richard E. Stren, eds. *The Social Sustainability of Cities: Diversity and the Management of Change.* Toronto: University of Toronto Press, 2000.

Preston, Ted. "Environmental values, pluralism, and stability." *Ethics, Place and Environment* 7, nos. 1-2 (March/June 2004): 73–83.

Punzo, Vincent. *Reflective Naturalism: an Introduction to Moral Philosophy.* New York: Macmillan, 1969.

Ransom, James W. 1995. "The Waters," Pp. 25–43 in Haudenosaunee [Six Nations Iroquois] Environmental Task Force, *Words That Come Before All Else: Environmental Philosophies of the Haudenosaunee.* Ahkwesahsne, Ontario: Native North American Traveling College.

Rawls, John. *A Theory of Justice.* Cambridge Mass.: Harvard University Press, 1981.

———. *Political Liberalism and the Reply to Habermas,* rev. ed. New York: Columbia University Press, 1996.

Reagor, Catherine, "When Phoenix, Tucson Merge." *Arizona Republic,* April 9, 2006. http://people.bath.ac.uk/mnspwr/Papers/JusticeSustainabilityParticipation.pdf (accessed 20 April 2007).

Reason, Peter. "Justice, Sustainability, and Participation: Inaugural Lecture." *Concepts and Transformation* 7, no. 1 (2002), 7–29.

Rees, Ronald. "The Taste for Mountain Scenery." *History Today*, 25 (1975): 305–12.

Regan, Tom. "The Nature and Possibility of an Environmental Ethic." *Environmental Ethics* 3, no. 1 (Spring 1981): 19–34.

Roaf, Sue, David Crichton, and Fergus Nicol. *Adapting Buildings and Cities for Climate Change: A 21st Century Survival Guide*. Burlington, Mass.: Architectural Press, 2005.

Roseland, Mark. *Toward Sustainable Communities: Resources for Citizens and their Governments*. Gabriola, B.C.: New Society Publishers, 1998.

———, ed. *Eco-City Dimensions. Healthy Communities, Healthy Planet*. Gabriola, B.C.: New Society Publishers, 1997

Rosenau, Pauline Marie. *Post Modernism and the Social Sciences: Insights, Inroads, and Intrusions*. Princeton, N.J.: Princeton University Press, 1991.

Rowe, Colin. *The Architecture of Good Intentions: Towards a Possible Retrospect*. London: Academy Editions, 1994.

Russell, Tom. "Can Reflective Practice be Taught?" *Reflective Practice* 6, no. 2 (May 2005): 199–204.

Ryden, Kent C. *Mapping the Invisible Landscape: Folklore, Writing, and the Sense of Place*. Iowa City, Iowa: University of Iowa Press, 1993.

Saddhatissa, Hammalawa. *Buddhist Ethics*. London: George Allen & Unwin, 1970.

Saegert, Susan and Gary Winkel. *Social Capital and the Revitalization of New York City's Distressed Inner-city Housing*. Sage Urban Studies Abstracts, 27(3) (1999).

Salingaros, Nikos A. "The Derrida Virus." *Telos* 126 (Winter 2003). 66–82.

Sandercock, Leonie. *Cosmopolis II: Mongrel Cities of the 21st Century*. New York: Continuum, 2003.

Sandercock, Leonie, and Ann Forsyth. "A Gender Agenda: New directions for planning theory." *Journal of the American Planning Association* 58. (Winter 1992): 49–59.

Sandlin, Gail. *Interstate-5 in Puget Sound: Issues of Airborne Pollution and Social Justice*. PhD dissertation. Seattle: University of Washington, 2008.

Sauer, Carl Ortwin. "The agency of man on the earth." Pp. 539–57 in *Readings in Cultural Geography*, edited by Philip L. Wagner and Marvin W. Mikesell. Chicago: University of Chicago Press, 1962.

Schaller, Frank. *Reclamation of Drastically Disturbed Lands*. Madison, Wis: American Society of Agronomy, 1978.

Scheler, Max. *Formalism in Ethics and Non-Formal Ethics of Values*. Evanston, Ill.: Northwestern University Press, 1973.

Schön, Donald. A. *Educating the Reflexive Practitioner: Toward a New Design for Teaching and Learning in the Professions*. San Francisco: Jossey-Bass Publishing, 1986.

Schwandt, T. A. "Evaluation ethics within cultures of accountability." Paper presented at the joint conference of the Canadian Evaluation Society and the American Evaluation Association, Toronto, October 2005.

Sharp, Daryl. *Personality Types: Jung's Model of Typology*. Toronto: Inner City Books, 1987.

Short, John R. *The Humane City: Cities as if People Matter*. New York: Basil Blackwell, 1989.

Singer, Brent A. "An Extension of Rawls' Theory of Justice to Environmental Ethics." *Environmental Ethics* 10, no. 3 (Fall 1988): 217–231.

Singer, Peter. *Animal Liberation: A New Ethics for Our Treatment of Animals*. New York: Avon Books, 1975.

Skirbekk, Gunnar, ed. *The Notion of Sustainability and its Normative Implications*. Oslo: Scandinavian University Press, 1994.

Skolimowski, Henry. Living Philosophy: Eco-Philosophy as a Tree of Life. London: Penguin Books, 1992.

Sommer, R. Social Design: Creating Building with People in Mind. Englewood Cliffs, N.J.: Prentice-Hall, 1983.

Soper, Kate. *What is Nature? Culture, Politics and the Non-Human*. Oxford: Wiley-Blackwell, 1995.

Spirn, Anne W. *The Granite Garden: Urban Nature and Human Design*. New York: Basic Books, 1984.

Stone, Christopher Stone. *Should Trees Have Standing? Toward Legal Rights for Natural Objects*. Portola Valley, Calif.: Tioga Publishing, 1974.

Sudjic, Deyan. "Green Utopias." *The Guardian*, October 27, 1974, 24–5.

Swearingen, Thomas Craig. *Moral Development and Environmental Ethics*. PhD dissertation. Seattle: College of Forest Resources, University of Washington, 1989.

Tashiro, Cathy. "Slippery Slopes and Shaky Ground: Being a HOPE VI Evaluator." Paper presented at the Place Matters conference, Seattle, October 28, 2006.

Taylor, Paul W. *Respect for Nature: A Theory of Environmental Ethics*. Princeton N.J.: Princeton University Press, 1986.

Thayer, Robert, L., Jr. *LifePlace: Bioregional Thought and Practice*. Berkeley and Los Angeles: University of California Press, 2003.

Thomashow, Mitchell. "Toward a Cosmopolitan Bioregionalism." Pp. 121–32 in *Bioregionalism: The Tug and Pull of Place*, edited by Michael Vincent McGinnis London: Routledge, 1999.

Thompson, Ian. "Aesthetic, Social and Ecological Values in Landscape Architecture: A discourse analysis." *Ethics, Place and Environment* 3, no. 3 (October 2000): 269–87.

Thompson, J. William, and Kim Sorvig. *Sustainable Landscape Construction: A Guide to Green Building Outdoors*. Washington, D.C.: Island Press, 2000.

Trachtenberg, Zev. "The Takings Clause and the Meanings of Land." in *Philosophy and Geography* 1 (1997): 63–90

Trudgill, Stephen T. *Barriers to a Better Environment: What Stops Us Solving Environmental Problems*. London: Belhaven Press, 1990.

Twombly, Robert. *Power and Style: A Critique of Twentieth-Century Architecture in the United States*. New York: Hill and Wang, 1996.

U.S. Census Bureau. 2003. "Income, Poverty, and Health Insurance Coverage in the U.S.: 2003." www.census.gov/hhes/www/income.html.

U.S. Census Bureau. "Poverty." www.census.gov/hhes/www/poverty/povdef.html.

U.S. Census Bureau. www.cia.gov/library/publications/the-world-factbook/index.html.

U.S. Department of Housing and Urban Development. "Notice of Funding Availability." Washington, D.C., 2003. www.hrsa.gov/homeless/pdf/pa5_carlile_handout.pdf.

U.S. Department of Transportation, Federal Housing Administration, Federal Transit Authority. *Environmental Justice Case Studies*. Government Document 0982-0-05. Washington, D.C.: 2000-2008.

U.S. General Accounting Office (GAO). "Siting of Hazardous Waste Landfills and Their Correlation with Racial and Economic Status of Surrounding Communities." Washington, D.C.: General Accounting Office, 1983.

Vale, Lawrence J. "Empathological Places: Residents' Ambivalence toward Remaining in Public Housing." *Journal of Planning Education and Research* 16, no. 3 (1997): 159–75.

———. *Reclaiming Public Housing: A Half Century of Struggle in Three Public Neighborhoods.* Cambridge Mass.: Harvard University Press, 2002.

Varela, Francisco J. *Ethical Know-How: Action, Wisdom, and Cognition (Writing Science).* Stanford, Calif: Stanford University Press 1999.

Ventre, Francis T. "Regulation: A Realization of Social Ethics." *Via* 10 (1990): 51–61.

Versluis, Arthur. *Sacred Earth: The Spiritual Landscape of Native America.* Rochester, Vermont: Inner Traditions International, 1992.

Violich, Francis. *The Bridge to Dalmatia: A Search for the Meaning of Place.* Baltimore: Johns Hopkins University Press, 1998.

Warren, Karen J. "The Power and the Promise of Ecological Feminism." *Environmental Ethics* 12, no. 2 (Summer 1990): 125–46.

Wasserman, Barry, Patrick Sullivan, and Gregory Palermo. *Ethics and the Practice of Architecture.* New York: John Wiley & Sons, 2000.

Watkin, David. *Morality & Architecture Revisited.* Chicago: University of Chicago Press, 2001.

Watson, Jeremy. *American Parks: Pilgrimage and Restoration.* PhD dissertation. Seattle: University of Washington, 2008.

Weber, Max. "Politics as a Vocation." In *From Max Weber: Essays in Sociology,* edited by H. H. Gerth and C. Wright Mills. New York: Oxford University Press, 1946.

Weiss, Michael I. *The Clustering of America.* New York: Tilden Press, 1988.

Wescoat, James, Jr. "Muslim Contributions to Geography and Environmental Ethics: The Challenges of Comparison and Pluralism." Pp. 91–116 in *Space, Place, and Environmental Ethics,* edited by Andrew Light and Jonathan M. Smith. Lanham, Md.: Rowman & Littlefield, 1997.

Williams, Daniel R., and Susan I. Stewart. "Sense of Place: An Elusive Concept that is Finding Home in Ecosystem Management." *Journal of Forestry* 96, no. 5 (1998): 18–23.

Yeang, Ken. *The Green Skyscraper: The Basis for Designing Sustainable Intensive Buildings.* New York: Prestel Publishing, 1999.

Zammito, John H. *A Nice Derangement of Epistemes: Post-Positivism in the Study of Science from Quine to Latour.* Chicago: University of Chicago Press, 2004.

Index

About the Authors

Robert Mugerauer is a professor in the Departments of Architecture and Urban Design and Planning in the College of Urban Design and Planning at the University of Washington—of which he is Dean Emeritus—and is also an adjunct faculty member in Landscape Architecture and Anthropology. He has taught ethics in a variety of settings: medical ethics at the Michigan State University, College of Medicine-Grand Rapids; medical, architectural, and planning ethics at the University of Texas at Austin, and the latter two at the University of Washington. He has published on environmental interpretation and the impact of technology on the built environment. Currently his research is centering on the "arc of life," ranging from the cellular, through organisms, to the human body and social community—with a special focus on the interrelationships of organism and environments at all scales.

Lynne Manzo is an associate professor in the Department of Landscape Architecture in the College of Architecture and Urban Planning at the University of Washington in Seattle, where she is also affiliate faculty in the Ph.D. Program in the Built Environment. She received her Ph.D. in environmental psychology from the Graduate Center of the City University of New York. She specializes in the study of place attachment, meaning and identity, affordable housing, and the politics of place. Her work appears in such journals as *Housing Policy Debate*, *Journal of Environmental Psychology,* the *Journal of Planning Literature,* and the *Journal of Architecture and Planning Research,* and she has presented her work at the annual conferences of the Environmental Design Research Association, the Council of Educators in Landscape Architecture, and Urban Affairs Association, as well as at a number of universities and professional design firms.

387